DIVERGENT CAPITALISMS

DIVERGENT CAPITALISMS

The Social Structuring and Change of Business Systems

RICHARD WHITLEY

OXFORD

UNIVERSITY PRESS

OXFORD

UNIVERSITY PRESS

Great Clarendon Street, Oxford OX2 6DP

Oxford University Press is a department of the University of Oxford.
It furthers the University's objective of excellence in research, scholarship,
and education by publishing worldwide in

Oxford New York

Auckland Bangkok Buenos Aires Cape Town Chennai
Dar es Salaam Delhi Hong Kong Istanbul Karachi Kolkata
Kuala Lumpur Madrid Melbourne Mexico City Mumbai Nairobi
São Paulo Shanghai Taipei Tokyo Toronto

Oxford is a registered trade mark of Oxford University Press
in the UK and in certain other countries

Published in the United States
by Oxford University Press Inc., New York

British Library Cataloguing in Publication Data

Data available

Library of Congress Cataloging in Publication Data
Whitley, Richard.
Divergent capitalisms: the social structuring and change of
business systems/Richard Whitley.
p. cm.
Includes bibliographical references (p.).
1. Capitalism—Case studies. 2. Business enterprises—Case
studies. 3. Economic history—20th century. I. Title.
HB501.W495 1999
330.12'2—dc21 98-43685
ISBN 0-19-829396-8 (Hbk.)
ISBN 0-19-924042-6 (Pbk.)

5 7 9 10 8 6 4

Typeset in Times
by Cambrian Typesetters, Frimley, Surrey
Printed in Great Britain
on acid-free paper by
Biddles Ltd, Guildford and King's Lynn

PREFACE AND ACKNOWLEDGEMENTS

This book developed from a meeting in Copenhagen in 1996 at which Kari Lilja suggested that a single volume dealing with the comparative-business-systems framework was needed because of the way this approach had evolved in a number of theoretical and empirical contributions since 1991. A major reason for writing this book, then, is to present this framework for describing and explaining differences between systems of economic coordination and control in as systematic and integrated a manner as possible. I have also taken the opportunity to discuss other analyses of different forms of capitalism as a way of showing how the business-systems approach differs from some of these and builds upon others. In its concern with differences between forms of economic organization and their contested nature, for example, it contrasts with much of the so-called new institutionalism in organizational analysis.

In Part Three of the book I analyse the distinctive systems of economic organization in post-war East Asia and post-1990 Eastern Europe and how these are changing. These chapters show how the comparative-business-systems framework can be applied both to the analysis of concrete industrial economies and to the understanding of how they change as a result of internal and external alterations. They highlight both the path-dependent nature of large-scale economic change and the often-contradictory effects of institutional transformations. Additionally, this part draws attention to the important roles of different kinds of collective actors and the interests they represent during periods of significant political–economic change. The discussions of Hungary and Slovenia also indicate how the comparative analysis of established market economies can be extended to understand transformation processes from state socialist ones.

Previous versions of the ideas and results in this book have been presented at a number of Colloquia of the European Group for Organizational Studies, Annual Conferences of the Society for the Advancement of Socio-Economics, Workshops of the European Science Foundation's Programme on European Management and Organizations in Transition, and at seminars held at the Academia Sinica, Taipei, Harvard University, the Massachusetts Institute of Technology, Tunghai University, Taiwan, and the University of Lancaster. I have also discussed them with colleagues in the continuing East Asian Capitalisms Group and the Social Systems of Production Group. I am grateful for all the comments and suggestions made by participants at those meetings and hope that the present volume addresses at least some of their concerns.

Laszlo Czaban, Marko Jaklic, Hari Tsoukas, and Eleanor Westney have also read previous versions of these chapters. Their suggestions have been especially useful in revising and improving both the ideas and their presentation. As usual, any errors, lacunae, and obfuscations remain my responsibility.

A previous version of Chapter 4 was published under the title 'The Social

Regulation of Work Systems: Institutions, Interest Groups, and Varieties of Work Organization in Capitalist Societies' in Richard Whitley and Peer Hull Kristensen (eds.), *Governance at Work: The Social Regulation of Economic Relations,* published by Oxford University Press in 1997, and an earlier version of Chapter 5 formed part of 'Internationalization and Varieties of Capitalism' published in the *Review of International Political Economy,* 5 (1998), 445–81.

I am grateful to the British Economic and Social Research Council and the European Union's ACE programme for funding the research that formed the basis of Chapters 8 and 9 in this book. Laszlo Czaban, Marko Hocevar, and Marko Jaklic conducted most of the fieldwork in Hungary and Slovenia with student assistants. I am also grateful to Judith Hollows, Cheng-shu Kao, James Liu, and Gordon Redding for arranging company visits in China, Japan, Korea, and Taiwan in 1992, 1996, and 1997.

R. W.

Manchester
June 1998

CONTENTS

LIST OF FIGURES

LIST OF TABLES

ABBREVIATIONS

ASEAN	Association of South East Asian Nations
BOAL	Basic Organization of Associated Labour
CEO	chief executive officer
CEPR	Centre for Economic Policy Research
CFB	Chinese family business
CMEA	Council for Mutual Economic Assistance
COAL	Composite Organization of Associated Labour
EBRD	European Bank for Reconstruction and Development
ESOP	Employee Share Ownership Plan
FDI	foreign direct investment
GATT	General Agreement on Tariff and Trade
GDP	gross domestic product
GNP	gross national product
IMF	International Monetary Fund
KMT	Kuomintang
LDP	Liberal Democratic Party (Japan)
MNC	multinational company
NIC	newly industrialized country
OECD	Organization for Economic Cooperation and Development
OEM	original equipment manufacturing
SCAP	Supreme Commander for the Allied Powers (Japan)
SHC	State Holding Company (Hungary)
SME(s)	Small- and medium-sized enterprises
SOE	state-owned enterprise
SPA	State Property Agency (Hungary)
UNCTAD	United Nations Conference on Trade and Development
WB	World Bank
WO	Work Organization
WTO	World Trade Organization

PART ONE

INTRODUCTION

1

Varieties of Capitalism

During the twentieth century a number of quite distinctive forms of capitalism have become established and continue to be reproduced as different systems of economic organization. Despite numerous claims of growing convergence and the 'globalization' of managerial structures and strategies, the ways in which economic activities are organized and controlled in, for example, post-war Japan, South Korea (henceforth Korea), and Taiwan differ considerably from those prevalent in the USA and UK. They also vary significantly between themselves (Orru *et al.* 1997; Wade 1990; Whitley 1992*a*). Equally, substantial variations in types of dominant firm, customer–supplier relations, employment practices, and work systems remain across the regions and countries of Europe, despite the efforts of 'modernizing' élites in the post-war period (see e.g. Herrigel 1996; Kristensen 1996, 1997; Lane 1992; Maurice *et al.* 1986; Sorge 1991). Convergence to a single most effective type of market economy is no more likely in the twenty-first century than it was in the highly internationalized economy of the late nineteenth century (Hirst and Thompson 1996; Kenworthy 1997; Koechlin 1995; Wade 1996).

Indeed, in so far as the international economy does continue to become more integrated, it can be argued that societies with different institutional arrangements will continue to develop and reproduce varied systems of economic organization with different economic and social capabilities in particular industries and sectors. They will, therefore, 'specialize' in distinctive ways of structuring economic activities that privilege some sectors and discourage others (Hollingsworth 1997; Hollingsworth and Streeck 1994; Sorge 1991). An example of such specialization is the late-twentieth-century UK economy, which has strong international capabilities in financial services and architecture (Winch 1996) but relatively weak ones in complex assembly manufacturing and construction.

The different varieties of capitalism that have developed over the course of the twentieth century have been characterized and analysed in a number of quite different ways from varied perspectives. Some, for example, have contrasted rather broad models of cooperative or 'Rhenish' capitalism with the excesses of neo-American capitalism (Albert 1993). Others have extolled the virtues of competitive managerial capitalism in the American mode over the more 'personal' variant in the UK and, less emphatically, the 'cooperative managerial' one in Germany (Chandler 1990).

Many observers of twentieth-century capitalism have proclaimed the fading of 'Fordism' as the prevalent system of mass production and mass marketing, together with its various associated regulation regimes (Boyer 1990; Boyer and Durand 1997). In a number of accounts, the rigidities of such large-scale production of standardized goods for homogenous markets have been contrasted with the virtues of the flexible production systems that have developed in some societies (e.g. Boyer and Hollingsworth 1997; Piore and Sabel 1984; cf. Hirst and Zeitlin 1991). In some instances, these analyses combine discussions of production and marketing competitive strategies with organizational differences within and between firms to delineate different kinds of economic organization which have dominated different economies in different periods (e.g. Best 1990; Chandler 1977, 1990; Lazonick 1991).

There is a tendency in such contrasts of systems of economic organization to assume that later forms of capitalism are superior to earlier ones, and/or that competition between alternative economic coordination and control systems inexorably selects the more effective one. Some versions of transaction-cost economics, for example, claim that the relative efficiency of hierarchies over markets in terms of reducing transaction costs determines whether authority- or price-based coordination mechanisms dominate an industry (Williamson 1975; cf. Dietrich 1994). However, as many have pointed out (e.g. Granovetter 1985; Langlois and Robertson 1995), this sort of approach both elevates market forces to a *deus ex machina* role operating in a social vacuum, and is essentially static, ignoring dynamic costs and learning.

It also fails to specify exactly the ways in which competitive pressures select particular ways of organizing economic activities in different circumstances, and how they continue to do so. All too often, a form of functionalist reasoning is implied that asserts that, because a pattern of organization has become established and survived, it must, therefore, be efficient and/or perform a useful role for the overall economic system. This type of argument is similar to that of sociologists who have suggested that certain social rituals, such as the British coronation ceremony, have continued because they contribute to social cohesion. It ignores both historical contexts and the active role of interest groups and collective actors in structuring economic relations, selection criteria, and market organization.

Such a view may be justifiable if it can be demonstrated that historical circumstances, institutional arrangements, and collective actors are irrelevant to economic processes and outcomes—or at least make little or no difference to them. To do that requires the systematic specification of the purely economic mechanisms that operate in isolation from their societal contexts to generate and select more efficient forms of economic organization in all market economies. Since prevailing social structures and conventions not only have major consequences for the ways that particular systems of economic coordination and control develop, but also greatly influence the 'rules of the game' according to which individuals and organizations make 'rational' decisions about investments and compete (see e.g. North 1990), this seems a rather utopian intellectual goal.

Essentially, it presumes the existence of some systemic rationality governing economic activities that lies beyond, and separate from, any specific set of social arrangements. Exactly how such a universal logic has become established and so powerful that it imposes itself on economic processes everywhere remains unclear.

Since a number of quite distinct forms of economic organization have developed and continue to be reproduced as separate variants of industrial capitalism since the early nineteenth century, I suggest that it would be more productive to try to understand the processes underlying such divergence. These processes include the ways in which different patterns of industrialization developed in contrasting institutional contexts and led to contrasting institutional arrangements governing economic processes becoming established in different market economies. For example, the ways in which industrial capitalism developed in Britain, Denmark, and Germany differed significantly as a result of variations in their political systems and the institutions governing agricultural production and distribution. Partly as a result, the structure and practices of state agencies, financial organizations, and labour-market actors in these countries continue to diverge and to reproduce distinctive forms of economic organization (Kristensen 1997).

The comparative analysis of current systems of economic organization, therefore, requires consideration of how they developed in contrasting ways during industrialization. It also involves identifying the processes that reproduce divergent ways of coordinating and controlling economic activities in different institutional contexts. Given, that is, the existence of varied forms of economic organization, why do they persist and how do they change? This, in turn, requires the specification of the interdependencies between particular characteristics of these distinctive forms and the dominant institutional arrangements that govern them. Variations in such characteristics, I suggest, are to be understood in terms of the prevailing institutions dealing with the constitution and control of key resources such as skills, capital, and legitimacy.

In this book I present a framework for identifying the central differences between established systems of economic organization and control in twentieth-century market economies that explains these in terms of specific features of their institutional environments. This framework is, then, used to analyse the development and change of different forms of economic organization in post-war East Asia and Eastern Europe. The *comparative-business-systems* approach outlined here seeks to explain how and why forms of economic organization diverge in specific ways, and to identify the factors involved in their change. It assumes that economic relationships and activities are socially constituted and institutionally variable, such that the ways competitive processes operate, and the nature both of the actors engaged in them and of their outcomes, vary significantly between societal contexts. The logics governing economic decision-making and actions are inherently structured by dominant institutions, and so are variable between different conventions and 'rules of the game', in the view presented here.

In this sense the business-systems framework is consonant with many institutionalist analyses of organizational forms and allied comparisons of coordination mechanisms, types of production systems, and business groups across countries and historical periods. Before presenting it in detail, then, in this introductory chapter I discuss the major ways in which these and other studies of economic organization have conceptualized forms of economic organization, and accounted for differences and changes in them. The four chapters in Part Two will outline the basic framework, the nature of firms' governance systems and capabilities, the nature of work systems, and the implications of globalization. Finally, the last four chapters in Part Three explore the development of different kinds of economic systems in Korea, Taiwan, Hungary, and Slovenia, and the changes in these in the 1990s.

In the next section I shall focus on how historians and others have characterized very broad changes in forms of capitalism since the Industrial Revolution to highlight the key differences they identified. Next, I shall consider the more specific studies of 'societal effects' on patterns of work organization and control and other aspects of firm behaviour in European economies, as well as the more extensive 'institutionalist' analyses of organizational forms and structures. Thirdly, the more explicitly comparative accounts of economic organization in Asia, North America, and Europe will be discussed. Finally, I shall highlight some general points arising from these studies for the comparative analysis of forms of economic organization.

THE DEVELOPMENT OF DIFFERENT TYPES OF MANAGERIAL CAPITALISM

One of the most detailed accounts of large-scale change in the organization of economic activities in a single country is Chandler's *The Visible Hand* (1977), which describes the rise of managerially coordinated big business in the USA. In this *competitive managerial capitalism*, large managerial bureaucracies integrated mass production with mass marketing and distribution of standardized goods to large, relatively homogenous markets. By concentrating on reducing throughput time and costs through using specialized machinery and semi-skilled workers, the successful firms were able to out-compete more specialized producers with lower fixed costs but greater unit costs in the medium to long term. Having learned how to manage the complex coordination of production chains in vertically integrated hierarchies, managers later extended the range of activities these hierarchies coordinated by diversifying into new product lines and markets.

Other aspects of twentieth-century US capitalism identified by Chandler (1990) included: the separation of asset owners from managers, the expansion of production sites under unified managerial control, investment in R&D, reliance on retained earnings for most new investment, and a gradual move to the multi-divisional organization structure. *Personal capitalism* in Britain, in contrast, remained dominated by family-owned firms that invested little in new technologies, management, or marketing and often relied on cartels and federations to reduce risks. The third variety, *cooperative managerial capitalism*, in Germany combined some aspects of the US managerial system, such as large managerial hierarchies integrating production chains, with much continued family control, inter-firm cooperation, and greater paternalism towards the workforce. German companies also tended to compete more on quality than price in many industries and often had more flexible production processes with greater reliance on skilled workers, although this is not much discussed by Chandler.

Essentially, then, the three varieties of late-nineteenth and early twentieth-century capitalism identified by Chandler are distinguished in terms of four key characteristics: first, the extent to which leading firms established large managerial bureaucracies to coordinate a wide variety of activities and transactions; secondly, the separation of owners from managers; thirdly, the degree of integration of large-scale production with mass marketing; and, finally, the extent to which competition was driven by economies of scale and scope. Primary sources of, and conditions of access to, investment funds, the flexibility of production processes, and labour-management strategies also differentiated these three forms of capitalism but seemed less significant to Chandler.

The presumption that managerial capitalism developed in the USA because it was more efficient, and was in that sense inevitable, has, of course, been attacked by many writers. Amongst other criticisms, some of these have pointed to the various ways in which business élites—especially those in capital intensive sectors—sought to control risk and uncertainty before the large-scale mergers of the early twentieth century (e.g. Fligstein 1990). Additionally, Dobbin (1994) has demonstrated the importance of state regulatory policies in the development of different economic ideologies and coordination systems in the US railroad industry. Overall, the historically and institutionally contingent nature of managerial capitalism in the USA is increasingly accepted, as is its less-than-universal manifestation across all manufacturing sectors (Hollingsworth 1991).

None the less, much of Chandler's characterization of this form of capitalism, and its overall significance, remains important to the analysis of twentieth-century economic history, especially that dealing with the different varieties of 'Fordism' and their putative successor production regimes. Fordism is usually understood as the system of production that produces standardized goods in very large quantities for mass, homogenous markets with dedicated, rigid production machinery and semi-skilled workers who are tightly controlled by production engineers and managers (see e.g. Boyer and Durand 1997). It implies high levels of managerial integration of economic activities.

The increased organizational integration of the economy represented by the rise of US big business in the early twentieth century has been emphasized by Lazonick (1990, 1991; Lazonick and West 1998) in his formulation of a more general approach to economic development and competitiveness. He highlights three varieties of capitalism which differ significantly in the extent to which economic activities are organizationally integrated and firms pursue innovation-based competitive strategies: *proprietary* (e.g. British), *managerial* (US), and *collective* (post-war Japanese).

Proprietary capitalism was dominated by vertically and horizontally specialized firms which coordinated their inputs and outputs through market contracting. These firms had little distinctive organizational capacity to pursue innovative strategies, and typically delegated control over work processes to skilled workers who were managed through piecework-based reward systems (cf. Kristensen 1997).

Managerial capitalism, in contrast, is dominated by large vertically integrated, and often horizontally diversified, firms run by salaried managers organized into authority hierarchies. These firms often developed their own innovation capabilities through establishing R&D laboratories and competed for much of the early twentieth century through innovation-based strategies for mass markets. They also tended to exert strong managerial control over work processes through formal rules and procedures and mechanization. High levels of managerial integration in such firms did not extend to the manual workforce, nor to suppliers and customers (Lazonick and West 1998).

Collective capitalism exhibits even higher levels of organizational integration of economic activities through extensive long-term collaboration between firms in business groups and networks, both within sectors and across them. Additionally, integration within firms is greater in this form of capitalism because loyalty and commitment between employer and employee extend further down the hierarchy than in either of the other two types. Lazonick (1991: 36–45) sees this investment in male manual workers as being crucial to the development of innovative organizations, since it encourages employees to improve products and processes on a continuing basis.

In addition to varying in the degree of organizational coordination and innovation-based competition, these ideal types also differ in the extent and mode of owner control, the delegation of work control to skilled workers, and, relatedly, the location of organizational segmentation boundaries. In the case of Britain, this segmentation primarily occurred between generalist top managers and managerial specialists—as well, of course, as between skilled maintenance workers and unskilled operatives. In the USA it was, and remains, concentrated between college-educated managers and manual workers, while in Japan it occurs between male, core employees and female, temporary workers as well as between large firms and their subcontractors.

The increasing degree of planned coordination of innovation and learning represented by the development of managerial and collective capitalism is superior to classic market coordination, according to Lazonick (1991: 328–34), when three conditions obtain. First, technical change becomes more complex and dependent on previous codified knowledge. Secondly, the specialization of technical skills grows and, thirdly, the fixed costs of generating product and process innovations become ever larger and necessitate cumulative, dynamic, and collective learning. In turn, such planned coordination requires more substantial and longer-term commitment on the part of employees and capital providers, which itself depends on the institutions governing employment relations, the provision of investment funds, and ownership relations. Thus, where dominant institutions in a country do not encourage long-term commitments, cumulative and collective learning processes to reduce uncertainties in production processes will not be widespread. Similarly, where the state or other systems of collective organization do not help to reduce market uncertainty, successful investment in long-term innovation strategies will be difficult to develop and sustain.

In a similar vein, Best (1990) has contrasted the 'new competition' that focuses on innovation and quality with the old competition of post-war Chandlerian adaptive bureaucracies that focused on standardization and price/cost reduction. Essentially, he sees the two types of capitalism as varying in the type of dominant firm, the organization of production chains and of sectors, and the type of industrial policy adopted by the state. Whereas many US firms in the twentieth century have adapted to the demands of existing markets, competed on price, and economized on throughput times, more 'entrepreneurial' ones in post-war Japan and Italy seek to restructure competitive domains. They do this by introducing new and higher-quality products at the same time as economizing on process times and reducing product development and changeover times.

Inter-firm relations in production chains similarly vary between zero-sum adversarial competition and more collaborative obligational contracting and exchange of information in this view. These differences are encouraged and reproduced by different state structures and policies. In particular, regulatory states that act as arm's length system regulators are contrasted with developmental ones that pursue more active market shaping and strategic coordinating roles, following Johnson's (1982) distinction.

These characteristics of very broad and wide-ranging models of capitalism in terms of competitive processes and organized coordination of economic activities suggest a number of important dimensions for comparing systems of economic organization across market economies. These include, first, the variety of resources and activities integrated through managerial hierarchies, and, secondly, the organization of ownership and control. A third important aspect of market economies that is highlighted by these accounts is the degree of cooperation between suppliers and customers and between competitors. A fourth one is the extent of organizational integration of employees and long-term interdependence between employers and employees. Finally, some of these models also emphasize the varying extent to which firms pursue price-based competitive strategies as opposed to innovation and quality ones. I shall draw upon these contrasts in developing the comparative-business-systems framework in Part Two. Additionally, the historical summaries of the development of different organizational forms in the USA, Germany, Japan, and the UK provided by Best, Chandler, Lazonick, and others suggest a number of institutional factors that are critical for different kinds of capitalism to become established.

However, the logic by which these factors generated and inhibited specific characteristics of economic organization in particular societies is not always systematically presented, and the pressures encouraging, say, the new competition to be effective at the end of the twentieth century in specific industries remain rather obscure. Exactly how and why dominant forms of competition changed in different societies and sectors remain to be explicated in detail. Furthermore, a degree of economic functionalism seems pervasive in some of these accounts, as if collective capitalism were inevitably going to arise once consumer demand became more heterogeneous and technical change speeded up and grew in uncertainty.

There is also a tendency to play down the possibility of organizational alternatives to currently dominant paradigms of economic organization, such as the combination of specialized firms with mobile workers organized along craft lines in strong unions pursuing innovation strategies characteristic of the Danish machinery sector (Kristensen 1996, 1997). Finally, the effects of conflicts between interest groups, sector élites, and various organized associations on forms of capitalism are sometimes ignored in these broad comparisons.

THE INSTITUTIONAL STRUCTURING OF ORGANIZATIONAL FORMS IN
CAPITALIST ECONOMIES

These rather diffuse contrasts and characterizations of forms of capitalism have been complemented by more detailed studies of the processes by which particular systems of economic coordination and control developed their distinctive features in different countries. Rather than identifying the broad features of different stages of capitalist development and their prevalent organizational forms which seem to be effective at different times, most of these recent analyses focus on differences in particular aspects of economic organization and how contextual—especially institutional—factors might account for these.

For example, the well-known studies of work organization and control in German and French—and, later, British—manufacturing enterprises conducted by Marc Maurice and his colleagues identified considerable national variations in how firms in the same industry and using similar technologies structured and controlled work processes. These resulted, in large part, from differences in skill development and certification processes and in union structures which were—and remain—highly varied across these three societies, thus exemplifying 'societal effects' on work systems (cf. Sorge 1991, 1996).

Many of these comparative studies of organizational variations between societies conflict in their assumptions and style of research with the dominant school of organizational analysis in Anglo-Saxon academia in the 1970s and 1980s: contingency analysis (Hickson *et al.* 1979; Maurice 1979). In a comparable way to the disputes within economics, many of these disagreements concerned different conceptions of the goals and nature of social scientific research. They also, though, reflected different understandings of the nature of organizations, and these were partly the result of important variations in firm type and behaviour across economies.

Three aspects of these conflicts are particularly worth raising in the context of the comparative analysis of economic organization. First, the theoretical logic underlying much contingency analysis remains obscure. In particular, the causal mechanisms leading from variations in production technology, size, etc., to differences in formal structures have rarely been specified with sufficient precision to permit systematic empirical research, let alone to justify normative recommendations to managerial élites. Correlations *per se* do not, of course, indicate causality, and, since *ceteris paribus* clauses are rarely expressed very clearly in much of this literature, it is difficult to draw strong inferences from most empirical studies.

Despite these points, and the difficulties involved with functionalist explanations in general (Elster 1984: 28–35), many advocates of this approach continue to believe that organizational survival implies economic effectiveness, if not efficiency. Additionally, statistically significant correlations are often thought to represent generalizable and efficacious connections between certain indicators of formal bureaucratic structures and production technologies, etc. These beliefs have underpinned claims that a universally valid organization science was being developed that could serve as the basis for rational organizational design in all capitalist economies (Donaldson 1985; Pfeffer 1993).

Secondly, much of this search for correlations between abstract properties of formal organizations presumed that they were well-defined and bounded social systems which had to adapt to certain contingencies if they were to survive. Essentially, they were viewed as relatively well-ordered and separate structures which were largely reactive to market forces in a way that is reminiscent of orthodox economists' presumption of firms being 'islands of planned co-ordination in a sea of market relations', as Richardson (1972) summarized it. Both assumptions of discrete well boundedness and passive adaptation to market pressures have been criticized extensively in recent years with the rediscovery of 'networks' between firms and awareness of the significance of strategic choices of managerial élites in Anglo-Saxon societies (Child 1972; Ebers 1997).

Thirdly, it is important to note that this style and focus of research was most institutionalized in Anglo-Saxon countries. The development of a generalizing organizational science based on statistical correlations of abstract properties of formal structures was highly consonant with prevailing conceptions of 'science' in such cultures. More significantly, it made much more sense as an intellectual programme in economies where firms combined both units of common ownership and units of authoritative integration and also tended to operate at arm's length from each other in a largely adversarial mode. This school can, then, be seen as reflecting the dominant Fordist production regime that was strongly institutionalized in the USA. It is perhaps curious that an intellectual endeavour so concerned to establish a universally valid science of organizations should adopt basic assumptions that restrict its application primarily to formal organizations in a single type of economy at one period in its historical development.

In contrast, where ownership units are more interconnected, cooperate as well as compete, and are able to share risks with financial partners, it is difficult to believe that organized coordination of economic activities occurs only within firms' boundaries, and that markets are fundamentally disorganized. Consequently, building the science of organizations on the analysis of standard, discrete, and well-bounded social units characterized as formal organizations is much more problematic for social scientists in much of continental Europe and Asia than it appeared to be to Anglo-Saxon ones (Hamilton and Feenstra 1997).

There have been a number of different approaches to the analysis of how societal institutions structure organizational forms in capitalist economies. Perhaps the two most influential ones in the 1970s and 1980s have been the largely European 'societal effects' school and the more US centred 'new institutionalism' (Scott 1995). An important feature of the former approach was its emphasis on (*a*) the varied ways in which social groups were constituted inside and outside organizations, and (*b*) their continuous competition for control of resources. The rules of the competitive game within and between organizations were seen here as being constructed and contested by a variety of occupational and other groupings rather than imposed by an external and asocial market. These groupings are themselves societally constituted by different state structures and policies, forms of association, and prevailing patterns of collective mobilization, and so differ significantly between institutional contexts.

Formal organizations, in this view, are more arenas for competing social groups to seek control over priorities and resources than stable authority hierarchies establishing distinctive routines and procedures separate from the rest of society. Especially in many continental European societies, the 'breaking down the walls of the organisation' (Callon and Vignolle 1977) reflects the horizontal presentation of many organizational activities by broadly based groupings and ideologies (cf. Kristensen 1996, 1997).

Such comparative analysis of 'societal effects' on organizational structures and operations has more recently been extended to issues of strategic choice and patterns of firm development. Distinctive logics of industrial structure and competitive strategy have been identified in the same industry in different European societies and reconstructed as the consequences of distinctive institutional arrangements and historical patterns of industrial development (e.g. Campagnac and Winch 1997; Sorge and Warner 1986). Relatedly, Herrigel (1993) and others (e.g. Lazonick 1990) have shown how variations in skill levels, union control, and policies were linked to differences in industrialization processes and state policies in Germany and the USA to affect the development of mass production in the machinery industry in the twentieth century. Here, the societal context, broadly conceived, structured the strategies and actions of managers, owners, and different groups of workers to generate quite different outcomes in the two countries.

Some of these comparative analyses of economic organization have been broadly characterized as 'institutionalist'. Together with related studies of how varied regulatory regimes and state policies have resulted in different patterns of firm organization and strategic behaviour (e.g. Dobbin 1994; Fligstein 1990), they have been labelled as part of the 'new institutionalism' in organizational analysis (see e.g. Powell and DiMaggio 1991; Scott 1995). While in very broad terms this attribution is not inaccurate, in so far as most authors are concerned to show how different societal institutions and agencies generate different kinds of economic actors pursuing different strategic logics, it conflates rather different concerns and approaches.

Much of the self-styled 'new institutionalism' in North America focuses on how organizations reproduce particular templates and forms which are authorized by central agencies and dominant ideologies as being legitimate, efficient, best practice, and so on. Initially concerned with publicly supported organizations in the USA, many studies showed how these were coerced or guided to change their structures and ideologies to fit prevailing norms of effective organization and governance, regardless of their 'technical' efficiency, however that was assessed. As Scott (1995: 35–45), DiMaggio and Powell (1991), and others have noted, the bulk of this work has focused on how various institutions have generated and reproduced particular taken-for-granted cognitive assumptions about appropriate organizational forms and the nature of legitimate social actors. In particular, they have emphasized the constitutive roles of institutions that establish the kinds of social collectivities that can claim resources and legitimacy. Dominant conceptions of rationality and effectiveness are seen as generating distinctive templates for organizations that constrain their structures and strategies if they are to be widely accepted as legitimate social actors. As a result, organizational forms tend to become remarkably uniform within societies dominated by particular institutional conventions.

In early contributions this sort of institutionalist account of organizational uniformity among public organizations was contrasted with more 'technical' explanations—or, more accurately, assumptions—of structural similarities among privately owned economic actors arising from competitive pressures. However, this restriction of institutionalist analysis to organizations in non-competitive environments has been dropped in the 1990s, at least among some researchers. Indeed, competitive logics themselves are now seen as institutionally constructed, not least by regulatory changes, in a number of accounts which attempt to subsume economic rationality in the narrow sense under wider-ranging institutional norms and conventions (Dobbin 1995; Fligstein 1996; cf. Scott 1995: 128–30). Standards for evaluating organizational performance and prevalent criteria for judging firms' strategic priorities vary significantly across institutional regimes and cannot be derived from a single universal market rationality (Boyer and Hollingsworth 1997).

This work has been useful in emphasizing the socially constructed nature of social and economic actors such that their boundaries, structures, and control become matters to research rather than generalized from a single type. It has also shown how their ability to act legitimately varies significantly across institutional contexts. However, it has been criticized for reifying an overarching and highly coherent notion of rationality that imposes itself upon formal organizations and other social actors. At least in some accounts, this set of institutionalized expectations appears almost as a *deus ex machina* rationalizing forms of social organization into a Weberian iron cage without much systematic specification of the circumstances in which, and processes by which, such expectations become established and reproduced in particular organizations and economies (see Scott 1995). In particular, the contested nature of many constructions of rationality and 'governance' norms is often ignored, as is the considerable variation across societies in how different social groupings are constituted and compete for control over the definition of economic rationality and market structures (see e.g. Kristensen 1997).

Furthermore, it is not at all obvious why many of the US 'new institutionalists' privilege cognitive norms and conventions as the central forces constituting and structuring organizational forms instead of what Scott (1995: 35–45) terms regulative and normative (i.e. values and norms) institutions. In practice, it is difficult to see how variations in systems of economic coordination and control across market economies can be adequately understood by considering only the role of dominant rationalities, not least because these are often entrenched in formal rules and procedures dealing with, for example, property rights, contractual obligations, and work jurisdictions. In explaining the different forms of East Asian capitalism, Hamilton and Biggart (1988; cf. Whitley 1992*a*) naturally had recourse to all three modes of institutional structuring, and, indeed, it is not very clear what is gained by positing them as distinct and separate, except perhaps to emphasize their different disciplinary and historical affinities.

There are, additionally, considerable differences in the objects and types of explanation sought in many of these 'institutionalist' analyses. Much of the North American literature focuses on characteristics of formal organizational structures and changes in these, without considering how these structures are themselves constituted as economic coordination systems competing and cooperating with each other in competitive markets, partly no doubt because of a strong tendency to study non-profit and/or public-sector organizations. While Dobbin (1994, 1995), Fligstein (1985, 1990, 1996), and others have examined changes in industry and firm structures in the USA from more or less avowedly 'institutionalist' perspectives, their main concern has been to show how business ideologies and practices altered more in response to changing regulatory and other institutionalist environments than as a result of competitive pressures to become more efficient. Cognitive legitimacy *per se* seems to have been less significant in these accounts than changes in the legal framework governing market control and the long standing US aversion to visible concentrations of power—whether in the economy or in the political system. Relatedly, the mechanisms adduced by many students of economic organization are as often coercive and normative as mimetic, and, in any case, these are scarcely mutually incompatible (cf. Hamilton and Biggart 1988).

If, then, 'institutionalist' analyses of organizational forms are only those which study how formal organizational structures follow dominant cognitive templates through some sort of imitation, most comparative accounts of economic coordination and control systems are not institutionalist in that sense. If, on the other hand, the term is stretched to include all studies of the coordination of economic activities that attempt to show how macro social institutions and agencies structure, reproduce, and change such phenomena, it becomes so broad and diffuse as to be of very limited use in delineating a distinctive form of economic and organizational sociology. Whatever label is applied to such studies, it seems important to clarify the nature of their intellectual concerns and how they are being addressed if we are to identify how they have illuminated our understanding of how and why different ways of organizing capitalist economies have developed and continue to be distinctive. In the light of these comments I now turn to a brief examination of some more general comparative studies of economic coordination and control systems across a number of societies that are broadly 'institutionalist' without being constrained by the assumptions of much of the 'new institutionalism'.

COMPARING CAPITALISMS: CONTRASTING CHARACTERISTICS OF ECONOMIC COORDINATION AND CONTROL SYSTEMS

Comparative analysis of how different forms of economic organization have become established, reproduced, and changed in different market economies has focused on a wide range of phenomena from work organization and control to production and accumulation regimes, business groups, and 'industrial orders' (Herrigel 1993, 1996). It has also invoked an equally wide range of explanatory factors. Units of analysis have varied between industrial sectors, geographical regions, nation states, ethnic networks, and 'global' capitalism. I shall focus here on some of the more systematic comparative analyses of economic organization in different market economies in order to identify common focuses and differences in their conceptualizations of the central phenomena to be explained, as well as in the sorts of accounts offered.

This will suggest the need for a more comprehensive framework for comparing and contrasting systems of economic coordination and control that attempts to identify the critical processes by which they become established, reproduced, and changed as relatively integrated and distinctive business systems. The 'societal-effects' approach and many of the broadly defined institutionalist analyses discussed above showed that differences and changes in central institutional arrangements and agencies have had significant and quite long-lasting consequences for the ways in which firms organize and control work, establish networks, and develop growth strategies. However, relatively few comparative studies have focused on how they have led to the development of distinctive systems of economic organization more generally.

Three particularly interesting sets of studies are (*a*) those concerned with different kinds of business groups in East Asia (Hamilton and Biggart 1988; Orru *et al.* 1989, 1991), (*b*) Herrigel's (1989, 1994, 1996) analysis of 'industrial orders' in Germany and the USA, and (*c*) the series of sectoral and country studies of forms of economic coordination and governance undertaken under the broad rubric of 'social systems of production' (Campbell *et al.* 1991; Hollingsworth *et al.* 1994; Hollingsworth and Boyer 1997*b*). These specifically focus on different systems of economic action and organization—as distinct from particular characteristics of firm behaviour and/or type—and seek to identify the processes by which these various systems became established and reproduced in societies with distinctive institutional arrangements. They therefore contribute both to how the central components of such systems vary, and to the explanation of the major differences between such distinctive varieties of capitalism.

The series of analyses of post-war East Asian capitalisms by Biggart, Hamilton, Orru, and their collaborators focused on the ways that enterprise groups have been organized in Japan, Korea, and Taiwan as central features of their distinctive forms of economic coordination and control. Such groups of variously interdependent firms coordinate different kinds of economic resources and activities in the three economies and constitute distinctive modes of authoritative coordination in them. They developed in contrasting ways as a result of pre-industrial legacies, patterns of industrialization, and twentieth-century state structures and policies.

The major characteristics of these business groups identified by Orru *et al.* concern: ownership relations, intra-group networks, inter-group networks, subcontracting relations, investment patterns, and growth patterns. The key characteristic of intra-group networks here is the degree to which, and ways in which, economic activities are coordinated within each group, while inter-group networks concern the amount and prevalent mode of economic coordination between them. Subcontracting relationships are analysed in terms of their formalization and stability, while investment patterns refer to vertical and horizontal integration and diversification. Finally, growth patterns concern mostly the sources of finance-for-growth strategies.

The considerable isomorphism of business groups within each economy in terms of these characteristics, and the marked variability between them, are explained by Orru *et al.* (1997: 184) as the product of particular 'fiscal, political, and social institutions that limit and direct the development of organizational forms ... business relationships ... represent enactments of socially acceptable, institutionalized forms of economic behaviour'. In particular, they are governed by different fundamental principles of control which are drawn from the state, the family, and the community. These are summarized as a communitarian ideal in Japan, a patrimonial principle in Korea, and the familial network in Taiwan.

While this set of comparisons highlights many of the important differences in East Asian capitalisms and shows how these are connected to major societal institutions, it is not entirely clear why the rather vaguely defined enterprise groups are taken to be the central components of these economies or, indeed, whether they can be validly conceptualized as equivalent units of analysis. This uncertainty stems from some ambiguity in the relations between 'firms' and 'groups'. Enterprise groups are defined as relatively stable and identifiable aggregates of firms that have patterned interdependent relationships between themselves (cf. Granovetter 1996). Since, however, firms are not specifically defined and it is unclear how we are to distinguish such groups of them from unrelated aggregates, the precise nature of business groups remains rather vague.

Furthermore, if firms are supposed to represent relatively autonomous units of economic decision-making and control under common ownership, then the separate legal identity of the Korean *chaebol*'s subsidiaries matters less in deciding whether they constitute distinct 'firms' than the parent companies' control of shares, investments, and senior managerial personnel. Given the high degree of hierarchical direction of subsidiaries' activities in these enterprises, it seems more reasonable to characterize the entire group as the firm, in which case there are no major groups of firms in Korea to compare with those in Japan and Taiwan. This point highlights the importance of being clear about the unit and level of analysis in comparing systems of economic organization, especially when a central focus of such comparisons concerns the ways in which different institutions and agencies constitute different kinds of collective entities as economic actors, as will be elaborated in Chapter 3.

A more general outline of three distinctive forms of capitalism, *alliance*, *dirigiste*, and *familial*, was later sketched by Orru (1997). This contrasted the economies of Japan and Germany, Korea and France, Taiwan and Italy in terms of six features. These were: the dominant economic units, modal economic interactions, modal means of organization, inter-firm relations, formalization of transactions, and the extent of non-contractual enforcement. Variations in these are portrayed as being closely related to three distinct 'rationality contexts of economic action' and to three types of political system, but unfortunately Orru's early death prevented further elaboration and justification of these concepts and their application to distinct societies. While suggestive as to how one might go about comparing and explaining differences between broadly conceived forms of capitalism, this sketch remains too brief to offer a systematic and coherent framework.

Differences in the organization of production chains and firms' strategies during the development of mass production, and the later growth of flexibility in large-scale production in the machine-tool industry in Germany and the USA, have been studied by Herrigel (1994, 1996) as outcomes of contrasting 'industrial orders'. He sees the prevalent 'governance mechanisms' controlling economic transactions in a particular industry and/or geographical region as the products of 'the peculiar social, political, and legal framework constructed over the course of the industrialization process that shapes the way that producers serving given product markets collectively define the legitimate boundaries of industrial practice' (Herrigel 1994: 97). Essentially, he contrasts the growth of large firms mass producing special purpose machine tools in the USA with the continued domination of relatively specialized small and smaller runs of more general purpose machine tools in Germany. These specialized German firms subcontracted more of the production process than their US counterparts and developed quite complex and stable networks of connections between themselves, whereas inter-firm relations in much of the US machine-tool industry were at arm's length and adversarial throughout the twentieth century.

Herrigel explains these differences in industrial organization and production and market strategies in terms of the contrasting 'ground rules for acceptable practice' in the two countries. These rules became institutionalized during the political and social conflicts between social groupings that occurred in the period of industrialization. These ground rules are constitution-like frameworks that establish (*a*) exclusionary rules, (*b*) dispute adjudication procedures, and (*c*) the nature of industry boundaries and of firms within these.

The first set of rules excludes certain kinds of activity or practices and encourages others. For instance, the regulatory inhibition of inter-firm collusion and cooperation in the USA encouraged the stabilization of competition through mergers. The second set of procedures governs how conflicts between competing firms are to be resolved—for instance, through formal association rules in Germany or through market competition between different production and pricing strategies in the USA. The third concerns the structure and organization of industries, particularly the degree of vertical integration of economic activities within authority hierarchies and the ways they coordinate economic activities between such hierarchies. While this contrast focuses on a single industry, Herrigel claims it represents more general differences in organizational forms and industrial orders between parts of Germany and the USA which apply to a number of sectors.

Herrigel (1996) also suggests that different kinds of industrial order have characterized different regions of Germany in the late nineteenth and twentieth centuries as the result of significant variations in pre-industrial legacies and local state structures and policies. The 'decentralized form' of industrial production focused on small volumes of specialized products in Baden-Württemberg, part of the Rhineland, and other areas, whereas the 'autarkic form' incorporated more production activities within private hierarchies and dominated the Ruhr region, north-east Westphalia, and much of Prussia (Herrigel 1996: 20–1).

As different systems of economic organization and conceptions of industrial order, these forms competed for domination of the unified German economy throughout much of the twentieth century. This competition structured the sort of production system and its institutional framework that we now take as characteristic of the post-war German economy (cf. Lane 1992). The conflict between contrasting ways of structuring economic activities was also, of course, a conflict between interest groups, industrial sectors, and their political allies that affected, and was affected by, the development of the German state and its policies. Industrial orders are thus closely connected to processes of modern state formation and change, at both regional and national levels, and not infrequently have political associations. The ways in which economic activities are organized and controlled in any one national territory at a particular historical period, then, are often the results of earlier, and continuing, competition between alternative conceptions of economic organization and different collective actors combining economic with political objectives.

The competition between autarkic and decentralized industrial orders in Germany, and similar battles between conflicting groups and their conceptions of economic organization in Denmark and elsewhere (Kristensen 1992, 1996, 1997), emphasize both the contested nature of 'national' systems of economic organization and the importance of national political arenas in establishing and reproducing particular 'rules of the game' for economic actors. In characterizing any one form of economic coordination and control as 'the' dominant one in, say, post-war Japan, this example of intra-national competition highlights its contingent and often conflictual nature as well as its linkages to particular interest groups and political–social arrangements. There is, therefore, no overwhelming reason to expect the current system to be uniquely and permanent 'Japanese', or to rule out the possibility of internal and external pressures and conflicts combining to transform it into a different one. Distinctive varieties of capitalism develop from economic and political competition between different kinds of social actors and are always subject to further conflicts and reformulations from different groups and rationalities.

Such conflicts remain highly national in their focus and organization, however, because nation states constitute the prevalent arena in which social and political competition is decided in industrial capitalist economies. As systems of economic organization are closely connected to particular kinds of interest-group formation and conflicts—between, for example, family firm owners, financial intermediaries, technically competent managerial élites, technicians of different kinds, skilled and unskilled workers—they both reflect and reproduce the ways those groups compete for control over resources, jurisdictions, and legitimacy in particular political systems (Kristensen 1997). Since this competition takes place in essentially national institutional arenas, patterns of economic organization are more structured by nationally organized collectivities and conflicts than by regional or international ones.

If the primary level of political and interest-group mobilization and competition were to move from the national to, say, the continental, then of course we could expect distinctive industrial orders and associated ways of structuring economic activities to become established at international levels. However, these would be greatly contested by current groupings and established national structures and so would inevitably reflect such battles for dominance. Just as the nature of any future European political system, for example, will be the outcome of competing national interests and political arrangements, so too will any pan-European system of economic coordination and control reflect the struggle between national and sectoral economic élites and interests and the particular forms of economic organization they help to constitute.

More general comparisons of economic coordination systems and their institutional supports have been undertaken by Boyer, Hollingsworth, Streeck, and colleagues in a series of collaborative volumes over the past decade (Campbell *et al.* 1991; Hollingsworth *et al.* 1994; Hollingsworth and Boyer 1997*a*). Initially focusing on the comparative analysis of governance mechanisms in eight different sectors of the US economy, and how these have changed, later studies examined variations in sectoral organization across countries. These distinguished a number of complexes of economic organization and societal institutions, termed social systems of production, that varied in their economic outcomes.

The early studies of changing forms of sectoral organization in the US economy focused on how the prevalent rules and conventions governing transactions between organizations within industries became established and transformed. These 'governance mechanisms' are characterized in terms of two dimensions: the degree of formal integration of transactions and the number of organizations in the sectors concerned incorporated into a particular governance regime (Lindberg *et al.* 1991: 13–14). Formalization is here divided into three categories of intensity. First, informal and often tacit conventions govern many exchange relationships in markets and among competitors. Secondly, variously organized networks of obligations and alliances between suppliers, customers, and competitors display greater stability and formalization of control procedures over the behaviour of organizations than do many markets, as in profit-pooling and production-allocation federations (cf. Daems 1983; Feldenkirchen 1997). Thirdly, formal bureaucratic structures represent the greatest degree of systematic integration of transactions, whether within a single enterprise or across sector members.

When combined with variations in the range of exchanges and actors encompassed by governance regimes, these three degrees of formal integration generate six distinct types of governance mechanism: markets, obligational networks, hierarchies, on the one hand, monitoring, promotional networks, and associations, on the other hand. Changes in the prevalent governance mechanisms in different sectors of the US economy over a century or so are explored as the result of changing perceptions of efficiency, technologies, and state policies. They also reflect changes in the political and economic powers of major collective actors, as well as alterations in other aspects of domestic and foreign political–economic conditions (Campbell and Lindberg 1991).

This concentration on how transactions between firms within industrial sectors are structured and controlled reveals considerable variety across industries in the USA and in how they change. The organization of exchange relationships in telecommunications, nuclear energy, railroads, steel, automobiles, meat-packing, dairy products, and healthcare clearly differs considerably, both in the late nineteenth and early twentieth centuries and in recent decades. To a considerable extent, these variations reflected the actions of state and federal governments (Lindberg and Campbell 1991; cf. Dobbin 1994; Fligstein 1990). However, by concentrating on exchange transactions between organizations, these analyses do not consider how firms themselves became constituted as discrete economic actors with variously defined boundaries and changing strategic priorities, nor how variations in the nature of firms were connected to how they managed transactions with each other and with employees. They therefore did not consider the systemic nature of these phenomena.

Relatedly, focusing on exchange regulation at the sectoral level limits consideration of how sectors themselves develop and change, or how firms come to coordinate activities across sectors and alter sectoral boundaries as they diversify and seek new markets. It also, of course, obscures more general features of economic organization that become institutionalized across sectors, especially in capital-intensive manufacturing industries. These develop interdependently with society-wide institutions, as analysed by Hollingsworth (1991) in his contrast of the Fordist system of mass production in the USA with the 'post-Fordist' system of diversified quality production, which some see as characteristic of post-war Japan and parts of Germany.

In a similar way to Lazonick's (1991) and Best's (1990) systematization of the Chandlerian visible-hand model of capitalism and its successor forms of competition and organization, this contrast combines differences in dominant-firm type and prevalent labour-management practices with variations in the nature of product markets and technologies and inter-firm relationships. It, therefore, goes beyond simply examining exchange relationships on their own. Additional aspects of the business environment which are seen as being linked to the predominance of either mass-production or flexible-production systems in a particular sector concern the education and training system, modes of capital formation, and state regulation of business combination, together with state support and coordination.

Despite the considerable differences, then, in sectoral organization in the twentieth-century US economy, important aspects of the ways that economic activities are coordinated and controlled seem to be more similar across industries within this national territory than vary between them. This similarity reflects those features of its political, financial, and education systems that have become nationally standardized. This is especially so when contrasted with those dominating the post-war German and Japanese economies. Rather than focusing on sectoral variations in governance mechanisms controlling transactions between organizations within a single country, this contrast of production regimes highlights the need to consider systematic characteristics of economic coordination and control relationships across national boundaries.

Cross-national variations in governance mechanisms in nine industries have been examined by Hollingsworth, Schmitter, and Streeck (1994), together with their colleagues. Still focusing primarily on the ways in which transactions between economic actors are controlled within particular sectors, these studies revealed considerable national differences in the prevalence of markets, hierarchies, networks, states, and associations as institutions regulating economic exchanges. Such variations reflected long-standing contrasts in the characteristics of national legal systems, political and financial systems, and policies and the institutions governing the development and control of various skills.

As Hollingsworth and Streeck (1994) point out in their concluding essay, the technological and economic contingencies shaping sectoral organization across societies through defining possible economies of scale and scope leave considerable room for national institutions to structure governance regimes and other aspects of economic coordination and control systems. Indeed, the nine studies of sector organization in eight states presented in their book demonstrate the considerable commonality of many characteristics across industries engendered by particular features of the national business environment, especially state structures and policies. The ways in which firms organize production chains, labour relations, trade associations, and competition in the chemicals, cars, steel, shipbuilding, electronic-components, machine-tools, consumer-electronics, dairy, and securities industries seem more similar within these environments than between them.

This emphasizes the national nature of many significant variations in forms of economic organization. Technical and market factors are less significant in structuring these differences than are societal institutions and agencies. Many important aspects of governance regimes, including the relative economic and political significance of individual industries in an economy, have been and remain nationally distinctive and constitute particular kinds of social systems of production (Hollingsworth and Boyer 1997*b*). These configurations of particular kinds of societal institutions dealing with the organization of labour power, capital, and state policies encourage the development and reproduction of different kinds of economic coordination mechanisms, and thus the dominance of specific production regimes. Essentially, the nature of core national institutions is seen as structuring the environment of economic actors so that distinctive economic logics become established which are associated with particular kinds of production systems. These latter consist of mutually interdependent combinations of production techniques, products and market types, forms of the division of labour at the workplace, authority structures, and reward systems.

The Fordist mass production of standardized goods for large homogeneous markets is perhaps the most obvious of these in the twentieth century and is contrasted here with various forms of flexible production. Four of these latter are distinguished: customized production, adaptive production, diversified quality mass production, and flexible diversified quality production (Boyer and Hollingsworth 1997). These are formally differentiated in terms of three dimensions: volume of production, speed of adjustment to changing market conditions, and whether competition is primarily on the basis of quality or price.

Different combinations of these characteristics are associated with variations in the importance of particular governance mechanisms for coordinating transactions, such as markets, networks, and firms, which develop interdependently with broader societal institutions. Thus, production systems develop complementarities with their societal contexts so that a limited number of different ones become established and, once dominant in a particular society, they are slow to change. The development of mass production in Anglo-Saxon societies, for example, has relied upon the combination of classical market contracting and large ownership-based managerial hierarchies in relatively impoverished institutional environments which inhibited cooperation and collective action by firms.

Many forms of flexible production, in contrast, are associated with extensive obligational networks between economic actors and considerable cooperation between competitors that developed and continue to be reproduced by particular state and private structures and agencies. In so far as changes in consumer tastes, forms of competition, production technologies, and skills are rendering mass-production systems uncompetitive, societies which lack the appropriate institutional infrastructure for encouraging flexible production and its associated coordination mechanisms will be disadvantaged in this view.

This approach focuses attention on the interconnections between product market strategies, coordination mechanisms, and societal institutions in different kinds of twentieth-century capitalism. It also highlights the ways in which different kinds of business environments can structure the sorts of governance mechanisms that dominate individual economies and thereby affect the relative economic performance of particular sectors facing various kinds of competition. In so far as there are general technical and market requirements for competitive success in different industries, then, the considerable variability apparent in institutional arrangements between societies in North America, Europe, and East Asia should encourage similar variations in the relative success of firms in these industries between countries.

Furthermore, since production systems, governance mechanisms, and societal institutions together constitute distinctive configurations that privilege some industries and interest groupings over others, it is unlikely that significant changes in these social systems of production will be rapid or free of considerable conflicts between different economic and political élites and groupings. Where, for instance, financial intermediation has been subordinated to rapid industrialization and the growth of export-oriented manufacturing industries, as in many East Asian and continental European societies, the growth of thriving financial-service organizations competing effectively in a world market dominated by Anglo-Saxon 'rules of the game' will be both slow and conflictual, as is evidenced by the banking crises of the late 1980s in the Nordic countries.

These analyses of social systems of production, then, summarize a number of important features of capitalist economies and suggest some connections between societal institutions and economic organization. However, the concern with mechanisms governing transactions between economic actors tends to obscure consideration of how different kinds of actors develop and control resources in different institutional contexts—and on what basis. As comparative analyses of firms and networks have shown, how economic actors are constituted and bounded varies considerably between forms of capitalism. This means that 'firms' as ownership-based units do not always combine authority founded on private property rights with formal organizational structures. Ownership and authority boundaries cannot, then, be assumed to be the same across societies (Hamilton and Feenstra 1997). Additionally, the processes by which particular configurations of state, financial, and labour systems become established and structure both dominant governance regimes and production systems are not always systematically articulated in these studies. It is also unclear how the degree of coherence and integration of social systems of production varies and can be expected to change.

THE COMPARATIVE ANALYSIS OF ECONOMIC ORGANIZATION

The comparative studies of business groups, industrial orders, and social systems of production have highlighted the close connections between firms' competitive strategies and their internal structures and external relationships. They have also emphasized the strong interdependence between dominant forms of organizing economic activities in particular regions and economies and the nature of the institutional contexts in which these developed. How economic transactions are organized between different kinds of economic actors and related to particular production systems differs significantly between institutional environments so that they constitute qualitatively distinct systems of economic organization that are unlikely to converge into a single one.

Such analyses also suggest, together with the institutionalist and other comparative studies discussed above, a number of ways of conceptualizing the key characteristics of systems of economic coordination and control and explaining their variations that could develop a more general approach to the comparative analysis of economic organization. Such an approach would identify the crucial ways in which market economies vary and show how particular institutional features and agencies can explain these variations. It would specify the distinctive nature of particular forms of capitalism conceived as systems of economic organization, and suggest the explanatory logics by which these become established and reproduced in different societal contexts. The studies discussed above suggest six general points that need to be taken into account in developing the comparative analysis of economic organization.

First, while the identification of the key characteristics of economic systems enables a limited number of coherent and distinctive 'ideal types' of economic organization to be conceptualized, the extent to which these become established in any particular economy remains limited. This is because the features of dominant institutions that affect these characteristics rarely reinforce each other consistently to encourage a single type of economic coordination and control system to develop. Typically, they generate contradictions and conflicts between competing principles of economic organization. Such contradictions and conflicts do, though, vary in degree and scope, so that some institutional contexts lead to more coherent and integrated patterns of economic organization than do others.

Post-war Japan, for instance, exhibits greater interdependence between institutional arrangements and business-system characteristics than the US economy (Hollingsworth 1991; Whitley 1992*a*).

The interdependencies between the business-system characteristics and features of dominant institutions that I shall outline in later chapters are to be understood, then, as tendencies that become realized in concrete economies when appropriate conditions obtain. As Herrigel (1996) has emphasized, the establishment of any one dominant 'industrial order' in a society reflects the outcome of competing groupings and structures, and cannot be assumed to remain uncontested. In principle, any framework for analysing economic organization in different contexts should be able to identify the processes by which such competition and contestation take place and result in particular outcomes.

Secondly, the comparative analysis of economic organization also has to encompass different kinds of economic actors and ways in which they cooperate and compete. As the above discussion has emphasized, units of economic decision-making and control vary considerably in their constitution and organization across capitalist economies and so their distinctive characteristics need to be explored rather than assumed to be identical. 'Firms' are by no means the same sorts of economic actors in different economies. This means that the ways in which private ownership is organized and connected to authority hierarchies—as well as how these latter are structured, of course—are central to any comparative analysis of economic organization.

Thirdly, variations in prevalent standards for evaluating economic performance and preferred strategic objectives across economies need to be analysed. As many of the authors considered here have emphasized, these vary greatly between societal contexts, not least as a result of differences in financial and political systems that encourage contrasting ways of managing risk and uncertainty. In addition to the usual distinction between growth and profit goals, different kinds of competitive strategies, innovation priorities, diversification preferences, and modes of growth are encouraged and discouraged by different business environments in ways that need further exploration.

Fourthly, many of these studies have additionally emphasized the varied ways in which organizational integration can occur between ownership units, and indeed the importance in many economies of authoritative networks or federations which are empowered to direct their member firms (e.g. Hamilton and Feenstra 1997; Lazonick and West 1998). Authority over economic activities is by no means restricted to units of financial control based on unified ownership— or 'firms'—but is often entrenched in various collective associations which are able to delimit production and pricing levels and coordinate investment decisions of legally autonomous entities. Such collective entities, on occasion, develop distinct and superior decision-making powers, with or without ownership ties, so that they become more significant as economic actors than legally defined firms do. Economic systems thus vary in their concentration or diffusion of decision-making and control between kinds of collectivities. Relatedly, the considerable differences in how supply chains are organized across institutional contexts have been highlighted in numerous studies of 'obligational' and arm's length contracting. These reflect both institutionalized expectations about reciprocity and fair dealing and established arrangements for controlling market entry and exit and the generation of various forms of trust.

Fifthly, considerable attention has been paid to different ways of managing employment relations and of involving the manual workforce in the development of organizational capabilities, especially by those concerned with flexible production systems and the 'new competition' (Best 1990; Lazonick 1990, 1991). In addition to the simple contrast of Taylorized work processes and various forms of delegated responsibility to skilled work that underlay much of the deskilling debate (e.g. A. Friedman 1977), this focus encompasses differences in the nature of employment expectations and practices, training, mobility, and internal versus external 'careers' for the bulk of the manual workforce. It is closely connected, of course, to types of national education and training systems, skill definition and control institutions, union structures and policies, and the legal framework governing labour relations, as well as more diffuse norms and values concerning authority, loyalty, and identity.

Finally, in many of the studies of different types of economic organization considered above, the precise reasons for particular variations have been difficult to identify, and the relevant societal institutions not always specified in a systematic way. In particular, the manner in which, say, political regulations have developed interdependently with the workings of the financial-system and/or labour-market institutions to guide the development or change of particular features of economic coordination mechanisms has often not been clearly spelled out. Nor have the processes by which conflicting pressures from different institutional arenas and agencies affect firm behaviour and structure been explored across countries on many occasions. In principle, the comparative analysis of economic origination has to show how variations in particular societal—or regional, or supranational—institutional agencies and structures helped to generate distinctive forms of economic coordination and control and continue to reproduce differences between them.

The comparative-business-systems approach presented in this book is an attempt to develop such a framework for comparing forms of economic organization that identifies their key characteristics and differences and explains these in terms of variations in particular kinds of societal institutions. It suggests how distinctive ways of organizing economic activities in industrial capitalist societies vary and why they do so. While not incorporating all the aspects of economic systems discussed by the studies considered in this introductory chapter, it does include most of them, albeit sometimes under different descriptions, and also draws on many of the explanatory linkages adduced by these authors.

Arising from an attempt to describe and explain the major differences found in the economic systems which have become established in East Asia since the Second World War (Whitley 1992a), this approach has been modified and extended to take account of the many different ways of coordinating economic activities in Europe (Whitley 1992*b*; Whitley and Kristensen 1996, 1997) and of the development of market economies in Eastern Europe since 1989. By highlighting the key characteristics of economic organization and their interconnections in market economies, and linking these to variations in political, financial, labour, and cultural systems, it emphasizes how different kinds of market economies have developed and continue to vary, and why they are unlikely to converge the same type in the future.

The next three chapters outline the general framework for comparing and explaining characteristics of business systems across market economies. In each one I first describe the basic characteristics of the economic coordination systems being analysed, that is: business systems, firms and work systems, and their interconnections. Subsequently, I identify the major interdependences between these characteristics and specific features of their institutional environments. Essentially, I suggest that differences in societal institutions encourage particular kinds of economic organization and discourage other ones through structuring the ways that collective actors are constituted, cooperate, and compete for resources and legitimacy, including the standards used to evaluate their performance and behaviour.

In Chapter 2, the basic ways in which business systems vary as coordination and control systems are described and the key institutional features that impinge upon these identified. Similarly to the analyses of Lazonick, Orru *et al.*, and others, a central concern here is the extent and mode of organizational coordination of economic activities. As many of the broadly institutionalist studies discussed above have suggested, the major institutions affecting this govern the organization and access to key resources such as capital and labour power, as well as the constitution of collective actors and how they compete.

Chapter 3 focuses in more detail on the nature of firms as units of financial control based on ownership and of employment in different business systems, and how the institutional environments of various market economies generate different kinds of firm that pursue different strategies. The following chapter summarizes the major characteristics of five kinds of work organization and control that are prevalent in different business systems and suggests how variations in the organization of social groupings and societal institutions are related to these. Chapter 5 considers the implications of the growing internationalization of economic exchange and managerial coordination for business systems at regional, national, and international levels.

Part Three examines the development of different kinds of business systems in East Asia and Eastern Europe, and how they are changing interdependently with institutional shifts. Chapter 6 summarizes the processes leading to the establishment of the distinctive business systems of post-war Korea and Taiwan, while the following chapter considers the effects of changes in the international and national contexts of East Asian business systems in the late 1980s and early 1990s on their distinctive characteristics. Chapter 8 compares the emerging systems of economic organization in two former state socialist societies, Hungary and Slovenia, in the light of their legacies from the state socialist period and the particular ways in which market institutions were developed and established in these countries. Finally, Chapter 9 presents some detailed evidence about the extent of enterprise change in Hungary in the 1990s as the result of institutional transformation. As expected, this was rather less than many anticipated in the aftermath of the collapse of the Soviet Union, and some features of the late state socialist economy continue to be reproduced despite changes in ownership and control.

PART TWO

THE COMPARATIVE-BUSINESS-SYSTEMS FRAMEWORK

2

The Nature of Business Systems and their Institutional Structuring

The comparative analysis of varieties of capitalism involves the identification of the central phenomena of market economies in ways that are both (*a*) sufficiently standardized across them to enable comparisons to be made systematically, and (*b*) flexible and variable enough to incorporate the crucial aspects in which they differ. If, for example, we focus on the characteristics of privately owned firms, they have to be conceptualized in such a way as to include the considerable variety of enterprise types found in late-twentieth-century capitalism. This means that they cannot simply be assumed to be discrete organizational hierarchies defined by legal and financial boundaries, as in much Anglo-Saxon economics (Richardson 1972). Indeed, an important aspect of contrasting forms of capitalist economic organization concerns the identification and differentiation of units of economic decision-making and action in, say, French industrial groups, Chinese family businesses, and Japanese *keiretsu* (Bauer and Cohen 1981; Redding 1990; Westney 1996).

The defining characteristics of different economic coordination and control systems have, then, to be constructed so that variations in the nature and behaviour of 'firms' can be described and explained, rather than simply presumed to be identical across market economies. The boundaries and characteristics of firms are key variables that help to distinguish varieties of capitalism and need to be explained in any comparative analysis of market economies. As Hamilton and Feenstra (1997: 66) have emphasized, the 'boundaries of economic organization are determined by the reach of authoritative power and are not arbitrarily equated with the firm'. For instance, cartels, profit-pooling federations, business groups, and similar alliances of legally separate firms all represent distinct forms of authoritative economic coordination that are distinct from units of financial control based on ownership (Daems 1983; Feldenkirchen 1997; Kurgen-van Hentenryk 1997). Authoritative coordination is here taken to mean common obedience to established rules of conduct in the pursuit of collectively agreed goals.

The comparative analysis of economic organization encompasses ownership-based units, then, but deals with broader and more general phenomena. In this chapter I focus on the description and explanation of different kinds of economic coordination and control systems, summarized as business systems, as general patterns of economic coordination, and control in market economies. Variations in the constitution and behaviour of firms as units of financial control under common ownership within these systems will be discussed in Chapter 3. As has been emphasized by many of the comparative studies summarized in the previous chapter, both forms of economic organization in general, and the nature of firms in particular, depend on the significance of ownership and legal boundaries in the society at large, and these arrangements differ considerably between economies.

How, then, should we describe and contrast economic coordination and control systems? The major difference between varieties of capitalism identified by Chandler (1990), Lazonick (1991), and others concerned the degree of organizational integration of economic activities. Not only has the 'visible hand' of managerial capitalism increased the number and variety of inputs and outputs controlled by authority relations since the first Industrial Revolution, but these are also organized in quite different ways in different economies. The extent to which, and dominant ways through which, organizational routines, hierarchies, and institutionalized expectations coordinate economic decisions and actors in various market economies are, then, important differentiating characteristics of business systems.

The idealized Marshallian industrial district, for example, is composed of small, owner-controlled, narrowly specialized actors whose activities are mostly coordinated through short-term market contracting (Langlois and Robertson 1995). This sort of business system perhaps comes closest to the classical spot market form of economic coordination in which transactions are impersonal, frequently anonymous, singular, and overwhelmingly price based. It represents the lowest degree of organizational integration of economic activities.

The post-war Japanese economy, in contrast, has been dominated by large corporations which have extensive obligational networks between suppliers and customers and significant cross-ownership ties between members of horizontally diversified business groups (see e.g. Gerlach 1992; Westney 1996). In addition, the 'white-collarization' of core manual workers (Koike 1987) in these large firms extends organizational integration to the bulk of their employees, and thereby increases the innovative capacity of the economy according to Lazonick (1991; Lazonick and West 1998). In many respects this represents the most highly organized post-war economy in terms of the extent of non-spot-market-based coordination of economic activities. Such integration need not be, and often is not, restricted to managerial hierarchies under unitary ownership. Central characteristics of market economies are, then, the overall extent to which economic activities are authoritatively integrated, and the prime means by which this is achieved, especially the role of ownership.

Important related features concern the ways that differently constituted groupings of social actors control economic activities and resources. The organization of ownership and control of private property rights, for instance, vary across capitalist societies such that controllers of financial assets have different kinds of connection to salaried managers and the authority structures they dominate.

Additionally, managerial élites vary in their ties to particular organizations and in their relations with technical staff and other employees. Put simply, owners and controllers of capital, salaried managers, skilled manual and non-manual workers, and other employees are organized differently across varieties of capitalism. They also compete and cooperate with each other in contrasting ways. These differences mean that the nature of economic actors and their interrelations vary significantly across market economies.

Business systems are conceived here, then, as distinctive patterns of economic organization that vary in their degree and mode of authoritative coordination of economic activities, and in the organization of, and interconnections between, owners, managers, experts, and other employees. Differences in the nature of relationships between five broad kinds of economic actors are particularly important in contrasting business systems: (*a*) the providers and users of capital, (*b*) customers and suppliers, (*c*) competitors, (*d*) firms in different sectors, and, finally, (*e*) employers and different kinds of employees. These vary in both the extent of organizational integration and whether this is achieved primarily through ownership-based hierarchies, formal agreements, personal obligations, informal commitments, etc.

Ownership, for example, can be exercised directly over economic activities and resources as in the owner-managed firm, or may be delegated to trusted agents with varying degrees of interdependence and commitment. It may also integrate whole production chains through formal authority systems or be much more narrowly specialized. Similarly, inter-firm relations within production chains can be dominated by *ad hoc*, one-off, anonymous, and adversarial bargains, as in much pure market contracting, or by more repeated, particularistic, and cooperative connections, as in obligational contracting (Dore 1986; Sako 1992).

Competitor relations may likewise be almost entirely adversarial and zero-sum, or may in contrast encompass collaboration over a number of issues such as R&D, training, and union negotiations. Finally, employer–employee relations can vary considerably between the sort of adversarial zero-sum conflicts typical of early industrialization in many societies and the more institutionalized forms of cooperation represented by Germany's Co-Determination Acts, and large firm–core workers interdependences in post-war Japan.

The considerable number of possible types of economic organization described in terms of these five sets of relationships is restricted empirically by their interdependence with societal institutions. For example, those institutions that encourage adversarial kinds of relations between competitors are also likely to encourage similar kinds of connections between elements of production chains and between employers and employees. As a result of such interconnections, the number of highly distinctive business systems that do become established and reproduced over many decades is rather less than the possible number of combinations of business-system characteristics. A further point about this broad set of comparisons is that they have quite strong implications for the sorts of growth and risk-management strategies likely to be followed by firms' managers in different kinds of market economies. These points will be further explored after the basic dimensions for comparing business systems have been described more systematically.

CHARACTERISTICS OF BUSINESS SYSTEMS

The general characterization of market economies in terms of the degree and mode of organizational integration of economic activities, together with differences in the nature of controlling groups, suggest eight key dimensions for comparing business systems. These are listed in Table 2.1. Particularly important in such economies, of course, are the ways in which private property rights confer authority over the acquisition, use, and disposal of resources and activities, including labour power. The organization of these property rights, connections between their owners and controllers and delegated agents or managers, and between managers and other employees, are clearly crucial phenomena which are closely related to variations in ownership- and non-ownership-based modes of economic coordination. Three of these eight dimensions therefore deal with variations in the organization of ownership relations and the role of ownership in coordinating activities. A further three concern other forms of organizational integration in which authority does not depend on unified ownership. The last two summarize major differences in employment relations and work organization that reflect both the extent of integration within enterprises and the organization of interest groups in the wider society.

Ownership Coordination

If we consider first relations between owners and controllers of private property rights and controllers of economic resources and activities—i.e. salaried

TABLE 2.1. Key characteristics of business systems

Ownership coordination
Primary means of owner control (direct, alliance, market contracting)
Extent of ownership integration of production chains
Extent of ownership integration of sectors

Non-ownership coordination
Extent of alliance coordination of production chains
Extent of collaboration between competitors
Extent of alliance coordination of sectors

Employment relations and work management
Employer–employee interdependence
Delegation to, and trust of, employees (Taylorism, task performance discretion, task organization discretion)

---

managers—an important dimension for distinguishing economies concerns the extent of owners' direct involvement in managing businesses. Three major types can be distinguished here: (*a*) *direct* control of firms by owners, (*b*) *alliance* control, in which owners delegate considerable strategic decision-making to managers but remain committed to particular firms, and (*c*) *market* or arm's length portfolio control. Owner-managers of family businesses—whether artisanal elements of industrial districts or the massive Korean conglomerates (*chaebol*)—typify direct control. Bank and allied companies' ownership of some shares in Germany and Japan exemplify alliance control, while the Anglo-Saxon pattern of institutional portfolio investment demonstrates the market type of owner control.

These three broad types of ownership vary in terms of six important characteristics summarized in Table 2.2. In this table and in subsequent ones in this book, the degree to which a characteristic is expected to vary is normally described in terms of five levels: low, limited, some, considerable, and high. The first aspect of ownership considered here deals with the extent to which owners and controllers of financial assets are involved in managerial issues and decisions of particular enterprises. Secondly, the concentration of control over these assets is high in owner-managed firms, considerable in most instances of alliance ownership where owners/controllers of voting rights are effectively locked in to the destinies of particular firms, and typically very low in most market forms. As a result, they differ significantly in, thirdly, owners' collective knowledge of the technologies, products, and markets of the firms in which they have major shareholdings.

Fourthly, the different extent of owners' interdependence with specific firms means that they vary in their exposure to, and sharing of, these firms' risks. Fifthly, the breadth of interest that owners have in any particular firms differs

TABLE 2.2. Characteristics of owner-control types

Characteristics	Types of owner control		
	Direct	Alliance	Market
Involvement in management	High	Some	Very low
Concentration of ownership	High	Considerable of voting rights, some of share ownership	Low, but some concentration of control over shares by portfolio managers
Owners' knowledge of business	High	Considerable	Low
Risk-sharing and commitment	High	Considerable	Low
Scope of owner interest	High	Considerable	Low
Exclusivity of ownership	Considerable	Limited	High

from the narrowly financial return on assets held typical of market ownership, to the wide-ranging interests of owner-managers. Alliance-type owners and controllers of financial assets usually have broader business interests in their link-ages than do portfolio holders. For example, banks controlling shares and voting rights often seek deposits from employees and preferential access to opportunities for providing additional financial services.

Finally, the exclusivity and rigidity of ownership boundaries typically varies across these ownership types. This refers to the extent that ownership rights are seen as indivisible and difficult to share. Owner-managers, for instance, usually maintain firm control over organizational boundaries and identify them with their ownership rights. Control and shareholdings are not often shared with others, except within families or with those with whom family-like relationships have been established over a long time. Similarly, market types of ownership encourage strong ownership boundaries because capital holders focus on returns from relatively discrete and separate comparable units in making investment decisions and changes. Overlapping boundaries and diffuse, broad linkages between units of financial control make it more difficult for portfolio managers to compare returns from individual firms in the absence of detailed information about particular enterprises.

Also, given the predominantly adversarial and arm's length relations between economic actors in economies where market forms of ownership dominate, long-term cooperation and sharing of resources, activities, and ownership between firms are difficult to develop and reproduce. In contrast, alliance forms of owner-ship encourage permeability and overlaps of organizational and ownership boundaries to share risks, to improve flexibility, and to coordinate innovations, as in post-war Japan.

The scope of ownership integration of economic activities also varies greatly across market economies. Two further dimensions for comparing ownership relations across business systems, then, concern (*a*) the extent of *ownership integration of production chains* in a number of sectors and (*b*) the degree of *ownership integration of activities across sectors*. The largest *chaebol* in Korea are both vertically and horizontally diversified, but the smaller ones tend to focus on vertical integration rather than unrelated diversification (Fields 1995). In contrast, many large German firms are also quite vertically integrated but limit their horizontal diversification to technologically and/or market-related fields (Feldenkirchen 1997; Herrigel 1996). Chinese family businesses have been characterized as pursuing opportunistic diversification that is typically horizontal, although backward integration from retailing and distribution to manufacturing in light consumer goods industries is also quite a common pattern of development (Hamilton 1997; Hamilton and Kao 1990; Redding 1990; Wong 1988).

These three characteristics of ownership relations are often interrelated, in that alliance forms of owner control tend to inhibit unrelated diversification while market ones encourage it as a way of spreading risks that cannot easily be shared with business partners. Where owners become locked into the fates of particular firms, they tend to develop expertise and knowledge about their technologies and markets in order to manage their greater exposure to risk and uncertainty. Diversification into unknown fields increases owners' risks and so is unlikely to be encouraged by them. Portfolio holders in capital markets, on the other hand, can usually sell their assets on liquid secondary markets if diversification fails and so are unlikely to oppose it strongly.

Non-Ownership Coordination

The integration of activities through alliances, obligations, and similar non-ownership linkages applies to three sets of inter-firm relationships. First, there are those between members of a production chain: this can be termed the extent of *alliance coordination of production chains*. Secondly, there are those between competitors, which can be characterized as the extent of *collaboration between competitors*. Thirdly, there are alliances between firms in different industries, which can be summarized as the extent of *alliance coordination of sectors*. In each case, the key contrast is between zero-sum, adversarial contracting and competition, on the one hand, and more cooperative, long-term, and mutually committed relationships between partners and competitors, on the other hand.

Production chains, for example, may be quite fragmented in ownership terms, but exhibit strong networks of obligational contracting between relatively stable suppliers and customers—sometimes with limited exchanges of shares, as in Japan. Similarly, competitors may compete fiercely for customers and yet collaborate over the introduction of new technologies, employment policies, and state lobbying through various formal associations and alliances, as numerous studies have shown (Campbell *et al.* 1991; Hollingsworth *et al.* 1994). They may also form production and profit-pooling federations and interest groups, as in some European countries (Daems 1983; Herrigel 1996).

Thirdly, firms may develop alliances across sectors, of varying stability, scope, and depth, to enter new markets, reduce the risks of specialization, or acquire new technologies. Occasionally these may involve long-term exchanges of equity, as in the Japanese inter-market groups (Gerlach 1992), but more commonly they take the form of subsidiary joint ventures and partnerships focused on fairly specific activities. Inter-sectoral business networks therefore differ considerably in (*a*) the range of activities they carry out jointly, (*b*) the extent and longevity of their collaboration, and (*c*) the variety of linkages between members, with the Japanese *kigyo shudan* at one extreme, and short-term, opportunistic, narrowly based alliances at the other.

In comparing the role of inter-firm networks across sectors in different market economies, the crucial issue is the extent to which economic activities are consciously and repeatedly coordinated across sectors by these sorts of horizontally diversified business groups. The existence of some such groups in Taiwan, for instance, does not imply a high level of this form of coordination, because they tend to be quite narrowly focused and based on personal rather than long-term organizational commitments. Taiwanese groups also do not dominate the economy to the extent that their Japanese counterparts do (Hamilton and Kao 1990; Numazaki 1992). Their authoritative integration of activities and resources is thus much less than that of the inter-market groups in Japan.

These variations in non-ownership forms of economic coordination and control are linked to differences in ownership relations. For example, direct owner control of managerial decisions will often limit the scope and depth of collaboration with competitors because of the strong sense of personal identity with the enterprise and reluctance to share information or control, especially in cultures where trust in formal institutions is low. Similarly, market forms of owner control are unlikely to encourage inter-firm alliances and cooperation, since they are typically associated with capital market-based financial systems that develop strong markets in corporate control and hence unstable owner–firm connections. Establishing long-term and wide-ranging alliances with business partners is riskier and more difficult in this situation than in economies where owners are more committed to the future of particular enterprises.

Furthermore, since alliance- and ownership-based modes of coordination and control are functionally equivalent in many circumstances, the dominance of large, diversified firms tends to prevent the development of alliances within and across production chains.

Employment and Work Management

Finally, employer–employee relations and work systems vary in a considerable number of ways, as the extensive literature on Fordism, labour processes, and industrial relations shows. The key contrast here, though, is between those societies encouraging reliance on external labour markets in managing the bulk of the labour force and those encouraging more commitment and mutual investment in organizational capabilities. This can be summarized as the degree of *employer–employee interdependence*.

Organization-based employment systems, such as those institutionalized in many large Japanese firms in the 1960s and 1970s, represent perhaps the greatest extent of mutual dependence between employers and the bulk of the workforce. The Anglo-Saxon pattern of 'flexible' external labour markets and high rates of employment change, on the other hand, represents the other extreme of this dimension (Dore 1973; Whittaker 1990*b*). Intermediate employment systems combine greater mobility among manual workers than is common in large Japanese firms with considerable employer and employee investment in skill development and improvement and *de facto*, if not formally agreed, long-term commitments by both parties. The post-war German and some Scandinavian business systems perhaps come closest to this combination.

Patterns of work organization and control can be distinguished primarily in terms of the discretion and trust employers grant to the bulk of the workforce in organizing and carrying out tasks, summarized here as the degree of managerial *delegation to, and trust of, employees.* The pure case of 'scientific management' removes all discretion from manual workers and fragments tasks to simplify them for unskilled and easily replaced employees. 'Responsible-autonomy' strategies, on the other hand, trust manual workers to carry out tasks with more discretion and independence from managers.

This autonomy, though, need not extend to questions of work organization and task definition. Few Japanese companies, for example, and even fewer Korean or Taiwanese ones, delegate the allocation and organization of jobs to manual workers, while being keen to involve them in problem-solving activities and grant many considerable discretion over task performance. In many Danish, German, and firms in some other European countries, on the other hand, employees have substantial influence on work-organization decisions, both formally and informally, particularly skilled workers (Kristensen 1992, 1997).

Employment strategies and work systems are interrelated in that it is difficult to envisage a firm pursuing a radically Taylorist system of work organization and control at the same time as seeking long-term commitments from the manual workers and investing in their skill development. Taylorism and market-based employment systems would, then, seem to be highly consonant. However, it clearly is possible to combine considerable fluidity in external labour markets with reliance on highly skilled workers who exercise high levels of discretion over work performance, as Kristensen's accounts of Danish work systems (1997) and many Anglo-Saxon professional service firms illustrate. In the case of the Danish metal-working sector, it seems that limited levels of organizational integration are combined with a very highly skilled labour force and considerable innovation. However, it may be that the powerful trade unions and pursuit of reputations for high levels of competence among occupational communities together function as coordinating devices here (Kristensen 1996).

The connections between high mutual commitment employment systems and work-control practices are, on the other hand, clearer. As Lazonick (1990, 1991), Best (1990), and others (e.g. Aoki 1988) have emphasized, integrating the bulk of the workforce into large, dominant enterprises as loyal and committed partners encourages firm-specific skill development, functional flexibility strategies, and the delegation of considerable autonomy over task performance. It need not, though, and typically does not in Japanese firms, imply high levels of worker control over job definition and allocation (Kumazawa and Yamada 1989).

These eight dimensions are general characteristics of business systems that exhibit particular interdependences with each other to form quite distinct ways of organizing market economies, from the atomized Marshallian industrial district to the highly coordinated post-war Japanese business system. These links are summarized in Table 2.3, which separates direct, alliance, and market types of owner control to highlight the differences between them. Considering first variations in types of owner control, these have quite strong implications for a number of other business-system characteristics. Both direct and market forms of owner control tend to limit inter-firm cooperation within industries and between them because of the strong connections between ownership-based coordination and authoritative control in the societies where these control types are highly institutionalized. Typically, control over economic activities is difficult to share between ownership units on a stable, long-term basis in such societies and so collaboration within production chains and sectors, and across them, is restricted.

Alliance forms of ownership, on the other hand, presume risk-sharing and mutual dependence between owners/controllers of financial assets and enterprises, which implies the development of an institutional framework for coordinating inter-firm relations in a non-zero-sum manner. Such a framework encourages other forms of inter-firm risk-sharing within production chains and collaboration between competitors. Similarly, it can lead to greater employer–employee interdependence as investors, managerial élites, and employees become locked in to particular sectors and each others' destinies. Market-based ownership relations, conversely, are associated with limited commitment between business partners. The existence of liquid external markets in labour and capital enable owners, managers, and workers to exit easily from organizational ties.

To some extent, ownership-based vertical and horizontal integration of activities within production chains and across market sectors rules out extensive reliance on other forms of coordination between firms. Thus, economies dominated by large, vertically integrated and widely diversified firms are unlikely to exhibit much sustained inter-firm collaboration within or across industries. However, it is clearly possible to combine a fair degree of vertical integration within ownership units with collaborative links between them, as German and other continental European firms have demonstrated in the twentieth century.

Such collaboration between firms within sectors is likely to limit diversification across them—at least into widely different areas of expertise—as sectoral partners seek to retain commitments to the sector and further its growth together. Enterprises that have substantial interests and assets in quite different fields will

TABLE 2.3. Interdependences between business-system characteristics

Business-system characteristics	1	2	3	4	5	6	7	8	9	10
1. Direct owner control		−	−			−	−	−	−	
2. Alliance owner control			−			+	+		+	
3. Market owner control					+	−	−	−	−	
4. Ownership vertical integration						−		−		
5. Ownership horizontal integration						−	−	−	−	
6. Alliance vertical integration										
7. Competitor collaboration										
8. Alliance horizontal integration										
9. Employer–employee interdependence										+
10. Worker discretion and involvement										

be seen as less committed to any particular industry and therefore less worthwhile partners for long-term collaboration, technology sharing, and so on.

Inter-firm collaboration may also encourage employer–employee interdependence, since cooperative links between competitors and common commitments to particular industries often lead to joint skill development and certification activities. Employer dependence on particular sectors additionally encourages the development of firm- and industry-specific skills and reliance on skilled workers' commitment to product and process improvements in those industries, and this is obviously difficult to elicit if they do not retain them over business cycles. Furthermore, high levels of employer–employee interdependence are often associated with considerable worker discretion over task performance, and sometimes task allocation and organization. This is because employers developing such interdependence rely on workers' flexibility to manage market and technology changes, and can assume greater levels of commitments and responsibility for overall organizational purposes than if they pursued numerical flexibility labour strategies and a 'hire-and-fire' culture.

These interconnections suggest that a limited number of combinations of business-system characteristics are likely to remain established over historical periods, because contradictions between them can be expected to generate conflicts between social groupings and prevalent institutional arrangements. In particular, business systems combining adversarial competitor relations with alliance forms of ownership and long-term employment commitments are unlikely to be reproduced over long periods, because owners and employees who are locked into the fate of particular firms will attempt to control market risks. Similarly, business systems based on market types of ownership relations are unlikely to be supportive of long-term risk-sharing between suppliers and customers or employers and employees, because portfolio owners usually prefer liquidity to lock-in.

At least six major ideal types of business system can be identified as a result of these linkages. Four types of market economy can be distinguished in terms of (*a*) their degree of ownership-based coordination of economic activities, and (*b*) the extent of non-ownership or alliance form of organizational integration. First, there are those where both forms are low, so that the overall level of coordination is quite limited. These can be termed *fragmented* business systems. Secondly, *coordinated industrial districts* combine relatively low levels of ownership integration—and so are dominated by small firms—with more extensive inter-firm integration and cooperation. Thirdly, *compartmentalized* business systems are dominated by large firms but exhibit low levels of cooperation between firms and business partners. Finally, *coordinated* or *collaborative* business systems combine relatively large units of ownership coordination with extensive alliances and collaboration between them. These last two types can be further differentiated by owner control type, size of firm, and extent of alliance integration between firms and within them to generate a further two kinds of business system: *state organized* and *highly coordinated*. These are summarized in Table 2.4 and will now be discussed in a little more detail.

TABLE 2.4. Six types of business system

Business-system characteristics	Business-system type					
	Fragmented	Coordinated industrial district	Compartmentalized	State organized	Collaborative	Highly coordinated
Ownership coordination						
Owner control	Direct	Direct	Market	Direct	Alliance	Alliance
Ownership integration of production chains	Low	Low	High	High	High	Some
Ownership integration of sectors	Low	Low	High	Some to high	Limited	Limited
Non-ownership coordination						
Alliance coordination of production chains	Low	Limited	Low	Low	Limited	High
Collaboration between competitors	Low	Some	Low	Low	High	High
Alliance coordination of sectors	Low	Low	Low	Low	Low	Some
Employment relations						
Employer–employee interdependence	Low	Some	Low	Low	Some	High
Delegation to employees	Low	Some	Low	Low	High	Considerable

Fragmented business systems are dominated by small owner-controlled firms that engage in adversarial competition with each other and short-term market contracting with suppliers and customers. Typically, employment relations are also short term and dominated by 'efficient' external labour markets. Thus, organizational integration of economic activities is low both across and within units of financial control in these economies. Such low risk-sharing by firms with business partners and with employees is often associated with relatively short-term commitments to particular technologies, skills, or markets. In the case of Hong Kong, firms moved rapidly from making plastic flowers, to wigs, to toy manufacturing and to property development and financial services as market conditions altered, representing perhaps the most exemplary low-commitment economy in recent decades.

Coordinated-industrial-district business systems, in contrast, exhibit more organized integration of inputs and outputs within production chains as well as more sectoral cooperation. Ownership units remain small and owner controlled, but rely more on worker commitment and, especially, on employees' willingness to improve task performance and innovation. As the title suggests, these kinds of economies are exemplified by the post-war Italian industrial districts and similar European regional business systems.

Where ownership integration of economic activities is greater, so that leading firms are quite large in terms of activities controlled, considerable variations in non-ownership forms of economic coordination, types of owner control, and extent of ownership integration are both theoretically feasible and empirically observable. In *compartmentalized* business systems large unified ownership units integrate activities both within production chains and across sectors. However, they exhibit little commitment or collaboration between firms or between employers and employees. Usually, owner control is exercised at arm's length through financial markets. Firms are here islands of authoritative control and order amidst market disorder, as in the stereotypical Anglo-Saxon economy (Richardson 1972).

State-organized business systems are similarly dominated by large firms that integrate production chains and activities in different sectors through a unified administrative apparatus. However, they differ in their ownership patterns. Families and partners in these economies are typically able to retain direct control over large firms because the state supports their growth through subsidized credit. They are termed state organized because the state dominates economic development and guides firm behaviour. As post-war South Korea demonstrates, horizontal linkages between economic actors and employer–employee interdependence are limited in these business systems by strong ties of vertical dependence, both between firms and the state and within enterprises dominated by owner managers (Fields 1995; Janelli 1993; Kang 1997).

Collaborative business systems, on the other hand, manifest more collective organization and cooperation within sectors, but less ownership integration of activities in technologically and market-unrelated sectors. Owner control of these large firms is typically alliance in nature and they tend to focus on particular industries rather than diversify across quite different ones. They develop a greater degree of employer–employee interdependence and trust of skilled workers than employers in compartmentalized and state-organized business systems. Many continental European economies come close to this kind of economic system, especially the more corporatist kind.

Highly coordinated business systems are also dominated by alliance forms of owner control but exhibit even more organizational coordination of economic activities throughout the economy. This is achieved through extensive intra- and inter-sectoral alliances and networks coordinating a large variety of activities, as in post-war Japan's 'alliance capitalism' (Gerlach 1992). Within ownership units, large employers in these business systems additionally integrate the bulk of the workforce into the organization to a greater extent than in other kinds of market economy and so employer–employee interdependence is typically very high here.

This summary of key business-system characteristics emphasizes their general and relatively long-term nature. This implies that they do not change very quickly or in response to the behaviour of individual firms. Significant change in these characteristics clearly involves considerable restructuring of economic relationships and typically requires substantial institutional reforms of the kind associated with the Allied occupations of Germany and Japan after the Second World War or the transformations of the former state socialist societies. Even in these cases, substantial continuities in many aspects of economic organization remain (Clark 1979; Herrigel 1996; Whitley 1992a; Whitley and Czaban 1998b).

THE BOUNDARIES OF BUSINESS SYSTEMS

So far I have talked mostly of market economies and business systems rather than of countries and national economies. In principle, distinctive systems of economic organization arise wherever key associated institutions are both mutually reinforcing and distinctive from other ones. However, nation states often do develop distinctive business systems for a number of reasons. First, state-based legal systems usually define and enforce private property rights in capitalist economies. Secondly, the state is typically responsible for maintaining public order. Thirdly, nation states usually organize interest groups and the conventions governing their competition and collaboration. They also, fourthly, remain the dominant level of organization for regulating financial systems and organizing skill development and control.

Even where norms and values are reproduced by families and ethnic communities which are both subnational and international, as in the case of the overseas Chinese and many migrant communities, the significance of these informal social organizations for systems of economic organization remains dependent on the structures and policies of states and political economies more generally. This is because state actions determine how effective are legal and educational systems, and hence the role of formal institutions in governing many important aspects of economic coordination.

State boundaries are especially important in economies where national political systems structure the formation of interest groups and modes of conflict resolution. The organization and actions of owners, managerial élites, and other groups of manual and non-manual workers, for instance, have been, and remain, highly nationally distinct and primarily focused on national arenas since the rise of the nation state as the dominant unit of political mobilization and competition. As long as resources, legitimacy, and jurisdictions are primarily controlled and contested within national boundaries, interest groups and their conflicts will remain organized at the national level.

If, however, these groups were primarily organized regionally, or internationally, and the major institutions governing their formation, competition, and collaboration were also regionally, or internationally, distinctive, and cohesive at those levels of social organization, then they would constitute distinct sub- or international systems of economic organization. In the case of the post-war, or perhaps post-1960s, Italian industrial districts, for example, it is debatable whether the key political, financial, and labour institutions in north-east and central Italy are sufficiently cohesive, separate, and distinct from those in the rest of Italy to constitute a quite different unit of socio-economic organization which can be contrasted with that established in north-west Italy or the Mezzogiorno.

While regional differences clearly are important and encourage considerable variations in patterns of economic organization across parts of Italy, it is difficult to understand the development of these industrial districts without taking account of the development of the Italian state and banking system, or the changes that occurred in the large firms of Milan and Turin in the post-war period (Weiss 1988). The interdependences between both local economic actors and local institutions and those in other regions and at the national level are too strong and significant to regard these industrial districts as a wholly separate business system. On the other hand, they do constitute an important and distinctive part of the post-war Italian business system, just as the small firms of Jutland constitute a significant—and arguably defining—component of 'the' Danish system (Kristensen 1992, 1997).

These examples highlight the need to identify the dominant role of institutions at each level of analysis. Where regional governments, financial institutions, skill development, and control systems and broad cultural norms and values are distinct from national ones and able to exert considerable discretion in the economic sphere, we would expect distinctive kinds of economic organization to become established at the regional level. This is especially so if national agencies and institutions are less effective in coordinating activities and implementing policies.

It is also important to note that many 'national' patterns of economic organization are the result of conflicts between distinct regional ones. For example, in the case of Germany, Herrigel (1996) has emphasized the importance of competition between the 'decentralized industrial order', which developed in Baden-Württemberg, Saxony, and elsewhere in Germany, and the 'autarkic' industrial order characteristic of the Ruhr and other regions, for the development of the German state and its policies in the late nineteenth and early twentieth centuries. The 'national' German industrial order was constructed, in his view, from the struggles of two quite distinct regional ones with their own pattern of institutional arrangements and agencies.

As in Italy, particular patterns of industrialization and state development resulted in considerable regional differences in economic organization and in the ways that firms and economic networks were, and are, linked to regional state agencies, banks, unions, and educational and research institutions. The continued strength and interconnectedness of regional economies and governing institutions in Germany prevented the establishment of a single industrial order across the whole country, in contrast to other political economies where the national state and related institutions became established as the dominant forces structuring economic relationships.

The increasingly dominant role of the London commercial and merchant banks at the end of the nineteenth century, at the expense of the provincial banks that had developed closer ties to industrial companies, for instance, represented such a centralization and standardization of the financial environment of British firms (Ingham 1984). Similarly, the dominating role played by the central state in most successful industrialization processes, except those in some northern European countries and North America, has meant that business systems are more national than regional in the late twentieth century.

The national boundedness of distinctive systems of economic organization is, then, historically contingent and variable. Distinctive and cohesive kinds of business system can become established and reproduced at regional, national, and international levels of socio-economic organization depending on the strength and integration of the actors and institutions involved at each level. If, for example, owners, managers, unions, and other organized groups became structured at a European level, together with the emergence of a European state that dominated national and regional political systems and established standardized labour and financial systems across Europe, we would expect nationally distinct business systems to become less significant than the emerging European form of economic organization.

Such a novel system would, of course, bear the marks of the struggles between national groupings, agencies, and institutional arrangements, just as national and regional business systems currently reflect the historical processes that led to their establishment. Both the characteristics of any pan-European business system and the features of its institutional context, as well as the ways in which political, financial, and labour systems at the European level are related to that system of economic organization, would emerge from an extensive series of competitive conflicts between existing patterns of economic organization, forms of interest representation, and the rationalities they exemplify and reproduce.

THE INSTITUTIONAL STRUCTURING OF BUSINESS-SYSTEM CHARACTERISTICS

As this discussion indicates, business-system characteristics in different societies developed interdependently with dominant social institutions during and after industrialization, so that distinctive forms of economic organization have become established in particular institutional contexts. Additionally, the distinctiveness and cohesion of business systems reflect the extent to which dominant institutions are integrated and their features mutually reinforcing. Important features of the family, labour-market institutions, the financial system, and state structures and policies in post-war Japan, for instance, are more interdependent than they are in the UK and the USA. As a result, many characteristics of the post-war Japanese business system are more integrated than are their counterparts in the Anglo-American economies (Campbell *et al.* 1991; Clark 1979; Hollingsworth *et al.* 1994; Lane 1992; Whitley 1992*a*).

There are a number of key institutions that help to generate and reproduce different kinds of business system, but the crucial institutional arrangements which guide and constrain the nature of ownership relations, inter-firm connections, and employment relations are those governing access to critical resources, especially labour and capital. Also important are the ways in which different kinds of labour power are developed, in terms of both technical skills and individuals' attitudes and values. Differences in the norms and rules controlling the terms on which private property rights' holders can acquire and use human and material resources, and exchange inputs and outputs, additionally have major consequences for firms' policies and structures. Finally, variations in social structures that differentiate individuals' capabilities and develop particular kinds of competences at the expense of others are also significant.

These institutional features can be very broadly characterized and compared across market economies in terms of four major arenas: the state, the financial system, the skill development and control system, and dominant conventions governing trust and authority relations. These deal with both the kinds of resources—especially human ones—that are available to privately owned economic actors in any particular market economy, and the terms on which they are available, as well as, of course, with the sorts of people who become private property rights' owners. To some extent, the location of particular features in one of these 'systems' is a matter of convenience. For example, the degree of state regulation of labour markets can be seen either as part of the overall level of state regulation of markets or as a specific feature of the training and occupational system. However, they do together summarize the aspects of the institutional context that impinge most on forms of economic organization. Their central features are summarized in Table 2.5.

The State

There are, of course, many features of state structures and policies that influence forms of economic organization, but three summary ones are particularly significant.

TABLE 2.5. Key institutional features structuring business systems

The state
Dominance of the state and its willingness to share risks with private owners
State antagonism to collective intermediaries
Extent of formal regulation of markets

Financial system
Capital market or credit based

Skill development and control system
Strength of public training system and of state–employer–union collaboration
Strength of independent trade unions
Strength of labour organizations based on certified expertise
Centralization of bargaining

Trust and authority relations
Reliability of formal institutions governing trust relations
Predominance of paternalist authority relations
Importance of communal norms governing authority relations

First, the overall cohesion, prestige, and autonomy of the state executive and bureaucracy, sometimes referred to as the 'strength' of the state *vis-à-vis* social interest groups, landed élites, etc., can be combined with their commitment to coordinate economic development and willingness to share investment risks with private economic interests. This feature can be termed: the extent to which *states dominate the economy and share risks* such that businesses become dependent on state policies and actions. Some, such as many Anglo-Saxon states, have neither the wish to, nor the capability for, actively coordinating economic processes. Others, like perhaps the post-1950s Japanese, pursue 'developmental' (Johnson 1982) policies but do not commit large resources to sharing private-sector investment risks, while a few do both, such as the post-1961 South Korean state (Amsden 1989; Wade 1990). Clearly, where the state is both 'strong' and actively risk-sharing, then private firms have to invest considerable resources in managing relations with the executive and bureaucracy.

A second significant feature of political systems is the extent to which the state encourages the establishment of important intermediary economic associations between individuals, firms, and the state. This can be summarized as the degree of *state antagonism to intermediaries*. Some European states, for instance, appear unable to tolerate such groupings, while others, such as the German and Austrian, seem positively to encourage their formation and to develop quite strong corporatist forms of intra- and inter-sectoral organization. Clearly, inter-firm cooperation, alliances, and cartelization will be easier in the latter sets of states than in the former.

Thirdly, there are significant differences in the extent to which states directly or indirectly regulate market boundaries, entry and exit, as well as set constraints on the activities of economic actors. They are here termed the extent of *formal regulation of markets.* In many countries, for instance, states regulate which sorts of organizations can offer financial services and how they can sell them, as well as where they can do so. Similarly, licences to undertake certain trades are often issued by national and local state agencies only when appropriate skill certificates have been acquired. In other countries, such powers are sometimes delegated to industry associations and quasi-statutory bodies. Product, capital, and labour markets, then, are variously regulated across states, and this affects their segmentation, the intensity of competition, mobility of resources, and flexibility of firms.

The Financial System

Financial systems also vary on a number of dimensions, but the critical feature here deals with the processes by which capital is made available and priced. In particular, is it allocated by capital markets through competition, so that lenders and users remain relatively remote from one another, or is it provided by some set of intermediaries that deal directly with firms and become locked into their particular success? *Capital-market-based financial systems,* as characterized by Zysman (1983), mobilize and distribute capital largely through large and liquid markets which trade and price financial claims through the usual commodity-market processes. Because many, if not most, investors and fund managers deal in portfolios of shares that can be readily traded on secondary and tertiary markets, they are only weakly committed to the growth of any single firm they own shares in. As a result, they have only a relatively short-term and narrow interest in its fortunes. This encourages a strong market for corporate control in capital-market financial systems, as ownership rights are easily traded and owners have little incentive to retain shares when offered considerable price premiums for them by acquisitive predators.

Credit-based financial systems, on the other hand, typically have weak and fairly illiquid or thin capital markets, which play only a minor role in mobilizing and pricing investment funds. The dominant institutions here are either large, 'universal' banks, as in Germany, or a combination of commercial banks and long-term credit banks coordinated by state agencies and ministries, as in France, Japan, and some other countries (Cox 1986). Because of capital shortages during high-growth periods, and/or state control of interest rates to support economic development, demand for investment funds often exceeds supply to a considerable degree in these systems. As a result, banks and/or the state allocate capital through administrative processes to particular sectors and activities, such as export industries or the heavy manufacturing sector. Since shares are not easily traded, owners, bankers, and trust managers become locked into particular borrowers' fates and so have to be more involved in decision-making and the detailed evaluation of investment plans than they do in capital-market-based systems.

This, in turn, means that they have to deal with a considerable amount of information about their customers' businesses and develop considerable expertise in them. Once that expertise has been developed by financial intermediaries, they have a vested interest in using it to provide new services and play a more active role in firms' growth planning. They thus become even more committed to particular enterprises and develop a common community of fate with them. Although a number of financial systems do not fit neatly into this broad dichotomy (see e.g. Iterson and Olie 1992), this basic contrast between two major kinds of financial systems has strong implications for firms and markets and is a critical feature of the institutional context of business systems.

The Skill Development and Control System

Thirdly, there is the system for developing and controlling skills, which has two broad and interrelated sets of institutions. First, there is the system that develops and certifies competences and skills: the education and training system. Secondly, there are the institutions that control the terms on which the owners of those skills sell them in labour markets and how those markets are organized. In comparing education and training systems, two aspects are especially important. First, the extent to which practical skills are jointly organized and certified by employers, unions, and state agencies. Secondly, the degree of integration of practical learning in firms with formal learning in educational institutions. In their comparison of work organization and control practices in France and Germany, Marc Maurice and his colleagues (1986) drew a contrast between unitary and generalist education systems, such as the French and Japanese, and dual, specialist ones, such as the German and some other continental European ones.

In the former, children are successively filtered by academic examinations in the general educational system and only 'failures' enter state practical training organizations, which are often poorly funded and have low social prestige. In the latter, practical skill training integrates theory and practice, as well as employers, unions, and state education, and is seen as a different, but not greatly inferior, form of education to the grammar-school system leading to university entrance. The 'dual' or specialist training system, at least in Germany, combines some elements of traditional apprenticeship with college-based formal instruction and is cooperatively managed by representatives of labour, capital, and the state.

While the specialist–generalist contrast is too simple to summarize all the important differences between education and training systems, there are two critical differences between these systems that impinge greatly on business-system characteristics. First, there is the extent to which they develop publicly certified, relatively standardized, broad practical skills that combine currently usable capacities with more general knowledge and aptitudes that facilitate future learning and improvement. Secondly, the extent to which employers, unions, and the state are jointly involved in developing and managing such training varies considerably. These two dimensions can be summarized as the extent to which there is a *strong, collaborative public training system* that develops broad, cumulating, publicly examined, and certified skills.

There are three critical features of the organization and control of labour markets. First, the extent to which the availability of skills and capabilities are controlled by trade unions and professional associations. Secondly, how such associations are organized. Thirdly, the way that bargaining is structured. The first dimension can simply be summarized as the *strength of independent trade unions*. Their overall power and significance is obviously an important factor in employers' ability to change strategic priorities, technologies, and markets as well as affecting their labour-management strategies.

Secondly, the extent to which unions and other forms of collective representation are *organized around certified expertise and are strong*, as opposed to being based on industries or enterprises, has significant consequences for the internal organization of work process and the division of labour. This has been amply demonstrated by the history of demarcation disputes and professional specialization in Britain (e.g. Child *et al.* 1983; Lane 1989). Where, on the other hand, they are industry or sector based, employers are also likely to develop strong forms of intra-industry collaboration, as in Germany, and employer–employee cooperation across the industry may be easier to develop, as it is when enterprise-based unionism is prevalent.

Thirdly, the extent to which *bargaining is centralized* affects the internal cohesion and coordination of employers' groups and union federations. In order to be effective representatives of collective interests, central federations typically gain control over constituent members in highly centralized bargaining systems and usually firms develop interdependent linkages with each other in dealing with industrial-relations issues. In general terms this facilitates collaboration between economic actors, as they have to work together on a continuing basis.

Norms and Values Governing Trust and Authority Relationships

Finally the norms governing trust and authority relations are crucial because they structure exchange relationships between business partners and between employers and employees. They also affect the development of collective identities and prevalent modes of eliciting compliance and commitment within authority systems. Variations in these conventions result in significant differences in the governance structures of firms, the ways in which they deal with each other and other organizations, and prevalent patterns of work organization, control, and employment.

How trust is granted and guaranteed in an economy especially affects the level of inter-firm cooperation and tendency to delegate control over resources. While there are significant variations in how competence, contractual, and goodwill forms of trust (Sako 1992) are developed in different cultures, the key feature here is the strength of formal social institutions generating and guaranteeing trust between relative strangers. In particular, the extent to which property rights' owners, and the economic actors they control, feel able to rely on impersonal institutionalized procedures when making business commitments is a crucial factor in the establishment of collaborative relations within and between firms. It also affects the perception and management of risk (Zucker 1986). Where such procedures are weak or judged unreliable, personal and particularistic connections become especially important in organizing exchange relationships (Hamilton *et al.* 1990; Redding 1990).

Superordinate–subordinate relations are typically governed by a number of different norms and rules, as Eckstein and Gurr (1975) have shown, so that a considerable variety of authority patterns has developed across cultures and political systems. At least six dimensions that affect subordination relations in work organizations have been identified by a number of authors. The first concerns the extent to which superordinate discretion is governed by formal rules and procedures, and the second refers to the degree of reciprocity expected of supervisors in return for deference and obedience. The third dimension concerns the appropriate social and moral distance between leaders and led, while the fourth summarizes the degree of autonomy and independent status of subordinates (d'Iribarne 1989). The final two concern the mode of legitimizing access to superordinate positions, such as elections or formal credentials, and the extent to which common interests can be invoked successfully in claims for compliance with superiors' instructions (Beetham 1991).

These dimensions can be combined in a large number of different ways in different empirical situations, but one far-reaching distinction can be drawn between *formal* and *paternalist* political cultures. The former (*a*) restrict superordinate discretion through formal rules and procedures to a fairly narrow range of issues and actions, (*b*) acknowledge the independent and autonomous status of subordinates as individuals able to make rational decisions, and (*c*) involve subordinates in the choice of superordinates and in decision-making to some extent. The latter typically treat subordinates as children who cannot be expected to know their own best interests and act accordingly.

Paternalism in turn can be divided into two major kinds: *remote* and *reciprocal*. Remote paternalism implies a high degree of social and moral distance between leaders and their followers with little direct reciprocity expected of superordinates in return for subordinates' deference. Common and shared interests are rarely invoked as the basis for compliance and superiors often claim a moral superiority which requires no further justifications, as in the virtuocracies of Confucian China and Korea (Pye 1985; Silin 1976). Reciprocal paternalism, on the other hand, involves much closer links between superordinates and subordinates, with reciprocal services expected of superiors through direct patronage and a strong belief in both leaders and led sharing a common community of fate, as in modern Japan (Haley 1992; Iwata 1992; Rohlen 1974).

Formal types of authority can also be further subdivided into a number of different kinds, but perhaps the most significant contrast is between *contractual* and *communal* forms of authority. This distinction focuses on the extent to which authority rests upon widespread and diffuse appeals to common interests as opposed to highly specific and narrow agreements between discrete and separate contractors. Communal forms of authority imply relatively high levels of mutual trust and commitment, with shared understandings of priorities and interests, and often rely on expertise as a key quality of superordinates, while contractual authority tends to presume more adversarial relationships and a dominant pursuit of self-interest. The former seems to have become institutionalized in some Scandinavian and continental European countries, while the latter is found more in Anglo-Saxon societies (Lodge and Vogel 1987). D'Iribarne (1989) suggests the prevalent form of authority in France constitutes a further kind of authority—the quasi-feudal—in which reciprocity is low and social distance high between superior and subordinate, but the autonomy and rationality of the latter are emphasized.

Just as the characteristics of business systems are interconnected in particular ways, so too are these features of institutional structures interrelated. For example, societies in which strong states play a major role in coordinating economic development and share risks with the private sector tend not to develop strong intermediary associations. Employers' associations and labour unions are, then, usually weak in such countries. Market regulation, on the other hand, is often considerable, since this is a major way in which state agencies coordinate development. These kinds of states tend to be associated with credit-based rather than capital-market-based financial systems for two reasons. First, because they are typical of late industrializing economies where capital is scarce and more readily mobilized through the banking system, and, secondly, because it is easier for the state to influence economic development through the financial system when it is dominated by banks rather than capital markets (Zysman 1983).

This combination of features can be characterized as a *dirigiste* type of business environment in which business development is highly dependent on the state. Where the state is less directly involved in the economy through ownership and/or credit allocation, and coordinates economic development with more independent industry associations, business is more autonomous. In these *state-guided* environments, intermediary associations are often encouraged by state agencies to take on coordinating and regulating functions, although these do not always include labour organizations.

Conversely, low levels of state risk-sharing and economic coordination are often combined with capital-market-based financial systems in what might be termed *arm's length* or differentiated business environments. In these contexts, institutional arenas and élites are organized quite separately from each other according to their own particular logics. Social relationships tend to be regulated by formal rules and procedures that treat actors as discrete individuals pursuing their separate interests, as exemplified by classical contracting. Authority and trust relations are here governed by formal institutions that limit mutual obligations to contractually specified duties. Collaboration between employers, unions, and other groups is difficult to establish in such societies, because collective actors are typically adversarial in their relations with each other.

On the other hand, where strong intermediary associations have developed, often with state support, they tend to be involved in regulating market entry and exit. They typically engage in bargaining and negotiation with each other on a continuing basis, with strongly institutionalized procedures limiting opportunistic behaviour. Such procedures depend on considerable trust between social partners and widespread beliefs in their joint dependence on cooperation for gaining group objectives. Commitment to relatively impersonal associations and an institutionalized ability to mobilize loyalties to collective goals beyond purely personal ones are important features of these kinds of societies. When combined with strong public training systems, as in many continental European countries, these institutional features are conducive to collaboration between economic actors and so can be termed *collaborative*.

Finally, cultures where trust in formal institutions is low and loyalties are focused on the immediate family rather than more impersonal collectivities limit the growth of intermediary associations and the development of exchange relationships governed by formal procedures. Capital markets are unlikely to be significant sources of investment funds in such societies and the largely personal nature of authority relationships will restrict the development of strong labour unions. Social relationships in these cultures tend to be highly personal and particularistic, and so can be described as *particularistic* business environments.

INTERDEPENDENCES BETWEEN INSTITUTIONAL FEATURES AND BUSINESS-SYSTEM CHARACTERISTICS

These differences in dominant institutions develop interdependently with particular business-system characteristics to generate and reproduce distinctive forms of economic organization. The establishment and change of divergent varieties of capitalism, then, are closely connected to variations in their institutional contexts. Before continuing to outline the particular ways in which the eleven features of institutions summarized in Table 2.5 are linked to business-system characteristics, it is important to bear in mind two points. First, the most direct connections between institutional features and business-system characteristics often occur when institutions display particularly strong features at extremes of the dimensions being considered. Relatedly, the connections are often not reversible in the sense that the negative relationship may not hold to the same extent. Secondly, interdependences between single institutional features and forms of economic organization are tendencies which, in practice, are modified by other aspects of dominant institutions and by a variety of historical contingencies.

The effects of particular political, financial, labour, and cultural institutions on the form of economic organization that becomes established in a specific market economy are often most marked when the strength of a particular feature is very high or low. For example, the link between a strong, developmentalist state and the prevalence of growth goals is not a linear, continuous one but rather is particularly significant—and dominates other factors—when the level of business dependence on the state is especially high, as in post-war Korea (Amsden 1989; Fields 1995; Whitley 1992*a*; Woo 1991). Similarly, the effect of weak institutions governing trust relations on inter-firm alliances and sector organizations is most evident when formal institutions are very weak and/or widely regarded as unreliable, as in many expatriate Chinese economies (Redding 1990; Silin 1976).

Additionally, these direct connections between particular institutional features and business-system characteristics often do not apply in reverse. Where, for instance, the state is relatively weak and/or does not pursue developmentalist policies, firms' strategies may or may not follow growth goals. Although, then, the strong, developmental French state in much of the post-war period has, amongst other factors, encouraged large firms to pursue growth goals, the weaker and less cohesive post-war federal German state has not led German companies to pursue profit-maximization priorities. This is because of other institutional features, such as the financial system and strong intermediary organizations, that encourage growth goals (Lane 1992). Similarly, the existence of an effective legal system governing contractual trust does not necessarily lead to extensive delegation of control to salaried managers by owners, although the lack of such formal institutions is likely to encourage strong owner control.

This point highlights the interdependence of these institutional features in structuring business systems. In any particular market economy, the prevalent form of economic organization will reflect the influence of all dominant institutions as they have developed in conjunction with each other during and after early industrialization. The explanation of differences between individual business systems, and of changes in their characteristics, then, clearly depends on an analysis of all the key institutions and how they interdependently structured the specific form of economic organization that developed. The peculiarities of the prevalent business system in Britain, for example, cannot be adequately understood without taking into account the combined consequences of the interconnected pre-industrial state and financial systems, their links with the development of the training 'system' and organization of labour markets, and the pervasive and long-established cultural norm of individualism (Lane 1992; Macfarlane 1978).

The linkages between institutions and business-system characteristics discussed in the following pages are, then, tendencies which are most likely to occur when institutional features are particularly distinctive and other features reinforce, rather than conflict with, them. Table 2.6, summarizing institutional influences, therefore describes them in terms of their strongest and exemplary features. The positive and negative signs in this table indicate that, other things being equal, the presence of such features is likely to encourage, or to inhibit, the development of the specified business-system characteristic. Given the complexities and interdependences of any concrete market economy, it is often easier to be clear about the business-system characteristics discouraged by specific institutional arrangements than about those that will become established in practice. This is because the detailed pattern of firms and markets that comes to dominate any one market economy at any one time is quite contingent on a

TABLE 2.6. Connections between institutional features and business-system characteristics

Institutional features	Business-system characteristics								
	Direct owner control	Market owner control	High ownership vertical integration	High ownership horizontal integration	Low alliance vertical integration	High competitor collaboration	Low alliance horizontal integration	High employer–employee interdependence	High delegation to workers
The state									
Dominant, risk-sharing state	+	−	+		+	−	+		
Antagonistic to intermediaries					+	−	+	−	
Formal regulation of markets				−		+		+	
Financial system									
Credit based		−	+	−		+		+	
Capital-market based		+		+	+	−	+	−	
Skill development and control system									
Strong public collaborative training system						+		+	+
Strong unions				−				+	+
Strong skill-based groupings						−		−	+
Centralized bargaining by sectors				−		+			
Trust and authority									
Low trust in formal institutions	+	−			+	−	+	−	
Paternalist authority relations	+	−							
Communitarian authority relations				−				+	+

variety of idiosyncratic factors, such as wars, the distribution of natural resources, and geopolitical developments.

Considering first the connections between institutional features and forms of owner control, direct owner control is strongly encouraged in societies where trust in formal institutions governing relationships is low and authority is predominantly paternalist in nature. Without strong mechanisms ensuring that owners can rely on managers to carry out their instructions and act in their interests, it is unlikely that they will readily delegate control over their property to salaried employees. Similarly, if authority in a society is more personal and direct than formal and procedural, owners will be expected to exercise direct control over employees. A high level of state dependence also encourages direct control, because owners typically manage political risks directly with decision-makers and would find it difficult to implement agreements through third parties. Since state coordination and guidance are usually not transparent and public, remote owners would be disadvantaged if they left political negotiations to managers, and so they have to become directly involved.

Conversely, market-based forms of owner control are feasible only when trust in formal procedures is high and authority predominantly procedural. They are less likely in credit-based financial systems, because these typically lead to considerable interdependence and lock-in between the owners/controllers of financial assets and managers of enterprises. They are, though, strongly linked to the existence of liquid capital markets in which assets can be easily traded and managed as items in a portfolio. Relatedly, they are unlikely to be widely institutionalized in economies with a dominant risk-sharing state because of political risks.

Ownership-based integration of production chains usually involves investment in capital-intensive facilities, and hence considerable fixed costs and associated risks. It therefore will be encouraged by state risk-sharing and by a financial system that locks capital providers into capital users. Credit-based systems do this, as do some capital markets dominated by individual shareholders who do not trade their shares easily and frequently. Capital markets where control over assets is concentrated in the hands of salaried fund managers competing for assets on the basis of relative performance of the portfolios under their care, on the other hand, are more liquid. They institutionalize a market for corporate control driven by short-term financial returns in which final beneficial owners are separated from nominee controllers (Lazonick and O'Sullivan 1996). Large-scale investments whose returns are long term and uncertain are unlikely to be encouraged in these sorts of markets.

Horizontal diversification within ownership units, on the other hand, will be more encouraged by capital-market-based financial systems than by credit-based ones, because risk management is internalized by firms in these economies and they are not constrained by alliances with banks and/or other controllers of voting rights. Additionally, whereas capital markets facilitate the acquisition of firms in quite different sectors, credit-based financial systems tend to inhibit hostile takeovers because of the greater interdependence between banks and firms. Formal regulation of markets will also inhibit such diversification into technologically and market-unrelated fields, as will strong unions and centralized bargaining on a sectoral basis, since these institutional arrangements restrict industry entry and exit as well as increasing the level of interdependence between firms and sector-based skills. Communitarian conceptions of authority additionally restrict unrelated diversification, because managers depend on employees' perception of their commitment to particular industries and skill bases for their own authority in such cultures.

Alliance forms of economic integration are, broadly speaking, discouraged by strong, risk-sharing states antagonistic to intermediaries between citizens and the state. This is essentially because high levels of business dependence on the state inhibit horizontal associations and collaboration between social and economic collectivities that might be seen as threatening state dominance. They are also unlikely to be widespread as long-lasting and wide-ranging coordination processes in societies where reliance on formal procedures and agreements is low because trust between strangers is difficult to develop and sustain. Alliance-based coordination and integration of activities between ownership units requires an ability to rely on organizational commitments rather than short-term informal and personal reciprocity. Relatedly, since capital-market-based financial systems facilitate strong markets in corporate control, and hence radical changes in ownership and strategic direction, alliance-based forms of economic coordination are unlikely to be significant where such markets dominate.

Similar arguments apply to variations in the degree of collaboration between competitors, but other institutional features also impinge on this characteristic of business systems. In general, such collaboration is encouraged and facilitated when industry membership is stable and widely known, because reputations for implementing or breaking business agreements are directly affected by firm behaviour and are important for business success. Market regulation thus encourages competitor collaboration by stabilizing entry and exit, as do credit-based financial systems and strong sectoral bargaining structures. Cooperative public training systems and centralized bargaining additionally favour such collaboration by forcing employers to work together in implementing and jointly controlling these systems. This emphasizes their interdependence and common interests within particular sectors.

High levels of sector commitment and focus can additionally encourage employers to develop long-term connections to employees. As firms concentrate on competing within particular industries, they increasingly come to rely on firm- and sector-specific capabilities and skills. Where entry and exit are regulated and constrained by training and bargaining systems, investment in employee development and quality-focused innovation strategies will not be so threatened by free riders and price-based competition as in economies where barriers to entry are low and ownership and control of businesses readily traded on capital markets. The combination of market regulation, credit-based financial systems, and strong sectorally based training and bargaining systems, then, encourages considerable employer–employee interdependence. Similarly, where the state has established a strong public training system that produces high level skills with employer involvement and the unions are strong, employers are both encouraged and forced to develop long-term linkages with employees.

Additionally, state antipathy to intermediaries will limit the growth of powerful unions, and so employers' need to make long-term commitments to their core labour force. Low levels of trust in formal institutions also reduce employer–employee interdependence, since owner managers in such cultures are reluctant to rely on the continued support of their staff without personal connections to them. Finally, strong skill-based groupings inhibit the development of such interdependences, because occupational expertise and identities dominate organizational loyalties in these societies.

High levels of certified skills and strong unions also encourage considerable delegation of task performance to workers, especially where employers are involved in the definition, development, and assessment of expertise. Skill-based groupings also encourage high levels of skill development—at least as defined by practitioners—and so imply considerable delegation to staff which is further encouraged by professionals' ability to influence if not control labour markets. Communitarian authority relations additionally favour employee discretion by reproducing common identities and loyalties so that managers can rely more on workers' perceptions of joint interests than where authority is purely contractual. Paternalism and low trust, conversely, discourage such delegation, because workers are viewed as needing instruction and being unreliable in following organizational interests.

THE INSTITUTIONAL CONTEXTS OF DIFFERENT BUSINESS-SYSTEM TYPES

These connections enable us to identify the sorts of institutional contexts that are associated with the establishment and reproduction of the six types of business system outlined in Table 2.4. As Table 2.7 indicates, the overall level of organizational integration of economic activities in any one economy is connected to the existence and nature of general coordinating institutions in the wider society. In particular, low levels of state risk-sharing, weak intermediaries, and low market regulation, coupled with weak unions, a poor public training system, and low trust in formal institutions limit the degree of organizational integration in an economy. Fragmented business systems, then, develop in particularistic business environments with low trust cultures where formal institutions are unreliable, risks are difficult to share, and the state is at best neutral, and at worst predatory.

More organizationally integrated business systems, on the other hand, develop in societies where institutional mechanisms for managing uncertainty and trust are more strongly established, and the political and social order encourages collaboration between social actors. Coordinated industrial districts, then,

TABLE 2.7. Institutional features associated with different types of business system

Institutional features	Types of business system					
	Fragmented	Coordinated industrial district	Compartmentalized	State organized	Collaborative	Highly coordinated
The state						
Strength of state's coordinating and developmental role	Low	Considerable locally, limited nationally	Low	High	Considerable	High
Strength and incorporation of intermediaries	Low	Considerable locally	Low	Low	High	High
Strength of market regulation	Low	Considerable locally	Low	High	High	High
Financial system						
Capital market or credit based	Low risk-sharing by banks	Some local bank risk-sharing	Capital market	Credit	Credit	Credit
Skill development and control						
Strength of public training system	Low	High	Low	Limited	High	Limited
Union strength	Low	High	Low to some	Low	High	Some
Dominant organizing principle of unions	Varies	Skill/sector	Skill	Employer	Sector	Employer
Centralization of bargaining	Low	Low	Low	Low	High	Low
Trust and authority						
Trust in formal institutions	Low	Some	High	Limited	High	Some
Paternalist authority	Some	Variable	Low	High	Low	High
Communitarian authority	Low	Limited	Low	Low	High	Some
Contractarian authority	Limited	Variable	High	Low	Low	Low
Typical business environment	Particularistic	Locally collaborative	Arm's length	Dirigiste	Collaborative	State guided

develop and continue to be reproduced in localities where both formal and informal institutions limit opportunism and provide an infrastructure for collaboration to occur. Local governments, banks, and training organizations typically work with quite strong forms of local labour representation in these situations to restrict adversarial, price-based competition in favour of high-quality, innovative strategies based on highly skilled and flexible labour. Various forms of market regulation at the local level limit both firm entry and large customer attempts to enforce cost reductions and price-based competition, as David Friedman (1988) suggests was the case in the machine-tool industry in Sakaki township. Firm size is limited in these localities by strong preferences for direct owner control by 'artisanal' entrepreneurs and consequent high levels of skilled labour mobility, often coupled with preferential tax and credit arrangements for small firms.

Compartmentalized business systems, in contrast, develop in arm's length institutional contexts where there are few institutions at either the national or the local level for encouraging cooperation between firms. Large and highly liquid markets in financial assets and labour power encourage considerable mobility with little regulation of market entry and exit. Effective and widely relied upon formal procedures governing exchange and authority relations enable transactions to be carried out at arm's length and impersonally. Typically, such procedures also limit informal and 'non-transparent' forms of collaboration between ownership units to ensure market openness and universal accessibility to information. States are here regulatory rather than developmental, and often quite internally differentiated. Similarly, capital is usually allocated by price and at arm's length from its users through impersonal market competition. These sorts of business systems are also associated with weakly developed skill training and control systems. Unions may be influential at times but are usually organized around craft skills rather than industries, and bargaining is decentralized. Practical manual worker skills are not highly valued and training in them is typically governed by *ad hoc* arrangements with little or no central coordination.

This lack of integration and systematic coordination of activities both within and across institutional arenas is a general feature of the societies that establish compartmentalized business systems. They are quite pluralistic in the sense that each sphere of society operates as a largely separate social space with its own norms and routines, processes of élite recruitment and selection, and standards for evaluating performance. Coordination between them is more *ad hoc* and occasional than continuous and systemic, and relationships between élites are often adversarial rather than cooperative, as exemplified by the separation of powers between the judiciary, executive, and legislature in the US constitution. Such a relatively impoverished institutional infrastructure restricts organizational integration between ownership units and leads to a strong reliance on ownership-based authority relations for coordinating economic activities (Hollingsworth 1997).

State-organized business systems develop in less pluralist, *dirigiste*, environments where the state dominates economic decision-making and tightly controls intermediary associations. Unions are typically weak and/or state controlled in such societies and bargaining is decentralized—where it takes place at all as an institutionalized activity. Coordination in general is greater in these societies than in arm's length ones, but is centralized by the state. Firms and their owners are highly dependent on state agencies and officials here. As a result, they delegate little to employees and find it difficult to develop long-term commitments with business partners or competitors.

In contrast, both collaborative and highly coordinated business systems are established and reproduced in more collaborative institutional contexts that encourage and support cooperation between collective actors. The state here performs a greater coordinating role than in the previous case, and additionally encourages the development of intermediary associations for mobilizing support and implementing collective policy decisions. Markets are typically quite regulated in these societies, with entry often governed by licensing procedures and/or through alliances and agreements between firms, banks, and other intermediaries.

Similarly, these kinds of business systems are much more likely to develop in economies with credit-based financial systems in which the providers of capital are strongly interconnected with its users and cannot easily exit when conditions alter. Both are effectively locked into each others' destinies in these systems. Such interdependence leads to high levels of mutual coordination and monitoring of activities and decisions, as many authors have noted (e.g. Zysman 1983).

Corporatist-type bargaining arrangements based on strong unions often lead to considerable employer–employee collaboration here. Labour markets are often strongly regulated, formally or informally, and the combination of legislative restrictions with union pressure tends to limit skilled worker mobility. Often organized around strong public training systems in which strong sectoral or enterprise unions cooperate with employers, labour systems in these economies encourage investment in high levels of skills which are cumulative and linked to organizational positions. Flexibility and cooperation within employment units are additionally encouraged by shared beliefs in the interdependence of managers and employees.

Such beliefs are, of course, enhanced by the predominance of communitarian or reciprocal paternalist authority relations in a society, and, conversely, inhibited by a reliance on contractarian notions of authority. Additionally, societies where trust in the efficacy of formal institutions governing exchange relations and agreements is considerable are more likely to encourage joint commitments between the bulk of the workforce and management to enterprise development than those where trust is overwhelmingly dependent on personal obligations.

What, then, is likely to lead to differences between these two kinds of business system? Essentially, I suggest that these result from variations in the extent of institutional pluralism across societies, especially with regard to those governing the organization and control of labour power, and the concomitant dominance of the state's coordinating role. Highly coordinated business systems are more likely to develop and continue in societies where the state dominates the coordination of economic development and the regulation of markets, as distinct from those where banks, industry associations, and similar organizations perform coordinating functions independently of state guidance. Collaborative business systems are not, then, likely to develop in societies where the state assumes responsibility for guiding economic development.

Perhaps even more important in separating these two types of business system, though, are the autonomy and influence of unions and other forms of labour representation in policy-making processes. This is because strong unions at the national level limit the capacity of state–business coalitions to coordinate and integrate economic development and restructuring on a significant scale. The more pluralist and differentiated are institutional arenas, the more difficult it is for state agencies to integrate decisions across sectors in a top-down fashion, and the more these decisions are outcomes of lengthy bargaining. Collective associations represent more diverse and potentially opposed interests in these kinds of economies than where unions are either weak or else largely based on enterprise units.

It is especially where sector-based unions are strong and involved in national policy networks that state coordination of economic changes across sectors is likely to be limited and difficult to implement. Additionally, powerful national unions coupled with strong public training systems limit worker dependence on particular employers. This, in turn, restricts the extent of organizational integration of manual workers within firms. Most continental European economies, consequently, do not exhibit the same degree of employer–employee interdependence that has developed in large Japanese firms in the post-war period. However, centralized bargaining, collaboration in the management of training systems, and other factors do, of course, encourage greater integration of the bulk of the workforce in many firms in continental Europe than in the Anglo-Saxon economies.

To summarize the main points of this chapter, major differences between business systems concern the degree to which, and modes by which, economic activities are coordinated through organizational routines and authority relations. Such organizational integration is distinct from, and typically opposed to, spot-market forms of economic coordination, although of course in practice these do shade into each other as links between business partners become more market-like and many markets become more organized. The critical difference in modes of organizational integration lies between that achieved through unified ownership and employment, on the one hand, and those dependent on collective agreements and long-term collaborations, on the other hand. Business groups, obligational contracting, and cartels are examples of the latter. A third important aspect of business systems that varies considerably across market economies concerns the nature of economic interest groups and how they collaborate and compete with each other. Owners, managers, and different groups of employees are organized and connected to each other in quite varied ways that affect risk-management strategies and the organization of employment relations.

These differences in economic organization arise from contrasting processes of industrialization and are reproduced by different kinds of institutional contexts. In particular, variations in political arrangements and policies, as well as in the institutions governing the allocation and use of capital, have major effects on the extent of organizational integration and its limitation to ownership-based units. Equally, the ways that skills are developed, certified, and controlled exert significant influence on prevalent employment relations and work systems, as do the dominant norms governing trust and authority relationships. All these institutional arrangements additionally affect the management of production and market risks. They also, of course, structure the ways that dominant firms are organized and controlled in market economies, and the sorts of competitive strategies they pursue, as will be further considered in the next chapter.

3

The Social Structuring of Firms' Governance Systems and Organizational Capabilities

INTRODUCTION

In previous chapters I have emphasized the variety of ways in which economic coordination and control are achieved in market economies. In particular, the significance and role of ownership in the organizational integration of economic activities differ considerably between, say, post-war Japan and the USA, and are highly contingent upon historical circumstances and current institutional arrangements. Firms as units of financial control based on ownership are, then, part of the overall system of economic coordination and control that distinguishes any particular variety of capitalism. Their characteristics reflect those of each business system and vary between them. Differences in the nature of firms are important for understanding economic development because they affect both economic and financial decision-making and the sorts of distinctive organizational capabilities that become established in different economies. Because they are typically units of employment as well as financial control, firms are critical agents for developing particular kinds of collective competences that affect competitive outcomes.

Accordingly, in this chapter I consider the major ways that firms differ between business systems in greater detail and analyse how they are related to particular features of dominant institutions. In the next section I shall outline the nature of firms as a key type of coordination unit in capitalist societies and then summarize the primary ways in which they vary across economies. The following section considers how these characteristics are connected to dominant institutions and agencies so that certain kinds of firms become more established and prevalent in particular contexts.

THE NATURE OF FIRMS AND THEIR KEY CHARACTERISTICS

The significance of firms in capitalist economies lies in their combination of financial control over resources with employment. As ownership-based units of decision-making and control, they are clearly central collective actors in the mobilization, allocation, and use of assets, especially human labour power. Through the legitimacy granted to private property rights' holders and their agents in capitalist societies, those in charge of firms are authorized to acquire and control resources for private gain in competitive markets. Differences in the groups controlling firms and how they do so, then, have significant consequences for economic coordination and competition.

Relatedly, their primary role as employers means that firms dominate the development of organizational capabilities and knowledges. Because employment agreements are flexible and grant considerable discretion to employers over how work processes are to be organized and controlled, firms are more able to develop relatively diffuse and long-term idiosyncratic competences than where coordination is based on formal contracts (Langlois and Robertson 1995: 37–43). The flexibility and variability of employment agreements in capitalist labour markets enable firms to create collective knowledges and skills for dealing with highly complex and uncertain problems, and thereby facilitate systemic innovations that are highly interdependent. Of course, not all firms attempt, let alone succeed, in developing such capabilities, and this constitutes an important variable characteristic of firms.

In this framework, then, firms are understood as units of economic coordination and control under common, unified ownership that develop distinctive capabilities through the authoritative direction of employees on the basis of employment agreements. In these respects they are quite similar to Penrosian administrative structures that add value to human and material resources through the collective organization of work and are the locus of entrepreneurial decision-making (Penrose 1959). However, whereas Penrose tended to see the firm as the sole location of such coordination, the approach adopted here explicitly allows for extra-firm authoritative organizations to integrate economic activities and develop distinctive capabilities.

This view of the nature of firms suggests two sets of key characteristics that differentiate them across market economies. First, there are those dealing with the nature of the groups controlling dominant firms and their interests. The relative importance of owners, managers, different kinds of employees, business partners, and other groups in deciding on dominant firms' objectives clearly varies greatly across business systems and significantly affects their behaviour. These characteristics can be summarized as those dealing with 'governance' issues. At least four distinct governance characteristics of firms arise from variations in the roles of owners, employees, and business partners in deciding on firm policies and actions, and in the nature of dominant performance standards and goals.

Secondly, firms also differ in the nature of the organizational capabilities they develop and coordinate, as well as in the sorts of strategies they pursue with these capabilities. Capabilities are here seen as sets of organizationally specific experiences, knowledge, and expertise that confer competitive advantages in carrying out particular economic activities, what are sometimes referred to as firms' competences (Foss and Knudsen 1996; Langlois 1995; Teece *et al.* 1994; Winter 1988). At least three distinct aspects of firms' capabilities and strategies can be identified that vary considerably between institutional contexts. These concern the role of workforce skills, the development of collective competences concerned with efficiency or with innovation, and the extent of flexibility and responsiveness to customer demands. These seven characteristics are summarized in Table 3.1 and will now be discussed in greater detail.

Governance Characteristics

The direction and management of firms can be analysed in terms of the relative influence of different economic interest groups and their dominant objectives. In addition to the usual balance of control between owners and salaried managers, it is also important to consider the relative importance of employees and business partners. As numerous studies of European and Asian firms have shown, the behaviour and priorities of top managers in different countries can be quite constrained by particular groups of workers and linked organizations (e.g. Aoki 1988; Gerlach 1992; Kristensen 1996, 1997; Lilja 1997; Streeck 1997).

Considering first the balance of power and interests between shareholders and salaried managers, it is important to distinguish between types of owners and controllers of financial assets. Because of the growth of institutional fund management and shareholders, and the dominant role of trust banks and universal banks in controlling shares and votes in some societies, not only has share ownership become remote from the management of individual firms in many cases, but personal investment is increasingly separate from control over the use of shares. In particular, beneficial shareholders are often distinct from those who control the allocation of shares and votes through nominee accounts and as fund managers. Additionally, it is critical to note that the interests of different types of share controllers are often divergent. Portfolio holders and fund managers in liquid capital markets are evaluated in quite different ways and pursue different objectives compared to financial institutions that are locked into the destinies of their clients through substantial equity holdings, trust management, deposits, and loans.

TABLE 3.1. Key characteristics of firms

Governance characteristics
Degree and type of management control: high manager control, manager control constrained by strong capital markets, manager control constrained by credit controllers, owner management
Managerial decision-making constrained by employee interests and concerns
Managerial decision-making constrained by business partners' interests
Dominant goals and performance standards: family wealth accumulation, portfolio investor returns, growth, technical excellence.

Organizational capabilities and strategies
Contribution of employees to the development and improvement of organizational capabilities
Development of innovative capabilities
Development of organizational capabilities focused on responsiveness to changing and differentiated demands

These distinctions between types of share ownership and control over the use of shares suggest four major variants of owner–manager relationships that differ in the relative autonomy of top managers and the closeness of owning groups to managerial decision-making. First, where the owners of financial assets control shares directly but are highly fragmented in terms of the proportion owned in any one firm, incumbent mangers are likely to dominate decision-making and strategy-setting processes, particularly where hostile takeovers are difficult to accomplish. In this situation of fragmented control over shares, owners can be said to delegate considerable control to salaried managers so that they have high levels of discretion.

Secondly, where beneficial ownership is still fragmented, but control over nominee accounts and fund management is in the hands of banks and other financial intermediaries such as unit trusts, the ultimate owners effectively delegate control to these intermediaries. In liquid capital markets this delegation of control means that neither beneficial ownership nor nominee ownership nor control implies any commitment to the shares of individual firms beyond their generation of 'satisfactory' rates of return. Usually, the proportion of issued shares held by any individual intermediary is small, both for fiduciary reasons and to retain liquidity, so that they are not locked into the fate of particular firms and are exposed only to limited risks. Each fund manager, then, exercises only a small degree of control over the affairs of any one firm it invests in, and top managers are able to pursue their own goals and strategies, subject to meeting the financial rates of return demanded by share controllers. They therefore have considerable discretion from individual shareowners.

However, as Lazonick and O'Sullivan (1996) have emphasized, the growth in concentration of control over shares and votes by fund managers and related institutions in the USA and UK since the war has resulted in the interests of equity owners and controllers in general becoming stronger than before. Because these managers compete for mandates to manage portfolios of assets that can be switched between them at quite short notice, they are increasingly evaluated in terms of short-term performance measures. In turn, they impose these standards on the companies whose shares they control through the market for corporate control. Thus, although delegation of decision-making powers by owners to the managers of individual firms is high in this situation, the system as a whole imposes strong financial performance criteria on firms when control over share use becomes concentrated. Managers are less autonomous in these sorts of economies than where individual ownership is direct and fragmented.

Thirdly, where capital markets are less liquid and fund management is largely dominated by commercial banks who additionally provide the bulk of investment funds for firms, and often take direct equity stakes in their leading clients, concentration of control over the shares of individual firms is even higher. However, it is also longer term because of the difficulty of selling substantial holdings. Share controllers here have broader interests than simple portfolio managers, since they are major lenders to particular firms and they are locked in to a much greater extent. They are, therefore, exposed to greater levels of risk than fund managers in highly liquid capital markets and so are less likely to delegate high levels of strategic control to managers. In particular, they will be more inclined to intervene directly in managerial matters when performance drops significantly. Managerial control is shared more with share controllers in this case, but so too are some risks.

Finally, of course, direct owner management as discussed in Chapter 2 implies very low levels of delegation of control to managers, although family ownership *per se* does not always imply direct control. The interests of owner-managers, however, are not as simply determined as the traditional theory of the firm suggested. While some may indeed seek short-term profits and high personal incomes, others prefer growth over a considerable period of time (see e.g. Boswell 1983). Often family owners prefer to maintain personal and family control over key assets at the possible expense of profitability, as is arguably the case for many of the Korean *chaebol* (Janelli 1993). In general, then, four distinct types of salaried manager autonomy from owners can be summarized as: *high management control, manager control constrained by strong capital markets, manager control constrained by strong credit controllers*, and *owner management*.

The second major aspect of governance relations to be considered here concerns the broad influence of employees' interests on firms' actions and priorities. As has been extensively discussed in the literature on the post-war large Japanese firm (e.g. Aoki 1988, 1994; R. Clark 1979; Odagiri 1992), the long-term mutual interdependence of employers with male core workers in these firms means that labour costs are relatively fixed in the short to medium term and employees constitute key assets. Together with the considerable managerial autonomy from direct owner control and from remote, arm's length portfolio holders in post-war Japan, this means that insider interests are significant influences on firms' strategies. This does not imply that employees as a separate group necessarily have a substantial direct impact, but that priorities and performance standards reflect firms' dependence on employee skills and commitments.

Equally, the strong position of unions in general, and skilled manual workers in particular, in Denmark and some other northern European countries has helped to ensure that many firms depend greatly on the skills and flexibility of employees, especially in the machinery sector (Kristensen 1992, 1996, 1997). Managers who ignore this dependence and pursue strategies antagonistic to employees' interests run the risk of destroying the competitive competencies of their businesses as key workers leave or reduce commitment to upgrading their skills. In contrast, firms who treat labour and employees' skills as short-term resources, to be acquired or removed on flexible external labour markets as business cycles change, are clearly unlikely to pay much heed to employee interests in deciding priorities.

This characteristic combines the general significance of employee interests for decision-making and priorities, on the one hand, with the scope of those interests, on the other hand. In many companies in, say, the USA (Lazonick 1991; Lazonick and West 1998), white-collar employees are considered to be part of the firm in a way that manual workers are not, and treated differently as a result. Their broad interests may be seen as consonant with the firms', and so may be taken more notice of, than are those of less educated and less committed manual employees. In such firms managerial integration is greater than organizational integration. For the purposes of comparing the general level of influence of different groups and interests on firm behaviour, the significance and scope of employee interests can be integrated into a single characteristic of the extent to which *managerial decision-making is constrained by the interests and concerns of employees as a whole* in determining firms' objectives, strategies, and performance standards.

A high level of such constraint means that most employees are considered to be members of the enterprise with distinct rights and interests that have to be respected in making decisions. Whether these are formally enshrined in legislation such as the German Works Constitutions Acts is less important than managers' recognition that the firm depends greatly on the skills and commitment of its staff for its success and that developing these constitutes an important part of its performance. A medium degree signifies that such interests are restricted to managerial and technical employees, while a low degree implies that all employees below top management are regarded as disposable and readily traded resources that are unimportant for strategic development of the business.

The third important characteristic of firms' governance structures to be considered here arises from the earlier distinction between firms as ownership-based units of economic coordination and control and broader units of authoritative coordination, such as networks and alliances. As this point highlights, firms vary dramatically across market economies in the extent to which they share control and risks with other companies and agencies. The highly networked economy of post-war Japan is commonly contrasted with the USA in this respect, but other societies also manifest considerable differences in the scope, intensity, and stability of cross-firm alliances and federations (Daems 1983). Such authority sharing has major implications for the determination of firms' goals and strategies, as well as for the nature of their priorities and performance standards. As emphasized in Chapter 2, the key aspect of this characteristic of business systems and firm behaviour is the stability and authority of such networks, and thus the degree to which firms are locked in to them. This dimension can be termed the extent to which *managerial decision-making is constrained by the interests of business partners*.

These characteristics of governance structures of firms affect the sorts of dominant objectives pursued by the controllers of firms, and the criteria by which they judge success. In the traditional theory of the managerial firm (e.g. Marris 1964), growth goals were seen as dominating profit maximization ones, usually on the grounds of salaries and other rewards being tied to firm size. An additional factor encouraging the pursuit of large size in capital-market-based financial systems was its connection with increased security for top managers, although this safeguard appears to be less convincing after the merger booms of the 1980s. In practice, however, growth is pursued by most firms, subject to a profits constraint, both for competitive reasons and because managerial skills develop and generate increased resources for new activities (Penrose 1959). However, the extent to which growth is viewed as the pre-eminent objective, its preferred form, and the relative significance of other goals, do differ across market economies.

For example, in South Korea, and perhaps post-war France and Italy, the high level of business dependence on the state and ample provision of low-cost credit have encouraged firms to grow very large and to seek a dominant position in a variety of markets, with only a very limited profits constraint (Amsden 1989; Janelli 1993; Whitley 1992*a*). Such credit-funded growth also enabled family owners to retain substantial control despite the large size of these firms. In Japan, on the other hand, firms long pursued market-share goals and sought to grow in size within their sector, partly because of the hierarchical nature of the 'society of industry' (R. Clark 1979) and the benefits of large size in the economy as a whole. Perhaps more important have been the complex networks of mutual dependence between firms, suppliers, customers, banks, employees, and other organizations that restrict unrelated diversification but lead to strong collective interests in expansion (Abegglen and Stalk 1985; Fruin 1992; Gerlach 1992). Profit constraints may be more significant here than in Korea, but they are less strong than in the Anglo-Saxon economies because of the weakness of the market for corporate control and the multiple interests of share controllers—i.e. the large commercial banks and allied industrial firms.

In other economies, where firms are closely tied into large banks but are not so embedded in sector-specific obligational networks, as in Japan, growth goals are also likely to be dominant, because increased size implies greater demand for banks' services (Zysman 1983). Such growth may be more diversified than in Japan, but, where employees have a strong influence, as in Germany, growth through radical diversification is unlikely if it is perceived to be a threat to current skills and capabilities. Similarly, where firms have developed close links with the state, banks and important economic groups, such as forest owners and engineers in Finland (Lilja and Tainio 1996), they are unlikely to move quickly into quite different markets and technologies.

Conversely, where firms are much more isolated, and share controllers operate as portfolio holders at arm's length from the companies they invest in, the pursuit of growth goals is limited by the market for corporate control and the need to meet the targets and expectations of the capital market. Dividend pay-outs and growth in share prices are here more significant measures of corporate perfor-mance than growth *per se*, and those financial objectives are indifferent as to how profits are made. Effectiveness in these sorts of firms, then, is more a matter of achieving financial objectives than market-share goals, and large size without sufficient rates of return on capital employed to pay significant dividends is unlikely to appeal to shareholders. Because the owners of these companies do not have any other connections to them, and so benefit only from the direct rewards of holding their shares, they have a very narrow interest in them and one which, furthermore, is typically easily traded in the securities market.

Direct owner control can lead to a variety of dominant objectives being pursued depending on the context. Although many family owned and controlled businesses may seek growth as the means of achieving family wealth and social standing, others may limit it because of a reluctance to share control. They may also do so in countries where owners feel politically insecure and large size is seen as attracting the unwanted scrutiny from the state, as in Taiwan and many other countries where the Chinese family business is strongly developed as a distinct kind of firm (Gold 1986; Greenhalgh 1984, 1988; Redding 1990). Owner-managers, then, may concentrate on sectors where personal capital commitments are limited and direct personal control can be maintained. In Belgium, for example, differences between regions in state policies and patterns of owner control have encouraged the growth of low-capital-intensity industries in Flanders and more-capital-intensive ones in Wallonia (Iterson 1996).

In addition to growth, broadly understood, and profitability goals, some firms seek to develop strong reputations for technical excellence and the development of new knowledge and skills. While this is especially important for 'artisanal' type firms in the industrial districts of Italy, Jutland, and elsewhere, it is also a feature of many firms in highly innovative industries. The need to make profits is, of course, a constraint in such firms, but often this is subordinated to the search for technical excellence and innovative success. Together with the different combinations of profitability and growth outlined above, this suggests four major kinds of dominant goals and performance standards pursued by firms that can usually be distinguished. First, the pursuit of *personal and family wealth accumulation*. Secondly, *high returns to portfolio managers and shareholders*. Thirdly, *growth in assets, turnover, and markets*. Fourthly, *increasing technical excellence and reputation*. In practice, of course, these are usually combined, but one tends to dominate as a result of different interest groups' control over firms' strategic priorities and the nature of the broader institutional environment.

These four characteristics of firms' governance structures and prime objectives are, of course, interconnected. Generally, high levels of owner-management are unlikely to be associated with considerable authority sharing, whether between firms or with employees. The reverse, however, does not hold. Arm's length and remote connections between firms' managers and portfolio managers are not especially likely to encourage employee influence or inter-firm collaboration, although strong insider control with fragmented ownership may do so. Both considerable employee influence and authority sharing with business partners, though, encourage growth goals, because workers and business partners gain more from expansion than from increased profits, particularly when the latter is at their expense. Strong employee influence is additionally likely to encourage a focus on technical excellence and skill improvement, especially where it is combined with a strong skill-training system, as in Denmark and Germany, and workers develop careers based on increasing technical competence (Kristensen 1996, 1997).

Characteristics of Firms' Organizational Capabilities and Strategies

We turn now to consider how firms vary across market economies in terms of the kinds of competitive capabilities they develop and how they do so. A crucial characteristic stems from their role as employers. Through employment agreements firms are able to develop idiosyncratic and flexible collective competences by organizing people in a variety of ways to undertake a range of tasks. Authority based on labour-market relationships enables managers to coordinate economic activities in more flexible ways than contractual arrangements do, and so in principle improves their ability to deal with productive and market uncertainties.

However, the extent to which firms incorporate the skills and knowledge of their employees in the development of such organizational capabilities varies quite sharply across market economies and over time. In the standard Fordist employment pattern, of course, the contribution of most manual workers to firms' competitive competences is limited. They are typically treated as relatively standardized inputs that can easily be substituted without changing the distinctive nature of the organization. In many large post-war Japanese firms, on the other hand, workers' skills are much more organization specific and constitute important components of their competitive capabilities. In a different but equally significant way, the contribution of skilled workers to Danish and German firms' capabilities is considerable, especially where they are retained over some time.

This characteristic of firms has two aspects, then. First, there is the extent to which firms develop particular kinds of competences as integrated administrative structures, in contrast to functioning as loosely coupled collections of individuals or small groups coordinated in quasi-contractual ways. The so-called virtual firm which subcontracts almost all its operations to separate organizations represents an extreme instance of such loose coupling, while highly integrated Chandlerian and post-war Japanese firms represent the other end of this sub-dimension. The second aspect concerns the degree of involvement of employees in the organization and their contribution to the development and enhancement of its capabilities. It reflects both their skills and their inclusion as members of the firm. Together these aspects can be summarized as *the contribution of employees to the development and improvement of organizational capabilities.*

The next two characteristics of firms' capabilities concern the sorts of competitive advantages they concentrate on generating. Following the contrasts suggested by Best (1990), Lazonick (1991) and others that were discussed in Chapter 1, we can distinguish between firms that focus on competing within existing industry 'rules of the game' from those that attempt to develop innovative capabilities for changing them. The former pursue essentially adaptive strategies aimed at reducing costs and/or improving quality incrementally, while the latter try to generate new knowledge and ways of doing things that result in radical innovations. As Lazonick and West (1998: 251–2) put it: 'an innovative strategy entails investments that enhance the productive capacity of new combinations of inputs, thus making possible the generation of higher quality, lower cost outputs … in contrast an adaptive strategy does not attempt to upgrade and recombine the productive capabilities of the enterprise's accumulated assets and purchased inputs'.

These more 'entrepreneurial' strategies concentrate on achieving strategic advantages by continuously innovating in products, processes, and organizational abilities. They seek to destabilize current industry practices and competitive patterns by developing new ways of making products or delivering services, introducing new goods and services, and responding flexibly and quickly to customer demands on a continuing basis. As discussed in Chapter 1, such firms focus on reducing process times and product-development times in addition to the throughput times given priority by Fordist firms. This reshaping of technologies and markets can be achieved as much through continuous improvement of existing competences as by the development of different kinds of knowledge, but both capabilities are concerned to dominate markets by innovation rather than by price or incremental improvements in quality. This characteristic can be summarized as *the extent to which firms develop innovative capabilities*.

The third characteristic of organizational capabilities deals with the ability of firms to adapt quickly to changes in market demand and respond to customers' needs. As Storper and Salais (1997) among others have emphasized, producers vary greatly in their differentiation of outputs to suit particular kinds of demand. On the one hand, the classic Fordist strategy produces highly standardized products for all customers, while in contrast artisanal producers make highly individual goods. Even more responsive are Chinese family businesses in Taiwan and Hong Kong that are highly flexible not only in responding to market changes within industries, but also in changing sectors (Enright *et al.* 1997; Redding 1990; Shieh 1992). This capacity of firms can be termed their *responsiveness to changing demands and ability to produce differentiated outputs*.

These characteristics of organizational capabilities are connected in particular ways to the dimensions of firm governance outlined above. Where firms rely extensively on the contribution of the bulk of their employees to the development of distinct organizational capabilities, they will obviously tend to pay more attention to their interests and concerns than if they pursue Fordist employment policies. Growth and technical-excellence goals will likewise be given greater priority by such firms than portfolio returns. Similarly, highly innovative firms will pursue technical excellence and growth goals at the expense of short-term profitability, as they invest resources for long-term dominance. Often relying heavily on the commitment and flexibility of employees, managers in these firms are quite constrained by their interests. The risks involved in this kind of strategy are unlikely to appeal to portfolio investors whose performance is evaluated every quarter, and so firms subject to strong capital-market constraints are less likely to develop such capabilities than those in other situations.

On the other hand, firms pursuing efficiency and adaptive strategies will typically not feel constrained by employee interests, and probably not develop strong interdependencies with business partners. Market domination through producing large volumes of standardized goods at relatively low prices is the dominant objective for these firms and this usually encourages adversarial, cost-based relationships with suppliers and limited cooperation with competitors. Flexibility and responsiveness, of course, are not associated with such firms.

These connections between firm characteristics enable us to distinguish five 'ideal' kinds of firms which vary principally in how much owners and managers can share risks and commitments, and with whom, and in the sorts of strategies they develop. Their characteristics are summarized in Table 3.2. *Opportunistic* firms are atomistic enterprises highly dependent on the market, which minimize commitments to business partners and employees. They are typically dominated by their owners, who compete by being highly flexible and opportunistic in seeking business. Thus, their commitment to any one sector and expertise is quite limited. Organizational capabilities tend to be narrowly focused and rarely depend on substantial fixed investments. They adapt quickly to market circumstances and rely on others to produce innovations. Personal and family wealth accumulation is typically the dominant objective of these firms, which are characteristic of fragmented business systems and exemplified by Chinese family businesses in adversarial environments.

TABLE 3.2. Characteristics of five ideal types of firms

Characteristics	Firm type				
	Opportunistic	Artisanal	Isolated hierarchy	Cooperative hierarchy	Allied hierarchy
Governance					
Management control type	Owner	Owner	Capital-market constrained	Credit-controller constrained	Credit-controller constrained
Employee-interests constraint	Low	High	Low	Considerable	Considerable
Business-partner constraint	Low	Some	Low	Some	High
Dominant goals	Family wealth accumulation	Wealth and technical excellence	Investor returns	Growth	Growth
Capabilities					
Employee contribution	Low	Considerable	Low	High	High
Innovation focus	Low	High, but adaptive	Limited	Considerable	High
Responsiveness focus	High	High	Low	Limited	Considerable

Artisanal firms similarly tend to be quite specialized in their skills and capabilities and are also dominated by active owners. However, they depend much more on the skills of employees for their competitive advantages that focus on continual innovations and improvements. Authority is typically shared with business partners and competitors to achieve joint economies in purchasing, marketing, and distribution, as in many Italian industrial districts (Best 1990: 205–23). Strategic decisions are, therefore, constrained by commitments to such partners. While wealth accumulation is also important to these firms, the pursuit of technical excellence and innovation is often more central to their decisions. Competitive advantage is sought more through innovation than opportunistic flexibility, although flexible responses to changing markets are important to maintaining competitiveness. Such innovations tend to be adaptive rather than radical, since these firms usually lack the resources and organizational cohesion often required for systemic innovation. They typically constitute the main elements of coordinated industrial districts, such as those in north-east and central Italy.

Isolated hierarchies, on the other hand, are less able to share risks and commitments with business partners or employees. Relations between owners, managers, and employees are essentially market based, so that owners are remote from salaried managers and delegate considerable powers to them, but subject them to strong financial performance constraints. Employee and business-partner interests are generally not significant influences on decision-making in these kinds of firm. Such firms focus more on increasing investor returns than continuous innovations and rarely develop long-term-growth strategies, especially where fund management and control over shares are concentrated in liquid capital markets. The dominant arm's length and market relations between owners and managers in these sorts of firms also tend to characterize employment patterns. Commitment and mutual dependence are thus usually limited and the contribution of most staff to organizational capabilities is restricted. Flexibility and responsiveness to changing customer demands through employee adaptability and learning are also difficult to develop in such firms. More often they adapt through organizational restructuring. Isolated hierarchies usually dominate compartmentalized business systems, such as those that have developed in Anglo-Saxon societies.

Cooperative hierarchies, in contrast, combine substantial delegation of owners' powers with some risk-sharing and collaboration between firms' business partners, competitors, banks, and employees. Strategic decision-making is here quite constrained by employee and business-partner interests, which encourage growth goals rather than profitability and investor returns. Competitive strategies depend substantially on employee skills and involvement, without, though, these skills being highly firm specific. This involvement enables firms to develop strong capabilities for improving organizational competences and innovation. However, it may also limit responsiveness to changing demands where the skill development and control systems are rigid and slow to adapt to new industries.

These kinds of firms are characteristic of collaborative business systems, exemplified by many of those that have become established in the more corporatist societies of continental Europe.

Finally, *allied hierarchies* are even more interdependent with business partners and employees and share business risks widely. Alliances are often cemented with long-term mutual shareholdings. Employee interests are typically strong influences on strategic preferences here, since employer–employee interdependence is high and long term. Ultimate owners' interests in profits are, in contrast, rarely dominant, since shareholding and share-controlling intermediaries usually have broad interests in the long-term success and growth of firms. Similarly to the previous type, capabilities in these firms are strongly dependent on employees' skills, but these skills are typically more firm specific because of long-term commitments and frequent job rotation to develop overall firm competences rather than individuals' skills. This concern with organizational learning enables such firms to be more flexible and responsive to changing demands than many cooperative hierarchies, while also focusing on collective innovation capabilities as the major means of developing strategic advantages.

The major differences between this kind of firm and cooperative hierarchies concern, then, the variety of organizational capabilities and the firm specificity and breadth of employee skills. Allied hierarchies develop more alliances and obligational relationships with formally independent business partners that enable them to remain more specialized than cooperative hierarchies. By sharing market and production risks with business partners, including core employees, these kinds of firms are able to adapt to technological and market changes more readily than vertically integrated enterprises. They also rely more on developing skills and expertise within the organization, and expect greater employee flexibility, than do cooperative hierarchies. Typically, they occur in highly coordinated business systems, such as the one that developed in post-war Japan.

INTERDEPENDENCES BETWEEN INSTITUTIONS AND CHARACTERISTICS
OF FIRMS

These characteristics of firms vary interdependently with their institutional contexts in similar ways to the forms of economic organization considered in Chapter 2. The same basic set of institutional features is linked to the sorts of firms that dominate different market economies and the strategies they follow. As with the broader characteristics discussed above, these interdependencies are typically strongest at the extremes of the dimensions being considered and are not always reversible.

For example, high levels of business dependence on the state arising from a strong state directing strategies and sharing risks, as in Korea, limit owner delegation and the influence of employee interests on major strategic decisions. However, a weak state, or one that stands aloof from business strategies, does not necessarily encourage higher levels of delegation to managers or greater levels of employee influence on strategies. Similarly, while a strong public collaborative training system encourages authority sharing with business partners, the lack of one by no means rules this behaviour out, as the example of post-war Japanese firms indicates. Here, large firms recruit educated people who have few if any practical skills developed by the public training system, and develop firm-specific skills by extensive on and off the job training and rotation. Despite this absence of joint involvement in a strong public training system, firms have here established elaborate networks of alliances and associations in what Gerlach (1992) has termed 'alliance capitalism' (cf. Whitley 1992*a*). These interdependencies and others are summarized in Table 3.3 and will now be discussed further.

Considering first governance structures, high levels of owner delegation to salaried managers are clearly unlikely to be widespread in an economy where trust in formal institutions and procedures is low and the predominant authority pattern is paternalistic. In such cultures control is more personal than procedural, and owners cannot operate at arm's length if they wish to be sure that their interests are being followed. Similarly, a dominant risk-sharing state limits owner delegation, since owners cannot afford to be remote from state–firm negotiations in this situation. Where the state is powerful and has distinct interests, owners run the risk of being sidelined if they do not deal directly with the state and control firm behaviour.

Conversely, strong capital markets with fragmented ownership imply considerable owner delegation, at least by the ultimate beneficial owners, since they institutionalize liquid trading in financial assets at a distance from firms and their managers. However, as discussed above, where concentration of control over shares is high in such capital markets, managers are subject to quite strong constraints through the market for corporate control and cannot pursue growth goals irrespective of investor returns.

Employee interests are similarly unlikely to be significant influences on firms' strategies and actions when state dominance is high and trust in formal institutions is low. Major political risks focus attention on state interests and priorities so that other groups are subsidiary, except perhaps for a small cadre of senior managers. Equally, a culture in which trust in strangers is difficult to establish and maintain except on a personal basis is not likely to encourage reliance on employee skills and commitment to the organization as distinct from the individual owner-manager. Firms in this situation will not be greatly influenced by the needs of employees as a whole in making decisions.

Employers will additionally be discouraged from giving weight to the interests of the bulk of employees where these are highly fragmented along skill and occupational boundaries. In societies with strong skill-based groupings, identities and loyalties will be predominantly horizontal rather than vertical and often conflict with each other. This means that firms cannot easily assume that there are common interests across major employee groups, or that strong organizational loyalties can be developed. Capital-market-based financial systems are also

TABLE 3.3. Connections between institutional features and firm characteristics

Institutional features	Firm characteristics						
	Management control	Employee constraint	Business-partner constraint	Dominant goals	Employee contribution	Innovation focus	Responsiveness focus
The state							
Dominant risk-sharing state	Low	Low	Low	Growth	Limited		Low
Antagonistic to intermediaries			Low				
Formal regulation of markets			Considerable			Considerable	
Financial system							
Credit based			Considerable	Growth		Considerable	
Capital-market based	Considerable	Low	Low	Investor returns	Limited	Limited	
Skill development and control							
Strong public collaborative training system		Considerable	Considerable		High	High	
Strong unions		High		Growth			
Strong occupational groups		Limited	High		Considerable		Limited
Centralized bargaining		High		Growth			Limited
Trust and authority							
Low trust in formal institutions	Low	Low	Low		Limited	Limited	
Paternalist authority	Low						High
Communitarian authority	High	High			Considerable	Considerable	

unlikely to encourage firms to take much account of employee interests, since the strong market for corporate control here focuses managers' attention on financial rates of return in the relatively short term.

Strong unions, collaborative and effective public training systems, and communitarian authority relationships, on the other hand, do encourage more concern with employee interests. Where unions have strong legal and/or labour market powers, they are obviously in a position to insist on worker interests being taken into account when strategies are being developed and implemented. Equally, a strong training system both produces high level skills, which employers can rely upon since they are involved in developing them, and encourages employers to work with unions in managing skill development and certification. Employees are, therefore, more useful to firms in this situation than where skill levels in general are low.

Additionally, employers' commitment to the collaborative training system in such societies means that they cannot ignore the interests of workers in general as much as they can in economies where such cooperation is weak or non-existent. Furthermore, where managerial authority rests largely—or even partly—on perceptions that employers and employees share a common destiny, and are jointly responsible for the future of the organization as a whole, the significance of employee interests is likely to be considerable relative to economies where authority is more contractarian.

Business-partner constraints on strategic decision-making are likewise inhibited by dominant states, capital-market financial systems, and low trust in formal institutions. High levels of business dependence on the state, combined with considerable antagonism to intermediaries between the family, firms, and the central state, ensure that firms concentrate on developing close links with state agencies and compete with each other for state support, within and across industries. In such economies, it is clearly difficult for them to develop substantial and stable linkages with each other. Strong markets for corporate control in capital-market financial systems also inhibit alliances and networks, since ownership can change quickly in such markets, as can strategic choices and élite managerial personnel. For similar reasons to those mentioned above, an inability to rely on formal institutions for ensuring trust between firms limits the extent and stability of inter-firm networks, since alliances are based on personal connections and risks are difficult to share in such societies.

Conversely, where (*a*) the state encourages regulation of markets, either directly or indirectly, (*b*) banks and other financial intermediaries are locked in to firms' destinies, and (*c*) employers collaborate with the unions in managing the training system and with each other in centralized bargaining systems, firms will be encouraged to develop links with each other that are relatively wide-ranging and stable. All of these institutional features restrict the freedom of economic actors to change direction and act as short-term opportunists in terms of their immediate interests. They thus reduce the risks associated with making commitments to business partners, whether suppliers, customers, competitors, or employees, and enhance the likelihood of benefits accruing from them.

Growth objectives are more likely to dominate where both (*a*) dependence on the state is high and (*b*) risk-sharing by the state is considerable. This is because investment in capital-intensive technologies and developing large markets is often subsidized by state agencies in one way or another, and the larger the firm is, the more powerful it will be in dealing with the state. The growth of the Korean *chaebol* is perhaps the most spectacular example of this tendency, but post-war French economic expansion also illustrates it (Boyer 1997; Fields 1995; Woo 1991). Similarly, credit-based financial systems where banks and other financial institutions share investment and growth risks with leading clients encourage growth goals, because the larger their customers the more services they can supply them with and the faster will be their own growth. Capital markets with concentrated equity management, on the other hand, emphasize profit goals, since owners and fund managers are solely concerned with financial returns on their portfolios. Unions also prefer growth-focused strategies, because these provide more jobs and promotion opportunities.

Turning now to consider how institutional features are related to the sorts of capabilities organizations develop and their strategic focus, I discuss first the contribution of employees to developing and improving these competences. As before, dominant risk-sharing states coupled with low trust in formal institutions limit such contributions, because of the need to manage political risks and low levels of organizational loyalty among the bulk of employees. Where the dominant risks and opportunities arise from state actions and support, investment in developing employee skills and commitment is unlikely to be as high as that in meeting state demands and negotiating with officials. Similarly, in societies where trust is largely based on personal relationships and commitments, building organizational capabilities around the contribution of most employees on a long-term basis will be difficult in large firms, and highly focused on individuals' skills—as distinct from collective ones—in small ones. Equally, strong capital markets inhibit employee commitment and involvement because of the threat of ownership changes and subsequent organizational restructuring that limit continuity and the value of organization-specific contributions.

Conversely, strong public training systems in which employers, unions, and state agencies collaborate in developing and controlling skills are more likely to encourage employee contribution to organizational capabilities for three major reasons. First, most workers will be equipped with skills that employers respect and so can be expected to contribute usefully. Secondly, these systems typically encourage the linking of certified skills to organizational statuses, so that careers within firms are dependent on skill improvement and upgrading. This encourages both workers to develop new skills and employers to offer new opportunities in order to retain them. Firms therefore have significant incentives to involve employees in improving overall organizational competences. Thirdly, strong collaborative public training systems limit horizontal diversification and encourage mutual interdependence between employers and employees because they are usually organized on a sectoral basis and require cooperation between firms within industries. By institutionalizing collaboration between leading firms, unions, and state agencies in specific sectors, such systems focus firms' strategies on sectoral growth and domination. Since firms have to invest in skill development in particular sectors, they become committed to those industries and to competitive success based on employee skills in them.

Similar pressures come from centralized bargaining systems in which employers have to collaborate with each other to negotiate effectively with unions and that standardize employment conditions across firms. Such systems restrict both opportunistic competition based on low wages and reliance on numerical flexibility, so that employers are encouraged to rely on the skills of their current workforce in dealing with competition and change.

Likewise, communitarian conceptions of authority relationships encourage the development of organizational capabilities based on employee contributions, because managers' authority depends partly on their commitment to particular organizations and their success in generating competitive competences in them. In contrast to more contractarian cultures, managers here are relatively immobile between firms, especially across sectors, and so are more dependent on the growth of specific enterprises. Since most workers also have a strong interest in firm growth, both groups have more in common than in other cultures. This both encourages and enables managers to generate high levels of employee contribution to improving organizational capabilities.

These capabilities will be less innovative in societies where relations between owners, managers, employees, and firms are adversarial and arm's length. Generally, we can be sure that continuous learning by doing and innovations requiring employee participation are unlikely to be widespread where entry and exit barriers are weak and investment in organizational innovativeness is liable to be undercut by opportunistic competitors focusing on price. Low trust cultures where risk sharing with business partners and employees is difficult to institutionalize are also unlikely to encourage investment in developing innovative capabilities that require long-term and collective commitments.

On the other hand, considerable levels of market regulation coupled with bank interdependence, and strong collaborative public training systems, encourage the development of innovation-focused organizational competences. This is because sharing the risks of innovation in these circumstances is easier, technical skills are higher, and the threat of losing customers to new entrants is reduced. Additionally, predominantly communitarian authority norms both encourage and facilitate innovation strategies for the reasons adduced above. In general, institutional contexts that encourage collaboration in knowledge generation and use, both within and between firms, are more likely to lead to strong innovation capabilities than are those that reproduce adversarial and spot-market-type relationships between economic actors.

Finally, the development of responsive capabilities and organizational flexibility is linked to the extent of customer dependence, the ability to share risks with business partners, including the workforce, and the rigidity of skill boundaries.

Where the state dominates the economy and collaborates with firms to develop industries, strategies are typically producer driven and focused on making large quantities of standardized goods for relatively homogenous markets, as in classic Fordism (Boyer and Durand 1997). At the other extreme, small firms that are highly dependent on customer demands and unable to share major risks on a continuing basis with partners, but are able to change employees rapidly, will be highly responsive to market changes. The export sector in Hong Kong and Taiwan dominated by small Chinese family businesses exemplifies this kind of ultra-flexibility (Redding 1990).

Somewhat less flexible across sectors, but perhaps more able to respond to changing demands through improving the quality of outputs with employee cooperation, are the artisanal firms discussed above. These require a high level of employee skills and considerable internal or external labour-market flexibility. Where occupational groups based on narrowly defined skills are strong and bargaining arrangements are highly centralized, on the other hand, it will be more difficult for firms to adapt rapidly to changing demands, either by reorganizing the division of labour or by changing the skill mix through hiring and firing.

Greater levels of risk-sharing with business partners in general, as in post-war Japan, coupled with weak horizontal groupings in society, facilitate considerable organizational flexibility, as firms are more able to adapt to changing circumstances through both internal and external reorganization. High mutual dependence between employers, employees, customers, suppliers, and other partners enables firms to respond quite rapidly to market demands by changing activities and resources jointly without having to renegotiate contracts and agreements formally. In contrast, more contractual and arm's length economies inhibit flexibility because of the costs of reorganizing agreements when goodwill and common interests cannot be relied upon.

These relationships enable us to identify the institutional circumstances in which particular kinds of firms are likely to develop, and those that will inhibit their dominance in certain market economies. These are summarized in Table 3.4, which features the five ideal types outlined earlier. Opportunistic firms are the products of highly adversarial environments in which partnerships are difficult to establish or rely upon and cooperation discouraged. The state is typically remote and non-supportive of business development and innovation, and is frequently antagonistic to intermediary associations. Markets are usually weakly regulated and the formal financial system is distant from most enterprises. The public training system is often poorly developed and funded, with little or no involvement of employers and unions. Labour organizations are typically weak, not least because of state repression, and bargaining highly decentralized. Trust in formal institutions and procedures tends to be low, and authority patriarchal in these societies. Many developing economies where the state is essentially predatory or antagonistic to independent business development display these features and are dominated by opportunistic firms, often with state-owned or controlled ones reaping quasi-monopoly rents.

TABLE 3.4. Features of institutional contexts associated with five ideal types of firms

Institutional features	Firm type				
	Opportunistic	Artisanal	Isolated hierarchy	Collaborative hierarchy	Allied hierarchy
The state					
Supportive, risk-sharing state	−	+	−	+	+
Predatory state	+	−	−	−	−
Antagonistic to intermediaries	+	−	+	−	−
Considerable market regulation	−	+	−	+	+
Financial system					
Credit based			−	+	+
Capital market			+	−	−
Skill development and control					
Strong public collaborative training system	−	+	−	+	+
Strong unions	−			+	
Strong occupational groups	−				−
Centralized bargaining	−		−	+	−
Trust and authority					
Low trust in formal institutions	+	−	−	−	−
Paternalist authority	+		−	−	
Communitarian authority	−		−	+	+

Artisanal firms in contrast develop in more supportive environments. Typically, the state at national, regional, or local levels encourages coordination between firms and the development of joint associations for raising finance and developing marketing and distribution channels. Often it also supports the coordination of firm-based training and technological development with local public institutions. For these kinds of firms to flourish, markets need to be sufficiently regulated, so that large firms cannot drive them out on the basis of price, nor customers drive down prices so far that artisanal businesses cannot compete on the basis of quality and innovation. According to David Friedman (1998), the machine-tool industry in Japan has been developed successfully by many small firms in Sakaki Township with the help of such restrictions on market entry.

A further important institutional feature encouraging the development and success of artisanal firms is a strong public system for developing skills and strong unions ensuring that employers have to compete on the basis of innovation and improvements to products rather than by reducing wage costs. Danish machinery firms seem to prosper with highly skilled workers, who are continuously upgrading their skills and competing with employers for control of new technologies, according to Kristensen (1992, 1996). These 'skill containers', to use Kristensen's term, are highly dependent on their employees' skills, and the combination of this dependence with strong unions based on skills limits firms' ability to develop hierarchical controls over work processes and organization, as will be further discussed in the next chapter.

Artisanal firms additionally require a more trusting environment than is typically experienced by opportunistic firms. For firms and employees to rely on each other they have to assume that commitments will be honoured and that formally certified skills do guarantee competence in work performance and commitment to further improvement. While personal networks and reputations are usually quite important to such firms' success, their ability to pursue strategic advantages through continuing improvements and innovations does depend on an institutional infrastructure that generates trust between business partners and limits short-term opportunism.

Isolated hierarchies, in contrast, arise in more adversarial contexts, but ones where formal institutions are highly developed so that arm's length contracting is a reliable way of doing business. They typically dominate economies where the state is essentially 'regulatory' rather than 'developmental' (Johnson 1982), market regulation is weak, and financial systems are dominated by capital markets. Risk-sharing between business partners is difficult to establish and maintain in these circumstances. Often the public training system is poorly developed in these sorts of economies and does not require firms to collaborate with each other or with unions. Equally, unions are typically too weak to force firms to invest in training and retain their staff over business cycles. Where bargaining is systematically organized, it is typically decentralized to plant or firm level and does not require employers to work together in central forums. Reliance on external labour markets for hiring and firing discourages employers from relying on employee skills as the basis for strategic advantages, and the prevalence of contractarian authority relations inhibits the development of common identities and loyalties within firms.

Collaborative hierarchies, on the other hand, are encouraged by states that are supportive of intermediary associations and inter-firm alliances. Such states do not need to share risks directly with private firms for these kinds of enterprise to develop, but they often coordinate risk-sharing between firms and provide various forms of non-financial support. Markets are typically quite regulated in such economies, so that firms are conscious of sectoral boundaries and the identities of major participants. Reputations among competitors, suppliers, and customers matter more here than where entry and exit are facilitated by liquid capital markets and an emphasis on 'free' competition. Credit-based financial systems also encourage cooperation within sectors by facilitating risk-sharing and discouraging unrelated diversification.

Strong public training systems, which involve employers collaborating with each other and with strong unions, additionally encourage the establishment of such collaborative hierarchies. Unlike the situation in Denmark, though, unions in these collaborative societies are rarely structured around specialized skills and expertise. This means that firms are more able to integrate work processes through administrative procedures and rely on greater organizational loyalty. Communitarian authority relations also enhance such commitments and enable firms to establish stronger managerial integration of economic activities than seems to be the case in many Danish firms.

Finally, allied hierarchies develop where institutions encourage the establishment and continuation of alliances and collaborative linkages between firms, so that they can share the risks of new investments, information about opportunities, and new technologies without fear of opportunistic 'free riding'. Thus, state support for intermediary associations, state coordination of technological investments, recession cartels, and joint market development will all encourage these kinds of firms to form and grow. Market regulation likewise leads to greater willingness to cooperate by reducing uncertainty and increasing the effectiveness of reputational control of firm behaviour. Credit-based financial systems also facilitate this kind of firm growth by developing joint bank–firm risk and information sharing.

These kinds of firms focus on developing organizational capabilities for continuous improvement and innovation through long-term investments in employees that enable them to change jobs and roles quite frequently. Because employers and employees are highly interdependent, internal labour markets are highly flexible and changing business conditions are managed through functional rather than numerical flexibility. This requires commitment to the organization rather than to occupational skills and professions. Consequently, while strong unions are often important in developing such high lock-in effects in these firms, they are more enterprise than skill based. Equally, strong public training systems that develop and certify stable and relatively narrowly defined skills restrict the development of these sorts of firms, because they limit the flexibility of internal labour markets and focus identities on these skills rather than on employers. Similarly, centralized bargaining systems prevent allied hierarchies dominating an economy.

Both paternalist and communitarian authority patterns are consonant with this kind of firm being established, although the form of paternalism that is effective is more reciprocal than is typical of the Confucian cultures of China and Korea (Jacobs 1985; Pye 1985). Contractarian authority patterns, on the other hand, will inhibit such firms developing, because they limit joint identities and loyalties and focus on formally specified jobs and subordination relations, thus reducing flexibility and teamwork.

These connections between firm characteristics and institutional arrangements highlight the close interdependences between the overall features of institutional environments and the sorts of organizational capabilities developed by leading firms in an economy. As many writers have emphasized in recent years (e.g. Best 1990; Boyer and Hollingsworth 1997; Hollingsworth et al. 1994; Streeck 1997), the development of innovative and flexible organizational skills increasingly requires collaboration within and between enterprises and this in turn depends upon supportive institutional contexts. The sorts of 'rich' institutional infrastructures characteristic of locally and nationally collaborative and state-guided societies facilitate the institutionalization of cooperative coordination within and between organizations, and so the development of collective capabilities that draw on the skills and knowledge of a wide range of groups.

More adversarial and contract-based ways of organizing transactions in arm's length societies, on the other hand, may encourage Fordist types of organizational capabilities to be developed but limit the ability of firms to implement innovative and flexible strategies based on employee and business-partner contributions. Finally, highly anomic and predatory particularistic environments, such as those faced by many Chinese family businesses in Pacific Asia, restrict the growth of formal organizations—and hence of collective competences developed within them—while encouraging high levels of flexibility and responsiveness to changing markets.

So far this discussion has focused on the sorts of interests which dominate firms' priorities and set performance criteria for assessing their effectiveness, on the one hand, and the organizational capabilities they tend to develop, on the other hand. However, dominant firms in market economies additionally vary greatly in the prevalent ways they organize and control work as a result of differences in their institutional contexts, including variations in the organization of interest groups. In the next chapter I shall explore these connections in an attempt to describe and explain major differences in the sorts of work systems that become established and reproduced across business systems and societies.

4

The Social Structuring of Work Systems

INTRODUCTION

As has been shown in a considerable number of studies, the organization and control of work processes and of workplace relations in capitalist societies are complex, systemic phenomena that vary substantially between institutional contexts (e.g. Boyer 1991, 1994; Kristensen 1997; Lane 1989). While Taylorism or scientific-management principles were once thought to represent the only efficient way of structuring work activities, they are now seen to be historically and societally contingent patterns of work organization that depended on a number of circumstantial factors to become established in the USA, and that by no means dominated industrial organizations in Europe or Japan (Guillen 1994; Merkle 1980). It is also apparent that Fordist production systems have had many variants and have not always proved as effective as some adherents claimed (Boyer and Durand 1997; Hounshell 1995; Wood 1989).

Equally, the idea that these sorts of work system are being replaced by a single standardized form of work organization and control in the more 'advanced' capitalist economies, whether summarized as flexible specialization, neo- or post-Fordism or diversified quality production, is increasingly discredited. Rather, the prevalent ways in which work is organized and controlled, in different sectors, regions, and countries, vary considerably, and there is no reason to expect any particular pattern to become dominant across institutional contexts on the grounds of economic efficiency or through 'globalization' by multinational companies. As emphasized in Chapter 1, this suggests that we need to explore how and why such variations in patterns of work organization and control across business systems and societies develop and are reproduced over substantial periods.

To do this requires identification of the major ways in which these patterns vary between market economies to constitute distinctive work systems. Such systems are characterized by contrasting ways of structuring tasks and jobs, of controlling how work is allocated, performed, and rewarded, and of structuring employment relationships. As many authors have shown, these systems are linked to the nature of firms, interest groups, and dominant governance principles or 'rules of the game' in different societies, which in turn often stem from particular patterns of industrialization (see e.g. Iterson 1997; Kristensen 1997). The comparative analysis of work systems therefore necessitates both the identification of the processes by which major work-related interest groups are constituted in different societies and the associated conventions governing how they compete and cooperate in workplaces.

Differences between British and German managerial identities, skills, and practices, for instance, reflect variations in labour-market institutions and educational systems, as well as general conceptions of professional expertise and status that stem partly from different industrialization patterns (Stewart *et al.* 1994). The sorts of prevalent work organization patterns that have become established in different capitalist societies, then, reflect both the nature of interest groupings and the governance principles underlying their formation and interaction.

Drawing on the business-systems framework outlined above, this chapter compares and contrasts the key differences in these phenomena across capitalist societies, and suggests how we might explain the prevalence—or relative absence—of particular kinds of work system such as the ideal types of Taylorism and delegated responsibility. For ease of exposition, work systems will be presented in this chapter largely as the outcome of their institutional contexts, including the ways that interest groups are organized and compete, while recognizing that societal institutions are not immutable and do change over time. The emphasis here is on how particular institutions and types of social groups tend to encourage the development and reproduction of distinctive kinds of work organization and control and, perhaps more directly, discourage antithetical ones.

In the next part of this chapter, the two summary business-system characteristics of employment relations and work organization discussed in Chapter 2 will be elaborated into six basic characteristics of work systems for distinguishing the major ways in which work relations and labour management are structured in market economies. Subsequently, I consider how the organization of interest groups differs significantly between capitalist societies, and how these variations are connected to the development of different work systems. Finally, the ways in which key institutions affect the constitution and strategies of interest groups will be analysed, together with their most significant linkages to work-system characteristics, and the conditions encouraging and discouraging the adoption of contrasting patterns of work organization and control identified.

CHARACTERISTICS AND TYPES OF WORK SYSTEMS

Key Characteristics of Work Systems

Most comparative analyses of systems of work organization and control in capitalist societies implicitly or explicitly rely on an ideal type of Taylorism as the key reference point for contrasting types of task control and labour management (cf. Wood 1989). In discussions of 'genuine', 'flawed', or 'hybrid' Fordism, this focus on task control has been extended to broader organizational characteristics, such as the stratification of skills and statuses and the nature of reward systems, as well as to more macro-societal phenomena such as the welfare state and the 'social wage' (see e.g. Boyer and Durand 1997).

In seeking to understand why different kinds of work system have become established in different societies, and the roles of various groups in these institutionalization processes, it is difficult to isolate work-process control practices from more general employment and labour management strategies, since these are often mutually implicative, as the examples of scientific management and responsible autonomy illustrate (A. Friedman 1977). How tasks are structured and task performance is controlled is usually quite closely interlinked with recruitment, training, and reward strategies, and these in turn are often connected to firms' overall product and market strategies, as the contrast of British, French, and German practices shows (Lane 1989; Sorge 1991, 1996). Work systems, then, are conceptualized as distinctive patterns of interconnected characteristics of (*a*) task organization and control, (*b*) workplace relations between social groups, and (*c*) employment practices and policies.

Work processes are typically analysed in terms of task specialization or fragmentation, on the one hand, and worker discretion over task performance, on the other hand (see e.g. Lane 1989: 139). 'Taylorized' tasks are usually portrayed as highly standardized by external agents, highly simplified, and narrowly specialized with little or no scope for individuals to influence how tasks are executed—summarized as the separation of conception from execution (Guillen 1994: 42). Responsible autonomy or delegated responsibility task systems, on the other hand, allocate much greater independence to individuals or work groups as to how work is to be conducted, and tasks are usually more broadly defined and complex. However, it is worth noting that specialization and fragmentation of tasks is not always the corollary of simplification, as Kuhn (1989) points out, and that low discretion can accompany considerable task variety, as in the Chinese family business (Redding 1990). Thus, the first characteristic of work systems to be identified here, *task fragmentation and specialization*, should be distinguished from the second one, the *degree of worker discretion* over how tasks are performed and involvement in problem solving.

A further aspect of work processes which differentiates many continental European work systems from some North American and East Asian ones is the extent of worker influence over task allocation and definition, worker deployment, and work organization more generally. As Kumazawa and Yamada (1989) have emphasized, Japanese workers in large firms may have some discretion over task performance, and are involved in problem solving, but have very little say in what tasks they do or the conditions under which they do them. In contrast, German and Scandinavian workers since the war have had considerable collective influence over task allocation and worker deployment (Jürgens 1989; Kristensen 1996). This characteristic of work systems can be termed the *degree of managerial control over work organization* and allocation.

Related aspects of labour management strategies and employment policies concern management–worker relations and the ways that rewards are allocated. The Taylorist emphasis on separating task execution from conception according to 'scientific' work study and measurement, for example, was intended to facilitate job standardization and simplification so that skilled workers could be replaced by unskilled and cheaper ones who were in principle easily replaced. This standardization of jobs and organizational roles enabled rewards to be based on the amount of standard outputs produced by each role incumbent, as distinct from their specific skills or personal capacities, and did not reward—or seek to elicit—workers' initiatives in solving problems (Lazonick 1990). Most employees were expected to perform highly standardized tasks and paid according to their success in meeting the demands of the predetermined and narrowly defined role.

Managers in scientific-management work systems, on the other hand, were seen as knowledgeable and highly skilled—at least those that formulated, standardized and controlled work processes (i.e. Mintzberg's technostructure)—and so were quite remote and separate from the bulk of the workforce in terms of their expected commitment, competences, and substitutability. They were, and remain in many US and similar sorts of firms (Lazonick 1991: 43–5), organizationally segmented from other employees. Typically, manual and routine clerical workers were not considered to be members of the corporation in the same way that more educated managerial and technical staff were.

In contrast, the various responsible or delegated autonomy work systems tie rewards more to skills and/or individual capabilities, which are often quite broadly conceived and assessed over substantial periods of time. Here, workers' involvement in problem diagnosis and solving is seen as crucial to the organization's success, and their skills need to be broader to deal with complex tasks. Workers carrying out basic tasks in organizations are not, then, easily disposable or replaceable in such work systems, and their knowledge is usually continuous with that of management rather than being qualitatively different and very much inferior. Typically, reward differentials are lower in these organizations than in more Taylorized ones and less tied to job definitions (Lane 1989; Maurice *et al.* 1986). Segmentation here tends to occur between core and peripheral workers and firms rather than between managers and other workers.

This comparison reveals a further three important characteristics of work systems. First, the extent to which managers and workers are separated and opposed in their backgrounds and skills differs significantly between business systems. This dimension can be termed the *degree of separation of, and segmentation between, managers and workers*. Secondly, the *degree of employer commitment* to retaining their core workforce, as manifested in efforts to provide employment security across business cycles. Thirdly, the *basis of reward allocation and differentiation* in terms of the relative importance of job category, certified skills, short-term personal performance as evaluated by outputs and/or supervisors, and longer-term evaluations of personal contributions. Significant variations in these occur across Europe and elsewhere, as Kristensen (1997) has shown in his analysis of Britain, Germany, and Denmark.

Types of Work Systems

Together with the three aspects of work processes identified earlier, these characteristics constitute the key dimensions for comparing and contrasting work systems in capitalist societies. At least five distinct kinds of work system can be identified in terms of these six characteristics and are summarized in Table 4.1. These types are relatively internally consistent and develop interdependently with particular kinds of interest groups and rules of the game governing their interaction and control over resources. A *Taylorist* work system, for instance, combines high levels of job fragmentation, managerial control over task performance and work organization, strong manager–worker separation, low employer commitment to employment security, and job-based reward systems. It is unlikely to become widely implemented as a work system in societies where unions are strongly organized around skills, and/or managers share many of the experiences and skills of the workforce, and/or labour organizations are incorporated into state mechanisms for regulating conflicts between interest groups (Guillen 1994; Lazonick 1990). This kind of work system is more likely to be widespread in compartmentalized, and perhaps state-guided, business systems.

In contrast, *delegated-responsibility* work systems emphasize worker involvement in problem diagnosis and solution in dealing with complex tasks, and so require greater levels of mutual dependence and commitment between employers and their core workforce, including skilled manual workers. This is difficult to develop where managers and workers have quite distinct identities and backgrounds, are mobile between firms and industries, and owners do not share long-term risks with particular firms. A major difference between many work systems of this kind that have developed in continental Europe and in Japan and elsewhere

TABLE 4.1. Characteristics of work-system types

Characteristics	Work-system type				
	Taylorist	Delegated responsibility		Flexible specialization	
		Negotiated	Paternalist	Artisanal	Patriarchal
Task fragmentation	High	Low	Low	Low	Low
Worker discretion and involvement	Low	High	Considerable	High	Limited
Managerial control of work organization	High	Some	Considerable	Some	High
Separation of managers from workers	High	Low	Variable	Low	High
Employer commitment to employment security for core workforce	Low	Considerable	High	Limited	Limited
Rewards tied to:	Standardized jobs	Skills	Personal performance and abilities	Skills and personal evaluation	Personal evaluation of performance

concerns the degree of worker influence on work organization and allocation. Strong industrial or craft unions in much of post-war Europe have limited managerial control over work organization, and generated what are termed *negotiated* work systems here, in contrast to the enterprise-based unions in Japan and the relatively weak occupational associations there and in other countries. Relatedly, while rewards are usually linked to formally certified skills in negotiated systems, they are more based on personal performance and capacities as assessed by supervisors and managers over some time in more *paternalist* work systems. In general, we would expect negotiated work systems to be characteristic of collaborative business systems, while paternalist ones could develop in highly coordinated ones.

The third general type of work system discussed here is labelled *flexible specialization*, because of its emphasis on the flexibility of work processes and products, and of employing organizations generally, as well as the typical small size of organizations. These organizations combine fluid job categories and flexible employees, in terms of tasks undertaken and skills developed, with a high level of specialization on particular outputs and processes, and reliance on various forms of market contracting to coordinate inputs and outputs across the production chain. This emphasis on organizational flexibility typically implies much lower levels of mutual commitment between employers and employees than in most delegated-responsibility work systems, and a corresponding high level of inter-firm mobility—and indeed of firm birth and death, as in the fragmented and industrial-district types of business systems discussed in Chapter 2.

The two distinct forms of flexible specialization identified in Table 4.1 differ mostly in their authority relationships and the significance of formally certified skills. The *artisanal* form is typified by many European variants of industrial districts, whether Marshallian, Italian, or Danish, in which small firms compete and cooperate on the basis of workers' skills, flexibility, and innovativeness (Kristensen 1996; Langlois and Robertson 1995). Jobs and tasks are varied and wide-ranging, with considerable worker discretion—sometimes buttressed by strong unions (Trigilia 1990)—and owner-managers and workers usually share a common skill base. Managerial control over work organization is limited by the need to maintain skilled workers' commitment, as is managers' ability to allocate rewards personally and differentially.

In contrast, the *patriarchal* form combines much greater levels of managerial control over work organization, and sometimes over task performance, with a considerable separation of the owner-manager from the bulk of the workforce. Typified by the Chinese family business, it reflects many aspects of pre-industrial authority relations in newly industrialized countries in which patriarchal family authority patterns mirror, at least ideologically, those institutionalized in the state (Pye 1985). The lack of strong intermediary organizations between the family and the state in many of these societies, and usually of a strong public training system, encourages highly personal and direct control over work processes and limited employer–employee trust (Redding 1990; Whitley 1992*a*). This kind of work system is widespread in fragmented-business and state-guided business systems, where trust and authority relations are highly personal.

These characteristics of work systems, and their varying establishment in capitalist societies in the twentieth century, reflect the sorts of interest groups and collective actors that have developed in these societies. How these are constituted in different societies, and the dominant ways in which they compete for resources and control over jurisdictions, differ greatly as the result of variations in political, financial, labour, and cultural systems. In the next section I outline the major ways in which such interest groups are differently constituted across market economies in relation to their impact on work-system characteristics.

THE ORGANIZATION OF INTEREST GROUPS AND WORK-SYSTEM CHARACTERISTICS

Key Features of Interest Groups

Interest groups are seen here as organized collective actors representing particular social interests that compete for control over resources and socially valued activities. They differ in the extent to which they mobilize and represent particular kinds of interests in a market economy, how they do so, and on what basis they compete with each other. For example, the organization of skilled manual workers, technicians, salaried managers, financial intermediaries and organizations, and other occupational and sectoral interests as distinct and coherent groups varies greatly across Europe, North America, and Asia. The most significant differentiating feature of such groups across countries is the overall extent to which they mobilize interests throughout society and function as intermediary organizations between families and the state. Generally, industrializing societies are relatively weak in such forms of interest representation compared to most European countries, such as Finland, Germany, and the Netherlands (see e.g. Iterson 1997; Lane 1997; Lilja 1997). Relatedly, the importance of 'horizontal' forms of affiliation and collective action, such as unions and professional associations, clearly differs between, say, France and Germany, let alone between the Scandinavian countries and Pacific-Asian ones.

Three further differences between these interest groups are important. First, the scope of interests represented in dominant organizations varies between those based on narrow crafts and professional skills to those mobilizing broad categories of manual workers throughout a sector. Secondly, the degree of mobilization and organization of specific interest groups varies between informal and *ad hoc* associations and those that are much more formally structured and centralized in various corporatist systems. Thirdly, prevalent modes of competition and cooperation between interest groups also vary considerably between business systems.

These last vary from largely adversarial, zero-sum conflicts over distributional issues in which market power is the determining factor to more formally regulated disputes over a range of issues where groups combine collaboration over, say, training with competition and conflicts on a continuing basis. Competition between interest groups can, then, vary in terms of (*a*) the stability and formal recognition of the parties concerned, (*b*) the regularity and continuity of their interactions, (*c*) the formal regulation of conflicts, (*d*) the extent and scope of any cooperation between groups, and (*e*) the systematic structuring and integration of conflicts at different levels of the bargaining system and across industries and sectors in various forms of corporatism.

From this broad set of characteristics of collective actors and interest groups, three major ones can be identified that are particularly relevant to the analysis of work systems. First, there is the overall extent to which employees are in general mobilized around horizontal forms of interest representation. One of the most striking differences in the organization of work groups and collective actors within organizations between European countries and, *a fortiori*, between Europe, North America, and Pacific Asia, is the varied extent to which these are based on extra-organizational ties and identities which are more or less formally structured. Interest groups based on certified skills and union membership are clearly much more important in the German and Scandinavian economies than they are in Mediterranean Europe or Pacific Asia. Collective action by employees in the former societies is therefore structured more around extra-organizational identities and commitments than it is in the latter.

Of course, family, kinship, locality, and schools/university-based cliques and factions can and do function as the basis for collective identities within and between work organizations in many countries. These personal and particularistic groupings rarely, however, form stable and systematically organized interest groups that compete for control over resources and rewards in an institutionalized framework. An important distinguishing characteristic of interest groups, then, is their *strength in mobilizing horizontal interests across organizations and sectors*.

Secondly, where occupational interest groups are significant collective actors, the extent to which they are segmented and fragmented into a number of distinct strongly bounded and rather narrow groupings can vary considerably. Britain and Denmark, for example, seem to share a quite strong distinction between skilled workers' and 'general' unskilled workers' unions, whereas post-war Germany, Finland, and Sweden have more sector-based forms of labour mobilization and representation (Kristensen 1997). Additionally, Britain has a much more fragmented organization of high-level white-collar expertise in engineering, accounting, etc., than most European countries (Campagnac and Winch 1997; Geddes 1995). This segmentation and stratification of skill-based interest groups can have quite marked effects on the organization of work, particularly its specialization, as the separation of skilled maintenance workers from semi-skilled operators and of different professional groups in Britain indicates (Child *et al.* 1983; Maurice *et al.* 1980). This characteristic of interest groups can be described as the extent to which they are narrowly and strongly segmented around occupational identities or their *occupational specialization*.

Thirdly, interest groups vary in their legitimacy and prevalent mode of competing with each other. Unions, for example, have widely contrasting legal rights and duties, and quite different roles in conflict resolution, training, and general policy-making across Europe, let alone elsewhere. Relatedly, states have differed in their attempts to regulate industrial conflicts formally, and to specify the role of different groups. This aspect of interest-group structure and behaviour combines the recognition and regulation of them as appropriate collective actors with their involvement in a range of activities that typically require cooperation as well as competition.

At one extreme they may be only quasi-legalized and interact as essentially oppositional agents not only to employers but also to the state as a whole. In contrasting societies, they are highly institutionalized as full partners in a wide range of regulated activities in corporatist states such as Austria, the Netherlands, and Finland (Katzenstein 1985). This characteristic can be summarized as the *degree of incorporation of horizontally based interest groups* as legitimate and formally regulated social partners.

Further aspects of collective actors and interest groups in capitalist societies concern, of course, the organization of ownership and control of economic activities. As discussed in Chapters 2 and 3, there are a number of aspects to be considered here, such as the fragmentation of owners, the significance of family and broader kinship-based owning groups, the power of financial intermediaries, and the development of a distinct socio-economic stratum of senior managers separate from property rights' holders. Three interrelated ones are, however, particularly important in the context of work systems. These concern the dependence of owners and managers on the success and growth of particular firms and/or sectors and their associated interests, including, of course, their mutual interdependence or separation.

Let us consider first the organization and roles of property rights' holders: there are two characteristics of these which affect work organization and control patterns, both directly and through the interdependence of managerial careers with the fate of particular firms. First of all, there is the strong difference between market economies in which owners typically are directly involved in the management of economic activities and those in which they delegate control to non-owning managers. This obviously affects the extent to which ownership-based collective actors develop separately from those organizing senior managers' interests.

Secondly, amongst this group of non-managing shareowners and controllers there are significant variations in the scope of their interests in the firms in which they invest. In particular, the extent to which share ownership overlaps with other business relationships between companies differs greatly between capital-market-based financial systems, such as the Anglo-American economies, and bank-dominated ones such as Japan and Germany. As emphasized in previous chapters, in the latter societies owners are more often locked-in to the fate and success of the firms they invest in and so have much greater interest in their long-term growth.

They also have a variety of business ties and links with them, so that share owner-ship is just one aspect of complex and extensive interdependences. These two characteristics of the organization of property rights' holders can be summarized in a single dimension for the analysis of work systems as the range and strength of shareowners' and controllers' interests in the activities and success of particu-lar firms, or, more simply, the *involvement of owners in management.*

The third aspect of owners and managers that affects the organization of collective actors and work systems is the *dependence of senior managers on the growth of particular companies and/or sectors.* This affects the extent to which they see themselves as a distinct social group or identify themselves more with specific organizations and industries. The obvious contrast here is between the post-war Japanese economic system, where managers in the large-firm sector typically spend nearly all their working life in the same corporation, and so depend very largely on its growth and success for their own careers, and the common post-war Anglo-Saxon pattern of high rates of inter-firm, and often inter-sectoral, mobility (Lazonick and West 1998). Recently, of course, this mobility has become frequently based upon the possession of a general manage-ment credential such as the MBA degree.

In these latter cultures, 'management' is seen more as a generalizable set of skills and competences than as a set of industry-specific functions linked to more technical competences. Where access to élite managerial posts is tied to academic success in a small number of higher-education organizations, such as the *grandes écoles* in France, careers at the top of organizational hierarchies are also more governed by general credentials than by individual firm performance, but inter-firm and inter-sectoral mobility at lower levels is often more limited than in Anglo-Saxon labour markets (Boyer 1990; Lane 1989). The interests of élite managers in this situation are thus more general across the economy than are those of more junior staff.

These three aspects of ownership and management are interconnected. Low levels of direct-owner involvement coupled with purely financial interests, for instance, probably limit the dependence of managerial careers and interests on particular firms and sectors, because risk-sharing and mutual commitment between shareholders and managers are restricted in this situation. The market for corporate control is likely to be mirrored in such situations by considerable managerial mobility, as élite managers seek to reduce their 'exposure' to individ-ual organizations. As owners treat their holdings in individual firms more as elements of a liquid portfolio, in other words, so too we can expect managers to 'diversify' their career risks by developing general skills that can be applied across a range of organizations and sectors. This does, however, depend on labour-market conditions and the education and training system.

High levels of direct-owner involvement and broad interests in particular businesses are, though, consonant with varying degrees of managerial depen-dence on individual firms and sectors. While this combination is often associated with considerable managerial stability and an emphasis on the firm and industry specificity of valued managerial skills—as in Germany and Japan—it is not always so. This link is especially weak when strong and direct-owner control limits opportunities for managerial autonomy, and entrepreneurial skills are more highly valued than technical ones, as in economies dominated by Chinese family businesses. Here, as in many economies and/or sectors dominated by small firms, managers without strong family-like ties to owners frequently leave employers when they have learnt enough about the business to start their own firms, sometimes with the support of their previous employer (Shieh 1992; Wong 1988).

Connections between Interest-Group Features and Work Systems

If we turn next to the linkages between these five features of interest groups and work systems in market economies, it is clear that many characteristics of these systems depend on more general contextual arrangements, such as those governing labour markets and the development, certification, and organization of skills. There are, however, a number of direct connections that can be identified, and these are summarized in Table 4.2. Both the degree of job fragmentation and the managerial control of task performance are characteristics limited by strong horizontal groupings, especially skill-based ones, as Kristensen (1992, 1996) has emphasized is the case in much of Danish industry. Additionally, strong and direct owner involvement in management will often limit job fragmentation because most owner-managed firms are small and flexible, and do not have large production planning departments to Taylorize work practices.

Managerial discretion over work organization and allocation is also likely to be restricted by strong horizontal groupings, whether based on skills or on sectors. It is additionally limited by highly corporatist arrangements, because these often grant unions some negotiating rights over the power of managers to restructure organizations and transfer workers between jobs and plants. On the other hand, strong owner control is likely to encourage managerial insistence on the right to determine how work is to be organized and allocated because of the personal involvement of owners in day-to-day management, subject to the power of the unions.

High levels of manager–worker separation as implied in Taylorist systems are limited by corporatist regulation of interest groups, since this implies mutual recognition of employers and employees as partners across a range of activities and goes well beyond purely market relations. They are additionally restricted by high levels of owner and manager dependence on the success of individual firms, since this encourages belief in a common destiny and commitment to the same organization. On the other hand, they are likely to be enhanced where managers are clearly much better and differently educated from the bulk of the workforce, and have high-level credentials, such as the MBA, which enable them to transfer easily between firms and sectors.

Similarly, employer commitment to the core workforce is encouraged when

TABLE 4.2. Linkages between characteristics of interest groups and work systems

Characteristics of interest groups	Work-system characteristics					
	Task fragmentation	Worker discretion	Managerial control over work organization	Manager–worker separation	Employer commitment to employment security	Rewards basis
Strength of horizontal interest groups	Limited	Considerable for skilled workers	Limited		Considerable	
Occupational specialization		Considerable over specialized tasks				Skills where interest groups are based on skills
Incorporation of interest groups			Limited	Limited	Considerable	
Involvement of owners in management of specific firms	Limited		High except where unions are strong		Limited to personal commitments	Personal evaluation except where unions are strong
Managers' dependence on specific firm and/or sector growth				Limited	Medium	

organizational dependence of managers is high, corporatist arrangements are strong, and horizontal associations are powerful, because of the difficulties of disposing of workers in this situation and the greater significance of firm-specific competences for senior managers. Strong owner control, in contrast, may well limit such commitment where flexibility is at a premium, and trust is over-whelmingly based on personal, rather than organizational commitments. Finally, rewards will be based more on skills where these are strongly entrenched as the foundation of specialist groups, but more on personal qualities and performance where owners are in direct control of relatively small organizations.

SOCIAL INSTITUTIONS, INTEREST GROUPS, AND WORK SYSTEMS

Institutions and Interest Groups

Many of these connections are highly dependent on the broader institutional contexts in which they develop, particularly the institutions governing the development and organization of skills, the availability of capital, and trust and authority relations. Drawing on the general analysis of dominant institutions in market economies presented in Chapter 2, I here summarize the key relationships between particular institutional features of market economies, the characteristics of interest groups just discussed, and their joint structuring of work systems. First, I discuss how the central institutions governing skills, capital, trust, and authority relations are related to the organization of collective actors and then I consider how they combine to affect patterns of work organization and control.

The major institutions governing the organization of work-related interests in market economies concern the development and control of skills, the ways in which the state regulated workplace relations during and after industrialization, and the nature of the financial system, as well as prevalent trust and authority relations. In particular, the strength and organization of the public training system have substantial consequences for the sorts of skills that are developed and their connections to interest groupings. Work by Maurice *et al.* (1980, 1986), for instance, has shown the importance of a strong, widely accepted, and far-reaching public training system for work-organization patterns in Germany, and the system obviously also affects the development of occupational skill-based groupings, and their significance throughout the workforce.

Relatedly, the more unions and employers are jointly involved with state agencies in the direction and operation of the training system, the more likely the skills it produces will be regarded as useful by firms. Where, on the other hand, the public training system is weak, and formal educational achievements are regarded as crucial indicators of competence and ability, it is likely that the verdicts of the various levels of the academic educational system will stratify entry to—and perhaps limit movement between—labour markets, especially at élite levels. This academic stratification of labour markets limits the development of common identities within organizations and encourages the separation of status groups based on success in the formal educational system.

Also crucial to the establishment of strong occupational groupings are the strength and policies of the state during and after industrialization, and, in particular, the extent to which pre-industrial forms of skill development and control have been reinforced and reproduced by the state (Campagnac and Winch 1997). The major contrast here is between societies where the state has supported the establishment of independently organized associations which mobilize commitments and generate distinct collective identities, and those where it has destroyed pre-industrial associational forms and/or actively discouraged the development of horizontal interest groups mediating citizen–state relations. A third situation occurs in those countries, typically Anglo-Saxon ones, where the state has delegated substantial control over skill development to practitioner associations and educational organizations, but without formally integrating these processes or developing systematic procedures for organizing relations between associations and the state. Especially in Europe, these differences are quite strong and have had major consequences for interest groups and work systems.

As outlined in Chapters 2 and 3, there are two key features of institutions governing ownership relations. These concern, first, the extent to which owners are locked into the fates of the firms they invest in, and, secondly, their trust in the formal institutions governing property rights, control over economic activities, and economic exchanges in general—what has been termed systemic trust or 'confidence' (Luhmann 1979, 1988). The former is linked to the existence of large liquid secondary financial markets, upon which financial claims can easily be traded between anonymous actors, in capital-market-based financial systems. This enables owners to treat equity holdings as components of portfolios whose overall financial performance is to be maximized, and so reduces the risks attached to any single shareholding and owners' commitment to it. Capital-market financial systems, then, reduce the scope of owners' interests in particular firms' activities and, by enabling a market for corporate control to develop, also limit managers' dependence on the fortunes of any specific organization.

Relatedly, because such financial systems presuppose considerable trust in formal institutions governing exchange relations, the degree of systemic trust affects owner behaviour, especially the lack of it. The less trust that private property owners have in formal institutional procedures and in the good faith of their agents—what Barber (1983) terms fiduciary trust—the more direct will be their involvement in management and the broader will be their concerns.

The final institutional feature to be considered here is the nature of authority relations. A key aspect of subordination in market economies is the extent to which authority is linked to paternalism, because this affects the scope of connections between managers and workers as well as the legitimate ability of superiors to require compliance with a wide range of orders. As Beetham (1991) points out, paternalism implies parent–child authority relations in which the parties are inherently unequal and superiors are therefore expected to act in the interests of subordinates—since the latter are incapable of recognizing their true interests and acting appropriately. Paternalist authority relations thus encourage close owner involvement in management and broad owner interests. These connections are summarized in Table 4.3 and the effects of combining these features will now be discussed in a little more detail.

If we consider first the contrast of societies which combine a strong public training system with joint employer/union involvement in its control and operation against those without such a system, it is clear that the former are much more likely to generate distinctive occupational interests around certified expertise than are the latter. This is especially so when skill-based unions are strongly entrenched—as in Denmark. The combination of strong skill-based unions with a highly developed technical training system—partly controlled by the unions— seems here to have led to work groups being predominantly organized around externally certified skills and their interests being focused on the control of tasks and technologies through continued skill enhancement. Indeed, this seems to have limited the extent of managerial integration and control of work processes (Kristensen 1992, 1996). Where, on the other hand, unions are more sector based—as in Germany and other Scandinavian countries—this high degree of skill identification and competition seems less marked and managerial coordination correspondingly greater.

A well-funded and highly regarded training system jointly controlled through standardized structures by unions, employers, and the state also implies the development of expertise-based identities and interests among a large part of the working population, as opposed to these being restricted to élite groups or a limited number of roles such as maintenance workers. As a result, the majority of people in societies with such training systems expect to gain a certified skill and invest accordingly. In contrast, training systems for many skills in the Anglo-Saxon economies combine strong practitioner control over their definition, assessment, and certification, with the bulk of the workforce being excluded from the system altogether or else limited to low-status, narrowly defined skills. The delegation of responsibility for skill development and control by the state to unions, professional associations, and similar groups has led to a highly varied, weakly standardized system that covers only a minority of employees in some of these societies, and, as a result, specialization of interest groups is high.

In Britain, for example, the combination of practitioner élite control of the more prestigious 'professional' skills, with the limited or non-existent cooperation between professional associations, the education system, and employers in defining, developing, and assessing such skills, has had two major consequences. First, the professions have exercised quite strong control over the numbers of newly qualified practitioners, not least to maintain income levels. Secondly, they have restricted much training and certification to the reproduction of existing professional practices, particularly in accountancy (Geddes 1995). Because technical societies also function, in effect, as trade unions in many Anglo-Saxon countries, and originally controlled training through personal apprenticeships in

TABLE 4.3. Social institutions and the organization of interest groups

Institutional features	Characteristics of the organization of collective actors				
	Specialization of interest groupings	Strength of horizontal associations	Incorporation of interest groups	Strength and scope of owner involvement in firms	Managerial dependence on firms and sectors
Historical continuity and priority of skill-based groups	+	+			
State support for intermediary organizations	+	+	+		+
Scope and strength of public training system	–		+		
Employer/union involvement in public training system		+	+		
Academic stratification of labour markets	–		–		–
Capital-market-based financial system				–	
Degree of systemic trust				–	
Paternalist authority relations		–	–	+	–

many instances, they tend to concentrate on monopolizing particular work jurisdictions (Abbott 1988) and to develop skills for carrying out existing tasks in the
current 'best-practice' mode for those jurisdictions. Competition between these
occupational groups for control over problem-solving tasks encourages rather a
narrow identification of particular skills with particular jobs and roles, as the
groups seek to maintain their distinctive social identity and privileged position in
the labour market. The high degree of professional specialization in the British
construction industry stems partly from this competition between occupational
associations (Winch 1996).

Where, on the other hand, skill definition, development, and assessment are
carried out in more standardized ways involving state agencies and educational
organizations, and prestigious qualifications are not so directly linked to specific
roles and problem-solving tasks through professional associations' control of
work jurisdictions, skills tend to be less tied to current professional practices and
social identities less dependent on particular skill-based roles. Competences in
these sorts of societies are more broadly based and not so tightly connected to
specific jobs. However, since employers are involved in their definition, development, and evaluation, at least in the 'German' type of training system, they remain
organizationally useful.

In leading to distinctive occupational 'interests', then, such skills do not limit
these to particular, narrowly defined roles. Because they are not so tied to specific
jobs and tasks, these interest groups compete more broadly over a wider range of
competences than do the Anglo-Saxon professional associations and skilled
workers' unions, and seek to control areas of organizational activity rather than
protect particular positions. Collective actors in these countries are unlikely to be
so self-conscious of their distinctive 'professional' identity and interests as they
are in societies where practitioner élites dominate skill definition, development,
and certification.

In contrast, countries where public training systems are only weakly developed, have low status, and/or have little impact on the organization of labour
markets and the organization of work in firms, certified skills are unlikely to form
the basis of interest groups or to structure organizational roles. Instead, a combination of informal, personal groups and networks and the hierarchy of the general
education system become key influences on group organization within and across
firms. The role of kinship links, common geographical origins, and shared educational experiences in generating personal networks and common identities in and
between organizations is well known in Pacific Asia, most notably perhaps
among the expatriate Chinese (Limlingan 1986; Redding 1990), but also occurs
in Europe and elsewhere. However, such personal networks rarely structure
labour markets or organizational roles in a comparable manner to formally certified skills in societies with strong public training systems. On the other hand, the
selection processes of the general education system can play a significant role in
organizing careers and collective actors that transcend organizations and, sometimes, sectors.

The most notable example of educational stratification of labour markets and organizational hierarchies is perhaps the elaborate grading of *grandes écoles* in France, which strongly influences the careers of graduates and provides distinctive élite identities that are reinforced through the *grands corps*. Here, relative success in the formal public educational system has a strong, not to say the strongest, influence on individuals' life chances and differentiates access to jobs in large organizations. At the apex of the system, the small technically focused schools, including now the Parisian Commerce schools, provide high status identities and organized networks which control—or at least strongly influence— access to top posts in the state bureaucracy and in the private sector (Bauer 1987). The *grands corps*, and arguably the *grandes écoles* in general, constitute important collective actors in France that transcend firm, sector, and ownership boundaries. It is less clear, however, that the universities or the *lycées* perform similar roles, not least because of their much greater size.

The education system in France, then, filters and grades people in ways that structure their future careers, but perhaps only generates organized collective actors at the élite level and so limits the scope of formally structured horizontal interest groups to élite groups. Similarly, the Japanese education system organizes life chances and access to hierarchical positions in firms of different sizes, but does not itself generate distinctive, formally organized, interest groups that transcend organizational boundaries. While university attendance may structure factions and allegiances inside Ministries and large firms in Japan, collective interests are typically based around employing organizations rather than horizontal identities derived from the educational system.

These general points also apply to managerial groups, in that a strong and pervasive public training system will structure their identities and organization as well as those of manual and clerical workers, technicians, etc. Indeed, many continental European societies have not institutionalized distinctive managerial identities because of the strength of traditional apprenticeship and functional careers based on expertise in engineering, law, and other fields. As Stewart *et al.* (1994) have pointed out, a major difference between British and German managers lies in the fact that the former separate their managerial role from technical proficiency and involvement in task performance, while the latter conflate their managerial identity with their technical competence. This partly reflects the much more systematic, prestigious, and far-reaching training system in Germany, in which technical qualifications are cumulative and careers are what Offe (1976) calls 'task continuous'. Managerial skills and activities are viewed as building on existing technical competences, because these are widespread and highly regarded rather than being detached from them as a separate set of capabilities.

Additionally, however, the development of distinctive managerial identities and collective interests, separate both from other occupational roles and from the success of individual employers and industries, reflects general arrangements governing access to capital and the organization of markets through their impact on managerial mobility and organizational change. The more managerial élites move between firms and sectors, the less committed they will be to any one orga-nization and industry and the less they will view their particular expertise as being closely dependent on knowledge and experience of specific sectors. This is espe-cially likely when, as in many post-war Anglo-Saxon economies, firms are often seen as diversified businesses that can be run as a portfolio of separate units, to be bought and sold as their financial performance dictates. In such companies, managerial expertise and interests are clearly less identified with those of partic-ular divisions and industries than when senior managers spend most of their working lives in the same firm and/or sector and their careers depend on their success within it. A general set of managerial skills that are transferable across industries, such as those institutionalized in the MBA degree, is much more likely to be regarded as the basis for a distinctive identity and collective interest in the former societies than in the latter ones.

Following the analysis presented in the previous chapters, high rates of managerial mobility and discontinuous organizational change are more likely to develop in economies where the financial system is dominated by capital markets and the state is essentially regulatory and remote from firms and markets. Because investors are not locked in to the fate of any one company, they do not develop much expertise in its products, technologies, or markets and generally prefer to sell their shares than intervene when problems arise. Thus, capital-market financial systems generate strong markets for corporate control in which ownership can change quite rapidly and businesses are bought and sold in the same way as commodities in general. Any one company can, then, radically alter its subsidiaries and its ownership. Managerial skills and interests in these economies are clearly not so closely dependent on specific industries and activi-ties, since the nature of firms can change quickly.

Additionally, such change is also facilitated by 'regulatory' states that stand aloof from economic processes and actors (Johnson 1982). They tend to outlaw cartels and similar forms of market collaboration as being 'anti-competitive', do not encourage strong sectoral trade associations, and do not attempt to limit industry entry and exit. Here, firms are free to move into, and out of, any business sector, and so industry membership is fluctuating with little collaboration between companies and weak institutionalization of industrial norms and regula-tory conventions. The overall level of firms' mobility in and out of industries, and their cooperation in training, bargaining, and other areas, are, then, additional factors affecting managers' dependence on the success of particular firms.

Similar factors affect the strength and scope of owner involvement in firms' affairs, as analysed in Chapter 3. Where shareholders treat their property rights as a diversified portfolio of assets to be bought and sold on liquid secondary markets solely as their financial performance dictates, clearly their interest in the activities and capabilities of any individual firm they invest in is quite limited and narrow. Conversely, where banks and other investors are effectively 'locked in' to share ownership and/or share trusteeship of specific businesses, they have to develop longer-term and broader interests in the businesses' growth and development, both to provide other services and business relationships as firms expand, and to ensure their investments pay off in the medium term. Investors here develop more elaborate monitoring skills and knowledge about specific clients' products, technologies, and markets, so that they can evaluate particular risks more effectively and, over time, offer informed advice about opportunities and strategic choices.

A further factor encouraging close and wide-ranging owner interest in particular firms' activities is the lack of trust in formal institutions for resolving disputes and ensuring contractual compliance. Clearly, remote owner–manager relations are more risky for investors when there is no well-established and functioning regulatory system and information asymmetries are considerable. The less reliable are the institutions governing property rights, the flow of information about firms' activities, and control procedures, the more owners are likely to become closely involved in the affairs of their companies and be concerned with a wide range of issues. Whether in newly industrializing countries or in the former state socialist societies, this lack of institutional reliability limits owner delegation of control to managers and generally restricts the development of separate managerial roles and identities.

Even where owners do not themselves manage operations in these circumstances, they will develop much more detailed understandings of their firms' activities and capabilities than those in societies where formal institutions are regarded as being more reliable, in order to manage the greater risks more effectively. This need to be personally fully informed about particular firms' products, technologies, and markets—or to be limited to relying only on those partners with whom strong levels of personal trust have been established—limits owners' abilities to diversify widely and/or to manage complex businesses that require much specialist technical knowledge to be successful. Thus, many Chinese family businesses diversify only into fields, such as property development, where dealing skills are more important than detailed technical knowledge of products and processes (Redding 1990). However, these points do not apply in many of the former state socialist societies where managers are effectively able to act as owners because a separate and distinct group of property rights' holders has not yet become established as a powerful interest group (Jaklic 1997; Whitley *et al.* 1999).

Connections between Institutions, Interest Groups, and Work Systems

Turning now to consider how these institutional features and characteristics of collective actors are connected to work systems, I shall briefly discuss some of the key direct linkages between institutional arrangements and prevalent forms of work organization and control, before summarizing the ways in which particular combinations of these factors encourage and inhibit establishment of different kinds of work systems in different economies. In Table 4.4 I suggest that a strong and broadly based public training system in which employers and unions jointly play an important role will limit job fragmentation and

TABLE 4.4. Direct linkages between institutional features and work-system characteristics

Institutional features	Work-system characteristics					
	Job fragmentation	Workers' discretion	Managerial control over work organization	Manager–worker separation	Employer commitment to employment security	Reward basis
Strong continuity of skill-based groupings						Skills
State support for intermediate organizations			−			
Strong and broad public training system	−	+	−	−	+	Skills
High level of joint employer and union involvement in public training system	−	+	−	−	+	Skills
Strong academic stratification			+	+		Jobs
Capital market-based financial system					−	
Low trust in formal institutions		−	+			Personal evaluation
Paternalist authority relations	−	−	+			Personal evaluation

manager–worker separation. It will also probably encourage managers to rely on skilled workers for firm growth, effective task performance, and problem-solving, where firm, owner, and managerial mobility is limited. This is because certified skills are widely available and broadly based, and employers have confidence in their utility and flexibility. Together with strong state support for intermediary associations, these phenomena are also likely to restrict managerial control over work organization somewhat.

On the other hand, a high level of academic stratification of labour markets—which usually implies the absence of a strong, highly regarded, training system—limits employers' willingness to depend on skilled workers and increases manager–worker separation. This is because of both the lack of broad, publicly certified skills on which employers have had some influence, and the tendency for élite groups to regard those filtered out by the general education system as less worthy and competent overall than themselves. Skills are less likely to become the basis for reward allocation and differentials than organizational roles in this situation. Capital-market-based financial systems additionally inhibit such dependence because of the strong market for corporate control and the limited amount of owner risk-sharing.

Low levels of contractual and fiduciary trust in business partners—including employees—encourage direct supervision of work processes and an unwillingness to delegate control to managers through formal procedures. Thus, fully-fledged Taylorist work systems that rely on impersonal and formalized control processes are unlikely to become established in societies where systemic trust is very limited. Relatedly, paternalist authority relations will also inhibit the development of formal rule-governed systems of work control because of their emphasis on personal relationships between leaders and the led. Similarly, these personal connections will limit job fragmentation and rigidity, because the scope of superiors' authority is not restricted by impersonal rules. While unskilled work in Korean *chaebol* may, for example, be quite narrowly focused, supervisors may also be able to require rapid change to a variety of new tasks because of the lack of formal procedures delimiting obligations and job characteristics (Janelli 1993).

Combining these linkages with those involving characteristics of collective actors to explain the establishment of different work-system types, often makes it easier to see how particular combinations restrict the development of particular kinds of work organizations and control, rather than how they actively generate specific forms to become prevalent in a society. For example, high levels of job fragmentation, separation of task conception from task execution, and managerial coordination of work activities in Taylorist work systems are unlikely to be prevalent in market economies with strong horizontal associations, skill-based unions, and an extensive and highly regarded training system with strong practitioner influence. These negative relationships are summarized in Fig. 4.1 which highlights the major connections between institutions, interest groups, and work systems, omitting some of the relationships identified in Table 4.4.

Such connections are often strongest between extreme values of the variables

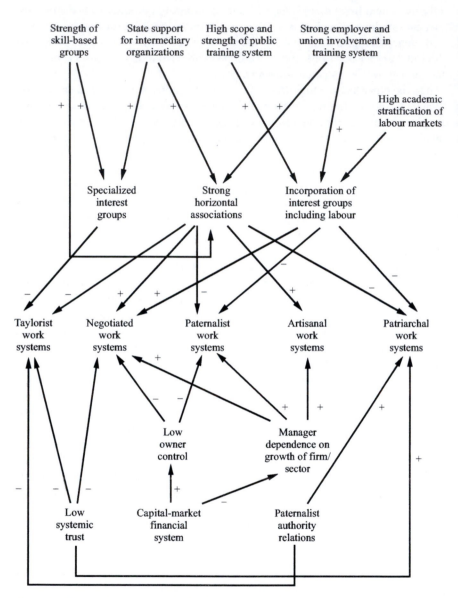

FIG. 4.1. Connections between institutional features, interest groups, and work-system types (omitting some direct links between institutions and work systems)

discussed here and it is important to note that reverse relations do not always obtain. In the case of Taylorism, for instance, the lack of strong institutions governing skill production, certification, and control in most East Asian societies has not led to the widespread reliance on highly fragmented tasks and jobs and formalized, rule-governed managerial coordination and control systems. Managers in East Asia do, though, often limit the level of worker discretion and tend to rely more on direct supervision of work processes than occurs in many European countries (Janelli 1993; Lincoln and Kalleberg 1990; Redding 1990).

Similarly, work systems that rely heavily on contractual obligations and elaborate managerial hierarchies to control and coordinate activities are not likely to develop in societies where authority is largely paternalist and formal institutions governing competence and contractual trust are regarded as unreliable—or simply non-existent. These conditions are, however, likely to limit owners' willingness to delegate responsibility for controlling work to a managerial bureaucracy and/or to grant workers considerable discretion over task performance. Again, though, the reverse situation is by no means going to encourage Taylorism, as many Central European countries demonstrate (Czaban and Whitley 1998).

Overall, then, fully-fledged Taylorist work systems seem most likely to become widely established in a capitalist society when the following five conditions are met. First, unions are weak and not based on formally certified skills. Secondly, there is a shortage of appropriately skilled labour but a surplus of unskilled workers because of the limited scope and strength of the public training system, which does not involve unions or employers in its management. Thirdly, managers are quite differently and better educated than the bulk of the workforce and are not closely dependent on the success and long-term growth of individual firms. Fourthly, contractual arrangements and formal procedures in general are widely relied upon to regulate behaviour, and, finally, the state does not involve labour organizations as legitimate partners in managing conflicts.

Additionally, of course, the investment required to establish such elaborate rule-governed work systems, and their relative inflexibility in facilitating product and process changes, limit their systematic use to economies where there is a large market for standardized goods and mass production can be effectively integrated with mass marketing through elaborate managerial hierarchies, as in the USA (Chandler 1980; Lazonick 1990, 1991). In general, these conditions are rarely all met and so the successful implementation of the whole set of practices has not been widespread, although some elements of Taylorist work-management principles, such as the use of work study and measurement, have been applied in a number of societies, as Guillen (1994) and others have indicated.

On the other hand, negotiated work systems in which skilled workers exercise considerable discretion over task performance and some influence over work organization, and in which there are quite strong continuities between them and middle managers, require a highly educated workforce. They are most likely to develop in societies with strong skill-based unions, a wide-ranging and highly regarded training system in which employers play an influential role, and a high level of managerial dependence on, and commitment to, the growth and success of particular firms and sectors. This, in turn, depends on owners not being too remote from the activities of particular firms and the market for corporate control to be limited in its impact on firm behaviour. In contrast, societies where the educational system directly stratifies labour markets, and the public training system is weakly developed and/or excludes employers and unions from influence on skill development and certification, limit continuity between workers and managers and make managerial coordination of work processes more likely.

Given these points, it may be wondered how large firms in the post-war Japanese business system developed such dependence on their core manual workforce with a high level of firm-specific skills being generated, or at least why the combination of academic stratification of labour markets, enterprise unions, and a weak public training system has not prevented the 'white collarization' (Koike 1987) of much of the manual labour force. While it is not possible to provide a full answer here, I suggest that the combination of the high level of risk-sharing between business partners in the large firm sector, the coordinating role of state agencies in managing economic and industrial change, and the high dependence of managers on individual firm growth and success has encouraged the incorporation of the core, male workforce into firms' long-term development (Whitley 1992a).

Additionally, the shortage of skilled labour during the high-growth period in Japan and the strength of unions in the 1950s and 1960s further encouraged employers to invest in employees and develop mutual long-term commitments with them. It is particularly the lack of an effective external labour market for males over 30 years old in large firms which has made both managers and other groups of employees highly jointly dependent on the success of 'their' firm, thus weakening if not entirely negating the differentiating effects of the educational stratification of labour markets in Japan. Thus, paternalist work systems are encouraged by a high level of manager and large shareholder interdependence with firms, considerable risk-sharing between organizations, their banks, and—in the Japanese case—trading companies, together with a strong coordinating role by the state, and the absence of strong skill-based unions. Risk-sharing and mutual dependence with the core workforce are helped here by the generally high level of cooperation in the economy and the close links between enterprise unions and employers in the large firm sector.

Work systems that combine more personal management of work processes, considerable dependence on relatively autonomous skilled workers, and continuity between workers and owner/managers develop in a variety of circumstances, such as the industrial districts of north-east and central Italy and western Jutland, but share a common rejection of extensive managerial hierarchies and formal systems of coordinating work processes. In Denmark this seems to arise from the combination of strong skill-based unions that exert considerable influence over the extensive and highly regarded state-funded training system with considerable continuity between skilled workers and managers and a lack of influence from capital owners beyond the entrepreneurial groups of owner-managers (Kristensen 1996, 1997).

In Italy, unions are also influential, especially in the Emilia-Romagna, but do not seem to be so strongly organized around skills or to exert such strong control over the training system. Here, the localization of work in specialized communities that have effective systems of reputational control and informal coordination processes buttressed by municipal and allied organizations facilitates internal cooperation and excludes outsiders (Storper and Salais 1997: 161–9). This enables small firms to integrate inputs and outputs without formal managerial procedures and ensures that both workers and owner-managers are jointly dependent on the success of the sector or part of the production chain. Effectively all the major groups in these industrial districts are locked in to each others' fate, so that they have to collaborate as well as compete in the short to medium term and so risks are shared throughout particular geographical areas (Langlois and Robertson 1995; Lazerson 1988, 1995; cf. D. Friedman 1988).

In contrast, patriarchal work systems are the product of an insecure, particularistic business environment in which trust and authority are highly personalized and formal procedures are rarely relied upon to control behaviour or resolve disputes. In societies where these are dominant forms of work organization and control, horizontal associations are weak and often based on kinship ties or similar ascriptive criteria so that workers have little collective influence. Given the overriding pursuit of flexibility and risk reduction by limiting commitments in many of the antagonistic and adversarial contexts where these work systems are widespread—for example, among the overseas Chinese (Redding 1990)—job and task fragmentation is usually limited. Paternalist political ideologies obviously reinforce these tendencies to highly personal and directive control over work processes by owner-managers (Deyo 1989).

CONCLUSIONS AND IMPLICATIONS

This analysis of the conditions encouraging and inhibiting the development and widespread adoption of different kinds of work systems emphasizes the importance of the 'societal effect', as opposed to the 'dominance effect' (Lane 1997; Smith and Meiksins 1995), in explaining variations in work organization and control across capitalist economies. The highly societally specific nature of many labour-market institutions, education and training systems, state structures and policies, and the other institutions discussed above has generated quite varied forms of interest representation and capital–labour relations and of prevalent patterns of work organization and control.

These institutions also significantly affect the transfer of managerial practices from one context to another, as the extensive literature on 'Japanization' indicates (e.g. Abo 1994; Botti 1995; Elger and Smith 1994; Hibino 1997; Sharpe 1997).

Just as technological innovations change over the course of their development and adoption, so too do social innovations, whether transferred from abroad or developed domestically, alter as their context changes and different aspects are accepted in different situations. As long, then, as the organization of interest groups and the prevalent rules of the game governing workplace relations vary significantly between societal contexts, the standardization of work systems around a single model of efficient production will remain limited. Rather, some features of work organization are being transferred across countries by some multinational firms, but these typically vary between firms and contexts as interest-group structures and institutional arrangements differ in nature and strength across contexts. Economic functionalist arguments that simply assume that competition will automatically standardize work systems are, then, inadequate.

This contextual interdependence of work organization and control patterns has a number of implications for the analysis of work-system change. First, it is clear that widespread and radical transformation of the prevalent system in any society is highly dependent on related changes in the most closely linked rules of the game and organization of interest groups. Changing the basis of reward systems in German organizations, for example, away from skills towards more individual evaluations by supervisors and personnel departments is most unlikely to become widely implemented without quite major changes in union structures and powers, and in the organization and prestige of the public training systems. Similarly, institutionalizing 'Japanese' levels of mutual dependence between employers and employees in Anglo-Saxon societies without also limiting the market for corporate control and increasing the 'stickiness' of external labour markets is likely to prove difficult, if not impossible, in the short term. The more integrated the work system is with institutional arrangements that are standardized and firmly established throughout a society, the more difficult such change will be (Schienstock 1997).

Secondly, as the Fordism literature indicates, many work-system characteristics are closely connected to other aspects of dominant business systems, particularly the nature of firms, and thereby further integrated with their institutional context. For example, the considerable employer commitment to employment security for the core workforce in large Japanese companies is linked to the general pattern of risk-sharing between firms, banks, and other agencies in Japan, and to their relatively low degree of diversification, broad owner–management connections, and focus on growth strategies (Whitley 1992*a*). Changing this characteristic significantly would, then, involve changing a number of important aspects of Japanese large firms and their interrelated institutional contexts, which is why the major recession in Japan in the 1990s did not result in substantial alterations to these employment policies in most large companies for a considerable time.

Thirdly, because the degree of institutional integration and mutual dependence in capitalist societies varies between, say, Britain and Japan, the variety of work systems and their susceptibility to change also differ substantially. Sectoral variations in how work is organized and controlled are more significant when labour-market institutions and interest groups are not highly standardized throughout a society but differ between industries. Similarly, changing such practices will be easier, in principle, where it does not involve challenging the entire national patterns of labour-market organization and highly institutionalized systems of interest-group organization.

Altering some aspects of British patterns of work organization in some sectors is, for example, more straightforward than it would be in Germany or some Scandinavian countries, because they are not as tightly integrated with national regulatory institutions. The extent of societal regulation and standardization of interest groups and workplace relations, and their interdependence with other institutional features, thus affects the variability of work systems between industries and the ease of changing them. The regulated and standardized nature of workplace relations and groups in state socialist societies continued to structure managerial practices in the 1990s, which helps to explain the limited extent of organizational change in many enterprises in these countries (Whitley and Czaban 1998*b*), as will be further discussed in Chapter 9.

Fourthly, just as the standardization and integration of key institutions affect the variability and susceptibility to change of work systems within societies, so too the varying strength and centrality of particular institutional arrangements and interest groups affect the likelihood that some characteristics of work systems can be altered more easily than others in different countries. The strength of the German public training system, for example, means that altering the basis of rewards is more difficult for firms operating in that country than it is in Britain, where the training system is more weakly institutionalized and standardized across industrial sectors. This, in turn, affects the systemic nature of work systems in different countries. Because of the nationally regulated nature of many aspects of workplace relations, interest groups, and training systems in Germany and some other European countries, work-system characteristics are more interconnected and standardized throughout the society than they tend to be in Anglo-Saxon countries, where the state does not play such a strong role in coordinating activities and the formal system of regulation is less elaborate. Work-system change in the latter countries is usually more piecemeal than in the former ones as a result.

Finally, although the systemic and institutionally interlocked nature of many characteristics of work organization in capitalist economies, and the associated institutional 'lock-in' effect (cf. Grabher 1993; Herrigel 1994), limit major changes to work systems in the short term throughout a number of societies, it is worth pointing out that some interest-group structures and institutions are more established and unlikely to change than others. Most obviously, perhaps, the nature of many formal rules and procedures is more susceptible to reform and influence by collective actors than are the conventions by which they are generated and altered. The rules of the game are usually longer lived and more deeply entrenched than are the specific policies and outcomes of conflicts that they govern.

For example, labour-law and training systems are typically more malleable than the structure of interest groups involved in battling over changes or the conventions according to which disputes are settled. Similarly, professional jurisdictions and expertise change more in Britain than the dominant conception of the profession as the primary mode of organizing high-level expertise and its practitioner controlled training and certification system, which has existed in some form for over 500 years. New skills and occupational groups continue to follow similar patterns that retain considerable prestige (see Geddes 1995). To change the nature of skill-based groups and the ways they compete in the workplace in Britain, especially in non-manual areas of work, is a very slow process and would involve major shifts in the roles of professional associations, the state, and educational organizations.

So too in Baden-Württemberg and other European regions, changing the policies of regional governments and developing new skills and technology institutes are relatively straightforward compared to altering the ways these activities are carried out and the nature of the groups involved. Where, then, particular rules of the game or background institutions are closely linked to patterns of work organization and control, these latter are unlikely to alter radically. In contrast, where the associated structures and conventions are more recently developed and linked to specific policies, such as the 1980s reforms of some Scandinavian financial systems, institutional lock-ins are less restricting.

5

Globalization and Business Systems

INTRODUCTION

The increasing domination of international trade by multinational companies (MNCs) over the past five decades has been seen by some to herald the establishment of new, non-national kinds of economic actors that behave differently from more nationally based competitors (e.g. Bartlett and Ghoshal 1989; Doz and Prahalad 1993; Hedlund 1993). Together with the expansion of international trade and growth of international capital markets, this increasing international managerial control of economic activities has been claimed to be leading to a borderless world in which national boundaries and the states controlling them have less economic significance than the decisions of transnational business élites and financial markets. Within Europe, such claims have, of course, been accentuated by the expansion of the European Union, moves to a single European market, and related efforts to standardize the rules of the game governing economic competition.

Some authors have additionally viewed these changes as intensifying the establishment of sectoral economic coordination and control systems on an international scale and the concomitant decline of national and regional ones (e.g. Hellgren and Melin 1992; Rasanen and Whipp 1992). Others have heralded the development of 'global commodity chains' as new kinds of global economic coordination and control systems (e.g. Gereffi 1994, 1995a; cf. Whitley 1996b). In general, such 'globalization' is seen as diminishing the significance of different kinds of national and regional forms of economic organization in favour of a new cross-national form of capitalism that is in the process of replacing them through superior efficiency. The basic tenets of the strong or 'radical' view of post-war globalization processes (Hirst and Thompson 1996: 10–13) can be summarized as follows.

First, national and regional economies are becoming dominated by a new global system of economic coordination and control in which competition and strategic choices are organized at the global level. Secondly, national and international firms are becoming subordinated to transnational ones that differ significantly from them and are accountable only to global capital markets. Thirdly, the ability of nation states to regulate economic activities is rapidly declining, and global markets increasingly dominate national economic policies. Fourthly, national economic policies, forms of economic organization, and managerial practices are converging to the most efficient ones as a result of global competition.

These tenets, and the empirical evidence claimed in their support, have been extensively criticized in recent years (see e.g. Hirst and Thompson 1996; Kenworthy 1997; Wade 1996). In particular, the extent to which national firms with international operations have been supplanted by the deracinated transnational company seems to be much more limited than enthusiasts have claimed (see e.g. Dicken 1998: 193–9; Hu 1992; Pauly and Reich 1997). Additionally, the internationalization of trade and investment flows has not, in many instances, exceeded those common before 1914, and, in any case, most international, let alone intercontinental, direct investment has been dwarfed by domestic investment over the past decade or so (Koechlin 1995). Similarly, cross-national ownership of corporate bonds and equities remains limited despite the growth of Eurocurrency markets and foreign-exchange dealings. Overall, as *The Economist* (1997*b*) recently concluded, global capital markets do not yet exist.

Additionally, the ways in which the increasing internationalization of competition and of economic coordination since, say, the 1950s has necessarily generated qualitative changes in established systems of economic organization, let alone lead to a new form of capitalism dominating them, remain unclear. Rather than simply assuming that 'market forces' will inevitably produce a new sort of transnational economic system that will outcompete current forms of capitalism, the advocates of the strong globalization thesis need to clarify the following points. First, what are the distinctive characteristics of such a system? Secondly, how is it going to develop and become established? Thirdly, in which ways, and under what conditions, will it succeed in dominating existing ones? A further point to be noted here is that the greater liquidity and size of international capital markets so far has not resulted in the sort of standardized macro-economic policies and institutional arrangements beloved of neoclassical economists. This remains the case even in Europe, where more sustained and collectively organized efforts have been made to coordinate state policies than elsewhere (Kenworthy 1997).

While, then, the growth of international trade, foreign direct investment (FDI), and expansion of capital markets since the 1950s has been considerable (Dicken 1998), its significance and consequences for the different varieties of capitalism discussed in earlier chapters remain to be clarified. In particular, the conditions under which these changes are likely to result in the qualitative transformation of distinctive forms of economic organization require more detailed specification. Accordingly, in this chapter I examine the circumstances in which, and processes by which, these sorts of internationalization of economic activities and coordination systems could affect the central characteristics of established business systems and lead to changes in them. Initially, I summarize the recent evidence about the extent of such internationalization in the twentieth century. In the subsequent section I outline the conditions that would be necessary for this to change the nature and behaviour of firms such that they altered key characteristics of both their home business systems and those they invest in directly. Finally, I discuss the likelihood that internationalization could generate a qualitatively new type of cross-national business system that would come to dominate current ones, and so standardize economic coordination and control systems.

MODES AND DEGREES OF INTERNATIONALIZATION

The growing internationalization of economic activities is often seen as composed of three interconnected phenomena that have major consequences for existing forms of capitalism. First, the increase in international trade and competition from foreign exporters is considered likely to threaten many domestic ways of organizing economic activities. Secondly, the expansion of managerial coordination and control across national boundaries in multinational firms is viewed as changing both the nature of those firms and, by extension, that of the business system they developed within, as well as the characteristics of the host economies they invest in. Similar but weaker consequences could presumably be expected from the cross-national alliances and networks that developed in the 1980s and 1990s. Thirdly, the 'globalization' of capital markets has both reduced large firms' dependence on domestic financial institutions—and so might encourage some change in their strategic preferences and choices—and internationalized their ownership so that previous patterns and priorities may shift. In particular, such changes in the ownership and control of shareholdings might be expected to affect dominant criteria of performance assessment in business systems; for example, towards more profit-focused priorities.

International Trade and Competition

As we consider first the increase in international trade and competition since the 1950s, it is important to note that this is still lower as a proportion of GDP in many countries than it was in 1913 and has not increased greatly in the past two decades in a number of OECD countries (Hirst and Thompson 1996; Kenworthy 1997). In fact, the average proportion of exports and imports in GDP between 1974–9 and 1990–4 has fallen in the UK, Norway, Japan, Italy, and Finland, and risen by less than 5 per cent in Australia, Canada, Denmark, France, Germany, the Netherlands, New Zealand, Sweden, Switzerland, and the USA. Overall trade dependence is much greater in the industrializing countries of East Asia and the Middle East than in much of Europe or North America. Furthermore, much of the growth in the external trade of these countries has occurred within their geographical regions, especially North America and Europe. While, then, the openness of most OECD economies has grown significantly since the war, it has certainly not resulted in their becoming dominated by imports and exports, and indeed most remain little more or, indeed, less dependent on external trade than they were before 1914.

The effects of such increasing international trade on business-system characteristics seems likely to be limited when it is primarily conducted through spot-market, short-term transactions. While increasing domestic competition from imports may encourage firms to change products, cut costs, and search for new markets, the ways in which they adapt will reflect the overall characteristics of their business system and their roles within it. It could also intensify firms' willingness to look for and introduce technological and organizational innovations, especially from abroad, but such innovations were, and are, introduced in quite protectionist environments, as in the case of Japanese companies' seeking to transfer Fordist principles of production organization in the 1950s. The search for the 'best practices' of foreign economies to transfer to domestic ones, moreover, is often based on serious misunderstandings of actual managerial practices. Additionally, idealized procedures and practices are usually transformed considerably when they are introduced in the domestic economy (Boyer and Hollingsworth 1997; Hollingsworth and Streeck 1994). There is no particular reason, then, to expect that growing international competition, *per se*, will lead to radical business-system change, let alone that it will do so in a single direction.

Where trading relations are more stable and perhaps based on longer-term alliances between specific firms, we might expect some to adopt novel procedures and practices. However, the impact of this on domestic business systems is likely to be limited unless (*a*) a large number of leading firms engage in such alliances, (*b*) they form a major part of their activities for some considerable time, (*c*) such alliances are mostly with partners from the same kind of foreign business system, and (*d*) the practices being changed are not closely connected to powerful domestic agencies and institutions. These conditions are, I suggest, not going to be realized together very often.

Furthermore, the capacity of dominant firms to develop such international alliances effectively itself depends on their previous success in doing so within countries, which in turn depends on the nature of the business system they are part of. Similar points apply to the sorts of firms they are successful in linking with, so that cross-national alliances will develop and be more effective when partners are both from business systems which are already characterized by substantial inter-firm connections. It follows from this that expanding international trading links to longer-term alliances is unlikely to alter domestic business systems significantly. Overall, then, both the extent and impact of trade internationalization and intensifying competition are less than is often thought, and are unlikely to result in radical changes to established business-system characteristics.

Cross-National Coordination and Control

The growth of FDI since the 1960s has been seen as leading to the creation of a distinctive global system of economic coordination and control. Particularly in the 1980s, the rate of FDI grew quite dramatically, at an average annual rate of 34 per cent between 1983 and 1990 compared to annual global trade increases of 9 per cent in that period. However, it fell slightly in 1992 and 1993, and still forms a small proportion of total investment in many countries. Between 1985 and 1991, for example, the average annual rate of overseas direct investment as a percentage of total investment was only 5 per cent in the USA, 7 per cent in Japan, Germany, and France, and 17 per cent in the UK (Hirst and Thompson 1996). Again, the total stock of foreign investment of most richer countries as a proportion of GDP was less in 1996 than in 1914, and only amounted to 6 per cent of their total domestic investment in 1996 (*The Economist* 1997a). While, then, the growth of FDI since the 1960s has been quite considerable, its overall significance is still limited.

Similarly, although the percentage of firms' sales and assets located outside their native frontiers increased in the 1980s and 1990s, the bulk of these remain in the home region. Leading MNC manufacturers from the Netherlands, for example, sell only 12 per cent of their turnover to domestic customers, but another 50 per cent goes to West European ones. Similarly, French MNCs in 1992–3 made less than half of their total sales to domestic customers, but a further 31 per cent went to European ones. Even UK MNCs made 65 per cent of their total sales to European customers as a whole. As might be expected, Japanese and US MNCs were even more focused on domestic customers at 75 and 64 per cent respectively (Hirst and Thompson 1996).

Similar results were found for the location of leading MNCs' assets. According to Hirst and Thompson (1996: 90–6), 54 per cent of large French firms' assets were in France in 1992–3, with a further 31 per cent in the rest of Europe; 39 per cent of equivalent UK firms' assets were similarly in the UK, and a further 23 per cent were elsewhere in Europe. Again, the vast bulk of US and Japanese firms' assets were situated within their national boundaries. Although, then, some increase in foreign sales and foreign investment of assets has undoubtedly taken place, its extent and importance are considerably less than is often claimed by advocates of globalization. Additionally, as we shall see, the consequences of such cross-national coordination of economic activities for the nature of firms and business systems are also less radical than is sometimes suggested.

Internationalization of Capital Markets

As mentioned above, one of the most marked aspects of economic internationalization in the last few decades has been the growth in cross-border capital flows and currency trading, as many countries have liberalized exchange controls. Not only has the total stock of international bank lending grown from $265 billion in 1975 to $4,200 billion in 1994, but the annual amount of capital raised through issuing bonds and equities on international capital markets grew from $36.2 billion in 1976–80 to $521.7 billion in 1993 (Hirst and Thompson 1996: 40; Kenworthy 1997). Foreign-exchange transactions have also grown dramatically, from around $15 billion a day in 1973 to nearly $1,300 billion a day in 1994/5.

However, these high growth rates should not obscure the fact that the international financial system still remains less integrated than it was before 1914 in many important aspects. For example, the overwhelming majority of the shares quoted on the world's stock markets are still held in domestic securities, and leading fund managers in Europe and the USA had only 11.4 per cent of their holdings in foreign assets in 1991. American investors, for instance, remained overwhelmingly committed to domestic securities, which accounted for 94 per cent of the value of the US exchanges (Hirst and Thompson 1996: 37; Kenworthy 1997). Furthermore, as *The Economist* (1997*b*) has recently pointed out, real bond yields continue to diverge considerably across countries, national savings and investment rates are still highly correlated, and capital mobility in the 1990s remains lower than in the thirty-year period before 1914 (Wade 1996). There is no single global interest rate and no integrated capital market across the world. While, then, international financial flows have grown considerably since the 1950s, their overall importance is much less than the enthusiasts of global capital markets have claimed, and remains lower than in the gold-standard period.

In sum, the growth in international trade, investment, and financial flows towards the end of the twentieth century forms a strong contrast with the immediate post-war decades, and even more so with the inter-war period. It does not, though, herald a radical break with all previous periods of capitalism, and can indeed be seen as a return to many aspects of the pre-1914 situation. Furthermore, it is important to note that it resulted from national decisions to deregulate financial systems and delegate substantial powers to international agencies such as the GATT and WTO, as well as to the European Commission. Although facilitated by reductions in communications and transport costs, it was these political choices that enabled this growth in internationalization to develop and, as we saw during the slump, such decisions can be reversed, as Hirst and Thompson (1996), amongst others, have emphasized.

Additionally, the nation state remains the primary focus of political loyalties and battles, as well as the dominant regulating and policing agency. Cross-border economic flows and coordination processes depend overwhelmingly on national state legal systems, enforcement mechanisms, and institutional arrangements to manage risks and uncertainty sufficiently to enable strategic decisions to be made. Internationalization, then, remains highly interdependent with national agencies' and institutions' structures and actions. As a result, its effects on established systems of economic organization and firms are greatly guided and limited by variations in these national institutions, as I will now discuss.

CONSEQUENCES OF INTERNATIONALIZATION FOR BUSINESS SYSTEMS AND FIRMS

The growing internationalization of economic activities is often thought to result in major changes to existing forms of capitalism in three ways. First, by changing the nature and behaviour of firms that engage in large-scale international coordination and control, which in turn could transform the characteristics of their home business system. Secondly, by inward FDI and capital-market internationalization altering current rules of the competitive game, and the nature of firms and introducing more 'efficient' practices. Thirdly, by generating a new supra-national level of economic organization and competition that in time will come to dominate national and regional ones. These do, of course, overlap and interact, but it is useful to separate them analytically for purposes of discussion.

Accordingly, I first specify the factors that affect whether multinational firms become transformed into qualitatively different kinds of companies from their domestically based national competitors as a result of their cross-border operations. The processes through which changes in the nature of MNCs could impinge upon their domestic business systems will also be examined here. Next, I consider how the growing internationalization of trade, investment, and capital might affect host business-system norms and characteristics. Thirdly, the likelihood of a separate and distinct international system of economic organization becoming established and dominating national ones will be discussed.

The Effects of Internationalization on MNCs and their Domestic Business Systems

The expansion of firms into foreign locations and markets could affect their governance structures and capabilities in four major ways. First, it might enable top managers to develop greater autonomy from domestic pressure groups, especially state agencies, banks, and other shareowner/controllers and unions. Secondly, it might similarly increase their distance from domestic business partners, as MNCs find new ones abroad. Thirdly, such autonomy from domestic pressures could lead to changes in dominant objectives, as managers have to deal with more varied interest groups from different societies with contrasting priorities. This greater variety of 'stakeholders' and interests in turn may well encourage increased organizational complexity, as MNCs attempt to manage conflicting expectations by establishing special groups to deal with them.

Finally, the growth of business units in geographically and institutionally diverse environments could decrease organizational cohesion and integration, which in turn might reduce the ability of firms to develop distinctive innovative strategies through continuous collective learning. Just as market and technological diversification can limit the continuing improvement of distinctive organizational competences, so too the diversification of operations and units across societal contexts may restrict MNCs' innovative abilities. In so far as they do focus on such 'entrepreneurial' organizational strategies in their domestic contexts, large-scale internationalization will encourage either substantial reorganization or separation of this domestic capability from most foreign subsidiaries, as is arguably the case in many Japanese MNCs.

The extent to which these consequences are likely to follow from outward FDI depends on six factors. First, the size of such foreign investments and operations relative to domestic ones clearly affects their impact on firm structures and strategies. For instance, Dutch firms which located on average 20 per cent of their total investments in 1985–91 abroad are, on the whole, more probably going to be influenced by their internationalization than, say, US (5 per cent) or Japanese ones (7 per cent) (Kenworthy 1997). To deal with a significantly more varied environment, they may restructure their organization and take more account of different interest groups than their less internationalized competitors.

Second, and more significant than the relative amount of foreign assets, is the nature of their location, specifically their concentration in a particular kind of business system. Other things being equal, the more a company's key assets and activities are located in a distinctive and different environment from its domestic one, the more likely it will adapt its structures and strategies to the prevalent pattern in that type of business system. If, for example, some large Japanese firms located over 50 per cent of their core assets and activities in Anglo-Saxon economies, we might reasonably expect them to develop in more Anglo-Saxon than Japanese ways. So far, though, this degree of outward concentration does not seem to have happened in most countries. Indeed, there appears to be considerable evidence that large firms investing abroad tend to be more committed to countries that share key institutions with their home society than to those that are strongly contrasting (Koechlin 1995; Pauly and Reich 1997).

Thirdly, the effects of outward FDI on a firm's characteristics are more likely to be significant when it invests a large proportion of its resources in more technologically advanced and wealthier markets, not least because of the greater power of dominant interest groups and institutions in these economies and their overall significance in the world economy. Japanese, Korean, and Taiwanese FDI in China, parts of South-East Asia and Eastern Europe, for instance, is less likely to affect these firms' general policies and practices than large-scale investments in Western Europe and North America. Indeed, this relocation of facilities and activities in relatively less industrialized economies may result more in the generalization of domestic business-system characteristics to those economies than in significant changes to firms' strategies and capabilities.

Fourthly, firms are going to be more affected by large-scale foreign investment when it is concentrated in economies with strong, cohesive business systems closely linked to integrated institutions than when host business systems and institutions are weakly structured and poorly integrated. This will be especially so if their domestic business system is relatively fragmented, and dominant institutions are as much contradictory as mutually reinforcing in their implications for economic relations. British investors in Japan, for example, are more likely to adapt to the local way of managing the workforce and supplier relations than are Japanese firms in Britain. Similarly, foreign firms investing in Germany have to adapt to the highly institutionalized training system and consultation procedures, since these are quite standardized, legally regulated, and enforced.

This also affects the kinds of changes that are made by MNCs in their foreign operations. Practices that are most closely linked to strong local agencies and institutions are most likely to be implemented by foreign firms. The New Economic Policy in Malaysia, for instance, had more effect on foreign investors' managerial practices than many other features of the Malaysian political economy, because it was a central focus of the state's development plans and affected state–business relations in a wide variety of ways. This does not, though, mean that such changes will be 'repatriated' to their domestic economies, or even transferred to other subsidiaries.

The extent to which such local adaptation influences firm behaviour more generally depends on the factors listed above, together with, fifthly, the dominant way in which foreign subsidiaries are integrated into the parent organizations. The more managerially integrated into the whole firm are foreign operations, the more likely are changes in these to affect the domestic enterprise, and, of course, the less easy will it be to implement them. Where multinational firms are organized as holding companies, with foreign subsidiaries primarily controlled through financial targets and results and granted substantial operating autonomy, they are likely to display considerable local variety of managerial practices, but these will have only limited effects on the domestic organization. Kristensen's (1994) account of how a Danish subsidiary was able to preserve considerable autonomy after being taken over, for example, at least partly reflects the financially oriented control systems of its new British parent. More integrated and centrally controlled enterprises, on the other hand, are less likely to tolerate wide fluctuations in procedures and choices, but once innovations are accepted in one subsidiary they may well be generalized throughout the organization.

In general, British firms have invested more in foreign facilities than have German ones for much of the twentieth century, and have also tended to rely on financial controls while granting subsidiaries substantial discretion on how they achieve general targets. German firms have, in contrast, preferred to export from their domestic facilities and integrate operations more closely (Pauly and Reich 1997). However, when some of these latter companies invested abroad in new 'lean production' factories—partly because they considered it would be too difficult to do so directly in 'Standort Deutschland'—this was intended to serve as a model for restructuring their domestic production system. To some extent, then, foreign innovations could result in some changes to the basic organization of German firms (cf. Mueller and Loveridge 1997).

Such repatriation of novel practices from foreign subsidiaries is, finally, dependent on their interdependence with central characteristics of the domestic business system and dominant institutions. Many Japanese firms, for instance, have had to adapt some of their employment and labour-management strategies to local conditions, especially on brownfield sites (Botti 1995; Sharpe 1997), but it is most unlikely that these modifications will be transferred back to their domestic operations given the central role of their labour management policies in their overall development and business system, not to mention the active involvement of the state in limiting enforced redundancies. Similarly, British and US firms operating in Germany would find it difficult to implement local training and work-system practices in their domestic operations given the very different institutional environment they face at home—although their experience may, of course, encourage them to try to change that environment.

In summary, then, internationalizing firms seem unlikely to change their key attributes and practices substantially unless the following conditions are met. First, foreign operations, assets, and profits constitute a large proportion of the total. Secondly, they are concentrated in a different kind of business system, which, thirdly, is more developed than the domestic one, and, fourthly, is more cohesive and linked to strong, more integrated institutions than the domestic one. Fifthly, they integrate foreign subsidiaries closely to domestic operations, and, finally, these attributes are not highly interdependent with strong domestic agencies and institutions. These conditions are not likely to be realized together very often, and so the extent of radical organizational changes as a direct result of outward FDI seems rather less than is sometimes suggested.

The circumstances in which the changing characteristics of internationalizing firms might affect the distinctive nature of their domestic business systems, if they did indeed alter as a result of cross-national managerial coordination, are also significantly affected by many of the factors just discussed. Three broad sets of influences are particularly critical. First, the number and centrality of the firms and sectors involved for the domestic economy, as well as the degree to which they have changed, are clearly critical to any qualitative change in business-system characteristics. Major changes in, say, the degree of vertical integration of the largest Finnish forest-sector firms would imply a much more significant shift in the organization of the Finnish economy than growing foreign investments of smaller firms in light industry or their increasing exposure to international capital markets (Lilja and Tainio 1996).

Secondly, because business-system change implies a reorganization of economic coordination and control relations, it involves the restructuring of interest groups outside as well as inside the firms concerned, and often a reshaping of sectoral strengths. Thus, significant institutional shifts and changes in dominance relations between major social groupings are typically associated with qualitative changes in business-system characteristics. For internationalizing firms to effect such shifts in the organization of their domestic economy, then, they would have to be allied to powerful groups and interests.

Business systems dominated by export-oriented manufacturing industry, for example, may begin to change as a result of outward FDI and reliance on foreign capital markets if the owners and managers involved become detached from their domestic alliances and create international ones at the same time as previously dominant allies in the state and economy begin to lose ground to new groups based on, say, financial services and domestically focused industries. In the absence of such sectoral- and interest-group shifts, business-system changes are unlikely to be very significant.

Thirdly, any important shifts in economic organization, whether due to internationalization or not, also imply some change in associated institutions, which is less probable where those institutions are strongly established and highly integrated. Changes to firms' skill-development practices and labour strategies in Germany, for example, are much more difficult to implement than in Britain, because the German training system is more standardized and regulated throughout the economy than is its British equivalent. Strong and cohesive institutions are even more likely to limit any changes introduced by internationalizing firms where they are linked to quite different kinds of institutions and patterns of economic organization.

The innovations achieved by Mercedes and BMW in the USA, for instance, are likely to be considerably modified when they attempt to repatriate them to the domestic economy, because of the strength of associated institutional arrangements. As a result, their overall impact on 'the' German production system will be considerably restricted by the established institutional order and the interest groups concerned to reproduce it (cf. Herrigel 1996; Mueller and Loveridge 1997). In contrast, business-system characteristics linked to peripheral, weakly integrated institutions and groups are more susceptible to change as a result of internationalization by powerful firms and sectors, especially if those firms are supported by state agencies.

In summary, then, significant change in the dominant system of economic organization in a particular region or country as a result of firms' outward FDI depends on four quite demanding conditions being met. First, the firms concerned have to be substantial and central to the business system and, secondly, to have qualitatively changed major attributes and strategies. Thirdly, they also need to have close ties to major interest groups that also seek change in the prevalent system. Finally, they have to be linked to institutional agencies and governance structures that do not prevent significant changes and/or are weakly integrated with the current institutional order.

The Effects of Inward FDI on Host Business Systems

The likelihood that inward foreign investment and control of economic activities, and the internationalization of financial flows, will significantly change business-system characteristics is similarly structured by the strength and cohesion of host economy institutions and their closeness to particular characteristics of the economic coordination and control system. If we consider first the impact of inward FDI on host business systems, the overall weight and relative significance of FDI is obviously a critical factor. Where foreign firms dominate an economy, it is unlikely to develop its own distinctive patterns of economic coordination and control. Additionally, though, the concentration of such FDI from a particular kind of business system will affect how much influence it has on an economy.

If, for example, the bulk of the total stock of manufacturing investment in a country was owned and/or controlled by foreign firms from the same type of business system, such as the Anglo-Saxon one, we would expect the host economy to display similar sorts of economic organization characteristics to those prevalent in the home economies of such firms. While high levels of FDI from a single type of business system are not a common occurrence in industrialized economies, the Australian economy may form an example of this phenomenon (Marceau 1992). In this case, of course, the colonial legacy has resulted in many of the key domestic institutions being 'Anglo-Saxon', so that the influence of inward FDI on its own is difficult to distinguish.

More common in the late twentieth century is inward FDI from a number of different kinds of business system so that no single type dominates, together with substantial domestic ownership and control of economic activities. The extent to which foreign firms have qualitatively changed established host business-system characteristics in these circumstances is limited. In industrializing countries, however, their impact may be more marked, especially when MNCs are predominantly from a single type of business system or the former colonial power.

Thirdly, the more dependent are foreign firms on domestic organizations and agencies, both within and across sectors, the less likely are they to change prevalent patterns of behaviour. Japanese firms linked to Japanese suppliers and financed by Japanese banks, for instance, are more independent from local practices than those from other countries that rely more on host economy companies. Such Japanese firms are, therefore, more able to maintain distinctive practices that deviate substantially from those current in the local business system than, say, US ones that become more interdependent with local organizations. Where such firms dominate particular sectors, they may well diffuse these innovations more widely.

Such change depends also, fourthly, on the overall integration and cohesion of the local form of economic organization and associated institutions. This factor helps to explain why much Japanese investment in Britain has had more impact in the particular sectors where it has been concentrated, mostly cars and electronics, than has British investment in Japan. As well as the level and sectoral concentration of the latter being less—and, of course, the overall level of inward FDI to Japan has been minuscule relative to GDP at 0.4 per cent in 1994 (UNCTAD 1996: 262)—the sheer strength and cohesion of the host business system and allied institutions greatly restrict the effects of foreign investment in Japan.

Relatedly, the impact of any change introduced by outside enterprises depends on, fifthly, the strength of the sector and its centrality to the economy, as well as on the strength of the particular institutions connected to different spheres of activity. Japanese manufacturing firms, for example, have probably been able to have more influence on British industrial companies than their counterparts in financial services because of the dominant role of the latter sector in the British economy and its closer ties to political and bureaucratic élites. Similarly, their effects on labour and production management in Britain have been more marked than on financial and ownership issues, and probably more so than in other parts of Europe, as a result of the weakened position of the unions and the decline of the manufacturing sector in general.

It should be noted, however, that the evidence for wholesale 'Japanization'—
however that may be interpreted—of the British and other economies is
extremely limited, as many authors have pointed out (e.g. Elger and Smith 1994;
Stewart 1996; Strange 1993). Even in the former state socialist societies of
Eastern Europe the impact of foreign-firm ownership on factory organization and
labour management has been limited by local unions and quite strong domestic
norms governing acceptable managerial behaviour (Czaban and Whitley 1998;
Globokar 1997; Mako and Novoszath 1995).

In sum, significant shifts in business-system characteristics as a result of
foreign firms controlling economic resources and activities in an economy
depend on those firms' investments being large relative to domestic ones, being
predominantly from one kind of business system, and remaining substantially
independent of local organizations and agencies. In addition, they are more likely
to occur in sectors that are peripheral to dominant interest groups and institutions
and/or in business systems that are quite fragmented with relatively weakly integrated institutions.

The Effects of Financial Market Internationalization on Business-System
Characteristics

The effects of internationalizing financial flows on business-system characteristics could be considerable under certain conditions. If, for instance, most of the
leading firms in credit-based financial systems were to raise the bulk of their
external finance from international capital markets instead of relying on their
usual business partners, this could alter the strategic priorities of these firms and
eventually affect the nature of their domestic business system. Since these international markets are typically Anglo-Saxon in their governance norms and priorities, we could expect a general move to market-based relations between large
shareholders and individual firms, more adversarial relations between firms and
between employers and employees, and more emphasis on profits than growth
goals.

However, this sort of change implies considerable shifts in established institutional arrangements, as well as in the relative influence and ability of interest
groups and organizations to control key resources. It, therefore, seems unlikely to
occur without substantial debate and conflict. Competing groups within both the
firms concerned and their financial partners, as well as those elsewhere in the
economy and society more broadly, can be expected to conflict over the desirable
direction of changes to established financial structures and relationships. The
outcomes of such conflicts will, of course, depend on the resources and legitimacy of different interest groups in different political economies and can by no
means be assumed to converge on the dominance of Anglo-Saxon capital market
rationalities.

Relatedly, it is not at all clear that the recent growth in capital market funding
will continue through the next recession, or that it will constitute the dominant

source of new investment funds in most economies. The more pension-fund managers and other institutional shareholders pursue Anglo-Saxon notions of transparency, shareholder value, and appropriate dividend payout ratios in continental Europe and East Asia, the more resistance can be expected from managerial élites anxious to preserve their autonomy and independence from both banks and shareholders.

It does not require a particularly cynical turn of mind to see the adoption of capital-market funding and globalization rhetoric by some European business leaders as weapons in their struggles to impose their goals and priorities on governments and 'social partners' within firms and across economies (cf. Hirst and Thompson 1996: 1–7). Depending on the balance of groups and forces in particular economies, such attempts will be more or less successful, as the contrast between, say, the Netherlands and France in the mid-1990s indicates. In terms of qualitative changes in business-system characteristics, though, the expansion of corporate fund-raising from international capital markets seems unlikely to lead to substantial shifts without other changes occurring in dominant institutions and social groupings.

In general, the effects of growing foreign portfolio ownership depend on similar factors to those already discussed. The more shares of firms in one economy are owned by foreign investors who overwhelmingly come from a different kind of business system, the more we would expect those firms to begin to change key characteristics and strategic priorities. The extent to which such changes would occur, though, depends on the overall distribution of share ownership in each firm, the prevalent nature of the financial system in the host economy, and the links between particular firms and industries with major institutions and agencies.

If, for example, a firm has substantial domestic shareholders and foreign shareholders are relatively fragmented, managers' responsiveness to alien shareholder preferences will be limited, particularly if there is only a weak market for corporate control, so that declining share prices do not usually generate hostile takeover bids. Relatedly, the effects of increasing foreign portfolio investment in a country will be restricted by high levels of interdependence between investors and firms in the financial system as a whole. Threatening to sell shareholdings will clearly be less effective in changing managerial behaviour in such economies than where investors act at arm's length from companies.

Additionally, the role of foreign portfolio investment depends on the overall role of the firms concerned in a particular business system and their connections to powerful agencies and groups. The responsiveness of Finnish paper firms to increasing overseas shareholding, for example, is likely to be less marked in the event of conflicts with managers than it might be for those less central to the economy and less integrated with the political and financial systems (Tainio 1997). In general, of course, the more cohesive and integrated are key institutions in a society, the less likely is foreign portfolio investment to affect business-system characteristics significantly, as the behaviour of the Japanese one in the 1990s indicates. Even in the transforming societies of Eastern Europe, the effects of such investment on, say, labour-management strategies has been less marked than some might have expected (Czaban and Whitley 1998; Whitley *et al.* 1999).

In sum, the growth of foreign portfolio investment in an economy need not, on its own, result in significant shifts in firm governance and behaviour. Even if it was on such a large scale, and so concentrated, as to alter the priorities and choices of some firms' dominant coalitions, this would not imply the qualitative change of a particular business system. That would require a reorganization of central institutional structures and relationships, as well as a restructuring of interest-group relations and, perhaps, of their constitution and organization. Particular characteristics of a business system could, though, be affected by such substantial transfers of ownership if they were (*a*) weakly standardized and regulated across the whole economic order, (*b*) relatively poorly integrated with other aspects of the business system, and (*c*) linked to rather peripheral groups and institutions in the wider society.

The Establishment of New Cross-National Business Systems

The growth of cross-border coordination and control of economic activities by managerial hierarchies and of competition between firms on a world-wide scale has led to suggestions that a new kind of international system of economic organization is becoming established. This system is dominated by distinctive 'transnational' (Bartlett and Ghoshal 1989) MNCs that have considerable autonomy from national institutions and agencies and are able to pursue competitive strategies on a global rather than a national or regional basis. Such firms develop characteristics that are more similar to each other than to those of their domestic competitors, and their strategies are also focused more on each others' resources and actions than those of domestic firms.

Relatedly, Gereffi (1994, 1995*a*, 1995*b*, 1996) and his colleagues have suggested that the development of consumer-driven 'global commodity chains' constitutes a new form of international economic integration. These sorts of suggestions are often made rather informally and the exact nature of such distinctively 'global' systems of economic organization remains unclear. However, it is worthwhile briefly considering the issues involved in distinctive and separate business systems becoming established at the international level, because they highlight the strong conditions required, especially if such international business systems were so to dominate existing national ones that they determined the latters' performance and key characteristics (Pauly and Reich 1997; Wade 1996).

Before examining the conditions required for such distinctive cross-national business systems to develop, it is important to distinguish these new kinds of international economic organization from the rather more frequent extension of existing systems of economic coordination to new geographical and institutional locations. For example, the generalization of dominant business systems—such as the Fordist one in the USA—over new territories through FDI and/or capital-market internationalization did not so much herald the creation of a separate and distinctive cross-national business system as the domination of an existing national or regional one over other economies. Rather than the growth of US FDI, and the expanding influence of the predominantly Anglo-Saxon capital markets in the post-war period indicating the emergence of a new kind of 'global' business system with its own actors and rules of the game, it would be more accurate to regard it as the internationalization of the US business system. The continued significance of different kinds of business systems in Europe and Asia despite the dominant role of the US economy in the post-war period demonstrates the limited changes induced by these developments, for the reasons outlined above.

For a new kind of business system to become established at the international level that was genuinely different from existing national ones, three requirements would have to be met. First, it would have to combine a particular set of characteristics that differed significantly from those of established business systems. In terms of the framework outlined in Chapter 2, this means that ownership relations, inter-firm connections, and employment relations would be organized together in distinctive ways across national boundaries. It also implies that different kinds of international firms exhibiting significantly different governance and capability characteristics from those of domestic competitors would become established as a direct result of coordinating economic activities across national borders. These novel characteristics of cross-national firms would increasingly become more similar, as such a new kind of international business system developed.

Secondly, such patterns would have to be fairly well established and stable, so that, say, distinctive ownership relations or supplier–customer connections would not change rapidly, and international cooperative/competitive behaviours would remain similar over business cycles. Distinctive governance structures and organization of international linkages would need to be reproduced over some time, if such a cross-national system of economic coordination was to be considered well established. It is not at all clear that either producer- or consumer-driven global commodity chains would meet these conditions. Rather, they seem to be characterized by rather short-term arm's length contractual relationships, especially the latter ones. They are also constituted by quite varied kinds of firms whose characteristics reflect more their domestic business systems than any distinctive international one.

Thirdly, the establishment of a separate and different kind of economic coordination and control system at the international level implies the concomitant emergence of distinctive and powerful international agencies, institutions, and interest groups. For new rules of the game and ways of organizing economic activities to become institutionalized cross-nationally, new institutional arrangements would have to develop to support and reinforce them. This, in turn, implies that existing, largely national, agencies and groups would either become more involved in international competition, cooperation, and conflicts, and/or delegate some of their powers and interests to international organizations and arenas. This has already happened to some extent in the areas of trade policies and financial intermediation, as well as politically and juridically in the case of Europe.

Such internationalization of regulatory agencies and institutions, however, typically involves considerable competition for control over their form, remit, and resources between national groups and interests, just as the establishment of national state agencies and political arenas did. This competition is not only a matter of personal and group aggrandizement, but also involves conflicts between different conceptions of how agencies and institutions should be organized and evaluated and economic activities structured. The nature and behaviour of the European Commission, for example, reflect the dominant groups involved in its establishment and subsequent development, just as many aspects of the IMF and World Bank reflect the assumptions and interests of élite groups in the dominant post-war economies, especially the USA (Ross 1995; Taylor 1997).

Furthermore, the autonomy of such agencies from national ones, and their ability to initiate programmes and implement new kinds of cross-national rules of the game, fluctuate considerably, as the history of the European Union demonstrates. The single European market has by no means resulted in standardized norms and rules governing economic activities across Europe, let alone the emergence of distinctly 'European' firms which operate quite differently from national ones (Whitley and Kristensen 1996). Indeed, the limited significance both of pan European institutions and agencies, on the one hand, and of European-level systems of economic organization, on the other hand, despite the existence of the European Economic Community and its successors for over forty years, reveals the tenacity of national institutional arrangement and national business systems. Equally, the influence of the US government on the IMF's strategies for dealing with the East Asian financial crises of the late 1990s reveals significant limitations to the latter's autonomy.

Similar points are involved in considering whether and how distinctive cross-national business systems—once they have developed—could dominate national ones to the extent that they determine the prevalent rules of the game. For this to happen, three conditions would have to be met. First, the world-wide institutions and agencies associated with such business systems dominate national and regional ones. Secondly, global competition between transnationals dominates competition at other levels, and, thirdly, transnational firms are able to dominate predominantly national or regional ones because of their 'global' operations and resources.

As the European example suggests, the first phenomenon is unlikely to occur quickly or be widespread. It clearly depends on the cohesion and strength of host economy institutions and the willingness of state agencies to accept the authority of supra-national organizations. The second point assumes that world markets are dominated by oligopolies which increasingly compete with each other across national economies, rather than with more nationally focused firms. However, the number of industries where such global dominance by a small number of firms has developed is still quite small, and competitive strategies remain national and regional in many sectors. Despite the growth of very large multinational firms in the white-goods industry, for example, markets and competitive advantages remain quite specific to particular territories (Baden-Fuller and Stopford 1991).

Similarly, the presumption of MNC dominance assumes that sheer size and the advantages of combining operations across countries outweigh the costs of managerial coordination of activities across institutional contexts. However, the increasing demands for flexibility in production methods and product lines, coupled with the difficulties involved in generating collective continuous learning and improvement in diversified enterprises, suggest that MNCs are often likely to be at a disadvantage compared to more focused organizations. Overall, then, the likelihood that distinctive, separate, and stable cross-national business systems will become established, and will dominate existing, strongly institutionalized ones, seems rather limited without much greater changes in national and regional institutions and firms than have yet occurred.

CONCLUSIONS

This discussion highlights five major points about the impact of internationalization of economic coordination and control on established varieties of capitalism. First, the conditions required for significant changes to take place in the nature and behaviour of firms as a result of their expanding their operations abroad are so stringent that late-twentieth-century patterns of internationalization are unlikely to generate qualitative step changes in the characteristics and strategies of leading firms in most economies. This is not to say that firms never alter when they internationalize—simply dealing with more diverse environments is likely to encourage some differentiation of structures and procedures—but to emphasize that they are unlikely to change central characteristics radically such that they become different kinds of economic actors. Modifying, say, some labour-management practices in some foreign subsidiaries or developing closer supplier links in Japan do not, in this view, signify significant changes in the control and strategies of, for instance, US corporations.

Secondly, even where some firms do develop differently because of their concentration of assets and activities abroad—and such changes are not, of course, likely to be only a result of internationalization—this need not, and often will not, herald qualitative change in the nature of the domestic business system. In terms of the framework present here, significant business-system change implies substantial shifts in ownership relations, the division of organizational labour, the level and/or type of non-ownership coordination processes, and/or employment and labour–management relations. Such changes are, then, large scale and far-reaching, requiring considerable institutional restructuring and realignment of major societal interests. They are unlikely to develop simply as a consequence of internationalization, or to occur within one or two decades. The significant but limited consequences of the institutional reforms imposed by the Allied occupation of Germany and Japan for the organization of those economies demonstrate the incremental and path-dependent nature of system change in industrial societies, as do the transformations of the former state socialist countries of Eastern Europe discussed in Chapters 8 and 9.

Thirdly, the impact of inward FDI and capital-market internationalization on a host business system is also mediated by local institutions and agencies, such that significant changes in core characteristics of industrialized societies are unlikely to be rapid consequences, even where this investment is concentrated in one or two sectors and is dominated by firms from a particular business system. The more cohesive is the host business system and its associated institutions, the less likely is that system to change just as a result of foreign firms developing a significant presence in that economy. Even in industrializing countries where a particular system of capitalist organization is in the process of being established, foreign investment does not necessarily determine the shape of the emergent economy, especially where the state plays a dominating role in organizing economic development and effectively controls the degree and nature of that investment.

Fourthly, the globalization of capital markets likewise has had only limited effects on systems of economic coordination and control. Some large firms have increased their financial autonomy from domestic intermediaries, but the overall functioning of credit-based financial systems does not seem to have changed greatly as a result of such growing independence. In particular, the considerable lock-in and mutual interdependence between large firms and banks in such economies has not yet been transformed into Anglo-Saxon forms of ownership organization and control. Given the major changes in related institutions and dominance relationships that such a shift would imply in most continental European and Asian economies, it seems unlikely to occur just as a result of capital-market expansion and internationalization.

Finally, the internationalization of managerial coordination and of capital markets has increased competition between predominantly national business systems and their associated institutions, rather than establishing a radically new cross-national system of economic coordination and control. As firms, states, and interest groups become more focused on international integration and competition, they seek to influence and control the emerging international norms governing the constitution of economic actors and the ways that their performance is evaluated and rewarded. In so far as there are such emergent international 'industrial orders', to use Herrigel's (1994) term, they will reflect this competition, and their characteristics will be strongly influenced by those of the leading economies, rather than the logic of an institutionally disembodied, idealized market.

Overall, then, globalization has been less significant in its scale and consequences than some enthusiasts have claimed. Furthermore, the ways in which the international coordination of economic activities is developing reflect established patterns of economic organization and competition, such that these structure any emergent properties of a new transnational business system. Similarly, the processes by which internationalizing firms develop novel characteristics over time depend on current ones and the distinctive contexts that generated and reproduced these. Internationalization, *per se*, is only one aspect of the development and change of business systems that is variously structured by different systems of economic organization and institutional contexts. How it occurs and the nature of its consequences therefore reflect these differences as path-dependent phenomena in the same way as other aspects of economic organization. The importance of such path dependence for understanding how distinctive business systems become established and how they change is exemplified by the development of different systems of economic organization and control in East Asia and Eastern Europe, as will be shown in the following chapters.

PART THREE

THE DEVELOPMENT AND CHANGE OF BUSINESS SYSTEMS IN EAST ASIA AND EASTERN EUROPE

6

Divergent Capitalisms in East Asia: The Post-War Business Systems of South Korea and Taiwan

INTRODUCTION

The wide variety of industrial capitalisms has become especially marked in the post-war period as a result of the widespread success of Japanese and other East Asian firms. It is widely recognized that these firms behave in quite different ways from many of those in Western countries, particularly North American and British ones (see e.g. Aoki 1988; R. Clark 1979; Kagono *et al.* 1985), and that these differences are connected to distinctive features of dominant institutions in these societies (Orru *et al.* 1997). However, while considerable attention has been paid to the particular characteristics of the Japanese enterprise system (see e.g. Fruin 1992; Gerlach 1992; Westney 1996), rather less effort has been devoted to analysing the nature of firms and markets in South Korea, Taiwan, and Hong Kong, partly because they are often viewed as being similar products of 'post-Confucianism' and not differing greatly from the dominant Japanese form of economic organization.

There are, though, significant variations in the ways that economic activities are organized in Japan and in other East Asian economies that are due to different patterns of industrialization and significant variations in national political, financial, and labour systems (Orru *et al.* 1997; Whitley 1992*a*). These differences in systems of economic coordination and control across East Asia are sufficiently marked to constitute distinctive business systems that can be analysed as contrasting forms of economic organization. In particular, while both South Korean and Taiwanese post-war capitalist systems share a common background of Japanese colonial rule, their distinct pre-industrial inheritances, post-war institutional structures, and policies have produced forms of industrial capitalism that are distinct both from the Japanese one and from each other in important respects. Thus, just as there are many forms of 'Western' capitalism, so too there are varied kinds of firm–market configurations in Pacific Asia that have become successfully established in different institutional contexts.

Because these forms of economic organization are both so distinct from each other and manifest such high levels of organizational isomorphism within national boundaries, as Hamilton and Biggart (1988) have emphasized, they constitute an ideal focus for comparative business-systems analysis. In this chapter I accordingly discuss the distinctive nature of the post-war business systems that have developed in South Korea (henceforth Korea) and Taiwan as different forms of industrial capitalism that developed in particular historical circumstances and institutional contexts. This account will focus largely on the characteristics of these business systems as they had become established by the 1980s, since I shall consider the extent and significance of changes to East Asian economies in the 1990s in the next chapter. Because many, if not most, of the business-system characteristics have continued into the 1990s, I shall mostly use the present tense in describing them.

After a summary contrast of the key characteristics of these two systems of economic organization, I describe the nature of the post-war Korean business system and then the Taiwanese one. Next, I discuss the dominant institutions that together help to explain these characteristics and how they do so. These include important pre-industrial legacies of Korean and Taiwanese societies that remained significant influences during and after Japanese colonialism. Finally, I briefly compare the business systems of post-war Korea and Taiwan to identify the key factors that account for their most significant differences.

The major distinguishing characteristics of the post-war business systems in these two economies are summarized in Table 6.1, following the framework outlined earlier in this book. This table reconstructs the dominant features of the particular form of economic organization that became established between 1960 and 1990 in Korea and Taiwan, much of which continued into the 1990s. As can readily be seen, some characteristics are quite similar in both business systems, particularly those concerned with employment relations and ownership control, but there are also significant differences between them and between both of these and the Japanese business system as discussed by Rodney Clark (1979) and Westney (1996), among others. These concern firm size, ownership integration, and horizontal linkages especially.

TABLE 6.1. The post-war business systems of Korea and Taiwan

Business-system characteristics	Korea	Taiwan
Ownership coordination		
Owner control	Direct	Direct
Ownership vertical integration	High	Low except in intermediate sector
Ownership horizontal integration	High	High in business groups, low elsewhere
Non-ownership coordination		
Alliance-based vertical integration	Low	Low
Alliance-based horizontal integration	Low	Limited
Competitor collaboration	Low	Low
Employment relations and work management		
Employer–employee interdependence	Low except for some managers	Low except for personal connections
Worker discretion	Low	Low

The Korean economy is dominated by very large family-owned and controlled conglomerate enterprises called *chaebol* (Amsden 1989; Cumings 1987; Fields 1995; Janelli 1993; Steers *et al.* 1989; Woo 1991). These quite diversified and vertically integrated firms have been the main agents of industrialization in Korea since the war under the strongly directive and coordinating influence of the authoritarian state. Competing fiercely for domination of a variety of industrial sectors and for political support, they have not developed the sort of long-term cooperative relationships with each other that characterize the post-war Japanese economy. Authority within these conglomerates is highly centralized and personal, with formal procedures often less important than personal relationships. Despite the high level of diversification, especially in the largest *chaebol*, most activities in the manufacturing sector are quite integrated, with frequent exchanges of managers and coordinated planning of activities. Employment relations are not nearly so interdependent as in large Japanese firms, and worker discretion is likewise much more limited (Janelli 1993; Wilkinson 1994).

Taiwan, in contrast, developed a large state-owned enterprise sector that dominates the capital intensive, upstream industries, together with a large number of small and medium-sized firms dominating the export trade in consumer goods (Gold 1986; Wade 1990). Business groups consisting of associated firms under common and shared ownership have developed in the intermediate-goods sector (Hamilton and Feenstra 1997). Privately owned Taiwanese businesses follow the traditional pattern of Chinese family firms, as highlighted by Redding (1990) and others (e.g. Hamilton 1997; Hamilton and Kao 1990; Wong 1988), which dominate many Asian economies. Most are limited in size, relatively specialized in particular industries, concentrated in light manufacturing industry and commerce, and enmeshed in highly flexible networks of suppliers, subcontractors, and customers. When successful they often engage in opportunistic, unrelated diversification. Most networks between family firms are not particularly stable or long lived, except where they are based on strong personal ties of mutual obligation and support.

Similarly to many family firms in other economies, authority in Taiwanese companies is highly centralized and personal, with little emphasis on formal rules and procedures. In diversified firms subsidiaries are coordinated through personal relationships and family domination of multiple top-management positions rather than by systematic planning or joint activities. Long-term employment commitments are restricted to these employees with whom the owning family has personal obligation ties, and workers tend to be closely supervised (Deyo 1989; Hamilton 1997; Wilkinson 1994). These points will now be discussed in more detail.

THE KOREAN BUSINESS SYSTEM

Ownership Relations

The largest firms in post-Second World War Korea are the fast-growing, diversified 'financial cliques' or *chaebol*, the largest fifty of which in 1986 controlled

547 firms, produced 21.4 per cent of non-agricultural value added, employed 22.1 per cent of all employees in mining and manufacturing, and accounted for 44.3 per cent of all sales in that category (Zeile 1991: 309). They dominate the heavy and chemical industries sector, with most fields of economic activity being divided between three or four *chaebol*. Even more striking is the domination of the largest five and ten *chaebol*. In 1981, the top five accounted for 22.65 per cent of all manufacturing sales and 8.4 per cent of manufacturing employment, the top ten for 30.2 per cent of sales and 12.2 per cent of employment (Woo 1991: 171). By 1991 they had sales of $116 billion, which was equivalent to just under half of Korea's GNP (Fields 1995: 35).

These also exhibited the greatest growth and diversification rates in the 1970s. The largest *chaebol* by assets in 1983, Hyundai, grew by 32.1 per cent in 1971–83, for example, and Daewoo—the third largest—grew by 46.3 per cent over the same period (Kim 1991: 283). In addition to dominating many manufacturing industries, the *chaebol* also dominate significant parts of the service sector. In particular, the construction industry became a favoured route to diversification and many *chaebol* are also active in transport services, insurance, and related financial services. Finally, seven large general trading companies which are members of the largest ten *chaebol* have come to dominate Korea's export trade (D.-S. Cho 1987; Zeile 1991).

The *chaebol* remain largely family owned and controlled, despite their rapid growth and state pressure to sell shares on the stock market (E.-m. Kim 1991; Shin and Chin 1989; Steers *et al.* 1989: 37–41; Yoo and Lee 1987). According to Kang (1997), the founder—or his successor—and his family on average owned 48.2 per cent of the shares of the largest five *chaebol* in 1994. While most of these holdings are indirect in the sense that owner control is exercised through a number of core companies rather than direct family ownership in all firms, in the cases of Hyundai and Sunkyung the owner and his family still had direct shareholdings in the whole group of firms of 16.8 and 16.6 per cent respectively in the 1990s. The smaller *chaebol* are even more dominated by family owners. This continuance of high levels of family ownership despite the rapid expansion and very large size of these conglomerates was facilitated by most of their expansion being funded by state-subsidized debt which did not dilute family shareholdings (Orru *et al.* 1991; Woo 1991: 175).

Family ownership in Korea continues to mean largely family control and direction, with most of the leading posts held by family members and/or trusted colleagues from the same region or high school as the founding entrepreneur (Janelli 1993; C. S. Kim 1992). For example, in 1976 a study of the largest 100 *chaebol* found that 13.5 per cent of their top executives were related to the founder by blood or marriage and occupied 21 per cent of the top managerial posts. In Hyundai in 1989 the founding family still held exclusive possession of the highest-ranking positions (Fields 1995: 40). As the *chaebol* have grown in size, direct family domination of the top management posts has become difficult to maintain—though not impossible, as the Hyundai example indicates—and shared regional origins and/or common high school/college backgrounds have grown as ascriptive substitutes for family ties. Daewoo, for instance, has largely eschewed the use of family top managers, but nine of the managers had attended Kyunggi High School in Seoul in the late 1980s (Fields 1995).

In addition to family ownership being associated with highly particularistic managerial appointments, it also implies strong central control over decision-making. The situation in Samsung is typical of the larger *chaebol*. In Kang's (1997: 51) words: 'the owner's family holds the final responsibility. That is, all the managers have to account to the owner. Owner Lee and his family participate in the management directly ... the final authority is President Lee.' This high level of direct owner control is implemented by substantial central staff offices that intervene extensively in subsidiary affairs. These offices typically deal with financial, personnel, and planning matters, including internal auditing and investment advice, and some have as many as 250 staff. The extent of direct owner involvement in management in the largest *chaebol* is illustrated by the personal participation of Samsung's founder, Lee Byung-chull, in all new employee interviews between 1957 and 1986. As Fields (1995: 41) comments, this means that he must have attended over 100,000 interviews in that time.

These strongly owner-controlled large groups of firms are highly diversified, both vertically and horizontally. According to Hamilton and Feenstra (1997), most are vertically integrated, with many individual *chaebol* business units themselves being quite integrated and the network of firms increasing this even more so. Over a fifth of the sales of all the firms in the largest forty-three *chaebol* went to other group member firms. Horizontal diversification is also considerable. By 1983 'the average *chaebol* had firms operating in five different manufacturing industries' and a 'quarter of its manufacturing workforce employed in industries altogether unrelated to its primary manufacturing activity' (Zeile 1991: 307). Furthermore, the top *chaebol* were even more diversified, with their average diversification indices being 'one and a half to two times as large as the averages for the top fifty *chaebol*' (ibid.). Samsung's fifty-five firms, for example, were active in textiles, electronics, fibre optics, detergents, petrochemicals, shipbuilding, property development, construction, insurance, mass media, health care, and higher education in the early 1990s (Fields 1995: 37).

The high level of centralized decision-making encouraged considerable integration of economic activities, as capital, technology, and personnel could be centrally allocated and moved between subsidiaries (E.-m. Kim 1991). For example, Hyundai Shipbuilders acquired managers, engineers, and supervisors from Hyundai Construction and other firms in the Hyundai group when it was established (Amsden 1989: 274–90). As mentioned above, an important role in this central direction and coordination of the *chaebol* is played by the secretariat or planning group, which is the key corporate staff unit under the direct control of the chairman. It is largely responsible for coordinating plans and mobilizing resources across the whole *chaebol*, so that these diversified conglomerates are in fact managed as cohesive economic entities with a unified group culture focused on the *chaebol* owner. As Biggart (1997: 234) suggests: 'the secretariat maintains control of the career paths of middle and top management, reinforcing management's orientation to the patrimonial centre of the *chaebol*, not to the company in which they are employed.' In this respect *chaebol* are quite different from those conglomerate holding companies in which the central office functions more like a bank than as an integrated planning and control agency, and subsidiaries are simply set annual financial targets as separate, discrete entities.

The *chaebol* have grown extremely fast since the 1950s. Samsung, for example, had an average annual sales growth rate of 35.5 per cent between 1963 and 1992, whereas the nominal GNP growth rate over the same period was 23.7 per cent. This high growth was usually at the expense of profitability. Although there are considerable difficulties in relying on the public financial statements of Korean companies (Janelli 1993: 124–9), detailed analyses of the *chaebol* suggest that 'the objective of the firms of the large *chaebol* is not to maximize profits but to maximize sales' (Jung Ku-Hyun 1987, quoted in Janelli 1993: 91). Janelli's own analysis of the *chaebol* he studied suggested that, 'since 1970, its profits have barely kept pace with its dividends' (1993: 94). This is because ownership rights are held for control purposes more than for income, and growth has been financed by state-provided and subsidized credit rather than out of retained profits. Also critical, of course, is the extra influence with the state that large size can provide and the fierce competition between the *chaebol* for being the largest enterprise group (E.-m. Kim 1989, 1991). The economic crisis of the late 1990s in Korea has highlighted this strong growth priority of the leading *chaebol*, as well as their reliance on debt financing.

Non-Ownership Coordination

The large size and self-sufficiency of the Korean *chaebol* mean that they exhibit low interdependence with suppliers and customers and are able to dominate small and medium-sized firms. Typically, their relations with subcontractors are predatory. As Fields (1995: 125) comments: 'Core firms are able to increase their working capital by squeezing the subcontractors associated with the *chaebol* … the *chaebol* are able to keep the small and medium-sized contractors under their thumbs, pass recessionary shocks on to them, or even merge with them if it suits their plans.'

Relations between the *chaebol*, and between ownership units in general in Korea, tend to be adversarial, with considerable reluctance to cooperate over joint projects, such as complementary R&D programmes (Wade 1990: 315–16). This is exemplified by the rivalry between Samsung and Lucky-Goldstar over domination of the electronics industry in Korea. Despite the second daughter of Samsung's Lee being married to the third son of Lucky-Goldstar's chairman Gu, Samsung entered this industry in a substantial way at the end of the 1960s. Indeed, Lee has disinherited this daughter, while giving his other daughters directorships in Samsung companies (Biggart 1997). New industries especially are often the site of intense competition for dominance, and the major driving force behind many new investments often appears to be corporate rivalry for the leading position in them, as in the expansion of the petrochemical industry at the beginning of the 1990s.

Overall, then, markets are not organized around long-term, mutual obligations in Korea but rather are characterized by predominantly short-term, single-transaction relations. These sometimes develop from personal contacts, as when subcontracting firms are set up by ex-employees (Amsden 1989: 183–4). Where cooperation does occur between firms, direct personal ties between chief executives are usually crucial to reaching agreement (Steers *et al.* 1989: 103–4). Alliance-based modes of integration, then, are weak in the post-war Korean business system.

The high degree of competition between the leading *chaebol*, which has been fuelled by the state's policy of selecting entrants to new industries and opportunities on the basis of competitive success, has severely limited the development of independent-sector-based organizations in Korea (Amsden 1989: 64–76; Wade 1990). With the exception of the cotton-spinning industry in the 1950s and 1960s, there have been few if any industry-wide autonomous associations and similar bodies promoting cooperation between firms and collectively lobbying the state (Moon 1994). Additionally, since the dominant economic actors are highly diversified, their interests in any one sector are less important than they would be in economies where firms are more focused on particular industries, and so the incentives to develop strong sector-based collectivities are correspondingly lower. In the 1980s and 1990s, however, the umbrella organization, the Federation of Korean Industries, together with a few other associations, attempted to diverge from and publicly influence state policies (Eckert 1993; Moon 1994).

Employment Policies and Labour Management

In most *chaebol* the level of employer–employee commitment is limited for manual workers. Although seniority does appear to be important in affecting wage rates, and employers do provide accommodation and other fringe benefits in the newer capital intensive industries, most notably perhaps at the Pohang Iron and Steel Company, Korean firms are reluctant to make the sorts of long-term commitments to their workforce that many large Japanese ones do (Amsden 1989; Bae 1987; Bae and Form 1986: Biggart 1997). Mobility between firms, both enforced and voluntary, has been considerably greater for manual workers— and some non-manual—than is common in the large-firm sector in Japan. Annual labour turnover rates of between 52 per cent and 72 per cent were quite usual in the 1970s in Korea, and were especially high in manufacturing industries (Michell 1988: 109).

Additionally, leading firms in Korea sometimes poach skilled workers from competitors rather than invest in training programmes (Amsden 1989: 275–87; Janelli 1993: 139). Even where workers do not leave very often, this is more because they are locked into their current employer through high levels of over-time pay than because they feel committed to the firm (Bae 1987). White-collar employees are more favoured and tend more to remain with large employers, not least because their pay and conditions are usually substantially better than they could obtain by moving (Janelli 1993: 153).

The centralized and personal nature of authority relations in the *chaebol*, and avowal of a paternalistic ideology, are accompanied by a largely authoritarian, not to say militaristic, management style. According to the Japanese managers involved in joint ventures with Korean firms interviewed by Liebenberg (1982), the Korean management system is characterized by top-down decision-making, enforcement of vertical hierarchical relationships, low levels of consultation with subordinates, and low levels of trust, both horizontally and vertically (cf. Bae 1987; Chung *et al.* 1988). Superiors tend to be seen as remote and uninterested in subordinates' concerns or their ability to contribute more than obedience. As Janelli (1993: 223) puts it: 'subordinates advanced the view that the company was like the army' and later on comments that 'in many ways my military experience served as a better guide to behaviour in the office than my understanding of American bureaucracies or South Korean villages and universities' (ibid. 226). Similarly, C. S. Kim (1992: 150) describes relations between supervisors and subordinates as 'formal, distant, and authoritarian' and cites some of the workers in Poongsan Corporation as viewing hierarchical relations as being worse than in the military.

This authoritarian management style encourages close supervision of task performance. Frequently, the physical layout of office furniture and workspace in general is carefully arranged so as to maximize supervisor surveillance of work processes (Janelli 1993: 164). In the company studied by Janelli in the 1980s, section chiefs and department heads also ensured control by narrowly circum-scribing subordinates' tasks and carefully monitoring all messages coming into the work unit and work outputs. Subordinates in general were seen as children, needing firm guidance and direction. As mentioned above, these aspects of the *chaebol* were also related to considerable social distance between superiors and subordinates and permitted considerable personal discretion to supervisors in evaluating the performance and worth of their juniors.

Such strong supervision of task performance was allied to considerable specialization of roles for manual workers. According to Bae (1987: 60), 90 per cent of the manual workforce at Hyundai Motors remained at their initial job level and were not systematically upgraded. Unskilled workers continued to carry out relatively narrow tasks without much movement between jobs and skill cate-gories. Similarly, C. S. Kim (1992: 209) found a considerable degree of worker specialization at Poongsan Corporation in the 1980s, with only 20 per cent having changed jobs more than once, and then nearly always in the same speciality.

However, non-manual workers do appear to be moved between tasks and sections, and sometimes develop more varied skills, in the larger and more diver-sified *chaebol*. Yoo and Lee (1987) suggest that job assignments are often unclear and overlapping by US standards and job rotation is quite frequent. Managers in particular are often transferred across subsidiaries and have more fluid roles and responsibilities. Job boundaries and the scope of formal authority relations are rarely tightly defined, or adhered to where they are spelled out, especially in senior managerial posts (Shin and Chin 1989). Because of the importance of personal authority in the Korean *chaebol*, jobs and responsibilities are determined more by superiors' wishes than by formal rules. Supervisory discretion means that the division of labour is less formally prescribed in the *chaebol* than in more rule-governed work systems.

THE TAIWANESE BUSINESS SYSTEM

Ownership Relations

The Taiwanese economy is dominated by large state-owned firms in the capital-intensive sector and small to medium-sized family-owned and controlled firms in the export sector, with the larger Taiwanese firms focused on making intermediate products (Hamilton 1997; Numazaki 1992). As Wade (1990: 176) points out: 'From the early 1950s onward Taiwan has had one of the biggest public enterprise sectors outside the communist bloc and Sub-Saharan Africa', and public enterprises contributed about twice as much to GDP at factor cost as their equivalents in Korea in the 1970s. Similarly their share of gross fixed capital formation was well over 30 per cent in that decade, when Korea's was under a quarter and Japan's under an eighth. Indeed the only Asian countries with a comparable public-sector contribution to capital investment were India and Burma.

In 1980 the Taiwanese Ministry of Economic Affairs owned firms in the power, petroleum, mining, aluminium, phosphates, alkali, sugar, chemicals, fertilizers, petrochemicals, steel, shipbuilding, engineering, and machinery industries, while the Ministry of Finance owned four banks and eight insurance companies (Chu 1994; Wade 1990: 178). These public enterprises were very large by comparison with privately owned ones and often dominated, if not monopolized, their sectors. Thus the state has retained ownership and control of the 'commanding heights' of the economy in Taiwan, especially the upstream capital-intensive sectors. As Hamilton (1997: 245) has suggested: 'state-owned enterprises primarily supply infrastructure and basic initial goods and services ... that all other companies might use, regardless of size.'

The private sector does have some large enterprises but is much less concentrated than its Korean equivalent. In 1976 there were only 176 manufacturing enterprises employing over 1,000 people, and 167 in 1981, and many of the largest of these were state-owned ones, such as China Steel and Chinese Petroleum (Wade 1990: 66–8). In contrast, in 1981 those employing under 100 people constituted 96 per cent of manufacturing firms and employed 60.3 per cent of the labour force. By the late 1980s, the proportion of employees in manufacturing establishments working in units employing less than 100 people was even greater at 62.9 per cent, while 22.8 per cent of them worked in units of less than ten people (Shieh 1992: 38). Furthermore, while the number of firms in the secondary sector increased 250 per cent between 1966 and 1976, the number of employees per firm grew by only 29 per cent, in strong contrast to Korea, where the employment total per firm doubled in the same period. Between 1966 and 1986 the number of reported firms in Taiwan increased by 315 per cent, but the average firm size grew by only 15 per cent, while in Korea the number of firms increased by only 10 per cent but average firm size increased by 300 per cent (Hamilton 1997).

These smaller companies dominate the export trade: those with under 300 employees accounted for 65 per cent of manufactured exports in 1985 (Wade 1990: 70). In 1990 this size group employed 70 per cent of the workforce and produced 60 per cent of Taiwan's exports (Fields 1995: 64). However, the production of intermediate goods tends to be more dominated by larger enterprises, often exercising quasi-monopoly control and also forming more diversified business groups (Hamilton 1997; Hamilton and Kao 1990). These groups are usually under common ownership, although this may be shared between a number of business partners who have established highly personal trust relations with each other (Hamilton 1997; Numazaki 1992).

Private firms in Taiwan are nearly all owned and controlled by families, as indeed are most Chinese businesses throughout South-East Asia (Redding 1990; Wu and Wu 1980). Of the largest ninety-seven business groups—i.e. multi-firm groupings of associated enterprises—in 1983, no less than eighty-four were majority owned by members of a particular family (Hamilton 1997). Owners are highly involved in the running of their firms and there are strong connections between ownership and direction of economic activities. Wong (1988: 170–2) has characterized the pervasive economic ethos generating this strong drive towards autonomy and proprietorship in Chinese communities as 'entrepreneurial familism', which has led to high rates of new-firm formation in Taiwan, Hong Kong, and elsewhere as families seek to be in control of their own businesses (cf. Gates 1987; Greenhalgh 1984, 1988). This emphasis on family ownership and control means that dominant goals are focused on the acquisition and growth of family wealth rather than on the growth of the firm as a separate entity. The pursuit of large size irrespective of profitability is not usually the dominant objective in these firms, especially if it could lead to the loss of personal control or to being considered a threat by the ruling party's interests.

Vertical integration is weak in most of these firms and they are rarely self-sufficient in terms of combining the management of key processes and activities in one organization. Instead, they are usually highly interdependent with other enterprises for inputs and for distributing their outputs and form fluid subcontracting networks (Hamilton and Kao 1990; Redding 1990; Shieh 1992). However, this interdependence is not usually accompanied by a willingness to share long-term risks with suppliers and buyers. Rather, more restricted and limited connections are preferred. Some Taiwanese business groups do, though, exhibit a greater degree of backward integration in the production of intermediate goods, but this is much less than in Korea or many Western firms (Hamilton 1997). Ownership-based vertical integration is, therefore, rather low in Taiwan.

Diversification of a horizontal nature—'opportunistic' in Hamilton and Kao's (1990) terms—is, however, more widespread in private Taiwanese firms, especially those forming business groups of associated companies. While by no means all successful firms develop into highly diversified business groups, including some of the largest, those that do diversify tend to move into a variety of sectors in a seemingly *ad hoc* and idiosyncratic way, often as the result of personal requests or obligations. According to Hamilton (1997), a common pattern of expansion of the leading Taiwanese business groups is to establish a dominant presence—quasi-monopolistic in many cases—in a particular sector supplying export-oriented firms, and then to set up a number of quite separate and unrelated businesses to be run by the patriarch's sons and other male relatives. Ownership-based horizontal diversification is, then, quite considerable in the intermediate sector, but less so in the capital-intensive state sector or the very-small-firm-dominated export sector.

An important point about such diversification and growth is that it is not usually associated with managerial integration but rather is achieved by setting up legally separate firms linked through common ownership and family top management. Diversification is informal and typically personal. Each firm, in the sense of a formal management structure, tends to be quite specialized in its resources and spheres of economic activities, but families may well invest in and control a variety of businesses. While leading managers of each firm in a business group may well be members of the same family, they are not usually structured into a formal hierarchy of authority relations. Rather, the core group of family members shares the top jobs in all group firms, so that each member may well have a considerable number of posts, sometimes into double figures (Hamilton 1997; Numazaki 1992).

Non-Ownership Coordination

The specialization and interdependence of Taiwanese family businesses mean that they have to rely on each other to obtain inputs for their products and services and to distribute and market them. Thus multiple market connections between firms are crucial to their operation. However, these are not necessarily long term or based on mutual obligations (Silin 1972). Rather, inter-firm links are often managed in such a way as to reduce risks, and so commitments to other economic actors are restricted. Exchange partners may, then, be numerous and selected on the basis of their personal reputations for competence and reliability, but do not usually form networks of long-term trust and reciprocal loyalty (Redding 1990). For example, the extensive use of subcontracting, especially in the export sector, means that a large number of firms deal with each other frequently, but little or no long-term commitment to continued orders is implied by such contracting—which

is usually informal (Shieh 1992). Similarly, trading companies may select a particular supplier to fulfil an order without any obligation to do so for successive
orders. Market relations can thus change rapidly and are quite fluid, and flexibility is emphasized over long-term risk-sharing (Hamilton 1997; Hamilton and Kao
1990).

Business partnerships, on the other hand, often do involve long-term reciprocal commitments and can lead to the development of elaborate networks of
personal obligation that structure strategic decisions and new ventures (Kao 1991;
Numazaki 1991, 1992). Where significant resources are involved and firms need
to undertake activities jointly, connections are highly personal and dependent on
trust between the owners. Without high levels of personal trust, such partnerships
cannot be formed successfully in Taiwan, and, as a result, many medium-sized
firms do not grow into large enterprises, because they are unable to find partners
they can rely on. While straightforward trading relationships, then, are quite
limited in their mutual commitment, more substantial alliances and joint activities involve considerable personal obligations, often on a long-term basis. Even
here, though, flexibility is valued and families will often prefer to establish new
ventures with a number of different partners rather than expand existing ones with
their current associates (Hamilton and Kao 1990).

Inter-firm connections are, then, highly personal, and form extensive networks
of mutual, albeit often asymmetric, obligations, without developing into the sorts
of long-term, wide-ranging inter-organizational linkages found in the Japanese
inter-market groups (Hamilton et al. 1990; Orru et al. 1989). Indeed, when the
Taiwanese state did try to encourage the formation of Japanese-style subcontracting arrangements, it failed (Hamilton 1997). Equally, attempts to establish
trading companies as long-term coordinating agencies in Taiwan have been less
successful than in Korea and there are few major intermediaries performing similar functions to the Japanese sogo shosha or German banks (Wade 1990: 160–5).
Thus, the extent of systematic, stable vertical and horizontal integration of
economic activities through alliances and long-term partnerships is limited in
Taiwan, although partnerships based on personal connections and trust seem
easier to develop and to be more sustained than in Korea (Numazaki 1992).

Sectoral cooperation is also limited by this concern with personal control, as
well as being restricted by the state's intolerance of independent intermediary
organizations, particularly those dominated by Taiwanese (Gold 1986; Wade
1990). Additionally, given the flexibility of most Chinese family businesses and
their unwillingness to commit major resources to any single industry or activity
for a long time, stable associations of industry-specific enterprises are difficult to
maintain. In Numazaki's (1992: 75) terms: 'the survival strategies of Taiwanese
small and medium enterprises ... (are to) ... catch the opportunities, take full
advantage of them, and leave (the industry) ... the result is the frequent entry and
exit of Taiwanese enterprises ... (they are) ... industrial nomads.' Collective organization and joint action by competitors are, therefore, low in Taiwan. However,
the high population density in Taiwan, combined with considerable cultural

homogeneity among the Taiwanese, has encouraged a strong reliance on reputations as the primary means of ensuring compliance with exchange commitments in the absence of an independent and reliable legal system (Gates 1987; Greenhalgh 1984, 1988; Silin 1972, 1976).

Employment Policies and Labour Management

The personal nature of authority relations in Chinese family firms and the strong ideology of paternalism encourage considerable expectations of reciprocity in employment policies and practices. However, these are considerably reduced when there is little prior basis for personal commitments and employees were previously strangers (Salaff 1991). In practice, obligations become more attenuated as connections become more distant from the basic family unit. Thus, the strongest ties and sense of commitment occur between family members, somewhat weaker ones between schoolmates, neighbours, and more distant kin, and weakest ones between those who were strangers before employment (Wong 1985). Long-term commitments and seniority-based promotion practices tend to be reserved for those workers with strong personal ties to the owner, while previously unknown staff hired through impersonal channels neither expect nor receive such commitments. In particular, young, female, semi-skilled, non-family workers in the light manufacturing export sector are expected to stay only for a short time and are rarely trained for more demanding posts (Deyo 1989; Gates 1987; Shieh 1992).

Furthermore, the intensely familial nature of these businesses restricts senior managerial posts to family members or those who have family-like connections to the owner. Thus, many skilled workers and managers prefer to leave and start up their own businesses once they have acquired business skills and some capital (Greenhalgh 1984; Tam 1990; Wong 1988), especially in the labour-intensive export sector, where subcontracting is widespread (Shieh 1992). Both the general cultural preference for personal business ownership over employment, and the unwillingness to trust non-family subordinates on the part of employers, limit the scope and length of employer–employee commitments in the Chinese family business, where obligations are restricted to close personal connections.

If we turn to consider task structure and control, the importance of personal relationships and authority in Chinese family businesses additionally means that formal specification of roles and positions is less important than in most Western societies. Equally, jobs and skills are not rigidly defined and separated by formal procedures, but rather are fairly broad and flexible (Pugh and Redding 1985; Redding 1990: 160–1). In the large Taiwanese firm studied by Silin (1976), roles were fluidly defined, many managers held multiple positions, and their responsibilities were liable to be changed suddenly at the behest of the owner. Similarly, many managers in Taiwanese business groups hold a considerable number of posts and are rarely restricted to a single specialized role (Hamilton and Kao 1990).

The strong commitment to patriarchal relationships in the workplace, and in society as a whole (Deyo 1989; Greenhalgh 1988), means that superior–subordinate relations are quite remote and distant, particularly those between the owner-manager and employees (Redding 1990; Silin 1976). Similarly, as in Korea, paternalism implies a lack of confidence in the abilities and commitment of staff, so that close supervision of work performance is a feature of Taiwanese firms, as is considerable personal discretion in how authority is exercised, especially at the top of the enterprise.

Overall, then, leading Korean and Taiwanese businesses in the post-war period shared a high level of owner control, highly personal and centralized authority relations, and a high degree of personal discretion over the exercise of authority. They were also able to move into new business areas quite quickly, but have rarely formed long-term sectoral alliances. They differed in the extent to which privately controlled economic actors dominated major economic sectors, were diversified and self-sufficient, and developed personal alliances between owning families, as well as in their commitment to growth and large size. The integration and interdependence of subsidiaries of firms also varied between these two economies, as did the rigidity of categories of employees and their employment conditions. I now turn to the consideration of the major institutional factors that help to explain these similarities and differences. The key institutional features of pre-industrial Korea and Taiwan that continued to influence their development during and after industrialization are very briefly discussed first, followed by a summary of the effects of Japanese colonial rule and the nature of post-war institutions, especially the state.

INSTITUTIONAL INFLUENCES ON THE KOREAN BUSINESS SYSTEM

The dominant institutions structuring the post-war Korean business system stem from both pre-industrial Korean society and the period of Japanese colonial rule, as well as the Korean war and the post-1961 period of military-supported rule. Particularly important features of the pre-industrial Korean political system that have continued to be reflected in post-war authority structures and state business relations are (*a*) the high degree of political centralization, (*b*) the Confucian legitimation of superior authority in terms of moral worth demonstrated by examination success, and (*c*) the highly competitive nature of factional struggles among the aristocracy together with the importance of aristocratic status itself and family ancestry.

From 1392 to 1910 Korea was ruled by the *Yi*, or *Chosun*, dynasty, which entrenched Confucianism as the official ideology (Haboush 1991). In this 'patrimonial' state (Jacobs 1985: 1–3), political power was highly centralized by the pseudo-bureaucratic élite, which claimed moral superiority over the population on the basis of examination successes. Because power was legitimated in terms of personal moral worth, the élite formed a 'virtuocracy' (Pye 1985: 22–4) that led by example and did not need to perform reciprocal services for subordinates to demonstrate its superiority. Additionally, by claiming personal superior moral status, members of the élite, the *Yangban*, sharply distinguished themselves from the rest of the population that was morally unworthy. As Cumings (1997: 56) puts it: 'The purified social order was one in which yangban were pure and everyone else was not.' This élite was awarded official posts by the king as a purely personal gift and at his discretion. Thus a major weapon at his disposal in the continuing battle between the king and the bureaucracy was his power to appoint and dismiss officials (Jacobs 1985: 15).

However, unlike China, access to the examinations was restricted to those of aristocratic status. In the earlier years of the dynasty this meant that a relatively small élite group was able to monopolize leading posts and to restrict the personal power of the monarch in Korea. An important institution in this restriction of royal power was the Censorate, which permitted moral criticism of official behaviour, including that of the king. Although individual officials and their families might be dismissed or banished, then, the aristocratic bureaucracy had more power in Korea than its Chinese counterpart and limited the monarch's ability to rule independently. The political system as a whole consisted of a set of checks and balances that kept most kings from accumulating despotic power (Cumings 1997: 73; Haboush 1991; G. Henderson 1968; Jacobs 1985; Koo 1993).

After the Japanese invasions of 1592–8, the number of successful candidates for the state examinations increased considerably, which meant that competition for official posts became intense and membership of powerful lineages developed as an important resource in this competition (Janelli and Janelli 1982: 10–11). The intense factional struggles between lineages were heightened in the latter period of the *Yi* dynasty by the expansion of the yangban class which formed 48.6 per cent of the population in 1858 (Haboush 1991; G. Henderson 1968: 41; Jacobs 1985: 192–202). Although the expanded junior ranks of the aristocracy did not usually gain access to the leading posts in the bureaucracy, which remained the preserve of the élite lineages (Palais 1975: 8), this growth further intensified concern with the relative status of each lineage and an obsession with ancestry.

Additionally, as Jacobs (1985: 202) has emphasized, because the possibility of obtaining a state office was always present for the Korean aristocracy—and these offices were reliable sources of privileged status and security in this patrimonial society—they were discouraged from developing non-official corporate interest groups at the local level. Instead, the pressures to seek official posts generated what Gregory Henderson (1968: 5–8) has termed a political vortex in which energies and loyalties were pulled towards the centre (cf. Palais 1975: 14–16).

Factional disputes between lineages, often suffused with Confucian moralism as competing groups attempted to demonstrate their superior virtue (Haboush 1991), were encouraged by the monarchy as a means of preserving its autonomy and limiting the development of local power centres. This autonomy was also maintained by the frequent rotation of officials, both in the capital and in the provinces. Towards the end of the *Yi* dynasty, senior officials were often changed daily and even in the more stable fifteenth and sixteenth centuries the Chief Censor was changed every few months and many officials held over 100 posts during their careers of thirty years or so (G. Henderson 1968). Élites thus combined influence and power with considerable insecurity and competition. Similarly, provincial officials were frequently rotated to prevent them forming alliances with the local aristocracy and there was little or no integration of local communities with broader political units.

The overwhelming dependence on central authority for state office and access to economic resources meant that rural élites had little or no interest in mobilizing local support and, indeed, usually relied upon the central power to support their extraction of rents and expropriation of common land (Jacobs 1985: 77–91). Villagers did not develop loyalties to local leaders, who were usually appointed by state officials, or to larger collective entities and were unable to retain the benefits of agricultural improvements, such as irrigation schemes, for themselves. They did not, as in Japan, control and manage collective resources (Fukutake 1967; T. C. Smith 1959).

The official antagonism to local power centres was echoed by consistent state opposition to private concentrations of economic power and wealth. In both pre-industrial China and Korea successful merchants were considered to be potential threats to the official élite as manifesting an alternative basis of prestige and power to the official examinations and constituting an independent source of power (G. Henderson 1968; Jacobs 1958, 1985). Private accumulation of wealth was officially regarded as an indicator of corruption and Confucian rulers established their ethical right to prevent it as part of their duty to preserve harmony and frugality. The merchant class was even smaller in Korea than in China and subjected to stricter surveillance. Traders were considered to be exploiters and pedlars were organized into a state-controlled guild to be used for political control of any threats to the established order (G. Henderson 1968: 51–3). As Cumings (1997: 81) suggests: 'The flinty scholar-officials who ran the Chosun state, however, wanted to nip commerce in the bud everywhere.'

At the end of the *Yi* dynasty, then, Korean society was highly politically centralized, riven by factional conflicts and yet remarkably stable because of the 'finely tuned mechanism of checks and balances' (Robinson 1991) between the leading aristocratic lineages and the monarch. Military institutions had atrophied and had little prestige in the Confucian dominated political culture; equally Korea lacked a strong commercial class. Power was justified in terms of moral superiority manifested by examination success in the Confucian classics and did not require the mobilization of commitments and loyalties among subordinates but rather depended on personal favours and factional success. There were few institutions capable of resisting foreign encroachments and Korea was formally annexed by Japan in 1910. Overall, then, the institutional legacy of the *Yi* dynasty can be summarized as one of highly personal authority relations, fierce competition between lineage-based factions, weak collective loyalties beyond kinship groups, moralistic claims to superiority, and considerable insecurity of merchants (Eckert 1993; Koo 1993).

The thirty-five years of Japanese rule and the subsequent US occupation of Korea intensified some features of the pre-industrial political system, such as its high level of centralization and dependence on the political executive, while modifying others. Perhaps the major changes involved the development of a formal administrative apparatus that enabled the state to control rural communities directly and enhanced the centre's power over the whole society. However, as Jacobs (1985: 162–70) suggests, much of this 'modernization' of Korean society by the Japanese retained crucial elements of the earlier patrimonial system and, in particular, the capricious and unpredictable behaviour of the executive. In his words (1985: 165):

although the Governor General proliferated formal, very modern commercial and industrial codes and regulations, he did nothing to shake the conviction of those Korean entrepreneurs who were emerging on the scene that the way to protect one's economic interests and service ... was still to be opportunistically self-serving and somehow come to terms with a dangerously capricious and heartless bureaucracy.

Similarly, McNamara (1990: 127–37), amongst others (e.g. Cumings 1997; Eckert 1993), has emphasized the insecurity and instability of indigenous enterprises during the colonial period that encouraged dependence on close family ties among top managers and the intensive cultivation of personal connections with the governing élite.

Thus, the Japanese occupation destroyed many of the political institutions of the *Yi* dynasty without developing new ones that were sufficiently rooted in the indigenous culture to survive the collapse and removal of the colonial regime. Consequently, when Korea recovered its independence in 1948 many of the traditional patterns recurred, especially the dependence on the centre and factional conflicts over access to power and the spoils of office (G. Henderson 1968: 126–47). A clear indication of this during Syngman Rhee's leadership was his frequent rotation of ministers and top bureaucrats. Within six months of taking office he changed half of his ministers and on average changed more than ten of them each year between 1948 and 1960 (Henderson 1968: 238–9). This pattern continued through the short-lived government of Chang Myon and the early days of military rule under Park Chong-hui, reflecting the desire 'to prevent the consolidation of groups, bonds, personal powers and vested interests in any province, ministry or board' (G. Henderson 1968: 239–40; cf. Steinberg 1989: 96).

As well as inhibiting the development of new indigenous political institutions, the Japanese occupation also prevented the growth of an independent Korean entrepreneurial élite and technical strata. Koreans were systematically excluded from middle- and senior-ranked posts in both the state bureaucracy and privately owned businesses that were dominated by Japanese. The few indigenous firms that did develop and survive were mostly in textiles and food-processing industries and were heavily dependent upon the toleration of the colonial administration (Eckert 1993). The bulk of the productive land, manufacturing, and industrial enterprises was owned and managed by Japanese and the forced industrialization of Korea in the 1930s and 1940s was directed almost entirely towards supporting Japanese military expansion in mainland Asia (Cumings 1984; G. Henderson 1968: 94–7; S. P.-S. Ho 1984; McNamara 1990). However, the Japanese did provide a model of how industrial enterprises and banks could be organized and did develop the physical and social infrastructure necessary for an industrial economy, albeit one designed to support the colonial power.

The disruption of the Japanese-instigated industrialization and urbanization was intensified and extended by the Korean War, so that dependence on the central government grew even more in the 1950s, especially after land reform weakened the landlord class and rural élites. In the commercial and industrial field, Rhee used this dependence to finance his political campaigns and traded licences and cheap credit for economic support (Woo 1991: 65–72). The new class of Korean entrepreneurs were essentially political capitalists who owed their fortunes to the favours of the President and followed his wishes. Particularly important was the virtual giving-away of the formerly Japanese-owned businesses between 1947 and 1957 to favoured businessmen. These firms formed the basis of many of the leading *chaebol* (Eckert 1993).

The high level of business dependence on the state, and especially upon personal relations with the chief political executive and/or bureaucratic élite, during the period of early industrialization became even more intensified after the 1961 military *coup* led by Park Chong-hui. Initially, Park rounded up the richest men in an anti-corruption campaign and charged them with illicit profiteering. After realizing that this would merely prevent the economy from developing and that it was not particularly popular, the military regime released the major business leaders and much of their property in exchange for paying fines in the form of establishing new enterprises and cooperating with the state in its ambitious industrialization plans (Moon 1994; Woo 1991: 83–4).

The one exception to this return of expropriated property was the banking system, which was systematically used to direct investment, reward exports and other achievements desired by the state, and punish inefficiency and/or political opposition (Jones and Sakong 1980). Thus, the state controlled the flow of cheap credit, and especially access to foreign loans and technology, to the fast-growing *chaebol* in favour of its developmental priorities, first in light manufacturing exports and later, in the 1970s, in heavy and chemical industries (Cheng 1990; Koo 1987; Koo and Kim 1992; Zeile 1991).

Big business in Korea was, and remains, highly dependent on the state, and especially the President and his closest advisers in the 'Blue House', for access to subsidized credit and the means to expand. In return for these resources, the *chaebol* diversified into heavy industry in the 1970s to fulfil state priorities and funded the political campaign of the ruling party. While their success and size may have enabled them to develop some autonomy, so that the business–state relation is now a little less one-sided (E.-m. Kim 1989), the dominant pattern of Korean industrialization over the past forty or so years has undoubtedly been one of state leadership and control. The effective destruction of the landlord class by

Japanese colonialism, land reform, and civil war combined with a military-backed authoritarian state to produce an autonomous political executive and bureaucratic élite that could pursue medium- to long-term development goals, with US support (Castells 1992; Cumings 1997; J. Henderson 1993; Moon 1994; Woo 1991). As Jun (1992) emphasizes, this 'strong state' grew out of both the pre-war Japanese regime and its American-backed successor.

The commitment by the military regime to rapid industrial development was a result of a number of factors. First, its legitimacy was low because of the long-standing Confucian disdain of military élites and civilian domination of the political system during the *Yi* dynasty. As Woo (1991: 97) puts it: 'the Korean variant of Confucianism long held the Man on Horseback in supercilious contempt and equated the ascendance of praetorians with national degeneration.' The military became committed to rapid economic growth as a prime means of gaining acquiescence to its rule. Secondly, the experience of Japanese colonization meant that there was wide support for policies based on the goal of catching up with Japan, however distant that might have seemed in the 1960s and 1970s. Thirdly, the military threat from North Korea provided a strategic justification for the state-directed growth of heavy and chemical industries in the 1970s. As a result, Park mobilized the business élite around the goal of, first, fast export-led growth and, secondly, the development of capital-intensive industries, which greatly increased the degree of diversification in the leading *chaebol* (Zeile 1991).

As mentioned above, the key weapon in this mobilization was state control of credit, both its availability and its price, together with access to foreign exchange and technology (Woo 1991: 149–75). Essentially, the military regime provided the funds for investment and expansion at highly favourable rates to the select few firms that could meet its objectives and supported it. The direct financial risks for the *chaebol*-owning families were, therefore, limited, since they did not need to find the capital themselves to dilute their control by selling shares on the stock market (Amsden 1989: 151; Eckert 1993). However, political risks were obviously very high, either for failing to meet state targets or for not supporting the regime, as some *chaebol* owners found when they flirted with opposition leaders (Cumings 1987, 1997; Fields 1995; Woo 1991: 165–75).

These political risks were managed in four major ways. First, by maintaining close personal relations with the President and his immediate advisers. Secondly, by diversifying across sectors so as to minimize the consequences of failure in any single priority area. Thirdly, by growing as fast as possible to maximize the political and economic consequences of failure and effectively to lock the state into the *chaebol*'s survival as well as ensuring that rival *chaebol* did not become significantly bigger and so have a greater claim on politically controlled resources. Fourthly, by maintaining strong central control over *chaebol* activities to ensure that state priorities were achieved and resources could be switched between activities quickly to respond to changes in these priorities. Because dependence on the political executive was so high, together with the highly personal and kin-based means of ensuring trust, the *chaebol* had to compete for its favours and so found it difficult to cooperate and collaborate amongst themselves.

A further way in which the state reduced the risks for the *chaebol* was by controlling and restricting trade unions and limiting real wage increases (Deyo 1987, 1989; Haggard and Moon 1993; Koo 1987; Michell 1988; Woo 1991: 11–13, 180–2). For political as well as economic reasons, the military regime maintained considerable control over the organized labour movement in Korea and often intervened in strikes and other industrial disputes. Attempts to set up enterprise unions along Japanese lines have not been successful in terms of gaining workers' trust and the capital–labour relations in large firms remain predominantly antagonistic—as was shown by the large-scale outbreaks of labour unrest in the late 1980s when authoritarian restrictions were relaxed (see Bae 1987; Brandt 1987; C. S. Kim 1992). The weakness of the trade unions in Korea has meant that *chaebol* owners have not had to gain their cooperation or make long-term commitments to workers. The plentiful availability of relatively cheap labour until the mid-1980s, due to population growth and emigration from the land to the major cities (Michell 1988: 106–79), also limited real wage growth and the need to gain workers' commitment to enterprise goals.

The general prestige of educational qualifications and their perceived necessity for high-status white-collar jobs have led to high levels of investment in education, both public and private. Indeed, so highly prized is higher education that, as Robinson (1991: 223) suggests: 'the rapid expansion of industry has been plagued by a shortage of skilled labour, but there has almost always been an oversupply of liberal arts trained college graduates', and Amsden (1989: 225) cites a Seoul National University survey that found that managers were one of the least scarce labour resources in large firms, whereas skilled and experienced workers were most scarce (cf. C. S. Kim 1992: 83). This imbalance is partly due to the greater prestige of traditional liberal arts degrees compared to engineering ones, and to the low status of specialist manual skills (see G. Henderson 1968: 226–36), and partly to the much greater rewards received by college graduates in large Korean companies. As Amsden (1989: 230–1) puts it: 'the gap in earnings between managers and production workers reflects a large gap in earnings related to educational level … in the case of returns to education, the well educated in Korea probably earn a premium by the standards of most developing countries.'

In general, then, levels of education in Korea are quite high but technical education is limited in provision and of relatively low status. The *chaebol* rely on the verdicts of the educational system in selecting managers and engineers, in a comparable manner to large Japanese firms, but do not invest greatly in training manual workers and do not make long-term commitments to them. Turnover among manual workers is greater in the *chaebol* than in Japanese *kaisha* and reliance on external labour markets for scarce skills is also greater.

The militarization of Korean society during and after the Korean War reinforced the highly authoritarian relations between superiors and subordinates developed during Japanese colonial rule (K.-d. Kim 1988). All Korean males have to serve two or three years in the armed forces and the military has served as the model for many large firms, especially with regard to norms of obedience, not least through the recruitment of senior officers to top managerial posts (C. S. Kim 1992; Janelli 1993; Steers *et al.* 1989: 44). Military notions of discipline have also supported traditional subordination relations based on Confucian conceptions of moral superiority and worth. Since these based claims to élite status on examination success, and emphasized the morally distinct nature of superiors, reciprocal services and close involvement in subordinates' tasks were not widely regarded as important components of the managerial role.

Overall, then, the military-backed regime reinforced many of the pre-industrial features of Korean society and combined them with the state coordinated and directed pursuit of rapid industrialization. As a result, the dominant institutional influences on the Korean business systems include both pre-industrial attitudes and belief as well as the legacy of Japanese colonialism and post-war authoritarian state structures. Their major features are summarized in Table 6.2 along the lines of the analysis presented in Chapter 2 of this book. In exploring their linkages with the characteristics of the Korean business system listed in Table 6.1, these features can be further reduced to seven key influences that together help to account for its distinctive nature.

First, the pervasive insecurity of the merchant class during the *Yi* dynasty—and its low prestige in official circles—was reinforced by Japanese colonialism and the authoritarian post-war regimes. The high level of business dependence on personal connections with political leaders, and the traditional devaluation of formal legal institutions which was further intensified by their association in the twentieth century with the colonial regime, have engendered a low degree of trust in formal institutions and procedures for settling disputes.

Secondly, the combination of weak collective loyalties beyond lineages in

TABLE 6.2. Dominant institutional influences on the post-war Korean business system

The state
Dominant and risk-sharing state
Antagonistic to independent collective intermediaries
Strong formal and informal state regulation of markets

Financial system
State-dominated, credit-based financial system

Skill development and control system
Weak public training system; no collaboration with unions
State-controlled official unions
Weak occupational associations
Little institutionalized bargaining

Trust and authority
Low trust in formal institutions and procedures
Patriarchal authority relations

many Korean villages with the massive disruptions and uprootings of the twentieth century inhibited the development of commitments to broader organizational
units on a non-personal basis. While aristocratic lineages may no longer be critical for political and economic success, as they once were, they still form an
important basis for group solidarity and resources for mobilizing support (Janelli
and Janelli 1982), as the example of President Park's support for Poongsan corporation illustrates (C. S. Kim 1992). In this role they have become complemented
by groups formed around secondary-school class membership and common
regional backgrounds. Trust, cooperation, and loyalty in Korea remain largely
focused on groups constituted by predominantly ascriptive criteria and/or shared
collective experiences.

Thirdly, many characteristics of the pre-industrial patrimonial state buttressed
by Confucian ideology and ethics have continued into and through the twentieth
century (Jacobs 1985). In particular, the exercise of political authority remains
highly personal and relatively unconstrained by formal rules and procedures.
Constitutions and regulatory structures have frequently been changed by new
leaders and have typically not been seen as independent, autonomous institutions.
Relatedly, although Confucianism has been periodically rejected and denigrated
during the twentieth century as the ideology of the backward *Yi* dynasty, parts of
Confucian doctrine have also been used by both the Japanese regime and post-
war governments to buttress their authority (K.-o. Kim 1996; Robinson 1991).
The military-backed regime, in particular, alternately attacked Confucian indo-
lence and the prestige of the state bureaucracy while urging adherence to
Confucian norms of obedience to authority and acceptance of hierarchy.

Similarly, the Confucian emphasis on moral worth and leading through exemplary behaviour remains an important part of the Korean political culture at the
same time as Koreans are urged to be enterprising and competitive. This has
fuelled attacks on the *chaebol* owners, as they have become more powerful
(Eckert 1993). More broadly, Confucian values have encouraged widespread
belief in education (Cumings 1997: 59–61), especially in the humanities, as the
primary means of economic and social success, a strong preference for white-
collar, generalist, jobs—particularly in the state bureaucracy (Evans 1995: 51;
Moon 1994), and an emphasis on family solidarity and kin-based identity (Janelli
and Janelli 1982; Sorensen 1988). In general, then, the prevalent system of political authority and the legitimation of power can be described as one of remote
paternalism.

Fourthly, the post-war Korean state has clearly been a strong state dominating
the economy, as did its Japanese predecessor, especially since 1961. While the
chaebol may have become too large and economically important to treat as
simple subordinates, there is no doubt that the pattern of post-war economic
development in Korea has been dominated by the state and that business dependence on the political and bureaucratic élite has been high (Eckert 1993; Evans
1995; Moon 1994; Woo 1991). This dependence has, of course, been reinforced
by the fifth institutional feature: the high level of state commitment to economic

development and sharing of investment risks with private business. This became especially strong after the 1961 military *coup* and the state-directed development of heavy and chemical industries in the 1970s. A major instrument of this state direction has been the state-owned and controlled banks that channelled cheap loans to favoured *chaebol* and industries. Essentially, the whole financial system in the post-war period can be considered to be subservient to the political executive and its pursuit of economic development.

Sixthly, the modern Korean state has systematically followed the example of the colonial regime in repressing and strongly controlling labour organizations. As a result, unions have been weak and dominated by state agencies, where they have existed at all, at least until the late 1980s (Deyo 1989; C. S. Kim 1992). Labour relations have been firmly controlled by employers, often in conjunction with the authorities, and collective workforce negotiation remains regarded by most owners as an affront to their patriarchal authority (Eckert 1993). Finally, manual and technical skills have not been highly regarded or developed by a strong public training and certification system. The educational system remains primarily focused on academic success rather than practical competences, so that employers typically recruit on the basis of general educational qualifications and then train staff on the job as and when required (Janelli 1993; C. S. Kim 1992).

These seven key influences together help to explain the bulk of the characteristics of the post-war Korean business system listed in Table 6.1. For example, the combination of a strong authoritarian state, high levels of business dependence on political leaders and historical patterns of insecurity among merchants and entrepreneurs, low degrees of trust, and informal institutions of non-kin collective loyalty, together with traditionally patriarchal authority relations, encouraged high levels of owner control and of centralization within leading firms. Similarly, the willingness of the strong state to share major investment risks in new fields with particular businesses, and to punish those which do not support it, helped to produce large, fast-growing, widely diversified firms which focus on vertical relationships with the state rather than horizontal alliances within and across industrial sectors.

These combinations and their multiple consequences suggest that the interdependences between institutional influences and business-system characteristics could be further summarized by reducing the latter to a smaller set of three inter-related features. For instance, strong owner control is connected to high centralization of decision-making and control and a reluctance to become dependent on employees. Similarly, the high level of ownership-based vertical and horizontal integration is linked to strong growth goals, rapid movement into new areas of activity, and considerable separation of firms from each other, with relatively low levels of non-ownership coordination and cooperation. Thirdly, low levels of employer–employee interdependence and trust are connected to close supervision and control of narrow, circumscribed tasks, together with remote superordinates who are not particularly constrained by formal rules and procedures. These features are summarized in Fig. 6.1, together with their critical links to dominant institutions that will now be briefly discussed.

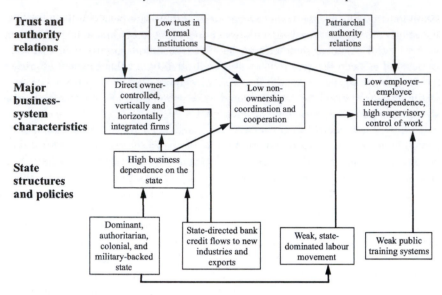

FIG. 6.1. Interdependences between institutions and the post-war Korean business system

The diversification and self-sufficiency of the leading *chaebol*—in terms of controlling ancillary upstream and downstream activities through managerial hierarchies—are linked to low levels of inter-firm collaboration as the result of the combination of the strong state pursuing rapid heavy industrialization with considerable distrust and insecurity. The dominance of political risks and state emphasis on industrial exports, followed by the move into heavy and chemical industries, encouraged the *chaebol* to diversify into new industries, both to retain political support and to reduce the risks of failure in particular sectors.

Additionally, by using state-subsidized credit to grow fast, they were able to become very large—and hence less vulnerable to state domination—without losing control through equity dilution. Given the pervasive insecurity of the entrepreneur in Korean society, and the lack of institutional mechanisms for generating trust and loyalty beyond the lineage, or similar personally based groupings, long-term obligations and alliances between firms are difficult to develop and maintain so that growth has been managed internally by *chaebol* owners rather than through extensive networks and business groups as in Japan (see e.g. Hamilton *et al.* 1990; Orru *et al.* 1989). The overweening power of the central state likewise prevented the establishment of powerful intermediary institutions to coordinate economic activities within and between sectors. The Korean 'vortex' (G. Henderson 1968) funnelled energies and resources towards the centre at the expense of private intermediaries.

The critical importance of political risk and insecurity also helps to explain the continuance of family ownership and control, high internal centralization and integration. Since the growth and success of the *chaebol* have been highly dependent on political support and access to subsidized credit, they have had to be able to respond quickly to changes in political priorities and shift resources into new areas. This encouraged centralization and integration. Furthermore, since power and authority are more personal rather than formally rule governed in Korea, and those in power retained considerable personal discretion over decision-making and resource allocation, in what Jacobs (1985) characterizes as an essentially patrimonial system, it is the personal connections between the *chaebol* owners and the President that were especially important in maintaining *chaebol* growth. Also, the major role of the *chaebol* in funding political campaigns encouraged personal control over their top management. Again, the difficulty of establishing long-term trust relations outside kinship or similar groupings in Korea inhibited the delegation of control to non-family managers in the *chaebol*, and this was reinforced by the importance of personal superior–subordinate relationships in authority structures.

Thirdly, *chaebol* owners did not have to develop long-term labour strategies for eliciting commitment and loyalty from their workforce because of the availability of unskilled labour and weak or non-existent unions. This latter feature was, of course, ensured by long-standing state control over, and repression of, the organized labour movement, together with the inability to tolerate intermediary institutions organizing commitments and loyalties in Confucian Korea. Again, the difficulty of establishing reliable long-term trust relations and collective commitments beyond kinship and similar groupings prevented the generation of 'Japanese-style' employment policies in the *chaebol*, despite the apparent wish of some car workers in Hyundai for them (Bae 1987).

Traditional conceptions of authority and subordination also help to explain the considerable distance between superiors and subordinates in Korean businesses and the authoritarian nature of managerial authority. This was reinforced by the lack of a strong labour movement and the authoritarian nature of the state, during both the Japanese occupation and the military-backed regime since 1961. Additionally, the weakness of formal rules governing the exercise of power and continued emphasis on the personal discretion of leaders limited the need of managers to justify their authority or involve subordinates in decision-making processes.

Confucian disdain for technical skills and specialized expertise in Korea (G. Henderson 1968; Jacobs 1985: 182) encouraged the pursuit of general academic qualifications at the expense of practical competences and limited the state's investment in technical training and certification institutions. Together with the low prestige of manual work—and the considerable supply of unskilled workers from the land in post-war Korea—this enabled employers to pursue segmented employment policies which limit the 'white-collarization' of manual workers in the Japanese mode (Koike 1987). Additionally, of course, traditional attitudes to female employment and careers buttressed the high levels of differentiation between male and female employment conditions in Korea (Janelli 1993; Michell 1988).

Overall, then, we can explain the dominant characteristics of the post-war Korean business system in terms of the combination of certain features of pre-industrial Korean society with particular features of the industrialization processes under Japanese rule and post-Korean war regimes. Despite the upheavals of the colonial period and the Korean War, many continuities in the operation of the political system and of cultural conventions have been maintained and substantially affected the nature of firms, their interrelations, and their internal structures and practices. In particular, the high level of political centralization, and the low degree of formalization of authority relations and of institutionalized trust, remained important features of Korean society that have strongly influenced the sort of business that became established. Some of these features are also found in Taiwan, but there are also significant differences that have resulted in a different kind of business system being developed there.

INSTITUTIONAL INFLUENCES ON THE TAIWANESE BUSINESS SYSTEM

Perhaps the most important feature of Taiwan's industrialization since the end of Japanese colonialism in 1945 has been the large-scale movement of the Chinese Nationalist government and its followers to Taiwan in 1949 following its defeat in the civil war. This take-over of Taiwan by Chiang Kai-shek and the Kuomintang (KMT) not only effectively created a new state but also established a major division in its population between the 6 million or so Taiwanese and the 1–2 million 'mainlanders' that had major consequences for the organization of the economy and control over economic activities.

In particular, it resulted in the exclusion of most Taiwanese from the state bureaucracy and political leadership as well as from the management of the large publicly owned industrial sector (Gold 1996). It also entrenched a large, linguistically distinct group as the ruling élite that claimed its authoritarian rule was justified by its imminent invasion of the mainland and reassertion of its authority over the whole of China. This domination of Taiwan society by outsiders continued the pattern established by the Japanese occupation in which the indigenous population learnt to obey and fear their rulers, and to develop economic activities within the context and framework established by an external power. Although, then, post-1945 Taiwan is a Chinese state, which has also had important consequences for its business system, it is a divided society and has developed a divided economy.

Before we consider this point, and the broad pattern of post-war development in Taiwan, in more detail, it is necessary to highlight two important features of pre-industrial Taiwan. First of all, it was quite different from Korea and Japan in never establishing a separate, distinct political system. The Manchu Ching dynasty gained control of Taiwan in 1683 from the retreating remnants of the previous Ming dynasty and made it a prefecture of neighbouring Fukien province. During the seventeenth and eighteenth centuries there was considerable immigration from the Chinese mainland, and the original inhabitants were pushed into the mountains from the more productive coastal plain. Patterns of land tenure and use became similar to those on the mainland, and a distinct gentry, landowning class developed with links to state officials and oriented to Confucian ethical norms and values.

However, the growing influence of the Western powers in the nineteenth century, and consequent development of trade in primary products, was more marked in Taiwan than on the mainland and its economy became more commercialized as a result (Gates 1987: 35–7; Gold 1986: 23–31). In 1895 Taiwan was ceded to Japan after the Sino-Japanese War and it remained a Japanese colony until the defeat of 1945. Thus, autonomous national political institutions and élites did not develop in Taiwan, and administrative and political structures before 1895 were basically similar to those elsewhere in late Imperial China.

Secondly, the incorporation of Taiwan into China and the growth of immigration from the mainland meant that by the nineteenth century Taiwanese society was essentially Chinese in all important respects, albeit rather more commercialized and less dominated by state officials than much of the mainland. Landlords and merchants were probably more powerful in Taiwan, and many Taiwanese engaged in waged employment or small-scale commerce and industry, but the Confucian ethical system had come to play a dominant role and especially its focus on the family. As Gates (1987: 104) puts it: 'the coincidence of kinship ties, economic advantage, and the Chinese state's age-old tendency to treat families as primary social units makes families central to Taiwan's culture ... Chinese strongly value, idealize and identify with their families.'

The great significance of the Chinese family as the basic unit of economic action and consumption, together with its distinctive authority structure, is an important element in the development of Taiwanese society and its business system, as many authors have emphasized (e.g. Gates 1987; Greenhalgh 1988; Hamilton 1997; Hamilton and Kao 1990; Silin 1976). In particular, traditional patterns of subordination and obedience within families, and acceptance of the overriding authority of the father, in accordance with Confucian doctrines, remain influential in Taiwan and structure authority relations within family-owned businesses. Thus the model of the ideal Chinese family as a patrilineal patriarchy remains important and serves as an idealized foundation for superior–subordinate relations in firms (e.g. Silin 1976).

Another important feature of the Chinese family that has affected the Taiwanese business system is the practice of equal male inheritance, coupled with the strong preference for self-employment over working for someone else (Wong 1985, 1988). Whereas Korean inheritance practices gave more of the family assets to the eldest brother—together with responsibility for carrying out ancestor worship rituals and other duties associated with maintaining the status and honour of the family—the Chinese pattern divides up the estate equally between the sons, each of whom frequently start their own businesses (K.-o. Kim 1996). To quote Gates again (1987: 77): 'the values of small business families permeate the rest of the working class. The desire for the independence and social mobility that small businesses make possible motivates the traditionally frugal, savings-conscious, hard working lifestyle of traditional Chinese families.' Thus, it is rare for large Chinese family businesses to survive more than two generations, as the centrifugal forces of equal inheritance and the desire of each son to establish his own patriarchal household business encourage fragmentation (cf. Tam 1990).

The importance of the family in pre-industrial China was reinforced by the Confucian state's unwillingness to tolerate broader units of collective action and resource control and, in particular, to allow large-scale concentrations of wealth owned and controlled by private interests to become established (Beattie 1979; Hall 1988; Jacobs 1958; Mann 1987). Families were regarded as the basic building block of society, whose organizing principles governed relations between them and the central state, to which household heads owed their loyalty, without any intermediaries such as feudal lords serving as focuses of loyalty and commitment. Essentially, Chinese society was regarded as atomistic, with stability ensured through strict and stable authority relations within families, on the one hand, and by the virtuous official élite maintaining harmony centrally by periodic visits, on the other hand. Additionally, central control was enhanced by making family fortunes dependent upon success in the official Confucian examinations. As King (1996: 232) puts it: 'The Confucian bureaucratic state had in effect prevented the emergence of civil society in China.'

Together with the increased commercialization of land tenure and use during the Ching dynasty, and the growth of the population which made competition for access to land more intense in the eighteenth and nineteenth centuries, this focus on the family and lineage at the expense of broader collectivities restricted social cohesion beyond family units and encouraged competitive relations between families within and between villages (Fukutake 1967; Jacobs 1958; Moore 1966). Trust and commitment are greatest within Chinese families as a result and decrease rapidly as proximity to the basic family unit reduces. In Pye's terms (1985: 70): 'the Chinese were taught to recognize a vivid distinction between family members, who could be relied upon, and non-family people, who were not to be trusted except in qualified ways.' Although cooperation among villagers from different families appears to have been greater in parts of Taiwan, largely for purposes of common defence during the nineteenth century (Gates 1987: 34), this basic pattern of distrust of non-family members—or of those with whom family-like links have been established (Hamilton and Kao 1990)—still seems strong in Taiwan (e.g. Kao 1991; Numazaki 1991).

An important feature of Taiwan's development was the Japanese occupation from 1895 to 1945. While perhaps not as brutal as that of Korea (McNamara 1986), it developed the economy to produce agricultural products—especially rice and sugar—for Japan and sought to assimilate the Taiwanese landowning class into Japanese society (Gold 1986: 34–45). Substantial investments in physical infrastructure were made to improve agricultural productivity, so that Taiwanese exports could support Japanese industrialization while most manufactured goods were imported from Japan, thus reorienting trade away from China towards Japan through the Japanese trading companies. The social infrastructure was also improved by making elementary education compulsory for the Taiwanese and so developing basic literacy and related skills as well as indoctrinating them in loyalty to Japan.

As in Korea, the Japanese severely restricted opportunities for advancement for the native Taiwanese, especially in the developing industrial sector. With the exception of a few landowning clans who were licensed to set up sugar mills and some trading companies, most Taiwanese remained in agriculture and petty commerce and Japanese dominated senior and middle management posts in most organizations (Numazaki 1992). When broader industrial development was encouraged during the late 1930s as part of the general militarization of the Japanese economy, it was firmly directed and controlled by the Japanese and no distinct Taiwanese industrial bourgeoisie became established (Gold 1986: 43–5).

However, it is important to recognize that the Japanese occupation did not remove the peasantry from the land—although it did increase land taxes and the effectiveness of their collection—but rather improved their productivity through infrastructural investment and upgrading agricultural inputs. Additionally, such industrial development as did occur was diffused through much of the island rather than being concentrated in a single, small area, so that most Taiwanese were connected to the relatively modern part of the economy, albeit as subordinates. At the time of retrocession to China in 1945, Taiwan had developed considerably as a productive, agriculturally based economy with better infrastructure and resources than mainland China (Wade 1990: 74). Indeed, many of Gates's (1987) working-class respondents looked back on the Japanese occupation as a period of order and stability in which rules were enforced and officials were firm but relatively fair.

After the departure of the Japanese, the Chinese Nationalist government treated Taiwan as a colony to be plundered as part of its civil war against the Communists. It then liquidated the bulk of the Taiwanese élite in the aftermath of the riots of 28 February 1947 (Gold 1986: 50–2). As a result, they became seen as an external occupying force little better than the Japanese, and in terms of their efficiency and orderliness considerably worse (Gates 1996). However, after their defeat and removal to Taiwan in 1949, Chiang Kai-shek and his followers eventually developed different policies to those that they had pursued on the mainland (Gold 1996). In particular, they implemented substantial land reform once the US government had decided to support the new regime in Taiwan and prevent its takeover by Mao after the start of the Korean War in 1950. This land reform redistributed most of the productive land to small owner-farmers and destroyed the bulk of the landlord class as an economic force, although some of the larger ones became significant investors in industry and finance (Gold 1986: 65–6).

By destroying much of the urban élite and dispossessing landowners, the KMT had few, if any, Taiwanese opponents to its authority and could pursue its objectives with little fear of organized dissent. The new regime constituted, then, a strong and authoritarian state that controlled the bulk of the Japanese-owned enterprises and dominated the economy (Chu 1994). However, its primary objectives at first were more concerned with maintaining its own control over Taiwanese society and revitalizing its military machine in order to attack the mainland rather than the long-term economic development of Taiwan. Partly as a result, it retained ownership and control of the bulk of the Japanese-owned enterprises and adopted an import substitution policy to improve self-sufficiency in manufactured goods as well as building up its capability in defence-related industries. In Gates's (1996) terms, it remained an essentially tributary state

Bolstered by US aid and military support during and after the Korean War, the regime became more secure during the 1950s and subsequently began to develop longer-term developmental policies that involved the promotion of the textile industry and the further encouragement of agricultural and processed food exports. However, most of the beneficiaries of these policies were mainlander families who had accompanied Chiang Kai-shek in 1949 and the larger Taiwanese landlords who had retained the government enterprise bonds given in exchange for land redistribution and invested in the new state-supported industries (Gates 1996: 221–5; Gold 1986: 67–73, 1988; Winckler 1988).

The lack of trust between the KMT and its mainlander followers and the Taiwanese, together with the military objective of retaking control of the mainland, which justified the continuance of martial law and the authoritarian state— at least in the eyes of the leadership—resulted in the state maintaining ownership of the larger, upstream, and capital-intensive sector of the economy, although the public-enterprise share of manufacturing production fell from 56 per cent in 1952 to 44 per cent in 1960 to 21 per cent in 1970 (Wade 1990: 88). This ownership extended to the banks and the bulk of the formal financial sector, and enabled the regime to provide jobs for its followers as well as influencing the development of the small-firm, Taiwanese-dominated export sector.

Additionally, many state officials and leading KMT politicians continued to regard the establishment of large privately owned concentrations of economic resources with considerable suspicion and a potential threat to their power, and so were reluctant either to privatize state enterprises or to encourage large Taiwanese firms to develop independently of the state (Gold 1986, 1988). This view was partly legitimated by Sun Yat-sen's economic philosophy, which emphasized the need for strong state tutelage of the economic system through state ownership and control of the banking system and heavy industry. Concentration of capital in private hands was regarded by Sun as a source of misery, but small enterprises were thought appropriate for private ownership (Wade 1990: 257–8). As the regime's legitimacy became more tied to economic development and its likelihood of invading China more obviously unrealistic, it became more systematically engaged in managing industrialization, but retained strong state direction of this process and preserved its control of the capital-intensive sector (Chu 1994; Cumings 1987; Haggard 1990: 88–94).

The traditional Chinese leaders' concern with limiting the power of private wealth holders, exacerbated in this case by the ethnic divide between the Taiwanese and the mainlanders, was expressed strongly in the conflict over liberalization of the economy and movement to a more export-oriented policy at the end of the 1950s. As Gold reports (1986: 77): 'many officials still disliked businessmen, and these (reform) policies would further the state's retrenchment from the economy and grant even greater rein to private capital. This would entail concentration of capital, something that Sun Yat-sen opposed.' However, more for political reasons than for economic ones, coupled with strong US pressure (Barrett 1988; Haggard 1990: 90–3; Wade 1990: app. B), Chiang Kai-shek supported the reform group in 1958, and Taiwan adopted a more liberal, though still state-dominated, approach to economic management.

This boosted the largely Taiwanese-owned export-oriented sector and confirmed the distinctive division of the political and economic system between mainlanders and Taiwanese. The former dominated the military, the political system, the bureaucracy, and the state enterprises, while the latter concentrated on building up family businesses in export-focused light manufacturing and commerce (Gold 1996). Although this division became attenuated in the 1980s as the proportion of mainlanders declined and economic growth increased the regime's security, it remains a distinctive feature of Taiwan's society and has had major consequences for the business system that has become established.

The KMT domination of the economy was different from that of the military-backed regime in Korea, in that it concentrated more on state ownership and control of tariffs, import licences, etc., than on direct control over the flow of credit to privately owned firms. Although the formal banking system in Taiwan has been owned and controlled by the state since the war, the regime has not used this control to direct the flow of capital to favoured private firms pursuing state priorities. Rather, it has been more concerned to prevent the growth of large Taiwanese enterprises that had close links to major banks and so has enacted legislation that prohibits banks from owning shares in borrowers' companies or forming holding companies that combine industrial and financial businesses (Wade 1990: 264). In general, the banks prefer to lend to the state enterprises and the largest privately owned firms that have good mainlander connections, since the risks are lower and function more as arms of the bureaucracy than as risk-sharing supporters of industry. Indeed they are popularly regarded as little more than pawnshops (Fields 1995; Wade 1990: 163).

As a result, the bulk of the firms in the export-oriented sector rely more on the informal 'curb' market and capital from family and friends for growth funds than on the formal banking system. This is especially true of the smaller and newer enterprises that have little or no collateral to support their applications for bank loans (Shieh 1992). As a result, most Taiwanese firms have to pay exorbitant rates of interest—often 50–100 per cent higher than bank loan rates in the 1970s—

and/or mobilize personal networks to raise capital. Additionally, since the banks are regarded as part of the state apparatus, many Taiwanese are reluctant to rely on them to a great extent and prefer to rely on informal means of obtaining credit. Consequently, informal, personal networks of trust and support are crucial to firms' survival and growth in Taiwan, and the development of large-scale capital-intensive industries is difficult without strong state support (Greenhalgh 1988; Wade 1990: 160–5).

The regime's antagonism to large privately owned enterprises that are independent of the state—buttressed by references to Sun Yat-sen and sharpened by the ethnic divide—has prevented long-term collaboration between the state and large-scale private interests, except in a few cases, such as Formosa Plastics. Instead, the private, Taiwanese-dominated part of the economy has been largely treated with official disdain, and relations between state officials and Taiwanese businessmen are often described as 'cool' and 'distant' in contrast to those between officials and the leaders of publicly owned enterprises (Chu 1994; Wade 1990: 274–6). As a result, the degree of direct dependence on the state of most Taiwanese businesses is limited, and the state has found it difficult to gain the cooperation of firms in a particular sector when it did want to achieve a specific objective through collaboration. This is exacerbated, of course, by the large number of small firms in most sectors and the traditional distrust of the regime and its agents (Greenhalgh 1984, 1988).

As in Korea, the Confucian emphasis on education has resulted in high rates of private and public investment in education. However, the exclusion of the Taiwanese from leading positions in the bureaucracy has meant that the private sector has been more attractive to college graduates than might be expected. Additionally, engineers have become a well-paid and prestigious group in Taiwan, and the state has invested heavily in technical training schools and colleges since the 1960s, so that the pool of highly skilled technically qualified labour in Taiwan is quite high. This is especially so in electrical and electronic engineering (Chou and Kirkby 1998). In the 1980s the universities graduated 70 per cent more engineers per head of the population than did those in the USA (Wade 1990: 64–6). Unlike Korea, then, there does not seem to be a surplus of liberal arts graduates in Taiwan, which may also be a consequence of engineers dominating the economic and planning bureaucracy for much of the post-1949 period (Wade 1990: 217–20). Although university education remains highly prized and competition to enter universities is highly competitive, traditional literary qualifications and official positions are not as highly regarded as in traditional Chinese society.

State control over the labour movement has been strongly enforced, as in Korea. The KMT maintained firm control over unions for political as well as economic reasons and the right to strike was prohibited under martial law. In addition, the combination of the strong preference for family entrepreneurship, close rural–urban linkages, and the relatively decentralized nature of industrial development throughout much of Taiwan has restricted the development of large concentrations of urban workers wholly dependent on employment. This, in turn, has limited the formation of a self-conscious working-class movement that could exert pressure on employers and the state (Deyo 1987, 1989).

Furthermore, the predominance of small to medium-sized family-controlled businesses, in which traditional conceptions of paternalistic management remained important, has inhibited the growth of unions, since they threaten the personal authority of the owner and the personal ties of obedience to him (Silin 1976). The significance of personal relations and foundations of trust in Taiwanese society limits the establishment of formal collective organizations representing workers' interests in favour of personal obligations and commitments. Skill-based occupational identities and organizations are similarly not important in Taiwan.

Overall, then, the dominant institutions in Taiwan during its industrialization combine some features from pre-industrial society—such as the strong identity with, and loyalty to, the family—with a number of quite distinctive features resulting from Japanese colonialism and the imposition of KMT rule after the war. These are summarized in Table 6.3, in a comparable manner to those listed in Table 6.2 for Korea. To explore their connections with the characteristics of the Taiwanese business system, these features can be further reduced to seven broad institutional influences that together help to account for its distinctive nature.

First, the state has been highly authoritarian and has dominated the economic system for most of the twentieth century. In this respect it is quite similar to Korea under Japanese occupation and since 1961. As a result, Taiwanese businessmen have been subordinated to the political and bureaucratic élite and have not developed as a

TABLE 6.3. Dominant institutional influences on the post-war Taiwanese business system

The state
Dominating state controlled by mainlanders; commitment to state-led development with little risk-sharing with Taiwanese firms
Antagonistic to independent collective intermediaries
Strong state control of upstream capital-intensive sectors, agriculture and new industries; low control of small firms in export sector

Financial system
State-directed credit-based financial system; limited state control of informal curb market in SME sector

Skill development and control
Stronger state technical training system for technicians and engineers than elsewhere in East Asia
State-controlled and repressed labour organizations
Weak occupational associations
Little institutionalized bargaining

Trust and authority
Low trust in formal institutions and procedures
Patriarchal authority relations

relatively independent business class. However, unlike Korea, the state has been dominated by an ethnically distinct group that has not encouraged the development of large privately controlled enterprises.

Thus, the second major institutional feature of Taiwan's industrialization has been the exclusion of most Taiwanese businessmen from access to power and the lack of large-scale risk-sharing by the state with the private sector. This combination of an authoritarian state dominated by outsiders and a lack of widespread cooperation between the state and private business led the Taiwanese to fear the power of the state, on the one hand, and to expect little assistance and understanding from it, on the other hand. Unlike the Korean *chaebol*, then, most Taiwanese firms have not, on the whole, developed close linkages to the political executive but rather remained distant from it and tried to make sure that they did not become too large and visible to the authorities and so become seen as a threat (Gold 1986: 88). Successful Taiwanese business owners preferred to set up a number of small firms connected through personal linkages rather than establish a single large enterprise that could excite the jealousy and anxiety of the mainlander élite.

The third major institutional feature is the low level of institutionalized trust between non-kin in Taiwanese society, together with considerable merchant insecurity, which is linked to the fourth major influence, the low levels of collective loyalty beyond kinship groups. While these phenomena stem from the traditional focus on the family and the lack of strong secondary institutions regulating relationships between non-kin in Confucian China, they have not been substantially changed by the process of industrialization in Taiwan, as the continued reliance on personal knowledge and reputations for organizing alliances and agreements shows (see e.g. Kao 1991; Numazaki 1992; Wade 1990: 269–70).

The considerable distrust of formal institutions, and the authorities controlling them, in China has been exacerbated in Taiwan by the experience of authoritarian rule by outsiders throughout the twentieth century and has led to an overwhelming concern with flexibility and limiting long-term commitments to business partners and employees. As a result, business networks are less permanent and stable than in Japan, and family firms prefer to develop alliances with a variety of different partners rather than become highly dependent on a small number. Similarly, political and economic risks are often managed by growing firms through opportunistic diversification into unrelated fields by establishing new subsidiaries run by family members. These firms are not usually formally integrated through a managerial hierarchy (Hamilton 1997; Hamilton *et al.* 1990; Numazaki 1992).

The fifth major institutional feature of Taiwanese society, the prevalence of remote paternalist patterns of authority, also derived from the traditional Chinese political system. The personal nature of leadership in Chinese society has been reinforced in Taiwan by the Nationalist emphasis on the dominant role of Chiang Kai-shek and the mobilization of commitment for military strength and, later, economic development (Wade 1988). The ethnic divide in Taiwan also limited the development of formal rules for regulating the use of power, since they could threaten the freedom of action of the KMT and its dominant position. As a result, the patriarchal and personal nature of authority in the Chinese family continued to dominate Taiwanese businesses, a phenomenon that has been reinforced by the difficulty of establishing long-term trust relations with non-family, and hence of delegating control to managers and relying on formal procedures.

This highly personal form of authority is, of course, also a result of the dominant Confucian legitimation of power, which stressed the moral superiority of leaders and hence the high degree of trust which could be placed in their personal integrity. This Confucian ethical system, and its justification of authority in the family and the state, has continued to be important in Taiwan, primarily through the Nationalists' reliance on the doctrines of Sun Yat-sen in their legitimating ideology (King 1996; Wade 1988, 1990: 234–46). This ideology justifies the tutelary role of the state in Taiwan and the wide discretion allowed to senior bureaucrats in managing the economy. As Wade (1990: 286) puts it: 'Those near the top of bureaucratic hierarchies are assumed to have reached their position by their superior knowledge and strength of moral character, which frees them from the constraints of formal law ... the imperial scholar-official tradition taught officials to feel superior to their business clients and to exercise leverage with them. Today's officials are descendants of that tradition.'

The emphasis on moral worth and superiority does, of course, imply a strong separation between leaders and the led, and a corresponding remoteness between superiors and subordinates in business where the dominant management style is seen as didactic, the business owner teaching wisdom and correct judgement through personal example and decision-making (Silin 1976). In this context it is not surprising that coordination and control in firms remain both personal and centralized.

The sixth major institutional feature of Taiwanese society to be discussed here is the weak labour movement and the lack of strong horizontal commitments and loyalties. As in Korea, unions and occupational associations have had little impact on skill development and standardization, and they have not affected the way work is organized and controlled in firms. Equally, state control over, and repression of, trade unions meant that business owners have not had to formalize employment procedures nor to elicit long-term commitments from employees, especially those to whom personal obligations are not due.

Finally, it is important to note that, while the public education system in Taiwan has produced large numbers of engineers over the past thirty years, and the appeal of technical subjects seems to have been greater then than in Korea, this has not been accompanied by the development of strong craft-based skills credentialled by public institutions that structure labour markets. As a result, Taiwan has had a large supply of school- and college-trained technical workers since the 1960s, but without their expertise being integrated into practical work processes by employers during training. How employers use these skills within firms has not, then, been constrained by specialized, publicly certified and standardized practical competences, but remains largely determined by individual firms' organization of tasks and on-the-job training. Consequently, the education and training system develops certified technical skills without standardizing jobs around them or institutionalizing highly specialized roles within firms.

These seven key institutional influences together account for many of the characteristics of the Taiwanese business system outlined earlier. As in the case of Korea, these latter can be further summarized as three general sets of characteristics of firms and markets in Taiwan which reflect, and are mutually interdependent with, these institutional influences. First, the high levels of owner direct control are combined with relatively limited levels of ownership-based vertical and horizontal integration in the economy as a whole, and very flexible firms in the export sector. Secondly, there is little long-term and stable non-ownership-based coordination and cooperation, although personal connections and networks help to mobilize investment funds and coordinate new activities in Taiwan. Third, employer–employee interdependence is typically low and coupled with low levels of worker discretion over task performance. The primary connections between these combinations of business-system characteristics and dominant institutions are summarized in Fig. 6.2 and will now be briefly discussed.

First, the close connection between ownership and strong, central, personal control of economic activities is a result of both traditional features of Chinese society that have continued to be significant in Taiwan, and the particular political system that has dominated since 1949. The difficulty of developing long-term trust relations and collective loyalties beyond the immediate family except on a highly personal basis, together with the personal nature of political authority

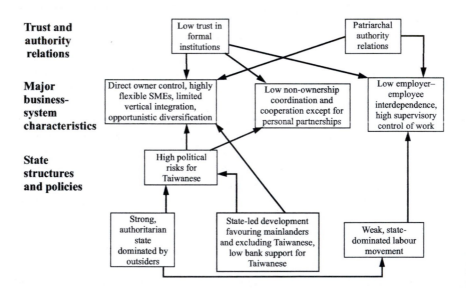

FIG. 6.2. Interdependences between institutions and the post-war Taiwanese business system

linked to the moral worth and superiority of leaders justified in terms of Confucian ethics reproduced through the education system and the Chinese family, encouraged the direct involvement of owners in the running of firms and reliance on personal ties in developing inter-firm agreements. Equally, delegation to non-family middle managers within firms has been discouraged by the lack of trust in formal procedures for ensuring control and the prevailing cultural emphasis on the personal qualities of the owner-manager (Silin 1976).

These features of Taiwanese society have been reinforced by the political insecurity and exclusion of most entrepreneurs from access to power throughout the twentieth century, and the widespread perception that large and autonomous integrated firms run by Taiwanese would be seen as a threat to the dominance of the KMT and hence subject to expropriation. The fear of political attack further intensified the pervasive insecurity of wealthy merchants in pre-industrial China, which encouraged considerable secrecy and a strong emphasis on personal trustworthiness in business dealings (see e.g. Godley 1981; Hamilton 1991).

Secondly, this insecurity and distance from the state also reinforced the traditional Chinese emphasis on flexibility and unwillingness to enter into long-term commitments, except on a highly personal basis. High levels of political and economic risks remain managed in Taiwan through limiting commitments to non-family, including employees, to whom personal obligations are not owed. Relatedly, interdependence between specialized firms is not here translated into long-term risk-sharing, as in Japan, because of the difficulty in developing trust and mutual commitment, and the unwillingness to rely on formal means of conflict resolution, especially those controlled by the state. The pervasive lack of trust also limited the scope, depth, and stability of partnerships and alliances, just as the fear of political and bureaucratic displeasure inhibited the development of vertical integration within sectors and encouraged opportunistic diversification across them, with reliance placed more on personal ties than as formal procedures for coordination purposes.

The strong focus on the family and pattern of equal male inheritance in Chinese society additionally encouraged the separation of growing family businesses into separate firms so that the sons could run quasi-independent entities without having to coordinate their activities formally. Additionally, the high level of population density in Taiwan, relatively low level of rural uprooting and disruption to established networks, and common ethnic identity among the Taiwanese all facilitated the development of effective reputational systems of control and monitoring of transactions.

Thirdly, the strong emphasis on flexibility in managing political and economic risks, combined with the difficulty of developing collective loyalties beyond the family, restricted the extent to which employers developed long-term commitments to employees, unless there were personal obligations to particular individuals or families. The lack of a powerful labour movement also reduced incentives to become interdependent with employees. This also meant that the traditional emphasis on the moral worth and superiority of political leaders, together with the remote nature of paternal authority in the Chinese family (cf. e.g. Gates 1987; D. Y. F. Ho 1986; Wolf 1970), encouraged a distant and didactic managerial style in private Taiwanese businesses.

THE KOREAN AND TAIWANESE BUSINESS SYSTEMS COMPARED

This discussion of the distinctive business systems that have become established in Korea and Taiwan since the end of the Second World War has highlighted both a number of strong similarities in the dominant institutions influencing business-system characteristics and some significant differences. It has also drawn attention to significant continuities in some institutions despite the upheavals of the twentieth century. In this concluding section I will summarize these and consider their implications for the comparative analysis of forms of economic organization.

It is quite clear from comparing Tables 6.2 and 6.3 and Figs. 6.1 and 6.2 that a number of important institutional features were, and remain, shared in twentieth-century Korea and Taiwan, and that these had major consequences for the kinds of business systems that have developed. In particular, the predominantly patrimonial character of pre-industrial Korea and China had a significant impact on the way industrialization developed in Korea and Taiwan, and continues to affect the operation of their political and economic systems at the end of the twentieth century. The heritage of strong and authoritarian government which repressed the development of intermediate organizations between the central state and families, and was intolerant of large privately owned concentrations of economic power, was reinforced by Japanese colonialism and continued to structure state–business relations during industrialization in both economies. As a result, business owners distrusted and feared political authority and have had to manage high levels of political risk. Additionally, the personal nature of patrimonial power has heightened the importance of direct personal commitments between entrepreneurs and the political and bureaucratic élite, as well as encouraging personal control of enterprises.

Relatedly, the strong emphasis on family identities and lineages found in both societies, together with the weakness of formal institutions for generating trust and reliability between non-kin, led to close owner control and involvement of family members in running firms, as well as a reluctance to delegate important decisions to outsiders or to rely on formal means of organizing transactions and connections between firms. Together with the traditional justification of political authority and pattern of family authority relationships, these legacies encouraged rather remote and distant managerial styles in firms with little sense of reciprocal obligations and responsibilities on the part of superiors, except where strong personal commitments have been established. However, the Korean War and the continued compulsory military service in Korea led to much greater formalization of hierarchical relationships in Korean enterprises than seems to be the case in Taiwan, as well as more insistence on military-like discipline.

Similarly, the combination of an authoritarian state, low trust in formal institutions, and state control of many markets limited inter-firm cooperation in both
economies. Although *guanxi* networks have been important informal means of
coordinating investments and organizing new activities amongst the Taiwanese—
to a greater extent than in Korea—these tend to be highly personal and limited in
stability and scope (Hamilton 1997; Numazaki 1992). Whilst business partnerships, then, seemed easier to form in Taiwan than in Korea, they were much less
stable and significant as economic coordination systems than inter-firm alliances
were in Japan (Fields 1995; Gerlach 1992).

Another common feature of the institutional context of Korean and Taiwanese
business systems has been the strong state control over organized labour as well
as the weakness of horizontally based collectivities and skill groupings. Together
with the weakness of public training systems for manual skills, these features
limited skill standardization and specialization, in addition to restricting
employer–employee commitments. These commitments have also been limited in
scope and degree by the difficulty of establishing strong loyalties to collectivities
beyond kinship groupings in both societies, partly because of their pre-industrial
patrimonial legacies, in contrast to Japan (T. C. Smith 1959; Whitley 1992a).

The major differences between the Korean and Taiwanese business systems
stem largely from variations in the nature and policies of the state, especially with
regard to the way in which industrialization was developed. These variations
affected the nature of political risks for firms and hence their responses (Fields
1995: 240–3). In turn, they arose from the contrasting circumstances in which
political leaders acquired power, variations in the patterns established by
Japanese colonialism, and the legacies of pre-industrial political systems.

The most important contrast between the processes of industrial development
in Korea and Taiwan was, of course, the level of state ownership and the related
willingness of the state to share risks with the private sector. In Korea the military-backed regime relied on the privately owned *chaebol* to industrialize the
economy rapidly and so manipulated their behaviour through a combination of
incentives and sanctions which led to large, hierarchically integrated, highly
centralized and diversified firms dominating the economy (Evans 1995; Jones and
Sakong 1980; Moon 1994). These enterprises managed political risks by culti-
vating strong personal links with the political leadership, using state-subsidized
credit to diversify into new industries and grow fast so that they became too
important to ignore or to be allowed to fail. They combined strong central control
with a high level of interdependence with the state that was eager for rapid industrialization.

In contrast, the KMT retained direct ownership and control of the
'commanding heights' of the economy in Taiwan and remained relatively aloof
from the large number of small and medium-sized Taiwanese firms. They did
not share risks with most of these firms and exerted direction of economic
development more indirectly than did the Korean state. As a result, most
Taiwanese managed political risks by remaining small, at least in terms of

public identity, and emphasizing flexibility over long-term commitments. In these respects they have followed the traditional pattern of Chinese family businesses (Hamilton 1991; Redding 1990). Interdependence between the state and most private Taiwanese firms has consequently remained low and diversification has been largely opportunistic, with limited vertical integration or formal integration of different activities. The distance between the KMT state and local entrepreneurs has reinforced the traditional preference for relying on family resources and personnel, together with personal links and obligations with business partners and distrust of more formal institutions.

These differences in the policies followed by the Korean and KMT states stem largely from the ways in which the post-1945 political leadership became established, together with some differences in the effects of Japanese colonialism. In Korea, the USA encouraged Syngman Rhee to sell the bulk of the Japanese-owned enterprises to private firms. In order to ensure a continued flow of funds for his political campaigns, he did this at low prices to his political allies (Haggard and Moon 1993). As a result, a quasi-autonomous group of private entrepreneurs had become established by the time the strong developmentalist military regime took over in 1961 and Park decided to achieve rapid industrialization through the state direction and coordination of the *chaebol* rather than by state ownership.

Conversely, the KMT was in many respects an external regime in Taiwan that had few or no indigenous élite groups with whom it had to compromise after the implementation of land reform. Equally, however, because of the ethnic divide between mainlanders and Taiwanese, it was unlikely to tolerate the establishment of a powerful Taiwanese business class and so did not encourage the growth of large indigenously controlled firms or share risks with them. Instead, industrialization, especially in the capital-intensive sectors, was achieved mostly through state firms managed by mainlanders.

Additionally, because of the important role of the Chinese peasantry in the civil war, and the perception that an important reason for the defeat of the Nationalist government was its identification with exploitative landlords (Wade 1990: 260), the KMT limited both the surplus extracted from the agricultural sector to fund industrialization and the movement of peasants off the land (Gold 1986; King 1996). The broad diffusion of agricultural improvements throughout Taiwan by the Japanese, and the consequent general growth in productivity, were matched by the decentralized nature of industrialization and the lack of a strong separation of industrial employment from agricultural work (M. Moore 1988). Small-scale industry developed throughout much of the countryside in Taiwan and the common availability of farming activities cushioned the consequences of market fluctuations, enhancing firms' flexibility.

Korean industry, in contrast, was more concentrated in urban centres and separate from farming households, both during and after the colonial period. As a result, agricultural workers who left the land tended to stay in factory employment and became more dependent on it (Sorensen 1988). The military-backed regime ignored the plight of rural households for some time and so encouraged the drift away from the countryside that generated a large pool of unskilled labour for the new industries. As C. S. Kim (1992: 191–2) suggests, this greater degree of rural 'uprootedness' in Korea compared to Taiwan has contributed to the higher levels of class consciousness and militancy among Korean industrial workers (cf. Deyo 1989).

In sum, although there were many commonalities between the import substitution and export-oriented economic policies followed by the authoritarian state in Korea and Taiwan (Cheng 1990; Cumings 1987; Fields 1995; Wade 1990), the particular way in which these policies were implemented in terms of business–state relations was quite different and as a result the nature of political risks and how these were managed by private firms varied also. The type of firm that dominated the industrialization process and its growth pattern in Korea and Taiwan followed contrasting logics as a consequence and so the overall configuration of firm–market relations in these two economies has developed in somewhat different ways, despite important similarities in some institutional features.

More generally, the development of both business systems highlights two important points about variations in forms of capitalism. First, there are significant differences in how state-led industrialization takes place, and these have important consequences for business-system characteristics. Secondly, both the processes of industrialization and the nature of dominant institutions in industrialized capitalist societies are shaped by pre-industrial legacies, and in that sense are path dependent. While frequently transforming key institutions of pre-industrial societies, both the nature of industrialization and the kinds of collective actors that play leading roles in it are greatly affected by the nature of these institutions (see e.g. Kristensen 1997).

In addition to the contrasting development of the post-war Korean and Taiwanese business systems demonstrating the variety of state-led industrialization patterns, and hence of resultant forms of economic organization, these two economies also highlight the significance of institutional and organizational pluralism. Unlike Japan, and much of continental Europe, pre-industrial and twentieth-century China and Korea had few, if any, independent collective organizations between the family and kin group, on the one hand, and the state, on the other hand. Civil society in the European sense was largely absent, as indeed it typically is in many twentieth-century industrializing societies. In particular, the private control of economic assets and the institutionalization of economic activities as an autonomous arena of decision-making and control were not tolerated by state officials before industrialization, and hardly so during it. In this respect, both the process of industrialization and the nature of the economic system that became established were quite different from those in Japan and Europe.

Tokugawa Japan, for instance, permitted merchant families to accumulate considerable quantities of wealth and to manage the economic system with substantial autonomy from the Shogunate (Hirschmeier and Yui 1981; Sakudo 1990). Additionally, the leaders of the feudal system delegated much more responsibility and power to the nobility and villages than did the contemporaneous Chinese and Korean scholar-officials (Jansen and Rozman 1986; Sato 1990; T. C. Smith 1959). They also did not identify élite status with moral superiority. Relatedly, Japanese industrialization was much less state directed than that in Korea and Taiwan, with considerable economic control decentralized to private families, most notably, of course, to those owning and controlling the *zaibatsu* (Allen 1981). While the militarization of the economy in the 1930s and 1940s undoubtedly increased central state control, the dominant pattern of state–business relations in Japan since 1868 has been more a matter of reciprocal consent (Samuels 1987: 8–9) than of state direction.

As a result, the Japanese business system has developed in quite different ways from those in Korea and Taiwan, particularly with regard to vertical and horizontal alliances between firms and collaboration between competitors (Orru *et al.* 1997; Whitley 1992*a*). As contrasting developments in Europe have also demonstrated, the extent of institutional and organizational pluralism before and during industrialization is, then, an important factor structuring the organization of economic activities in capitalist societies. Differences in this between the various state socialist societies of Eastern Europe have also affected the sorts of business systems that are emerging in these countries, as will be discussed in Chapter 8.

The second phenomenon highlighted by this comparison of Korea and Taiwan, as well as the contrast with Japan, is the continued importance of pre-industrial institutions and ideologies. As is also demonstrated by the continuing significant differences in economic organization across Europe, the institutional framework in which industrialization takes place has a major effect on how it does so, as well as on the nature of the leading actors involved, and of the resultant economic system (Whitley 1992*b*; Whitley and Kristensen 1997). It would be difficult to understand adequately the differences between British and French capitalism in the twentieth century, for instance, without an appreciation of the nature and policies of pre-industrial state agencies and financial institutions, let alone the contrasting patterns of political change, in those countries. The importance of pre-industrial institutions is even more marked when industrialization is as fast as it was in Korea and Taiwan, and as directed by the state.

Clearly, the organization of the industrializing state, its capacity to mobilize support and implement rapid economic and social change, and the beliefs and rationalities of those leading it, are all path dependent in the sense of reflecting pre-industrial political and bureaucratic arrangements, and their attendant legitimatory ideologies. The nature and capabilities of state actors during industrialization—as well as those of other collective actors—depend on their pre-industrial predecessors even as they transform them. The post-war Korean state, for instance, reflected both the experience and institutions of Japanese colonialism, as well as those of the Chosun state, at the same time as it was determined to overcome them. The differences between the business systems of Korea and Taiwan, and between both of these and that of Japan, in the post-war period are a product both of the particular state structures and policies of the past four or so decades and of the legacies of colonial rule in combination with certain features of their pre-industrial societies. Business-system characteristics, then, reflect industrialization processes and the nature of the institutions dominating them, but these in turn bear the mark of previous rules of the game and patterns of political and social organization and conflict.

7

Continuity and Change in East Asian Capitalisms

INTRODUCTION

The distinctive patterns of economic organization established in post-war Korea and Taiwan that were described in the previous chapter have been seen by some as changing significantly in the 1990s. In combination with the extended recession in Japan, the growing internationalization of Korean and Taiwanese firms, democratization, and other institutional changes have raised questions about the continued internal homogeneity and external distinctiveness of East Asian business systems. For example, the growth of intra-regional trade and investment in the 1990s (Chu 1995; Gangopadhyay 1998) and the increasing amount of Japanese and Korean investment in North America and Europe have encouraged suggestions that the nature and behaviour of firms in these societies are changing.

Additionally, the internal economic and political changes in many East Asian countries, together with shifts in the regional geo-political environment, can be seen as heralding substantial and systematic changes in the nature of East Asian capitalisms (see e.g. Clark and Kim 1995). The combination of increasing external interdependence and growing internal differentiation could encourage greater variability in organizational forms within these economies, on the one hand, and reduced contrasts between them, on the other hand. Finally, the financial crises of the late 1990s in some regional economies could be viewed as intensifying and extending these pressures for change.

These suggestions raise important issues about how distinctive and cohesive business systems change as a result of both contextual shifts and internal developments. Just as these systems of economic organization become established over time, reflecting particular struggles and historical circumstances, so too they develop and alter as their societal and international contexts change. The description and explanation of how distinctive business systems became institutionalized in particular market economies, such as those discussed in the previous chapter, need, then, to be complemented by accounts of how internal and external developments do, or do not, result in changes to them.

Rather than simply assuming that the growing internationalization of economic activities automatically leads to radical changes in business-system characteristics, for example, the conditions under which different forms of cross-national coordination are likely to generate substantial alterations in important aspects of economic organization need to be specified. In assessing the impact of recent changes in East Asia on the characteristics of the distinctive business systems in Japan, Korea, and Taiwan, then, it is important to clarify the circumstances in which they could alter particular ways of organizing economic activities. Especially critical here are the connections between 'internal' and 'external' pressures for change, and whether they typically reinforce or contradict each other in terms of the implications for business-system characteristics. In fairly cohesive and integrated societies, it seems improbable that external pressures on their own will effect significant alterations in political and economic structures in the absence of support from internal groups and institutions.

As outlined in Chapter 5, the growth of international managerial coordination of economic activities is likely to lead to qualitative changes in national systems of economic organization only when a number of quite strong conditions are met. In a similar way to the situation in Europe and elsewhere (Whitley and Kristensen 1996, 1997), it is not at all clear that the growth of outward FDI by East Asian firms, and of intra-regional trade, has been sufficient to meet the conditions required for large-scale transformations of prevalent business systems. Similarly, the undoubtedly significant internal changes in these societies over the last few decades have not obviously generated radical restructuring of their political economies, as the limited consequences of the Japanese political reforms of the early 1990s indicate.

In any event, the generally path-dependent nature of economic and social change implies that different kinds of political economies develop in contrasting ways, not least because the nature of dominant collective actors and their resources vary significantly. The organization and priorities of organized labour, for example, differ considerably between Japan, Korea, and Taiwan, and these variations can be expected to affect how they develop and act in the 1990s. Before assuming, then, that East Asian business systems are becoming more alike, let alone that they are developing Western characteristics, as the result of globalization and/or institutional changes, it is important to clarify how such processes might occur.

Accordingly, in this chapter I consider the conditions which would need to be present for the different East Asian models of capitalism to change their characters significantly as a result of (*a*) the growing internationalization of firms and markets, (*b*) changes in national political and economic arrangements, and (*c*) geopolitical shifts. A particular focus here is whether these alterations in the business environment are likely to generate qualitatively different kinds of economic organization, and if so how they will do so, as opposed to more evolutionary and gradual developments. The question being considered is not so much whether East Asian capitalisms are changing at the end of the twentieth century as whether these changes are resulting in fundamental alterations to their basic characteristics. Furthermore, if they are indeed changing significantly, does this mean that they are converging on a single 'successful' model or continuing to diverge in key respects?

First, I summarize the sorts of alterations in business-system characteristics that would imply qualitative changes in these varieties of capitalism. Secondly, I discuss the ways in which external and internal factors could generate such transformations. Next, I consider the relative importance of the external and internal changes that have taken place over the past decade or so in these economies, and finally I outline their likely consequences for the established business systems of Japan, Korea, and Taiwan. Essentially, I shall argue that the growth of outward FDI and institutional changes in East Asian economies, while important, have not yet resulted in the transformation of their post-war business systems. Rather, the differences in dominant institutions, interest groups, and patterns of economic organization across these societies have structured both internationalization processes and how political and other systems have altered such that current patterns of economic organization in East Asia remain both different and closely linked to previous ones.

BUSINESS-SYSTEM CHANGE

First of all it is useful to clarify the changes to the post-war Japanese, Korean, and Taiwanese business systems that would result in their transformation to new kinds of economic coordination and control systems. In terms of the comparative-business-systems framework outlined in the earlier part of this book, significant changes to dominant forms of economic organization in market economies imply the transformation of (*a*) ownership relations, (*b*) non-ownership coordination, and (*c*) employment policies and labour management practices. Considering initially the organization of ownership and control, radical shifts would mean the transformation of owner-control practices and of ownership-based vertical and horizontal integration. In the case of East Asian economies, this implies, first, that Japanese shareholders move either to direct control of 'their' firms, or to a more Anglo-Saxon 'market' form of control, and that Korean and Taiwanese owners become more distant from managerial decision-making and resource allocation.

Secondly, the extent of vertical integration of ownership units would have to alter considerably if the nature of the established business systems were to change. Japanese firms could, for example, incorporate their extensive *keiretsu* networks under their ownership, or, alternatively, might become much more specialized. Similarly, the *chaebol* might divest themselves of many suppliers and become more 'Japanese' in their organization of production chains. Finally, Taiwanese firms could integrate forward into export industries, and even backward into the state/KMT sector. Thirdly, the transformation of ownership relations would mean that horizontal diversification grew dramatically in Japan, declined in Korea, and became more 'related' in Taiwanese business groups—or that SMEs grew and diversified in the export sectors.

While some of these changes are clearly more likely to occur more readily than others, most imply considerable shifts in dominant institutions, especially in the structure and polices of the state and long-established norms and conventions governing trust and authority relationships. They are also quite interdependent and systemic, in that increasing, say, the degree of vertical integration within firms is clearly linked to the degree of non-ownership coordination, and diversification in general has strong implications for employment policies, as was discussed in Chapter 2.

Non-ownership coordination could similarly alter so that Japanese networks and alliances might dissolve, as many US trade negotiators would like, both vertically and horizontally. 'Alliance capitalism', in Gerlach's (1992) phrase, could become more Anglo-Saxon, or alternatively more like the post-war German pattern. On the other hand, radical change in Korea and Taiwan could mean the adoption of more Japanese-style groupings between customers and suppliers, business groups, and greater cooperation between competitors. Given the analysis presented in the last chapter, this would require substantial reductions in state dominance, encouragement of intermediary associations, and a significant growth in trust of formal institutions and procedures, as well as the development of institutions favouring collaboration, such as those common in much of mainland Europe.

Radical changes in employment and labour policies could mean the end of long-term employment commitments in large Japanese firms, as has been long heralded without actually arriving, as well as the development of such interdependencies between employers and the majority of employees in Korean and Taiwanese firms. They also imply the intensification of direct supervisory control over work performance in large Japanese firms—or alternatively their systematic Taylorization—and the delegation of much greater autonomy to manual and clerical workers in Korean and Taiwanese businesses. These sorts of changes seem most unlikely without major alterations to labour-market institutions and labour organizations, trust and authority relations. They additionally mean that the boundaries of firms and their stratification in terms of employment conditions, reward systems, and skill levels would change.

Similarly, major changes in employment policies and work organization among leading organizations and sectors are likely to be linked to shifts in strategic priorities, ways of dealing with risks, and the development of organizational capabilities, as was discussed in Chapters 3 and 4. For example, implementing 'scientific-management' labour-management strategies requires the following conditions. First, an ability to build up a managerial cadre that can be relied upon to systematize and control work processes in the interests of the owners. Secondly, to be able to apply largely formal and impersonal means of integrating and controlling organizational tasks and units in a predictable and stable manner. Thirdly, a large and relatively homogenous market for low-cost, standardized goods and services.

Equally, moving towards a more delegated responsibility form of work organization and labour-management strategy involves some risk-sharing with core workers, and this in turn is unlikely to occur without some ability to share risks and longer-term development with owners and/or suppliers and customers. Organizations and firms that remain islands of order in a sea of market disorder will find it difficult to delegate much responsibility for work performance and coordination to work groups because of their vulnerability to market changes and tendency to rely on numerical rather than functional flexibility. Major changes in prevalent ways of organizing work and employees are, then, unlikely without allied shifts in the nature of organizations, firms, and groups, although some innovation in working practices is, of course, feasible in countries where institutions are quite differentiated and pluralist, as the studies of 'Japanization' in Britain indicate (Wilkinson *et al.* 1995).

These sorts of significant, qualitative changes in business-system characteristics are dependent upon substantial institutional and/or international economic transformations, of the kind represented by the Allied occupations of Germany and Japan after the Second World War and by the collapse of state socialist regimes in Europe. Conceptualizing business systems as particular and distinctive forms of economic organization that structure and coordinate economic activities in specific, interrelated ways means that their change is a major socio-economic process requiring substantial changes in related institutions. Of course, some shifts in particular characteristics can, and do, take place frequently without affecting other ones greatly, but the interconnected nature of many of these phenomena means that altering some characteristics to the extent that they become quite different nearly always involves changing other ones, and this, in turn, is unlikely without significant contextual changes.

A few large organizations changing their employment policies, or firms developing technological alliances, do not, then, necessarily signify changes in the nature of a particular form of economic organization or its major components. For these to be significant they would have to represent qualitative shifts in the prevalent way of doing things such that new norms and institutionalized practices have replaced the previous ones. For leading Japanese *kaisha*, for example, to change their labour-management practices significantly they would have to develop new ways of recruiting, rewarding, training, promoting, and organizing their core employees—and of dealing with female and temporary workers—such that both employers' and employees' expectations about how major firms should behave had radically altered. While this is clearly possible, it is extremely improbable without major changes in state policies, family structures, and the education and training system, as well as in inter-firm relationships and, probably, firms' boundaries (Sako 1997).

In considering the conditions that might generate these sorts of large-scale shifts in business-system characteristics, it is useful to distinguish between those operating internationally, or across crucial institutional contexts and boundaries, and those mainly operating nationally, or within particular institutional contexts. This is especially useful in East Asia in the light of the strong state boundaries there since the war, and the periods of isolation in pre-industrial Japan and Korea. Accordingly, I first summarize the major changes in the international environments of these business systems that could affect their key characteristics, and then discuss how the important changes in their 'internal' political economies since the mid-1980s or so could be expected to impinge on their business systems.

In addition to the general increase in internationalization of competition and investment in East Asia, there have been three sets of geopolitical changes that can be expected to impinge upon their business systems. First, the considerable financial and military support provided by the USA at crucial stages of the economic development of these economies, especially through the Korean and Vietnam wars (Cumings 1997; Fields 1995; Woo 1991), has declined substantially. Relatedly, the willingness of the USA to open its borders to imports from East Asia without insisting on reciprocal access has, of course, come almost to a complete halt. The collapse of the Soviet Union further reinforced the declining importance of Japan's political support for US containment policies, which at one time was viewed as counterbalancing Japan's growing economic rivalry with the USA. As the crises of Pacific-Asian economies in the late 1990s have shown, the USA is increasingly insisting on widespread changes in the internal organization of many economies, as well as in trade relations, both directly and indirectly through multinational agencies such as the IMF.

These pressures can be expected to encourage shifts in particular business-system characteristics when they reinforce other tendencies and are allied to the priorities of powerful interest groups, or to those of new collective actors such as organized labour. They are unlikely to effect significant changes on their own, though, in the light of the considerable strength and cohesion of many national institutions in these economies. Where, then, the implications of changes in US policies and actions are reinforced neither by high levels of trade, financial, and military dependence on the USA, nor by the likely consequences of changes to dominant groupings and institutional arrangements, their impact on business-system characteristics will not be radical.

Secondly, the overall economic and military power of the USA in the region has declined as other economies have grown and increasingly compete on equal terms. While remaining the lone superpower and the largest national economy, the USA no longer dominates Pacific Asia as it once did. This means that its ability to impose its wishes on East Asian states is quite restricted, as is its capacity and commitment to defend them against external threats. Just as concerns about US support encouraged President Park to direct the *chaebol* into heavy industry in the 1970s, so too we can expect these shifts to increase national self-sufficiency and/or encourage regional cooperation in both economic and military matters. The latter tendency could encourage some coordination of financial policies, although this seems to be more discussed than implemented.

This relative decline in the role of the USA has of course been accompanied by the rise of China as a regional power, both economically and politically.

Together with the crisis in the North Korean regime, this may lead to greater instability in the region. In turn, that may encourage increased investment in military capabilities and emphasis on national security. Alternatively, Japanese, Korean, and Taiwanese firms may continue to invest in the coastal regions of China and seek to integrate these with their own economies. Either way, it seems unlikely that the growth of the Chinese economy will lead to radical changes in their distinctive national business systems, at least in the short term.

Thirdly, the very success of these economies, and their growing integration into the global trading system, have increased pressures on them to implement international trading norms and open their economies to foreign imports and FDI to a far greater extent than was the case in the 1960s and 1970s. The increasing importance of multinational agreements and agencies such as GATT, WTO, and OECD in establishing trading and investment rules and policing their implementation, together with their incorporation of the East Asian economies, could be expected to reduce the ability of state agencies to control imports and support targeted industries. This should reduce the degree of business dependence on the state in Korea and perhaps Taiwan, although the changes in the Japanese business system since the 1970s appear rather less dramatic than was expected earlier (Westney 1996).

Relatedly, the involvement of the IMF in managing the currency and financial crises of Pacific Asia has encouraged some Western observers to hope that 'real'—i.e. Anglo-Saxon—capitalism will now become established in these countries. However, the continuing variability of economic coordination and control systems in Western Europe despite long-standing membership of these agencies and European Commission attempts to standardize the rules of the game, suggests that resulting changes will not be radical, especially when they conflict with powerful institutions and interest groups (Whitley and Kristensen 1996, 1997). In any event, the ways that different élites and organizations deal with the IMF and the changing market environment reflect the distinctive nature of their business systems and societies, and so will vary considerably. Just as the different East European societies have responded differently to the political and economic collapse of the Soviet Union as a result of their contrasting state socialist legacies, so too will East Asian countries diverge in their response to the financial crises of the late 1990s.

Turning to consider how the growing international coordination of economic activities within East Asia and elsewhere is likely to affect the cohesion and distinctiveness of the Japanese, Korean, and Taiwanese business systems, I now discuss the implications of the analysis presented in Chapter 5 for these economies. There are three basic issues to be considered here. First, how outward investment and managerial coordination of activities in other economies might affect the nature and behaviour of East Asian firms. Secondly, how such changes of firms could alter particular characteristics of their domestic business systems. Thirdly, the ways in which foreign inward investment, both strategic and portfolio, could change these systems.

If Japanese, Korean, and Taiwanese firms are to change their distinctive characteristics—such as ownership control, the role of employees, collaboration, strategic priorities, and organizational capabilities—as a result of outward investment, six major conditions would need to be met, according to the analysis presented in Chapter 5. First, a high proportion, probably over a half, of their key assets, employees, and sources of profits would have to be located abroad. Secondly, these overseas assets would have to be concentrated in contexts that are both very different from their domestic ones and are highly similar to each other. For East Asian firms this would probably mean that the overwhelming bulk of their important investments would need to be in Anglo-Saxon-type economies.

Thirdly, these host economies would additionally need to be politically, economically, and technologically at least as advanced and powerful as the domestic ones. Fourthly, their business systems would also have to be as cohesive and integrated in their characteristics as the post-war East Asian ones, and to be as closely connected to equally integrated and mutually reinforcing societal institutions. In other words, firms investing in these economies have to adapt to their hosts' ways of doing things at least as much as they do in their domestic economies. Fifthly, these East Asian firms would need to integrate their overseas operations tightly with domestic ones so that, when they adapt to foreign institutions, these changes influence how they do business at home. Finally, any changes that internationalizing firms may implement as a result of their overseas commitments would be largely peripheral to their core characteristics, which are closely associated with dominant institutions and interest groups in their domestic economies.

As mentioned earlier, these conditions are quite strong and are not likely to be realized together on many occasions. In particular, given the cohesion of the post-war Japanese, Korean, and Taiwanese business systems, as well as their high degree of interdependence with major societal institutions, it seems rather unlikely that firms from these economies will locate the bulk of their key assets in economies that are even more cohesive. Equally, given the strong links between many of the distinctive characteristics of leading Japanese, Korean, and Taiwanese firms and dominant institutions and agencies in their domestic societies, condition six is not likely to be met very often.

Even if some firms from these countries did develop significantly different characteristics as a result of overseas investments, their impact on their home business system would depend on four further conditions. First, to change the prevalent form of economic organization, such firms would have to be significant in size and centrality to the business system. The leading Japanese corporations and the dominant Korean *chaebol* are examples of such firms. Secondly, they would have to have made major changes to their defining attributes and strategies. For example, relations between owners and managers in the largest enterprises would need to be radically transformed if the business system as a whole was to change significantly in terms of the organization of ownership relations.

These changes would need, thirdly, to be supported by important interest groups and élites if they were to make a marked impact on domestic business systems. Taiwanese banks with overseas subsidiaries that attempt to change aspects of the financial system in Taiwan, for instance, are unlikely to achieve very much in the absence of élite support for this part of the financial services industry and its growing influence in the economy as a whole. More broadly, we can emphasize that any qualitative change to the business-system characteristics of these economies is improbable without concomitant changes in the relative power of dominant interest groups and/or the establishment of major new élites representing new interests, such as organized labour (Evans 1995).

Finally, changing the prevalent conventions governing economic organization is obviously easier when central institutions and agencies' interests are not greatly affected. It is therefore more straightforward for British firms, for example, to alter labour-management practices than their financial strategies, given the greater power of capital markets relative to most trade unions in Great Britain. If, then, changing characteristics of leading East Asian multinationals are to affect their domestic business systems, they would need to be supported by other shifts in institutional structures and interest groups, and/or be limited to relatively minor changes. In sum, for outward FDI to have a significant impact on the distinctive business systems of East Asia, a considerable number of conditions that are unlikely to occur together have to be met.

Turning now to consider the possible effects of inward investment, I first discuss the impact of strategic investment by foreign firms that may increase over the next few years as a result of deregulation and IMF pressures. Again, this obviously depends on the relative magnitude of such investments compared to domestic ones. More important, though, are their provenances. Their influence on the host business system will be greater if they are dominated by firms from a different kind of business system. For example, if US firms had been able to dominate investments in the post-war Japanese economy, we would expect the business system there to have developed in quite a different way.

They are also more likely to affect business systems that are only weakly integrated and/or established, such as those in some developing countries, or where related institutions are fragmented and only weakly established. Multinational firms are thus more able to affect the shape of state–business relations, labour-market institutions, and other features of their environments in societies where the state is weak and/or still developing, or large-scale transformation is taking place, as in many of the former state socialist societies. Even here, though, their impact has been slower and less marked than expected, as the study of Hungarian firms reported in Chapter 9 shows (see, also, Whitley and Czaban 1998*b*).

Finally, where there is substantial foreign investment, its impact will be more marked in sectors that are peripheral to dominant interest groups and institutions. The influence of Japanese firms in the UK, for example, has been more significant in the electronics and vehicle manufacturing sectors, where it has been concentrated, than in the more powerful and successful financial-services sector. Even there, however, its impact has been rather less than is sometimes suggested (Elger and Smith 1994; Stewart 1996; Wilkinson *et al.* 1995).

As discussed in Chapter 5, foreign portfolio investment and increasing foreign ownership of domestic firms are likewise going to have major effects on host economy firms—and hence on business-system characteristics—only when the following three conditions are met. First, they are substantial relative to domestic shareholders. Secondly, they are concentrated in particular firms and sectors, and, thirdly, they come from business systems that organize ownership relations in quite different ways from the host economy. Highly diversified foreign share-holdings are unlikely to affect firm behaviour very much, especially when domestic owners have more concentrated holdings and if the dominant form of owner control is alliance or direct.

They are also going to be limited in their ability to impose their performance standards on firms if there is only a weak market for corporate control in an economy and/or owner–manager relations are strongly interconnected with powerful institutional arrangements and interest groups. Similarly, the impact of extensive foreign shareholdings on the business system as a whole may be much less than it is on particular firms if those firms are marginal to the economy and/or in sectors that are not regarded as central. In this connection it will be interesting to see how much influence the foreign portfolio owners are able to wield in countries such as Hungary compared to foreign firms that have taken over many large enterprises.

In the case of East Asia, where direct and alliance forms of owner control predominate and there is only a very limited market for corporate control, it seems unlikely that foreign ownership will generate much change in prevalent business systems, even if such shareholdings are considerable. Additionally, given the strong links between many large firms and the state and/or between firms in business groups, the ability of foreign shareholders to change attitudes and financial policies if they do build up a substantial ownership stake is likely to be severely limited, as Boone Pickens found in Japan. Overall, then, the effects of foreign ownership on host business systems in East Asia are likely to be quite restricted by the prevalent nature of ownership and non-ownership linkages and their close interdependencies with particular institutions.

DOMESTIC INFLUENCES ON BUSINESS-SYSTEM CHANGE

Considering next the sorts of national and regional changes which could alter some key characteristics of East Asian business systems significantly, I shall first discuss some general developments in these economies that could be expected to lead to changes in these characteristics and then analyse their major institutional developments. Among the most significant 'secular' changes that have either taken place in many of these economies over the past decade or so and/or will do so in the first years of the twenty-first century are (*a*) the gradual decline in growth rates as they become industrialized and 'mature', (*b*) the increasing complexity of the economy, (*c*) shifts in sector dominance that alter the balance of power between interest groups, and (*d*) the greater differentiation of demand (G. L. Clark 1995; Webber 1995).

In very broad terms, these changes herald the increasing autonomy of the privately owned and controlled economy from the state in many countries, and the intensification of market competition in both domestic and regional markets. While they will not happen immediately in all these economies—and indeed in some may not take place for some considerable time, owing to institutional pressures—macroeconomic phenomena in countries where industrialization has already been achieved on a substantial scale are clearly different from those where it is still rapidly taking place. The major consequence of these developments concerns business–state relations, in that the ability of state agencies, such as those in Korea, to direct business activities and strategies declines as leading firms become larger, and more experienced and knowledgeable about markets and technologies, as well as managing market risks internally. Business dependence on the state may well decline, at least in the largest and most successful enterprises, so that alliances and networks become more significant means of coordinating activities.

The extent of vertical integration may also decline as organizational knowledge and skills become more widely diffused in market economies, because firms can increasingly rely on suppliers to produce high-quality inputs at lower prices than they could themselves. As Langlois and Robertson (1995) have pointed out, market 'learning' often reduces the competitive advantages of vertical integration. Additionally, declining growth rates may alter firms' priorities and competitive strategies. Instead of seizing high-risk opportunities that promise fast growth in periods of rapid economic expansion, leading firms in more 'mature' economies may focus on improving the efficiency of existing operations and developing more specialized organizational competences. Opportunistic diversification may thus decline in favour of more technologically and market-related diversity. Entrepreneurial risk-taking in industrialized economies no longer dominates managerial efficiency to the same extent as in high-growth ones and firm-specific innovation capabilities can become more significant competitive advantages.

Furthermore, competitive price and quality pressures from imports and/or inward FDI could, when coupled with growing wage costs and better-educated workers' demands for improved conditions, encourage firms to search for new ways of generating growth. These might include: improving workers' skills, investing in new technologies, and/or moving production abroad (Webber 1995). Whether these changes lead to qualitative shifts in enterprise strategies and structures towards more innovative capabilities, or, on the other hand, encourage investments in cheaper production sites overseas where firms continue to compete predominantly on price, depends on parallel institutional changes. Indeed, all of these possible transformations of domestic business-system characteristics arising from successful industrialization depend greatly on the sorts of institutional changes that occur at the same time, especially in the fields of political competition, interest representation, and labour organization.

The importance of institutional factors in mediating the effects of macroeconomic changes highlights the general significance of institutional change in encouraging and guiding business-system change. If, for example, the structure and behaviour of the state radically alters, as in the former state socialist societies, we would expect significant changes in the nature of the economic coordination and control system, albeit over some considerable time period (Whitley and Czaban 1998*b*). Similarly, moving from a credit-based financial system to one dominated by large and liquid capital markets would greatly affect the nature and strategic behaviour of firms, as well as the organization of ownership relationships in general. However, these sorts of radical and far-reaching changes in dominant institutions are relatively rare in established market economies, except in cases of war and military defeat or internal regime collapse and/or revolution. Even in these circumstances, the long-term consequences of radical political–economic changes are strongly affected by institutional legacies and typically vary significantly from the intentions of their initiators, as the results of the SCAP reforms in Japan (Eccleston 1989: 8–28) and the transformations of East European economies illustrate.

Changes in the institutional features most connected to business-system characteristics are usually, then, more incremental and limited than radical and rapid. Their direct effects on broad patterns of ownership coordination, alliance integration, and employment practices are similarly likely to be incremental and restricted. The changing balance of power between private enterprise groups and the state in Korea and Taiwan, for instance, may signify a decline in the overweening dominance of the state in these economies, but it scarcely implies its transformation into a regulatory one (Chu 1995; Evans 1995). Neither does this reduction in state dominance seem likely to result in major shifts in patterns of owner control, inter-firm collaboration, or labour-management policies, at least not on its own and in the short term.

Additionally, institutional reforms and policy changes are often contradictory in their implications for business-system characteristics. For example, the combination of economic growth, educational expansion, and political democratization and liberalization might be expected to encourage some 'white-collarization' of manual workers—particularly the core group of skilled staff—and greater managerial efforts to develop employee commitment to employers, including more intensive training. Such shifts in prevalent employment and labour-management policies would, though, require supportive conventions governing the development of trust and loyalty among workers and managers, as well as the limitation of 'efficient' external labour markets. In practice, countervailing institutional pressures from the existing skill organization and control system, together with dominant cultural norms, may well limit the extent of such changes, at least in the short to medium term.

Similarly, the reduction of authoritarian political rule and the growth of successful private enterprises could herald a reduction in direct business dependence on the state. This may, in turn, assist the decentralization of control within enterprises, the separation of ownership from direct control over enterprise activities, and the development of more horizontal modes of economic coordination. However, these developments too require the existence of reliable means of ensuring formal and/or informal contractual compliance and minimal levels of trust and collective loyalty between groups, other than family-like ties and direct supervision. If not the 'rule of law', certainly some way of institutionalizing common standards of behaviour and realizing predictable common interests among business partners is required for them to become established. In the cases of the former state socialist societies, of course, these issues are even more critical, because of the delegitimation of the state and the substantial absence of established private business practices and linkages not dependent on state support.

These interdependences imply that radical changes to ownership relations and employment policies as a result of democratization and the legalization of unions should not be expected in societies where trust in formal institutions is low and authority relations are predominantly patriarchal. Similarly, state encouragement, or at least non-repression, of independent associations may not lead to an efflorescence of civil society, let alone extensive long-term and stable alliances between privately owned firms. The relative depoliticization of trade unions in, say, Korea will obviously take some considerable time, as will the establishment of new rules of the game governing capital–labour relations. How these processes develop, and the nature of the new governance structure that emerges, will reflect the existing organization of social actors and their ideologies as they compete for influence and resources in the new environment. Given the recent history of Korean labour relations, such competition is likely to be adversarial and conflictual.

In a similar manner, any reduction in state control over the formal banking systems of East Asia seems more likely to lead to an evolution of these financial systems along similar lines to the rest of the established business system than to radical changes in them. That is, in Korea the *chaebol* can be expected to include banks and other financial businesses in their octopus-like embrace (Moon 1994), and in Taiwan the established business groups are diversifying into financial services as one more opportunistic source of growth. The IMF's attempts to develop more Anglo-Saxon financial systems in the crisis-ridden economies of Pacific Asia are likely to be as unsuccessful as the similar SCAP reforms were in Japan.

Changes in skill development and control systems could lead to significant alterations in employment strategies and practices, especially if authority relations also changed. However, reforming public-training systems takes substantial time and effort, and is also long term in its effects. Similarly, developing centralized bargaining systems which mobilize the workforce sufficiently to enable agreements to be implemented effectively is not something that can be achieved overnight. Collaboration between employers, and with unions, is therefore unlikely to develop quickly, and certainly not in cultures where formal procedures are regarded as less reliable than personal connections.

The consequences of particular changes in dominant institutions for business-system characteristics, then, are interdependent with other features of the domestic business environment that may not change in consonant ways. Thus, the likely outcomes of institutional transformations in particular countries are quite situation specific and cannot readily be generalized across them. As can be seen in Europe, considerable variety in national political, financial, and labour systems can exist across a large number of 'mature', liberal democratic industrialized economies, and this variety has encouraged significant differences in certain characteristics of the business systems that have become established in different countries. These variations in turn have affected patterns of firm development and the ways sectors have adapted to technological and market challenges (Sorge 1991; Whitley and Kristensen 1996). There seems little likelihood, therefore, that newly industrialized countries (NICs) will follow the same path in response to these economic and institutional changes. Bearing this in mind, I now consider the major changes that have taken place in East Asia since the mid-1980s, and their consequences for the post-war business systems that have become established there.

CHANGES IN THE ENVIRONMENT OF EAST ASIAN BUSINESS SYSTEMS

First of all, I shall summarize the key changes that have occurred and could affect the nature of organizations, firms, and markets in the industrialized economies of East Asia—i.e. the four NICs and Japan. I then follow the analysis just presented to consider the likely consequences of these changes and their significance for the distinctive nature of the post-war business systems in Japan, Korea, and Taiwan, especially whether their key characteristics are changing.

The growth of internationalization of East Asian leading firms' operations in the 1980s and 1990s is well attested (see e.g. Dicken 1998; Emmott 1992). Not only have many Japanese firms invested heavily in North America and Europe—especially in cars and electronics; they have also—and over a longer period—established plants in many of the ASEAN countries (see e.g. Koike and Inoki 1990) and are now investing in China, Vietnam, and elsewhere in Asia. The largest Korean *chaebol* have more recently followed the same pattern and are now investing heavily in East and West Europe as well as the rest of Asia. Similarly, Taiwanese firms have invested substantial resources in South-East Asia, especially Penang, as well as in China (Chu 1995). However, Taiwanese investments in production facilities in Europe and North America have not, so far, been as extensive as those of the largest *chaebol*, let alone comparable to Japanese commitments.

Despite this growth of overseas investment from East Asia, the total amount of such outward FDI from Japan, Korea, and Taiwan remains quite limited as a proportion of GDP and of total investment. According to the 1996 *World Investment Report* (UNCTAD 1996), the outward flow of investment from Japan as a proportion of gross fixed capital formation in 1994 was only 1.4 per cent, down from 5.1 per cent in 1990, and from an annual average of 3.4 per cent in 1984–9. The equivalent figures for Korea were 1.9 per cent in 1994, 1.1 per cent in 1990, and 0.3 per cent in 1985–9, and for Taiwan they were 6.3 per cent in 1994, 15.0 per cent in 1990, and 9.6 per cent in 1985–9. Similarly, the total stock of overseas foreign investment as a proportion of domestic GDP in 1994 was only 6.2 per cent in Japan, 2.1 per cent in Korea, and 9.9 per cent in Taiwan.

These figures scarcely indicate a massive shift of assets to foreign locations by East Asian firms, let alone a wholesale transfer of their core operations to economies with quite different business systems and institutional contexts. According to Hirst and Thompson (1996: 93), no less than 97 per cent of the assets of leading Japanese multinationals were located in Japan in 1992–3, with only minimal proportions in North America or Europe. It is also worth noting that most of this outward FDI from Korea and Taiwan—as well as that from Hong Kong and Singapore—is driven primarily by labour cost-reduction strategies (W. B. Kim 1995), and has been predominantly located in less-industrialized economies. As Clark and Kim (1995) suggest, the bulk of the NICs' investments in China, as elsewhere in much of Asia, has been cautious, risk averse, and concentrated in small-scale, export-oriented, labour-intensive industries. Capital commitments in many of these countries tend to be limited in size, and pay-back periods are correspondingly short. In the words of one top manager of a Japanese multinational firm during an informal interview: 'we are renting space in China' rather than making major irreversible investments. The extent and location of outward FDI from these economies, then, seem unlikely to effect major changes in the characteristics of their leading firms or of their systems of economic coordination.

The openness of these leading East Asian economies to external investment, especially to international capital markets and foreign financial institutions, has been even lower. As Dunning (1993), among many others, has noted, the extent of inward FDI to Japan is much less than its outward FDI, and Korea and Taiwan have been similarly reluctant to permit large-scale foreign investment either in production facilities, except occasionally in export-processing zones and for specific industries, or in their financial markets (Haggard 1990). In 1994, for instance, the total stock of inward FDI expressed as a proportion of GDP was 6.6 per cent in Taiwan, 3.3 per cent in Korea, and only 0.4 per cent in Japan (UNCTAD 1996). Even if the role of foreign MNCs in manufacturing output is somewhat greater than these figures might suggest (Ramstetter 1998), East Asian domestic markets are scarcely dominated by foreign firms and their internationalization is considerably less than that of their leading firms. The role of foreign firms in Japan, Korean, and Taiwan has been, and remains, much less significant than it is in many European countries (Strange 1993), and the effective limitation of foreign ownership of financial assets has obviously restricted the degree of change brought about by internationalization in this respect.

In comparison, internal changes to these political economies seem more significant. With the collapse of the bubble economy in Japan, that economy has undergone a long recession and it remains depressed in the late 1990s. Korea and Taiwan have maintained their high growth rates into the early and mid-1990s, but at lower levels than in the 1980s, and the service-sector proportion of GDP outweighs that of manufacturing industry, as it has done in Japan for some years. The Korean financial crisis of the late 1990s has, of course, reduced growth rates dramatically and, with assistance from the IMF and the USA, may lead to some reforms of the financial sector.

While not resembling the economic and social structures of North America and Western Europe, these East Asian societies have clearly become more differentiated and complex than they were forty years ago and more remote from early industrializing ones. New social groupings have developed that are less inclined to identify their interests with those of export-oriented manufacturing firms or with state policies supporting these. Economic growth has also led to dominant firms generating substantial financial reserves, especially in Japan, which reduce their dependence on banks and, indirectly, the state.

The most dramatic internal changes in recent years have occurred in the political sphere, particularly in Korea and Taiwan. Together with some indications that the 'iron triangle' of mutual accommodation and coordination of big business interests, the LDP, and the bureaucracy is fragmenting in Japan, Korea, and Taiwan have developed more pluralist forms of democracy and begun to permit independent forms of labour organization and representation. Coupled with the end of rapid population expansion, and combined curbs on immigration, these have enhanced the bargaining power of employees in many sectors—particularly dramatically in Korea in the late 1980s—and limited the ability of employers to rely on the state to reinforce their control over their labour forces.

The expansion of the education system, and growth of a highly educated population, has not, though, been accompanied by the establishment of a strong public training system in any of these countries, and the formal, academically focused, education system continues to reign supreme. Nor have formal institutional means of resolving conflicts and generating trust become widely accepted in Korea and Taiwan, and, in general, these societies have not developed the intermediary associations and strong conventions governing obligations between collectivities that are so strong in Japan.

Overall, the extent of institutional pluralism has grown—and the central coordination function of the state correspondingly declined—in these societies, although this decline has been greater in Japan than in Korea and Taiwan and the state—especially the executive—is still the dominant actor in managing economic development in the latter two economies. Recent deregulation measures in Japan have somewhat reduced the Finance Ministry's control over financial markets in the 1990s (Calder 1993), as the growth and collapse of the bubble economy indicate, and financial scandals have tarnished the legitimacy of the central bureaucratic élite. This, in turn, has encouraged some politicians to exert more influence over economic decision-making. However, the discretionary power of most Ministries remains considerable and the faction-ridden LDP seems more likely to continue seeking favours than to mount a serious challenge to the dominant role of the bureaucracy. In general, I suggest that the state, while no longer as dominant as it was, remains more significant for large enterprises in all three economies than in most European or American ones.

CONSEQUENTIAL CHANGES IN EAST ASIAN BUSINESS SYSTEMS

Japan

The likely consequences of these internal and external changes for the organization of economic activities in Japan, Korea, and Taiwan depend on the distinctive nature of their established business systems and associated institutional contexts. Each country, therefore, has to be considered separately. In beginning with the recent changes in Japan, an initial issue to consider is whether the growth of Japanese FDI is leading to major changes in large firms and their obligational networks, or, alternatively, to the Japanization of the economies they have invested in.

In other words, to what extent has the internationalization of Japanese firms' activities made them less interdependent with Japanese institutions and ways of doing things, such that they have changed some of their key characteristics which made the post-war business system in Japan so distinctive? In particular, how would the growing number of overseas operations of some firms be likely to change the high level of organization-ownership identity, limited ownership diversification, incremental change, and high level of risk-sharing with business partners, including 'core' employees?

Since most large firms in Japan (*a*) have invested in a wide variety of countries, from the USA to continental Europe to South-East Asia, (*b*) have not relocated the majority of their key assets to a powerful and antithetical institutional context such as the USA, and (*c*) remain highly committed to the Japanese economy which, (*d*), has not undergone radical institutional transformation, they have not, I suggest, significantly altered their key features (see e.g. Hirst and Thompson 1996; Stewart 1996; Strange 1993). Pragmatic response to, say, external labour markets in the USA and the UK, or to the German training system, do not imply the wholesale reinvention of the Japanese corporation as a result of its investment in overseas facilities.

In fact, the size and dominant positions in particular sectors and countries of many internationalizing *kaisha*, and the relative weakness and differentiation of many institutions' agencies in host economies, have probably enabled them more to transfer many characteristics of the Japanese business system abroad than forced them to change their ways. Not only have they often insisted on developing Japanese work systems and ways of structuring workplace relations in South-East Asia, some European countries, and North America, but they have often developed *keiretsu*-like relations with domestic suppliers and/or transplanted Japanese suppliers (Kenney and Florida 1993; Strange 1993).

Similarly, many banking services for these firms' overseas subsidiaries and issues on international capital markets have been provided by group banks. To a considerable extent, then, these large Japanese firms can be considered to be exporting their distinctive patterns of economic organization to other economies, especially less developed and cohesive ones, rather than to be changing key characteristics to suit foreign conditions and then importing these changes to their domestic economy. As they invest more resources in the rest of Pacific Asia, especially China, relative to Europe and North America, this regionalization of many aspects of the Japanese business system can be expected to increase.

A similar pattern can be observed in ownership and control relationships. Despite the growth of foreign portfolio investment and, in some cases, direct foreign acquisition of substantial shareholdings in Japanese firms, the extensive networks of reciprocal shareholdings and broad business relationships between banks, trust companies, insurance companies, and inter-market group members remain important features of the Japanese economy, and share ownership between firms is more often an expression of long-term business commitments than a narrowly focused financial connection (Sheard 1994; Sher 1996). Moreover, substantial foreign share ownership has not conferred control in many cases, senior Japanese managers continue to enjoy high levels of autonomy from beneficial owners and are not subject to a market for corporate control. Despite low capital gains and dividend payouts in the recession, insurance companies and other large shareholders do not yet seem to have required radical changes in financial policies or managerial personnel.

Equally, the growth of outward FDI does not seem to have greatly weakened inter-firm ties within Japan. While the inter-market inheritors of the *zaibatsu* may have declined in significance relative to the vertically quasi-integrated *keiretsu* as new industries have developed, and the role of the general trading companies has changed to include third-party transactions, the overall importance of business groups and particularistic, obligational links between firms does not appear to have declined (Gerlach 1992; Sako 1992; Smitka 1991; Westney 1996; Yoshino and Lifson 1986). As large companies have relocated some of their plants to China and elsewhere in Pacific Asia, many suppliers have followed to maintain established ties.

The comparatively long recession and rise of the yen in the early 1990s encouraged considerable restructuring of many large firms and relocation of many plants to China and elsewhere. However, most of the labour surplus resulting from the 1980s expansion and its reverse has been managed by established procedures such as reducing overtime, 'lending' staff to subsidiaries and subcontractors, reducing bonus payments and the number of 'temporary' workers, encouraging early retirements, ceasing graduate recruitment, and moving people between jobs rather than engaging in widespread compulsory redundancies (Higuchi 1997; Sato 1997). Long-term interdependences between large employers and their core workforce seem to have survived the early 1990s, and established patterns of work organization and control also do not appear to have changed greatly (Koike 1994). Given the systemic nature of the post-war Japanese business system, and the limited degree of institutional change that has occurred in the last two decades of the twentieth century, this is perhaps not too surprising.

Overall, then, the combination of the following four phenomena has limited the extent of change in the post-war Japanese business system. First, the diversity of institutional contexts of outward Japanese FDI has remained considerable. Secondly, the dominant position of many firms in their sectors, often on a worldwide basis, has limited their need to change. Thirdly, continued commitment to, and dependence on, the Japanese economy and institutions, together with, fourthly, incremental and limited institutional change in Japan, have limited the significance of external investments and pressures to alter prevalent ways of organizing economic activities. A few business-system characteristics have been modified—such as the close interdependence between main banks and their major clients and the coordination role of the *sogo shosha*—as successful firms became cash rich and integrated forward into distribution and marketing. On the whole, though, substantial changes of the key dimensions discussed above have not yet occurred.

Furthermore, they are unlikely to do so as long as domestic institutions and dominant interest groups remain similar and leading firms continue to be tied to the Japanese economy and regional economies that they can dominate. Incremental change seems much more probable than discontinuous shifts in firm type and priorities. Certainly a move to Anglo-Saxon forms of economic organization is most improbable, given the limited influence of international capital markets in Japan, the low rate of US and UK FDI into Japan, and the success of many Japanese firms in exporting many aspects of their forms of capitalism.

If, of course, the relative influence of manufacturing exporting firms, their allied financial and labour organizations, the construction industry and its political allies, and similar interest groups declined substantially at the same time as foreign MNCs and capital markets became more important, we might reasonably anticipate more sustained and wide-ranging changes in economic organization. However, the extended recession does not yet (1998) seem to have generated any major shift in the power of these groups, let alone the rise of, say, powerful consumer interest groups, and the sorts of deregulation and restructuring measures urged by US politicians and other interested parties have yet to find major domestic champions.

Korea

In the case of Korea, the internationalization of the *chaebols'* activities has been less than in Japan. However, the election of Kim Dae-Jung and more open political competition in general, together with the growth of independent trade unions, represent considerable changes in the institutional context of the Korean business system that are likely to affect the ways the *chaebol* develop. Their impact will be reinforced by the growing international pressure against overt state financial support of the *chaebol* and against the bureaucratic regulation of economic activities. Furthermore, as Woo (1991) and E.-m. Kim (1989) among others have noted, the largest *chaebol* are not so dependent on the state as they were in the 1960s and 1970s, and manifestations of disobedience of state decisions and wishes have become more noticeable in the 1990s. Their limited response to state demands for restructuring during the current crisis reveals their self-confidence and increasing autonomy. Additionally, economic growth, educational expansion, and the decline of demographic growth have resulted in the increase of an educated middle class and a reluctance of many workers to undertake dirty and dangerous jobs at low wages.

The relative liberalization of state direction of the economy, together with the development of some political competition and of genuine labour representation, could encourage the development of horizontal links between them and some decentralization of control within the *chaebol*, as the degree of vertical dependence on the state declines. In so far as diversification was a response to this dependence, it may also decline, as, of course, the state has requested. However, since overall size remains a crucial feature of *chaebol* success and power, it seems unlikely that they will dispose of substantial subsidiaries, particularly if they think their rivals will acquire them. This is borne out by the reluctance of the major *chaebol* to restructure their businesses in response to the 1997–8 financial crisis. Relatedly, the strong emphasis on owner control—rather than passive portfolio management—on the part of the owning families in Korea (Janelli 1993) seems likely to limit internal decentralization, at least as long as trust in formal procedures and institutions remains low.

The mid-1990s expansion of overseas facilities and attempts by some *chaebol* units to compete more on the basis of advanced technologies and innovative products may, of course, encourage less directive and personal managerial practices as organizational complexity grows. However, the *chaebol* in general remain highly dependent on their home economy and institutions, so that the influence of foreign investments remains limited. Additionally, they too are investing quite heavily in China and other parts of Pacific Asia, so that they are not dependent on a single type of foreign location with its possibly sharply different institutional context. So far there seems little indication that family owners are willing to hand over the reins of power to 'professional' managers, despite some restructuring of top management and the reduction in size of the chairman's secretariat in a few *chaebol*. Similarly, the extent of risk-sharing between *chaebol* in new developments remains limited, despite state encouragement in some cases, as does their development of long-term commitments to smaller suppliers and SMEs in general.

Perhaps the most likely area of change in the Korean business system concerns labour management and work structure. Both institutional changes and the increasing complexity of operations and tasks might be expected to encourage some *chaebol* to develop more 'Japanese' forms of labour relations and flexibility—as

Amsden (1989) claims to have found at the Pohang Iron and Steel Company (POSCO). As labour markets tighten and workers' skills become more important in improving products and productivity, eliciting commitment from at least the core manual workforce to contribute to corporate goals and use their initiative in a positive manner gains priority over earlier managerial objectives (You 1994). Investment in training and internal career ladders for manual workers could thus be expected to grow, as can the use of bonuses and fringe benefits to retain skilled staff. Whether authoritarian supervision practices and tight control over task performance will change dramatically given recent Korean history and the continued military threat from the North remains questionable, but outright repression seems less likely to be effective as a labour management strategy.

An important factor affecting the development of new employment policies and supervisory practices is the role of the unions. In particular, the relative strength of independent unions, and whether they are organized on an enterprise, sector, or national basis, will obviously influence owners' and managers' investments in the 'white collarization' of manual workers. The highly political nature of union organization and competition in Korea since industrialization suggests that Japanese levels of employer–employee interdependence and commitment are unlikely to become institutionalized in the near future. While the new President may alter the state's role in managing labour disputes, the legacy of state repression and the continuing distrust between employers and employees resulting from authoritarian management practices and *chaebol* ties to the military-backed regime are likely to limit the development of radically new forms of labour management.

A further constraint on the incorporation of the male manual workforce into full membership of the corporate family is the traditional disdain of manual labour in Korea and the high prestige of, and returns to, formal education, especially in non-technical subjects (Amsden 1989; Cho 1994; Michell 1988). The labour force remains highly stratified by the formal educational system and manual skills in manufacturing continue to be regarded as less valuable than white-collar skills certified by higher education institutions. As Cho (1994: 93–4) puts it: 'the wide wage differentials between production and clerical types of work do not necessarily reflect differences in their respective productivity' (cf. You 1994). Despite the substantial increases in production workers' real wages since 1987–9, there seems little evidence that these distinctions and prestige rankings have changed significantly in Korea, and so the establishment of Japanese forms of employment commitment to manual workers remains difficult there. Indeed, the intensification of the *chaebol's* relocation of many production facilities to China and other cheap labour sites after the strikes and sit-ins of the late 1980s suggests that large employers in Korea find it easier to search for new, more docile workers than to implement quite different ways of managing current ones (Wilkinson 1994: 106–7).

Overall, then, the owner-controlled *chaebol* remain quite strongly tied to the Korean economy and the state, despite their growing overseas investment and the weakening of the state's control over the economy as it has become more complex and political liberalization has grown. The highly diversified, centralized, and risk-taking nature of the *chaebol* does not appear to have been greatly modified over the past decade, although some changes in managerial structures and practices have occurred in some of them. Despite government exhortations to support SMEs, and some policies to assist them, and periodic efforts to restrict the *chaebol*'s growth and range of activities, the Korean economy remains dominated by them and they continue to behave in similar ways in the 1990s as they did before (Cho 1994; You 1994). Significant changes to the Korean business system have not yet taken place, and probably would require much more radical changes in the role of the state and labour market institutions than have occurred so far.

Taiwan

In the case of Taiwan, the democratization of the state and the election of a native Taiwanese as president, coupled with the extensive outflow of investment to China and ASEAN countries, might be thought to reduce the differentiation of KMT-controlled upstream enterprises from Taiwanese Chinese family businesses (CFBs) in export industries and, perhaps, encourage a move away from original equipment manufacturing (OEM) strategies to more integrated manufacturing and marketing organizations. As the mainlander–Taiwanese divide declines in significance, and the state becomes more responsive to Taiwanese economic interests, the growth of more Taiwanese firms into large companies with state assistance, especially in R&D activities, could be anticipated, especially if the banking system is reformed and encouraged to invest in smaller firms.

Relatedly, the internationalization of operations and investment in distribution and marketing channels in North America and Europe by some CFBs can be seen as leading to the development of more integrated organizations, which, perhaps, are becoming less personally controlled by owning families. The liberalization of labour legislation and some loosening of KMT control over unions (Wilkinson 1994) might also herald less autocratic management practices and greater tolerance of worker autonomy and bargaining rights. Increases in wage rates and tight labour markets could also encourage paternalist employers to develop labour retention and development strategies to upgrade skills and products.

As in Korea, though, the relocation of many plants carrying out relatively routine activities overseas, and some investment in downstream activities, have been insufficient to 'internationalize' most Taiwanese companies in the sense of transferring their key activities and personnel out of Taiwan, and have not been accompanied by major foreign investment in the domestic economy—as distinct from the export processing zones. Similarly, although some firms, such as *Acer* and *Mitac*, have developed brand names and tried to move away from a concentration on OEM activities, their success has been mixed and their impact certainly not as marked as that of the Korean *chaebol* in North America and Europe.

While state support for Taiwanese-owned firms has increased in the 1980s and 1990s, especially in electronics (Wade 1990), the state, and the KMT, still seem to dominate the heavy industry sectors of the economy. In contrast, the dynamic export industries remain the preserve of small firms. Businesses employing less than ten people, including the self-employed, still employed 51.6 per cent of all employees in 1990 (Wilkinson 1994: 139). Similarly, the high degree of individual business unit specialization, and considerable ownership diversification in the larger CFBs and business groups, seem to have continued into the 1990s in Taiwan (Hamilton 1997; Numazaki 1991, 1992). The importance of entrepreneurial familism (Wong 1988, 1996), and its associated low level of trust between owners and non-family employees—or employees with whom family-like relationships have not been established—remains considerable and discourages organizational integration of complementary economic activities.

Relatedly, the combination of strong owner control, close supervision of work processes, and a reliance on authoritarian paternalism as the prevalent way of managing labour relations seems to continue as a distinctive feature of Taiwanese enterprises (Wilkinson 1994: 142–3). As in Korea, many CFBs in Taiwan have preferred to export their dominant management-style and work-control practices to locations where employees are cheaper and less demanding than to develop new ways of managing. Additionally, when they have established operations in Europe and North America—which are not numerous—anecdotal evidence suggests they have been much less successful than Japanese firms, partly because of difficulties in adjusting to different managerial and workforce expectations.

The continued pervasiveness of personal relationships and networks in organizing business activities and controlling work in Taiwan seems to be echoed in the emerging political system. The partial dismantling of the KMT party state has opened opportunities for Taiwanese politicians and interests to affect state policies and thereby reduced the overall 'autonomy' of the developmental state. However, so far this has resulted more in the development of political factions based on personal loyalties and economic interests than broadly based political parties representing major sections of society (Chu 1994; Evans 1995). Domestic reforms have had only limited effects on the dominant interests structuring policy development and implementation and on how these processes occur. Their impact on the nature of Taiwanese capitalism is, therefore, likely to be similarly restricted (Hamilton 1997).

Overall, then, the political changes in Taiwan and the increasing internationalization of some CFBs' operations do not yet appear to have been so substantial as to modify radically established patterns of management and development. Even where manager-owners have been educated abroad—as many Taiwanese engineers have been—and state support for industrial development has been considerable, as in the electronics and information-technology industries, prevalent ways of managing risks and growth, and the labour force, remain dominant, and the traditional characteristics of Chinese family businesses continue to be reproduced in most Taiwanese firms (Deyo 1989; Wilkinson 1994). They seem unlikely to change significantly unless the nature of the Taiwanese family alters and the business environment becomes more formally regulated, such that owner-managers develop more trust in formal institutions and processes, as well as in key employees. While political risks in Taiwan have diminished, market risks in both product and labour markets remain high for most firms, and risk-sharing institutions are only weakly developed. The pursuit of flexibility is likely, there-fore, to remain a priority for most Taiwanese enterprises.

CONCLUSIONS

The general conclusion to be drawn from this brief discussion of changes in the context of East Asian business systems, and of possible changes in their key charac-teristics as a result, is that internationalization, growth, and institutional develop-ments have not constituted such strong and discontinuous changes as to lead to major shifts in dominant forms of economic organization in Japan, Korea, and Taiwan. Internationalization in terms of outward FDI has not been so great as to remove firms' dependence on domestic institutions or to encourage the adoption of different strategies and structures. In particular, it has not led to the concentration of key resources, activities, and personnel in quite different settings that would generate radically new logics of action and forms of economic coordination and control.

Furthermore, the outward flow of FDI has not, on the whole, been accompa-nied by a massive inflow of foreign investment that could provide alternative models and develop novel kinds of economic organization in the domestic econ-omy. Especially important here is the relative lack of significance of international capital markets and their performance standards. The role of foreign capital and ways of structuring economic systems remains quite limited in East Asia—except for Japanese domination of technology development and capital goods' flows. Given the considerable flow of Japanese, Korean, and Taiwanese capital to less developed economies and/or less cohesive and powerful sectors and countries, in fact, internationalization has probably resulted in the regionalization and export of domestic models of economic organization rather than the radical modification of those domestic models.

Similarly, the development of more differentiated and complex economies and societies has reduced the states' ability to direct and coordinate economic activi-ties, and increased large firms' autonomy from state agencies, without leading to radically new state–business relationships in East Asia, or to Anglo-Saxon levels of business independence. While the democratization of the Korean and Taiwanese states has limited the extent of authoritarian direction of economic development and firms' policies, the state remains the dominant collective agent of economic decision-making in these economies, and much more significant than it is in most European and North American societies. Although the way the state is structured and pursues economic development in Japan differs significantly from that in Korea and Taiwan, it continues to play an important coordinating role there too.

Other institutional changes, especially in education and labour relations, have modified employers' policies and practices to some extent, but have also encouraged capital outflows rather than qualitative and far-reaching organizational reforms and changes in labour-management strategies. The lack of strong intermediary organizations in Korea and Taiwan remains, as does the limited extent of collaboration between competitors over such issues as training, bargaining, and technological development. Risk-sharing continues to be highly developed in Japan—albeit with some shifts in its form—but largely absent beyond personal ties in Korea and Taiwan.

This broad conclusion highlights the large-scale nature of business-system change, especially in homogenous and distinctive societies such as those in East Asia, and the correspondingly large-scale nature of environmental and institutional change required for significant alterations in dominant forms of economic organization to take place. For the distinctive nature of organizations, firms, and groups in a business system to change qualitatively, substantial shifts in the features of closely interdependent institutions need to occur. Where business-system characteristics are highly integrated and interlinked, as in post-war Japan, such shifts will have to be even more radical than in more loosely coupled business systems where change in one aspect of economic organization is not so interdependent with changes in others. While these institutional shifts need not perhaps be as significant as those imposed by the occupying forces in Japan in the 1940s, nor necessarily as discontinuous, they probably require similarly substantial changes in élite structures, attitudes, and interests, as occurred in France in the 1940s. Democratization in Korea and Taiwan does not yet seem to have developed such radical discontinuities with the recent past as to generate major changes in business-system characteristics, although it may, of course, do so in the future.

Such discontinuities are relatively dramatic and easy to identify—although their consequences are often varied and unpredicted—but incremental change in institutional contexts may also result in qualitative shifts in economic organization that are less obvious. Okada (1996), for example, has suggested that the post-war Japanese business system has developed from a cooperative to a new cooperative-cum-competitive one, largely as a result of the oil price shock, increasing international competition in export markets and some deregulation. The issue here is how we decide that incremental changes in some characteristics have significantly altered the nature of the system as a whole; this, of course, depends on how we identify the key features of the system and its guiding logic. In the case of Japan, these would have to include, I suggest, the wide-ranging and often long-term connections between organizations and firms, and between financial institutions and firms, the quasi-integration of production chains through *keiretsu* and *sogo shosha* linkages, the preference for limiting organizational diversification and for incremental change, and the prevalent labour-management system. As long as these broad characteristics do not radically alter, it seems premature to claim that the Japanese business system has substantially changed.

Similarly, in the case of Korea the key characteristics would include the dominance of the owner-controlled, diversified, risk-taking *chaebol* pursuing strong growth goals and the weakness of inter-firm linkages and SMEs. As long as these do not change substantially—for instance, in a more Japanese direction—the fundamental character of the Korean business system as it has developed over the past four decades or so cannot be considered to have qualitatively altered.

In Taiwan, the separation of the state-controlled upstream industrial sectors from the fragmented Taiwanese export-oriented industries, the dominance of entrepreneurial familism and personalism in firm ownership, management, and interlinkages, pursuit of flexibility in products, technologies, and markets, and unwillingness to enter into broad, long-term commitments outside family-like ties are all central characteristics of the business system that substantially continue to be reproduced. Conceptualizing business-system change in this way, then, means that it is quite infrequent and far-reaching, and is unlikely to occur simply as the result of leading firms establishing some plants outside the domestic economy or incremental changes in the political system in the short term.

Change can, and does, occur, though, as a result of contradictions and conflicts within socio-economic systems and between institutions. No system is so cohesive and integrated that conflicts never occur, and the increasing complexity and differentiation of East Asian economies can be expected to intensify such divergence of interests and institutional arenas. For example, the conflicting interests of manager and employees in export-dependent manufacturing industries, financial services firms, domestic retailing, and public-sector organizations in Japan affect the degree to which, and ways in which, market deregulation is likely to develop there. Similarly, economic growth and the development of an educated middle class could lead to the development of influential consumerist and environmentalist pressure groups in democratizing societies. However, it is crucial to identify the processes by which such changes are likely to occur, and the conditions affecting these.

For example, the democratization of Korea and Taiwan will probably, in time, affect state–business relations sufficiently to alter some of the important characteristics of their business systems, including labour-management strategies, but these changes depend on geopolitical circumstances as well as family structures and priorities, the development of the financial system, and the overall extent to which intermediary collectivities and formal procedures and institutions independent from the ruling party become established in these societies. As is clear from the transformation of the former state socialist societies in Eastern Europe, such major institutional shifts do not occur overnight and the results of political–economic changes take considerable time to manifest themselves at the enterprise level (Whitley and Czaban 1998*b*).

Generally speaking, it seems reasonable to suggest that, where owners and managers are able to deal with changing economic and institutional circumstances more easily by extending established patterns of action and understanding to new locations by outward FDI than by revising and changing such patterns domestically, they will do so. Equally, where opportunities arise from political changes, it is likely that capitalists will seek to use economic resources to gain political influence in new ways as well as through established networks. Electoral competition on its own may enable owners and managers to gain more autonomy and influence, and so limit pressures to change prevalent patterns of economic coordination and control, in the absence of competing interest groups mobilizing strong support. In any case, the nature of business-system change, and the processes by which it occurs, reflect the peculiarities of current patterns of economic organization and the institutional arrangements that are interdependent with these, in East Asia as elsewhere. They are path dependent and variable, rather than merely following some abstract overarching economic logic.

8

Path Dependence and Emergent Capitalisms in Eastern Europe: Hungary and Slovenia Compared

INTRODUCTION

Just as the rapid industrialization of East Asian economies in the twentieth century highlighted the variety of economic coordination and control systems in market economies as well as their interdependence with societal institutions, so too the transformations of the former state socialist societies of Eastern Europe reveal the path dependence of political and economic change. As Grabher (1995), Offe (1997), and others have emphasized, differences in the nature of state socialist regimes and in their pre-war predecessor societies have greatly affected both how their political economies were transformed in the early 1990s and the nature of the economic systems that are currently being established. The command economies of Eastern Europe varied sufficiently in their political and economic structures to generate significant differences in how they introduced political and economic liberalization and in the resulting patterns of enterprise and market organization.

Analysing the impact of radical institutional change on enterprise development in these economies therefore complements the comparative study of East Asian business systems by showing how differences in previous political and economic arrangements structured enterprise types and interests during the state socialist period in addition to how these different types responded to the radical political transformations at the end of the 1980s and the collapse of the Comecon system in 1991. The 'same' geopolitical phenomena generated significantly different outcomes in different societies, because these arrangements varied, just as Japanese colonialism took different forms and had different consequences in Korea and Taiwan.

The divergent effects of different state socialist legacies are especially marked when comparing enterprises in countries that were integrated into the Council for Mutual Economic Assistance (CMEA), on the one hand, with those in the former Yugoslavia, on the other hand. The important differences in the nature of these state socialist regimes generated different sorts of enterprises that pursued distinctive policies and practices during and after the late state socialist period and therefore provide a useful contrast for exploring the relationships between institutional contexts and systems of economic coordination and control.

In this chapter I analyse the ways in which the contrasting nature of the state socialist regimes in Hungary and Yugoslavia produced distinctive patterns of political and economic organization before 1989, that in turn led to different kinds of economic systems developing in the 1990s. In particular, the structure and policies of the state in the 1970s and 1980s varied considerably between these two countries such that prevalent enterprise structures and policies also differed in ways that affected how they adapted to political and economic upheavals. This analysis extends the business-systems framework to non- or proto-market economies by including more details on state structures and policies but the central theoretical concern with how dominant institutions structure the organization of economic activities and change remains. Because the different republics of Yugoslavia varied considerably in significant respects before 1991, and of course had very different fates in the 1990s, I shall focus on the most prosperous and stable of the new states—Slovenia. This was also the most exposed to OECD markets and experienced in Western ways of doing business.

Initially, I summarize the key differences in the late socialist regimes of these societies and then explore their effects on enterprise development in the 1970s and 1980s. Next, the critical changes in their environments in the early 1990s are highlighted and then their consequences for enterprises in Hungary and Slovenia discussed. Because I compare two societies across historical periods, their main features will be considerably simplified and presented as relatively stable, in spite of the substantial changes taking place in the 1980s and, especially, the 1990s. In attempting to develop the logic of dominant institutions in different societies for enterprise type and behaviour, such simplification seems unavoidable.

LEGACIES OF LATE STATE SOCIALISM IN HUNGARY AND SLOVENIA

The major features of the enterprise environment during the late state socialist period—i.e. the 1970s and 1980s—in Hungary and Slovenia are summarized in Table 8.1. Most of these deal with similar issues to those discussed in Chapters 2 and 3 for market economies, but increased attention is paid to state structures and policies given their dominant role in the economy under state socialism. The key differences between these institutional contexts can be considered under the headings of (*a*) dominant values and norms governing authority, trust, and loyalty relationships, (*b*) the nature and policies of state agencies and élites, (*c*) the banking and financial system, and (*d*) the skill development and control system. In state socialist societies, of course, these last two areas are part of the state apparatus, but it is worth separating them here to clarify the ways in which they have—or have not—changed significantly in the 1990s.

Trust, Authority, and Loyalty

In general, authoritarian and totalitarian regimes generate low degrees of trust in formal procedures and institutions because these are subordinated to the interests

TABLE 8.1. Contrasting legacies of late state socialism in Hungary and Slovenia

Features of late state socialism	Hungary	Slovenia
Cultural conventions		
Trust in formal institutions and procedures	Limited	Limited
Authority relations	Low legitimacy of formal positional authority	Low legitimacy of formal positional authority
Collective loyalties	Low beyond nuclear family	Strong local attachments
State structures and policies in 1970s and 1980s		
State autonomy and cohesion	High but becoming more fragmented	Decentralized to republics and communes, declining central cohesion
State direction of enterprises and subsidization	Considerable but indirect and declining in mid-1980s when profitable	Considerable at the local level, but managers more autonomous
State control of imports and exports	High but declining in mid-1980s	Medium
State control of foreign exchange	High	Delegated to trading companies
State coordination of inputs and outputs	High, but declining in 1980s	Limited
State control and guarantee of demand	High for most large enterprises	Limited
Formal state decentralization of power to local workforce	Negligible	Considerable
State control over allocation of surpluses and investment funds	Considerable	Limited
Predominant pattern of industrialization	Rapid, extensive, heavy industrialization in urban centres	Polycentric after early 1950s
Banking system		
State control of banks	High	Shared with enterprises at republic and commune level
Dominant role of banks	Instrument of state control	Enterprise and local development
Labour system		
State regulation of wages	High	Intermittent
Role of unions	Political control and welfare services management	Political control and welfare services management
Training system	Extensive school-based system	Extensive school-based system with enterprise scholarships
Labour mobility	Indirectly restricted by the state	Low

and wishes of regime leaders. While the pre-war heritage of many central European countries may have encouraged more reliance on legal procedures for resolving disputes than has been common in parts of East Asia (Redding 1990; Upham 1987; Whitley 1992*a*), the subservience of the legal system and related procedures for regulating economic relations to the party state restricted trust in formal institutions in late state socialist societies (see e.g. Crawford 1995; Hall 1995; Lampland 1995; Sajo 1994). There seems little evidence that Yugoslavia differed much from Hungary in this respect (Lydall 1989).

In general, the legacy of the selective modernization carried out by the state socialist regimes in most East European societies has resulted in a form of ethical dualism in which a strong regard for the law is coupled with an unwillingness to be personally bound by it, and limited trust in others' obedience to it (Marody 1997). While systemic trust may have been slightly greater in post-reform Hungary than in Poland, as Swaan (1993) suggests, the extensive political control over the legal system, and the high discretion and lack of accountability of officials in managing the society and economy, are unlikely to have led people to put much faith in formal procedures for resolving disputes and enforcing agreements, especially when these involved state officials. Rather, bureaucratic bargaining and personal networks of obligation and influence seem to have been the primary means of dealing with problems.

Similarly, formal authority deriving from incumbency in hierarchical positions is unlikely to be regarded as legitimate in societies where such positions are tied to party membership and loyalty rather than attested expertise or more traditional criteria. Cynicism about the party leadership and the whole state socialist project seems to have been widespread in most state socialist societies by the 1970s (see e.g. Lampland 1995). There was also an increasing emphasis on formally certified expertise as state training systems were expanded in the 1970s and some party élites attempted to bolster their fading authority with technocratic expertise. In general, legitimacy for those in superior positions seems to have become tied to acknowledged expertise, in the absence of democratic selection procedures.

The one area of prevalent norms and values where significant differences have developed between Hungary and Slovenia concerns collective loyalties. In most of the CMEA countries forced industrialization in the 1950s resulted in rapid urbanization and migration from the countryside to heavy industry-based company towns and capital cities. Often, local ties and loyalties were severely disrupted and weakened in this process—as they were in South Korea—so that individual nuclear families became the primary unit of identity and commitment and social relationships became quite atomized (Csepeli and Orkeny 1992: 5; Lampland 1995: 1–4).

In Slovenia, in contrast, industrialization and economic development were much more polycentric and less concentrated in the major cities of Ljubljana and Maribor (Konjhodzic 1996). Together with the tradition of local house building and ownership and high levels of political, financial, and economic decentralization in the 1970s and 1980s, this encouraged considerable local loyalties to particular localities and inhibited geographic and labour mobility. Consequently, commitments to local enterprises and communes have tended to be much greater in Slovenia than in Hungary (see e.g. Jaklic 1997; Kristensen and Jaklic 1997; Svetlicic and Rojec 1996).

State Structures and Policies

If we now turn to consider the party-state regimes more directly, the major differences between the two economies concern the degree of centralization. Despite the post-1968 reforms in Hungary that delegated some control of enterprise activities to top managers, especially after 1984, the degree of political and economic central control by the party state remained much higher there than it became in Slovenia. The division of powers between the party, the government, trade unions, and other agencies did, though, become more marked in Hungary in the 1970s and 1980s (Berend 1990; Revesz 1990; Swaan 1993).

Constitutional reform in Yugoslavia in the 1970s decentralized political power to the provincial republics and local communes that took on many governmental functions (Smidovnik 1991). At the same time the large vertically integrated enterprises that dominated many parts of the domestic economy were decomposed into Basic Organizations of Associated Labour (BOALs), which were the smallest economic units capable of producing tradable commodities (Lydall 1989). While many of these subsequently recombined into larger Work Organizations (WOs) and Composite Organizations of Associated Labour (COALs), the political emphasis on workers' self-management at the smallest feasible organizational units ensured that these latter groupings were rarely fully integrated into a coherent managerial hierarchy (Dyker 1990; Jaklic 1997).

Thus, although the party state in both economies remained the dominant agent in economic coordination and control, in Hungary it was centralized in Budapest, while in Slovenia the central Yugoslav state in Belgrade was less significant for many activities than provincial and commune party élites and officials. This contrast also extended to control over foreign-exchange transactions that were more directly controlled by the central bank in Hungary than in Yugoslavia. Especially in Slovenia, enterprises were more able both to make profits from foreign-exchange transactions and to retain these profits within their organizations than they were in Hungary, not least because some of them established subsidiaries in Austria and Italy.

Correlatively, the degree of central state support of loss-making enterprises in Slovenia was less than in Hungary, given the Serbian domination of the Yugoslav bureaucracy and the considerable delegation of powers and responsibility to the provincial republics. The geographical and ethnic distance of Slovene enterprises from Belgrade meant that they were both more autonomous from the central state and received less support from it than their Hungarian equivalents (Whitley *et al.* 1999). While both states enjoyed 'soft budget constraints' (Kornai 1986) then, state support in Slovenia was much more localized and less directive than in

Hungary. Redistribution of profits between economic units, for example, occurred more within COALs and localities than through central state ministries.

The CMEA system itself contributed considerably to the central control of enterprise policies in Hungary. Even after the 1968 and later reforms, many large Hungarian enterprises were tied to long-term contracts for the whole CMEA market that were negotiated by governments rather than by managers. This encouraged narrow product ranges, and dependence on state authorities and on the former USSR (Csaba 1993; Daviddi 1993). In contrast, since many Slovene enterprises were oriented to OECD markets—while Serbian and Croatian ones focused on the former USSR—and were outside the CMEA system, they had to adapt to dealing shifts in demand and could not rely on planned allocations of customers. They did, however, have the not inconsiderable benefit of a protected domestic market, although their share of this was not fully guaranteed by state authorities. This protection enabled many firms to make considerable profits in dinars while also accumulating foreign exchange through selling their outputs on OECD markets at bargain basement prices (Kristensen and Jaklic 1997). They were also able to obtain foreign goods that could then be sold at higher prices domestically.

Similar contrasts arise in considering supplies to enterprises. Much CMEA trade was based on artificial prices and Hungarian enterprises often had to accept centrally decided deliveries of key inputs with major restrictions on imports from OECD countries. While the shortage economy was often circumvented by informal inter-enterprise connections in practice, the formal control of inputs by the central state was much greater than in Slovenia.

The Banking and Financial System

These differences also apply to the banking system. In the CMEA economies the state bank(s) were usually conduits for channelling investment funds to enterprises without any autonomy over lending decisions or ability to recover assets following delays in payments or defaults. As Kemme (1994: 41) puts it: 'the allocation and distribution of financial resources was ... left to the exact dictates of the appropriate central planning agency and the national bank.' Even after the introduction of the two-tier banking system in Hungary in 1987, which was supposed to separate the commercial banks from the central bank, dominant state ownership and central control of the banking system remained (Varhegyi 1993; cf. Bonin and Schaffer 1995). Because of the inherited enterprise loans, and further extensions to these at the end of the 1980s, most of which were either nonperforming or unlikely to be repaid, many of these 'new' banks were close to bankruptcy in the 1990s.

In Slovenia, on the other hand, while many banks were politically controlled, they were also decentralized to the commune level and were often established to channel funds to 'their' local enterprises by coalitions of local politicians and managers. They were not, then, simply agents of the central state or part of the central bank but rather integral units of local economies and under joint local political-enterprise control (Lydall 1989: 155–7), frequently indeed co-owned by leading firms.

The Development, Organization, and Control of Skills

Turning to consider the ways in which skills were developed, certified, and made available to enterprises, both economies had quite extensive secondary-school systems for developing practical skills, typically state controlled, funded, and managed. These systems produced a considerable number of skilled workers in a wide variety of occupations, but usually without much enterprise involvement in the definition and certification of skills, although a number of the larger organizations did develop training schools and offer work placements. The actual amount of time spent in practical work inside enterprises tended to be quite low compared to that spent in state schools, especially in the four-year vocational secondary schools (Halasz 1993).

The financial returns to these skills were, though, quite limited in Hungary by the wage regulation system. Despite the reforms of the late 1960s and the 1980s, this system restricted managers' ability to reward high-performing workers and effectively maintained centralized control of labour-management strategies and practices (Hethy 1983; Horvath 1977). Inflationary tendencies and mounting external debts, among other factors, ensured that delegation of control over the total wage bill and other aspects of labour management to enterprise managers was quite limited in Hungary (Berend 1990: 180–2).

In Slovenia, though, the political and economic decentralization of the 1970s and the ideological commitment to self-management restricted central control of wages and other rewards, despite a number of attempts to regulate wage increases and keep some control over inflation (Lazarevic 1994). Especially in the 1980s, managers formed coalitions with the unions and self-management leaders to maintain their position, often at the price of conceding considerable wage increases (Kovac 1991; Kraft *et al.* 1994). Although such inflationary tendencies may have been lower in Slovenia than elsewhere in Yugoslavia, the lack of effective central control over enterprises' reward policies meant that managers in Slovene companies had much more autonomy in their labour-management practices than their Hungarian counterparts. They also had greater incentives to develop enterprise-specific strategies in cooperation with local workers' representatives (Jaklic 1997).

Relatedly, although the official unions in both state socialist regimes were instruments of party control, as well as serving welfare-management roles, the greater decentralization of the Yugoslav system coupled with the self-management ideology meant that they were more enterprise focused there than in Hungary. Despite their function in the party state in both countries, some appeared to develop a limited degree of autonomy in the 1980s, and local shop stewards attempted to represent employees' interests at the enterprise level in some sectors (Stark 1989). This local role gained some of these official unions a limited degree of legitimacy, which resulted in their reformed successors winning a variety of elections in the 1990s and continuing to have by far the largest numbers of members in the new era of competition (Kuzmanic 1994; Lado 1994).

Finally, labour mobility between enterprises—and the associated degree of employer–employee interdependence—was limited in both Hungary and Slovenia, but for different reasons. Central control over wages in Hungary involved restricting workers' ability to move between enterprises in order to improve their pay and benefits, as well as standardizing wages across employers (Bonifert 1987). By the 1980s, labour turnover between the larger enterprises had been reduced to 20–4 per cent, of which 15–17 per cent was accounted for by voluntary mobility (Kollo 1993). While the weakness of such central control in Yugoslavia prevented such administrative limitation of mobility in Slovenia, the self-management system and pervasive local loyalties limited workers' willingness to change employers, even within the same town (Jaklic 1997; Svetlicic and Rojec 1996).

ENTERPRISE TYPE AND ORGANIZATION IN LATE STATE SOCIALIST HUNGARY AND SLOVENIA

These broad features of late state socialism in Hungary and Yugoslavia (Slovenia) generated significantly different kinds of enterprises in the two economies, which have continued to diverge in their key characteristics and policies in the 1990s. Their major characteristics in the 1970s and 1980s are summarized in Table 8.2 in terms of the dimensions presented in Chapters 2 and 3, modified to take account of the dominance of the party state and the absence of private ownership in these countries. Enterprise type thus focuses on governance and control issues within the system of state—or 'social'—ownership, as well as on the administrative integration of subunits and component production.

Similarly, employee interests were important in the shortage economy of the CMEA countries because of managers' reliance on employees to meet targets, but unions functioned more as agents of the regime than as mobilizers of workers' interests, albeit to different degrees in different countries. Managers were also more constrained by the wage-control system in Hungary and the political imperative to contain worker unrest. Employee interests were, then, significant in both countries, but in different ways.

Enterprise Type

The control of enterprise policies and behaviour was exercised by different groups and in different ways in Hungary and Slovenia. Despite the formal decentralization of the Hungarian economy since 1968, managers were in practice still highly dependent on state bureaucrats and party officials. As Revesz (1990: 98)

TABLE 8.2. Enterprise characteristics in late state socialist Hungary and Slovenia

Enterprise characteristics	Hungary	Slovenia
Enterprise type		
Extent of central party–state control	Considerable but mostly indirect	Limited
Extent of local interdependences and loyalties	Low	High
Significance of employee interests	Considerable, but mostly through central agencies	Considerable and direct
Dominant objectives	Target fulfilment, growth in size, export earnings	Employment growth, export earnings
Extent of backward integration into component manufacturing	High	Considerable in some COALs
Degree of administrative integration of subunits	High	Low in COALs
Product range	Very narrow in large SOEs	Limited to one sector or product type per BOAL or WO
Responsiveness	Very low	Varied
Innovation	Low	Incremental
Inter-enterprise connections		
Coordination of production chains	Indirectly by state, extensive informal links between managers	Within some COALS by managers, mostly by local informal links and market-based transactions
Collaboration between enterprises within sectors	Informal and personal	Low outside locality
Collaboration across sectors	Negligible	Very limited
Employment policies and work organization		
Employer–employee interdependence	High	High
Employer differentiation	Low	Low
Task specialization	Formally high, in practice rather limited for skilled workers	Limited
Superior control over work processes	Limited	Low
Supervisor distance	Low	Low
Supervisor discretion over rewards, work allocation, etc.	Limited	Limited

puts it: 'Following a course dictated by the market was risky (in Hungary) because the regulators might alter the rules of the game overnight ... confusion arose from the fact that taxation, wage regulations, credit and the like were controlled by different agencies, each issuing rules and granting exceptions from them.' The formal move to indirect regulation of the economy in Hungary did not result in substantial delegation of decision-making to enterprise managers because of the wage regulation system, Comecon export targets, and convertible currency targets. Top managers continued to concentrate on bargaining with state agencies, since these both generated and controlled the greatest uncertainty and access to resources, despite the apparent decentralization of control over the economy (Berend 1990; Revesz 1990). While, then, Hungarian enterprises did have more autonomy in the 1980s than, say, their Czech counterparts, they remained highly dependent on state agencies and decisions.

Slovene enterprises, on the other hand, were relatively independent of the central Yugoslav state in Belgrade but were more interdependent with local banks and officials at the commune and regional levels. As long, though, as they made few financial demands on local governments and maintained local employment levels, they seem to have had substantial autonomy in making investment and product development decisions, perhaps more than any other group of enterprises in Eastern Europe (Kristensen and Jaklic 1997). The self-management system, however, and the need to maintain union support in the decentralized Yugoslav economy meant that managers had to bear employee interests very much in mind when deciding priorities and allocating resources. Thus, while these interests were important factors in strategic decision-making in both economies, their influence was more direct and less constrained by central state agencies in Slovenia than in Hungary.

These differences affected the dominant objectives of enterprise managers in the late state socialist period. Continued state regulation of the economy in Hungary, albeit indirect, and the importance of export and convertible currency targets for many enterprises, meant that managers focused on meeting central targets and increasing the amount of the resources they controlled in order to improve their bargaining power with the bureaucracy (Batt 1988: 253–4; Swaan 1993). The decentralized Yugoslav political economy and the importance of employee interests, in contrast, encouraged Slovene managers to concentrate on maintaining or increasing employee numbers, ensuring financial independence and building up foreign-currency surpluses.

In terms of the vertical integration of economic activities through unified authority hierarchies, the differences in political and economic systems had major consequences for enterprise types in Hungary and Slovenia. The combination of a shortage economy with uncertain supplies, and soft budget constraints that rarely penalized inefficient producers as long as central targets were achieved, encouraged most large industrial enterprises in the CMEA economies to integrate backwards into component production as a means of assuring the availability of inputs of the required quality (Frydman and Rapaczynski 1993; Grancelli 1995;

Kozminski 1995; Myant 1993). Large vertically integrated combines were thus characteristic of most Eastern European states, especially where state planners themselves directly encouraged such sector centralization and integration (Amsden *et al.* 1994; Hirschhausen 1995). These combines were typically highly integrated and centralized in their management structures. The dominant organizational form was functional, although some had individual plant directors reporting directly to the general director (Dobak and Tari 1996). Decision-making was concentrated at the top of the elongated hierarchies, with all significant issues decided by the enterprise director, the party secretary, and the trade-union leader, together sometimes with the party youth leader (Hethy 1983).

In Slovenia, on the other hand, the much greater availability of imported supplies and the post-1974 break-up of the vertically integrated COALs, encouraged greater horizontal specialization among the BOALs and increasing reliance on market contracting for supplies. Large vertically integrated combines were not as significant here as in most of the CMEA countries, although some did exist and were more common in other parts of Yugoslavia. The COALs were less centrally integrated than the large Hungarian combines, because of the separate nature and rights of their constituent BOALs, although their top managers were able to redistribute surpluses between subunits with political support and to centralize foreign trading and employee training. Decision-making in the BOALs was shared between the top managers, worker representatives, and local politicians, although the more successful managers were able to dominate these organizations in practice (Dyker 1990; Jaklic 1997; Lydall 1989).

In both economies, though, final product ranges were narrow. The CMEA system encouraged high levels of production specialization whereby a very small number of producers were expected to supply the whole CMEA market with, say, buses or computers and thereby reap considerable economies of scale (cf. Amsden *et al.* 1994). As a result, *Ikarus* in Hungary concentrated on making three basic types of buses for the entire former Soviet Union and Eastern Europe—and nothing else. The BOALs in Slovenia were similarly focused on making a very small range of marketable commodities, since they were specifically designated as the smallest organizational unit capable of producing separate tradable outputs. COALs were more diversified but tended to concentrate on one industry, and often had quite limited product ranges, although they incorporated more varied activities in other parts of Yugoslavia. In many cases, the outputs of particular COALs were the result of power struggles between managers of different plants and organizations and local officials, as each BOAL tried to increase its independence from central control.

The CMEA planning system and central target setting discouraged enterprise innovation and flexibility, since changes to products and processes tended to create difficulties with suppliers and short-term disruptions to production runs, which in turn threatened target achievement and, often, managerial bonuses (Filtzer 1992). Additionally, producing new products without centrally guaranteed demand for them in the CMEA system might simply lead to penalties for missing targets. Responsiveness to customers' needs was, therefore, very low.

The greater involvement of Slovene enterprises in OECD markets and their greater autonomy in selecting suppliers and customers in the 1970s and 1980s meant that product upgrading and improvement were both feasible and encouraged in many enterprises. Markets—both domestic and foreign—were more competitive, with localities promoting the success of 'their' enterprises in the protected Yugoslav market (Lydall 1989: 78–9), and managers had to maintain local employment and remain profitable if they were to retain both the respect of the community and autonomy from political interference (Whitley *et al.* 1999). Innovation was here necessary to maintain demand, since losses invited intervention by local politicians and union leaders, as well as the loss of one's local reputation as a good manager. Decentralization and some limited competition between enterprises and communes thus encouraged incremental improvements, and responsiveness to changing market demands, especially in those enterprises most exposed to OECD markets.

Inter-Enterprise Connections

The continued, albeit more indirect, state control of the economy and enterprises in Hungary after the 1968 reforms meant that industry branch ministries, and their successors in the Ministry of Industry after 1981, exercised considerable formal coordination powers over inputs and outputs in production chains. In effect, they greatly limited enterprises' abilities to select suppliers and customers. The inflexibility of the CMEA system and the shortage economy, however, necessitated managers developing informal connections to obtain the required inputs and highly personal networks of obligations and favours between large enterprises became established (Frydman and Rapaczynski 1993). Because of the disruptive consequences of changing suppliers and customers, and resultant effects on target achievement and state evaluations, these connections tended to be quite stable and long term, although those with smaller suppliers were less significant and long lived (Berend 1990; Laky 1992).

Similarly, the continued importance of state connections and bargaining in Hungary meant that vertical links within industries were more significant than horizontal ones across them, and that enterprises competed with those in other sectors to obtain investment funds and exemptions from rules and taxes. Inter-enterprise relations outside the supply chain were, then, predominantly adversarial and little, if any, collaboration developed. This pattern was reinforced by the union structure that was—and remains—sectorally based.

In Slovenia, in contrast, inputs and outputs were more coordinated through quasi-market transactions. These were often based on personal bargains and linkages that stemmed from previously developed networks (Kristensen and Jaklic 1997). Communes and other local bodies frequently encouraged enterprises to obtain their inputs locally and thus tried to develop considerable economic autarky at the local level (Lydall 1989: 79). Unlike Hungary, though, the SME sector in Slovenia—but not necessarily elsewhere in Yugoslavia—did develop some longer-term linkages with large enterprises (Dyker 1990: 149), and inter-enterprise connections were more flexible.

However, connections across regions were—and remain—less developed, with considerable reluctance to develop close ties to Slovene firms in other parts of the republic. Even within some regions, the highly enterprise-focused loyalties and commitments encouraged by the self-management system limited cooperation between them. This was encouraged by the success of many Slovene firms in the protected domestic Yugoslav market, which encouraged the belief among many managers that they could compete effectively on their own (Konjhodzic 1996).

Work Organization and Control

In both countries managerial and worker mobility was low and managers had to rely on workers' cooperation to meet targets and deal with crises (cf. Kollo 1993). However, their ability to reward good performance was greater in Slovenia, although wide differentials were regarded unfavourably in Yugoslavia (Dyker 1990: 180). Employer–employee interdependence was, therefore, considerable in both Hungary and Slovenia. Managers' dependence on workers' goodwill—or acquiescence in the need—to manage shortages and poor quality of inputs, as well as machinery failures, generated considerable shopfloor autonomy in many Hungarian enterprises, as Burawoy and Lukacs (1985, 1992) have so graphically described. This autonomy—especially for skilled workers—limited task special-ization and Taylorization of work processes (Nagy 1989).

Although the shortage economy does not seem to have been anywhere near so significant in late state socialist Slovenia, considerable *de facto* worker indepen-dence and flexibility in how tasks were carried out seems to have been the norm in many plants, not least because of the self-management ideology and influence of worker representatives (Jaklic 1997). Similarly, supervisor–worker distance was low in both countries, partly because of the quite strong egalitarian ethos and partly because of the limited powers of supervisors. In general, their discretion over performance evaluation and rewards was quite restricted, because of central-ized personnel administration and the wage-regulation system in Hungary and the self-management system in Yugoslavia.

In summary, the late state socialist Hungarian economy was dominated by large enterprises—although not necessarily with large enough plants to reap full economies of scale, as Amsden *et al.* (1994) have pointed out—producing specialized final products and many components. Still dependent on state policies and regulations, as well as on worker cooperation to meet targets, managers had little autonomy in deciding strategies and implementing change. Process and product innovations in these combines were low and managers focused on achieving targets and acquiring resources from the state.

Hungarian enterprises developed quite close connections with suppliers and customers, usually on a personal basis, to overcome shortages and distortions resulting from centralized control over the economy. They did not, though, collaborate with those outside the industry, nor have particularly close links with the smaller cooperative suppliers. Organizationally they were typically highly centralized and functionally structured, with considerable employer–employee interdependence and labour-force stability. Managerial control of work processes and reward systems was limited and supervisors were usually promoted from the ranks of skilled manual workers.

These characteristics resulted from the nature of the state socialist system and its membership of the CMEA. As Fig. 8.1 shows, low managerial autonomy, high backward integration, narrow product ranges, and low innovation were largely products of continued state control, soft budget constraints, the shortage economy, and the CMEA system. Similarly, the nature of inter-enterprise relationships arose from the need to manage the uncertainties of the shortage economy and bureaucratic regulatory changes, on the one hand, and low trust in the formal system and authority relations, on the other hand. Additionally, the high levels of vertical dependence in the state socialist system, reinforced by the party-controlled unions, inhibited the establishment of strong horizontal linkages between enterprises on anything but an informal and hidden basis. A similar combination of central control, low trust, and soft budget constraints encouraged high levels of centralization within enterprises.

The shortage economy further affected employment policies and work control systems. In conjunction with the expanded training system, which produced large numbers of skilled workers, and the wage regulation system that restricted managerial authority and labour mobility, shortages enforced employer–employee interdependence. The low legitimacy of formal authority, coupled with the wage regulation system and dependence on worker cooperation to deal with machine breakdowns and shortages of spares, limited supervisor control over work performance and ability to reward superior skills or exceptional effort.

In contrast, the late state socialist Slovene economy was dominated by insider-controlled and relatively small organizations amalgamated into larger units that had limited control over their activities. Worker representatives played a significant role in deciding policies, so that maintaining employment levels was a central objective of managers, as was generating enough financial surplus to be largely independent of outsider direction. Vertical integration was lower than in Hungary, and incremental innovation in narrow product lines quite common. Local networks were important, both within supply chains and with banks, officials, and other managers. Production chains generally exhibited greater reliance on market contracting than in Hungary, although this was often organized around personal ties and informal groupings based on previous associations. Beyond local networks, inter-enterprise connections in Slovenia were often adversarial and remote, with cooperation being difficult to achieve in the absence of personal ties.

Many of these characteristics resulted from the much more decentralized political and economic system of late state socialist Yugoslavia and some liberalization

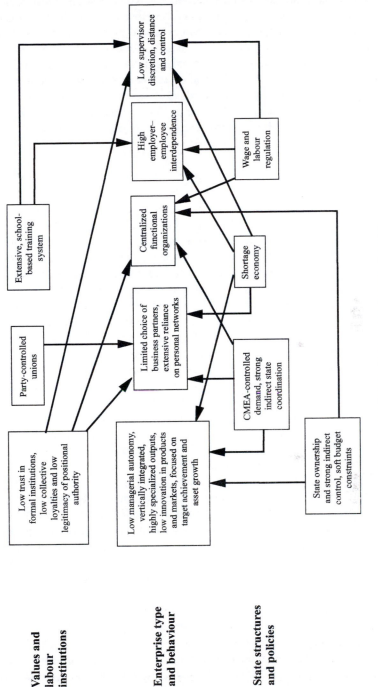

Values and labour institutions

Enterprise type and behaviour

State structures and policies

FIG. 8.1. Enterprises in late state socialist Hungary

of input and output markets, as illustrated in Fig. 8.2. The strong local orientation of most managers and enterprises, and interdependence with local agencies, encouraged cooperation within organizations, as did the ideology of self-management and the strong formal role of the unions. Equally, since the self-management system was concentrated at the smallest organizational level possible, loyalties to most COALs and their ability to control lower level managers were quite limited. Local attachments similarly encouraged local supplier–customer networks but inhibited obligational linkages elsewhere. Worker discretion and commitment were likewise encouraged by the self-management system, strong local loyalties, and a substantial school-based training system.

INSTITUTIONAL CHANGES IN THE 1990S

The key changes in enterprises' institutional environments in the early 1990s were, of course, the democratization of the political system through multi-party elections and the liberalization of market relations between them, together with considerable openness to both imports and exports and, later on, privatization. Essentially, the state withdrew from the active management of enterprise strategies—both directly and indirectly—and also became more responsive to emerging interest groups. At the same time the CMEA system collapsed and the Soviet Union disappeared, together with much effective demand for Eastern European products. In both Hungary and Slovenia, these changes meant that managers had to deal simultaneously with the loss of state support and of state coordination of economic activities as well as with the loss of many or most of their paying customers. Additionally, of course, the break-up of Yugoslavia and the outbreak of ethnic conflicts there meant that many Slovene enterprises lost suppliers, customers, factories, and other assets. Overall, enterprises became much more isolated and were left on their own to deal with a much tougher business environment and hard budget constraints.

These changes were less radical in Slovenia than in Hungary, because it had been outside the CMEA system and was more oriented to Western markets, although many firms were, of course, severely affected by the loss of the domestic Yugoslav market. Additionally, the lower extent of enterprise dependence on the state, and of state coordination of inputs and outputs, in Slovenia meant that many enterprises did not experience so great a transformation of their environment as their Hungarian counterparts. Thus, while both states moved from soft budget constraints and considerable enterprise support—whether at the national or the local levels—to much harder regimes which severely reduced risk-sharing, Slovene enterprises were more used to operating as quasi-autonomous organizations separate from the state. They, therefore, had more experience of managing commercial risks and were more able to respond proactively to the loss of domestic markets. In this, they were considerably assisted by state support in funding early retirements of their older and less skilled workers and, in general, appear to

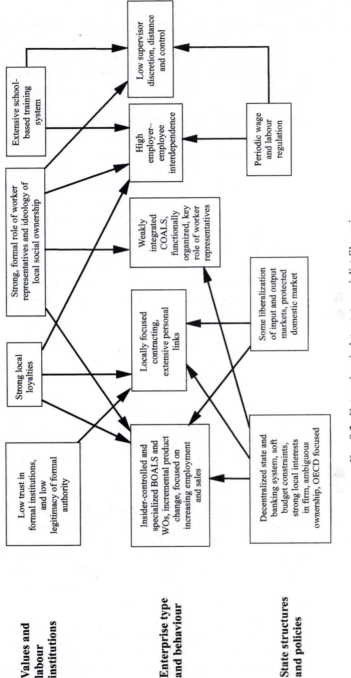

Values and labour institutions

Low supervisor discretion, distance and control

Extensive school-based training system

High employer–employee interdependence

Strong, formal role of worker representatives and ideology of local social ownership

Periodic wage and labour regulation

Weakly integrated COALS, functionally organized, key role of worker representatives

Strong local loyalties

Locally focused contracting, extensive personal links

Enterprise type and behaviour

Low trust in formal institutions, and low legitimacy of formal authority

Insider-controlled and specialized BOALS and WOs, incremental product change, focused on increasing employment and sales

Decentralized state and banking system, soft budget constraints, strong local interests in firm, ambiguous ownership, OECD focused

Some liberalization of input and output markets, protected domestic market

State structures and policies

FIG. 8.2. Enterprises in late state socialist Slovenia

have managed much of their reductions in employment through such means (Whitley *et al.* 1999).

In considering institutional changes in Hungary and Slovenia in more detail, it is important to bear in mind that these are still continuing and the new rules of the game remain to be firmly established. The major changes that had occurred by the mid-1990s are summarized in Table 8.3. Dealing with the transformation of the Hungarian political economy first, the most significant change was the great reduction of the state's indirect—but none the less dominant—role in coordinating economic activities in the early 1990s. However, the state as a whole remained the only collective agency capable of carrying out large-scale societal transformation and was both leading the transformation processes and being transformed by them (Csaba 1995; Holmes 1995). Despite being weakened and fragmented by the democratization and liberalization of Hungarian society, it was still the central agency coordinating social and economic change. Its responsibilities remained considerable despite its legitimacy, competence, and cohesion becoming considerably reduced.

In terms of the separate elements of the state and the political system, the executive—i.e. the cabinet—was relatively stable in Hungary and dominated both the bureaucracy and the legislature for most of the Antall government and the subsequent socialist government under Horn. The bureaucracy, as in most former state socialist societies, was weakened by many élite members leaving for private-sector posts or retirement and its low legitimacy from the past domination of party placemen (Dabrowski 1994). Although the legislature was obviously more powerful and politically significant than its predecessors, it remained less important than the executive for most of the early 1990s, except as an arena for the major political factions to compete for control. The Constitutional Court has, however, played a significant role in checking executive decisions and continues to review and reject government regulations and laws. Despite political threats to its powers and personnel, it seems sufficiently established to remain an important constraint on political actions and hence a contributor to the pluralization of the political system of Hungary (Csaba 1995: 132).

Additionally, the internal divisions of the political parties, and their often personally based groupings, have meant that the cohesion and integration of the political executive have been much more obviously limited than in the past. Conflicts and debates over transformation policies have been both factional and personal, and have involved the mobilization of parliamentary groups within the governing parties (Agh 1996; Cotta 1996). Thus, economic and social policies have decided and changed through bargains, trade-offs, and interest-group pressures more publicly and involving more kinds of collective actors than before. Policy-making and implementation have thus been more overtly political and the focus of conflicting pressures than under state socialism, and as a result rather varied, unpredictable, and subject to sudden changes (Henderson *et al.* 1995).

In particular, policies concerned with the management of enterprise debt, privatization, and loss-making enterprises have been the subject of considerable

TABLE 8.3. Major institutional changes in Hungary and Slovenia

Characteristics of major institutions in the early 1990s	Hungary	Slovenia
State structures and policies		
State executive dominance over bureaucracy and legislature	Declining but still significant	Low
State cohesion	Declining	Low
State control over enterprises	Declining but still significant	Limited
Central state financial control of local government	High	Medium
Extent of foreign debt and dependence on IMF and WB	High	Limited
Prestige and capabilities of bureaucracy	Limited	Limited
Power of the legislature	Limited	Considerable
Control of privatization	Centralized in government	Substantially delegated to enterprises
Dominant mode of privatization of large enterprises	Trade sales to foreign firms	Internal buy-outs plus investment funds and small external shareholders
Liberalization of imports and exports and of internal competition	High	High
Banking system		
State ownership/control of banks	High until sale in 1996	High
Bank–enterprise links	Becoming more remote	Formally weakening but still close in practice
Bank willingness to fund new large investments	Low	Limited
Labour system		
State regulation of incomes	Continuing, but more corporatist and less rigid	Continuing, but more corporatist and less rigid
Labour market reforms	Significant easing of restrictions on hiring and firing, weakening of official unions and of controls on differentials	
Role of unions	Liberalization of controls on unions, growth of new unions, revival of reformed socialist unions	
Recognized power of enterprise labour representation	Limited	Considerable
Reform of training system curriculum	Significant in both countries but little involvement of employers in development or credential assessment	

disputes and conflicts, with both leading personnel and decisions being rather unstable after the early decision to avoid Polish-style 'shock therapy' and rapid, discontinuous change (Kornai 1996). Relative political stability in terms of the governing parties and leadership has thus been accompanied by considerable instability and uncertainty in economic policies concerned with enterprises and microeconomic management in Hungary (Bunce and Csanadi 1993; Swaan 1993). The decision to avoid radical shock therapy, though, did not prevent the implementation of a draconian bankruptcy law in 1992, which soon had to be modified because of its large-scale destructive impact (Bonin and Schaffer 1995).

One of the key policy areas for all governments in the former state socialist societies has, of course, been privatization and changes in enterprise control and funding. In Hungary, the general approach has been incremental rather than radical, with various methods and structures being tried. After the brief period of 'spontaneous privatization' at the end of the 1980s, in which top managers were able to direct the restructuring and partial or total sale of many enterprises largely by themselves (Voszka 1992, 1995), the state recentralized control over the major enterprises and attempted to retain strategic decision-making powers for much of the early 1990s. This resulted in considerable political disputes over how, when, and what to privatize, together with frequent personnel and organizational changes (Szalai 1994).

By 1995, the end result was extensive foreign ownership of the largest enterprises (Figyelo 1995), not least because of the strong pressures to raise money to service the large foreign debt which had been inherited from the previous regime and the related influence of the IMF and World Bank. Voucher sales and similar methods of ensuring domestic ownership and control of large enterprises were, on the whole, less widespread and significant than elsewhere in Eastern Europe. In terms of state–enterprise relations, then, until foreign owners took control and/or dominant ownership shares, this meant that in the first half of the 1990s the state played a significant role in determining large enterprise strategies and their leading personnel. More so, indeed, than in the late 1980s.

In contrast, the new state of Slovenia was less dominated by the political executive, and the legislature has had greater control over policy choices than in Hungary. Governments have changed more frequently since 1991 and are more fragmented in terms of ruling coalition membership and turnover. The bureaucracy is limited in its powers and capabilities because of the greater influence of parliamentary factions and their leaders, as well as the brain drain to the private sector (Rus 1994). This has meant that central control over the economy has, on the whole, been less in Slovenia in the 1990s than in Hungary, not least because of the continuing strength of local government and identities.

Additionally, the ability of many enterprise managers to mobilize support against political control over organizational restructuring and their own appointments/dismissals has decentralized control over the economic transformation process to firms to a much greater extent than in Hungary (Kraft *et al.* 1994; Rus 1994). Because of this—and the broader political conflicts over privatization methods and policies—the transfer of ownership and control to private share-holders has been relatively slow in Slovenia and most enterprises of any size remain effectively controlled by internal coalitions of managers and other employees (Whitley *et al.* 1999). Where state ownership remains significant—as in many loss-making firms—this is usually vested in the Development Fund of the Republic of Slovenia that is responsible for restructuring and subsequently selling state enterprises.

The withdrawal of the state from economic coordination in Slovenia, and from direct state ownership, has, then, been less dramatic, because it was not so directly involved beforehand and because the process has been more decentral-ized. While state support for severely loss-making enterprises has continued, especially in the area of sharing redundancy and early retirement costs, enterprise dependence on the state has been lower than in Hungary and managerial auton-omy considerably greater.

An additional reason for the continuance of substantial internal control of most Slovene enterprises has been the relatively low external debt burden, and the correspondingly limited role of the IMF and World Bank. The Slovene economy was the richest of the former state socialist societies in 1990 and inherited propor-tionately limited foreign liabilities—although it has had to assume responsibility for a significant part of the former Yugoslav central bank's debts. This compara-tively healthy macroeconomic position, and the later success of the Bank of Slovenia in reducing inflation and managing the new national currency, the tolar, has meant that external pressures for radical shock therapy have been weak and largely ignored. On the whole, the enterprises have been left to cope with hard budget constraints and market loss on their own, without also having to restruc-ture their ownership and control relationships radically.

As for the banking system, and the financial system more generally, the high levels of enterprise and bank debt in both countries, and its often poor to bad qual-ity, meant that most banks could not be privatized as viable organizations before much of this debt had been reorganized in one way or another. In both countries a considerable proportion was effectively taken over by the state in exchange for government bonds and many banks were reorganized and merged, especially in Slovenia. Despite various debt consolidation programmes and restructuring of the financial sector, banks remained weak in terms of capital and assets in the early 1990s, particularly in Hungary (Abel and Bonin 1994; Bonin and Schaffer 1995). Partly as a result, they are unable or unwilling to engage in substantial new lend-ing for industrial investment or to support new firms. They have also preferred to invest in high-yielding and low-risk state bonds when they have had access to funds. The Hungarian government initiated a large-scale bank privatization programme in early 1996 and by the end of that year control over the largest commercial banks had been sold to foreign ones.

In Slovenia, on the other hand, the previously very close connections between local banks and enterprises may have been reduced by bank reorganization, but personal ties remain and anecdotally seem to bypass formal rules and procedures.

Foreign competition has become more significant in both countries, but most firms continue to have substantial borrowings from domestic banks and have not developed close connections to foreign ones based outside the country. On the whole, then, financial institutions in Hungary and Slovenia (*a*) remained state owned and/or controlled up to the mid-1990s, (*b*) continued to have non-performing loans outstanding to many enterprises, and (*c*) have been reluctant to finance major new investment. This reluctance, or inability because of lack of capital, has been mirrored in many cases by managers' unwillingness to take on major liabilities during a period of political and economic uncertainty.

The labour system has also been the focus of many reforms in both Hungary and Slovenia. New legislation has considerably facilitated dismissals, restricted political connections to workplace organizations, limited the role of unions and, especially, the privileged role of the communist/socialist party-based ones, and generally liberalized labour markets. Education and training systems have also been restructured, but obviously these changes will take some time to have significant consequences for firms.

At the same time, though, the state in both countries continued in the early 1990s (*a*) to limit wage increases through taxation, (*b*) to elicit the cooperation of unions in managing transformation processes, and (*c*) to restrict large-scale redundancies through imposing high costs in compensation payments. They did, though, sometimes assist employment reductions through other means. Additionally, the reformed and reorganized socialist unions have remained by far the largest and most important representatives of labour interests in the large-firm sector. Most of the 'new' and 'independent' unions have gained little support outside narrowly defined interest groups such as professional white-collar workers and other occupationally defined groups, which are especially notable in Slovenia (Luksic 1994).

As a result of these contradictory pressures and interests, the dominant institutions governing labour supply and management have by no means radically liberalized the labour systems in either Hungary or Slovenia. While managers unquestionably have much more discretion in managing work and employment relations than in pre-1980 state socialism, they still have to deal with significant union strength in the large-firm sector—and with works/enterprise councils—and with continued state intervention in wage policies. They also, of course, remain embedded in established conventions of fairness and appropriate standards of behaviour, especially concerning supervisor–subordinate relations and wage differentials.

The political and legal changes of the early 1990s have not, then, replaced rigid command economy labour institutions by Anglo-Saxon 'free' market ones. Rather, a variety of arrangements and controls have been succeeded by variously decentralized and delegated powers in more pluralistic institutional settings. The major difference between Hungary and Slovenia in these respects is the greater importance of enterprise-based unions and councils for managers' ability to implement changes—and indeed their own survival—in Slovenia. Close cooperation between top managers and workers' representatives has thus been crucial in achieving effective reorganization in Slovene enterprises, although it certainly has not been absent in Hungary.

This brief discussion emphasizes the different roles and policies of state élites and agencies in Hungary and Slovenia in the early 1990s. In particular, it highlights the more centralized control of privatization and enterprise restructuring in the former country. Additionally, there were different connections between local banks and firms, and more significant participation of the workforce in both privatization changes and firms' strategies in general in Slovenia. It is also apparent that the extent of radical changes in all the features of the institutional environments faced by enterprises in the late state socialist period has been somewhat less than might be expected. The implications of these changes and differences for enterprise type and behaviour will now be outlined.

ENTERPRISE CHANGE IN HUNGARY AND SLOVENIA IN THE 1990S

The liberalization of the economy and democratization of the political system in the former state socialist societies can be expected to affect enterprises in three major ways. First of all, the intensification of competition in domestic and foreign markets and the imposition of hard budget constraints encourage enterprises to search energetically for new customers—sometimes at any cost simply to keep cash coming in—and, eventually, to develop new products and processes to attract and keep customers. Such innovations do, though, require resources, both technological and human, which are typically in short supply in many state-owned enterprises (SOEs), especially in the light of the speed with which CMEA markets collapsed. Thus, the common response to market loss and the withdrawal of state support in the ex-CMEA countries was to seek customers for existing products rather than develop new ones, as well as trying to reduce employment and other costs where feasible and/or gain state help for keeping surplus staff employed. The plurality of political parties and factions sometimes enabled managers to gain political help in the search for state support, as was the case in one Hungarian enterprise we studied in the early 1990s (Whitley *et al.* 1996*a*).

Secondly, the increased availability of domestic and foreign supplies—and the improvements in their quality—could be expected to encourage vertically integrated enterprises to close down or sell their subunits producing components to cope with the shortage economy. Again, though, this disintegration may be limited by the desire to keep the workforce employed during the market turndown, and limit redundancy costs. It may, in effect, be cheaper to retain such subunits than to close them and search for new, untried suppliers, at least in the short to medium term (Swaan 1993).

Thirdly, the withdrawal of state support and of state guidance of enterprise activities meant that managers and workers had both more autonomy in dealing with economic crises and more responsibility for doing so on their own. In principle, then, managers had much greater independence and discretion in deciding what to do. However, this was in practice much more the case in Slovenia—especially in the profitable enterprises—than it was in Hungary, where the state retained more control over the privatization and restructuring processes. Slovene managers in the more successful firms developed coalitions with employee representatives to manage their 'privatization' and retain substantial internal control over strategic choices. Hungarian SOEs, in contrast, were more state dependent, and the state typically continued to exercise ownership rights quite directly, although managers did, of course, have more commercial autonomy than before. Where they had been sold to foreign firms or investors, Hungarian enterprises gradually became integrated into their international organizational structures with limited strategic autonomy, although this took several years in some firms, as is shown in the next chapter.

In considering how this variable increase in managerial independence can be expected to affect decisions about the direction and organization of leading enterprises in more detail, the first point to emphasize is that they were greatly affected by the availability of resources for modernizing production facilities and introducing new products. The 'decapitalization' of many plants in the 1980s meant that new investment was widely required in the 1990s, and yet domestic resources were difficult to obtain. Survival was thus a dominant goal in many large enterprises in both countries, but especially in Hungary. Radical change in technologies, products, or markets was additionally unlikely given the high dependence on skilled workers to keep machinery working and the common specialization of managers and workers in one industrial sector, if not indeed a single enterprise.

In this situation, we might anticipate attempts to improve product quality to meet OECD customers' demands, and some product upgrading and/or incremental innovation where resources were available. However, substantial discontinuities in economic activities or organizational capabilities would not be likely, given the lack of a market for corporate control and only gradually developing external labour markets. Substantial manager–worker interdependence remains in both countries and is likely to restrict both growth by acquisition and radical changes in markets or technologies.

This is especially probable in Slovenia, where the legacy of the self-management ideology and the formally recognized participation of the workforce in the appointment of top managers and strategic decision-making encouraged employees to consider 'socially owned' enterprises to be 'theirs' and so granted them some rights to decide over their disposal. In particular, managers have been able to mobilize employee support against outside owners, particularly the investment trusts, on the grounds that they will demand higher dividend payouts and so prevent necessary investment in firms. Such claims are obviously more convincing when enterprises are relatively successful and can offer employees a viable future in their present industry with current resources. It is in the more profitable firms in Slovenia, where managers are most autonomous and able to control strategic choices in cooperation with employee representatives, that little change in products, markets, and technologies is to be expected. In contrast, depending on the purpose of foreign firm takeovers, we could expect Hungarian firms owned by foreigners to have improved their production processes, introduced new products, and sought new markets to a greater extent than other types of firms in either country.

A further difference between some—if not most—Slovene enterprises and many Hungarian ones concerns their size, which in turn is related to their product specialization. The delegation of control to managers at the end of the 1980s and in the early 1990s in Slovenia extended down to the BOALs and their successor organizations and not just to the COALs. This enabled the more successful ones to secede from their 'parent' organizations and become fully-fledged autonomous firms that could keep their surpluses rather than have them reallocated to the less effective subsidiaries of the COAL. As a result, many, if not most, of the conglomerates in Slovenia broke up, and the typical Slovene 'firm'—or at least those that were profitable—became smaller and more narrowly focused on a limited range of products, often very narrow, such as *Iskra Emeco*, which manufactures electricity supply meters.

In contrast, Hungarian enterprises that remained in state hands—or under state tutelage—had every incentive to remain large, or even to grow, since this made them more powerful in bargaining with politicians and the bureaucracy. Additionally, large firms were more able to dominate the domestic market that was still significant for many SOEs (Swaan 1993; Voszka 1995). Generally, the larger the enterprise, the greater the rewards for managers and the more central it was to the economy, especially if it did not make large losses. Thus, those which were breaking even or making profits could be expected to remain large, while heavy loss makers—or 'crisis SOEs'—and foreign-firm-owned Hungarian firms would be more likely to reduce employment and the range of economic activities in line with market expectations.

These broad expectations for changes in enterprise characteristics are summarized in Table 8.4, and it can readily be seen that most are incremental rather than radical, and in many cases extend the pattern already developed in the late state socialist period rather than generating totally different ones. This is partly because the institutional transformations in both societies have not been quite as systematic, discontinuous, and all embracing as some would have liked, nor have they been achieved in dramatically short time periods—especially thoroughgoing changes in enterprise ownership and control. It also, though, reflects the high level of general political and economic uncertainty in the former state socialist societies in the early 1990s that inhibited significant changes in structures and strategies (Bunce and Csanadi 1993; Rus 1994; Swaan 1993).

While the previous rules of the game governing enterprise behaviour and rewards had been largely discarded by the end of the 1980s, new ones were still being developed, and so strategic decision-making was even more difficult than usual. Not only was it unclear how to evaluate the likely results of different actions, but the exceptionally fluid political and social environment made it difficult to decide which were the crucial interest groups and collective actors that

TABLE 8.4. Expected enterprise changes in Hungary and Slovenia in the early 1990s

Expected enterprise changes	Hungary	Slovenia
Enterprise type		
Managerial independence	Greater, but limited in crisis SOEs and foreign owned	High
Significance of employee interests	Reduced	High
Backward integration through ownership	Reduced	Reduced
Product range	Broadened where funds available but still limited	Limited
Size	Stable SOEs remain large	Smaller
Responsiveness	Limited	Increasing
Innovation	Limited and incremental, dependent on profits	Incremental
Dominant objectives	Survival, finding new markets, growth	Survival, increasing market share and internal growth
Inter-enterprise connections		
Coordination of production chains	Personal links in SOEs, market contracting in foreign owned	Informal links within localities, market contracting
Collaboration within sectors	Reduced	Low
Collaboration across sectors	Low	Low
Work organization and control		
Centralization	High, but should decline in private firms in medium term	Power shared with employee representatives
Integration of subunits	High but reduced	High
Employer–employee interdependence	Reduced	High
Employee differentiation	Growing	Limited
Task specialization	Increasing for semi-skilled workers, reduced for skilled workers	Low
Supervisor control	Increasing over semi-skilled workers, less so for skilled workers	Limited, but increasing
Supervisor distance	Increasing in private firms	Low
Supervisor discretion	Increasing in private firms	Low

were likely to influence outcomes. This was especially so in respect of privatization and state policies on debt management and personnel changes. Given this
uncertainty for both enterprises and top managers, there was little rational basis
for making major decisions and eliciting support for them from particular people
and organizations. Incremental developments through trial and error were, therefore, more to be expected than large-scale radical shifts in enterprise type and
behaviour. Even in the foreign-firm-owned and/or controlled Hungarian enterprises, changes were quite slow in being implemented and sometimes reverted to
previous patterns (Mako and Novoszath 1995).

Similarly limited changes can be expected in inter-enterprise relations. In the
case of Slovenia, of course, the extent of liberalization was less radical than in the
CMEA countries, although the loss of most of the protected Yugoslav market did
require many Slovene firms to reorient their sales policies. On the whole, though,
established patterns of coordination and collaboration—i.e. limited to local
regions and often market based—can be expected to continue in the absence of
effective state policies to encourage longer-term cooperation between Slovene
firms and the continuation of highly localized loyalties and institutions.

In Hungary, on the other hand, the liberalization of supply-and-demand relationships, the loss of predictable CMEA markets, and the decline of branch-based
state coordination might be expected to lead to a reshaping of supply networks
around market-based contracting and declining informal collaboration between
firms within production chains. This should be especially noticeable in consumer-
goods industries, where alternative sources of relatively standardized supplies are
more readily available and demand changes are more immediate and radical, as
well as in foreign-firm-owned enterprises that have to fit into already established
networks and relationships. While some changes along these lines had occurred
by 1993–4, the predominant impression in many large Hungarian enterprises was
of considerable stability in their most significant suppliers and customers up to
the mid-1990s, especially in those still domestically owned and/or controlled
(Whitley *et al.* 1996*b*). The larger, more capital-intensive firms continued to rely
on many of their larger suppliers and also retained some of their larger customers.

Similar differences in the degree and rate of change between Slovene and
Hungarian firms can be expected in the area of labour management and work
organization and control. Although both countries implemented quite similar
changes in the institutions governing labour relations and organization, their
impact on enterprise policies and practices in Slovenia has been less than in
Hungary because of the greater autonomy of Slovene firms in the 1980s and the
continued high level of manager–worker interdependence there. Thus, the liberalization of labour markets and weakening of unions, while increasing managerial control over work processes and labour management in general, has not
radically altered manager–worker relations in most Slovene companies. A crucial
reason for this has been that managers need workers' support during privatization,
and most unions have been supportive of managers' efforts to improve efficiency
and competitiveness, aided by generous early retirement schemes. Despite—or

perhaps because of—the high level of interdependence of managers and workers in most Slovene enterprises in the early 1990s, those in financial and/or market difficulties seem to have been able to implement considerable employment reductions (Whitley *et al.* 1999).

Furthermore, where employment expansion has taken place in Slovenia, this has often involved hiring workers on temporary contracts or other forms of flexible employment, despite some unhappiness among labour representatives. Similarly, some of the more successful Slovene firms have been able to implement more flexible working practices and production processes with the support of the unions—as they were already beginning to do before 1990—as long as established supervisory practices and norms continued. Foreign firms practising more 'top-down' and quasi-Taylorist management styles, on the other hand, have found considerable difficulties in making them effective, as Renault has found out (Globokar 1997).

In Hungary changes in labour-market institutions were more significant because of the greater extent of central state control over wages and unions. However, the resurgence of the reformed socialist unions in the large-firm sector has limited the extent of managerial autocracy, and the state continued to try to control the rate of wage increases in the early 1990s. In general, employee numbers have been quite markedly reduced in the severely loss making SOEs and many of the privately owned firms, but not nearly so much in the more stable SOEs (Czaban and Whitley 1998*b*; see also Chapter 9). Compared to Slovenia, reward differentials and the separation of managers from workers have increased in the 1990s, although managers' bonus payments were already growing quite fast in the late 1980s. So far, though, a distinct and 'efficient' market in managerial skills which would encourage substantial mobility between firms and sectors in the Anglo-Saxon manner has not developed and, given the similar lack of a strong market for corporate control, may not do so in the medium term in Hungary. This will limit the separation of managers' and workers' interests, except perhaps in the foreign-firm-controlled companies.

The limited extent of state delegation of control to enterprise managers has yet to encourage substantial decentralization of control within organizations. This is partly because the state recentralized control over privatization procedures in the early 1990s and still retains quite strong ownership rights and controls over 'its' firms, especially those making losses. In the privatized firms top management control similarly remains strong as the new owners and controllers seek to establish procedures they can trust before delegating day-to-day decision-making. Given the uncertain business environment and, in many cases, ignorance of exactly how these enterprises functioned, it is not surprising that new owners maintained highly centralized decision-making and control. As new control systems became established and top management's confidence in their understanding of organizational operations grows, we would expect decentralization to increase. Similarly, despite much talk of profit centres and separating subsidiaries with functional specialists as stand-alone businesses, many Hungarian enterprises remain highly integrated and directed through functional directors in top management. Some delegation of functional expertise to subunits has developed, but much less than is sometimes claimed.

Turning to consider work systems, we might expect a move to greater managerial control of work processes as pressures to cut costs and impose productivity increase, and perhaps to reorganize production processes in a more flexible and responsive manner. Because of the greater influence of employees—both as owners and as recognized partners in company development—in Slovenia we would expect less radical reorganization of work systems and supervisory control to be evident in Slovene firms. However, greater employee interdependence and commitment, given the low degree of labour mobility and strong local attachments, could also be expected to facilitate moves to enhance flexibility and the development of multi-task, integrated jobs, as happened in one company we studied near Ljubljana (Whitley *et al.* 1999). Thus, overall in Slovenia we would not expect greatly increased supervisory control of work processes or performance evaluation, but might well anticipate increased flexibility of production processes and willingness to trust skilled workers to manage changes in these and improve them.

In Hungary, on the other hand, greater differences between SOEs and private firms can be expected, especially between those SOEs financially breaking even or better and foreign-firm-controlled companies. Given the history of over-recruitment of skilled workers and little differentiation between them and less skilled employees in large Hungarian enterprises in the 1970s and 1980s (Czaban and Whitley 1998), together with quite loose supervision practices during the shortage economy (Burawoy and Lukacs 1992), we would not expect major differences in the treatment of skilled and semi-skilled workers in the more 'stable' SOEs in the 1990s, nor a move to much more directive and directly controlling supervisory styles in these enterprises.

In contrast, the foreign-firm-owned and controlled companies are quite likely to have differentiated between workers on the basis of their skills and contributions and be more directly concerned with increasing work efforts and output. Because they have access to a range of other ways of managing production and are able to invest in technological restructuring, they are quite likely to implement changes to production processes and to insist on greater supervisory control in order to gain a significant return on their investment. Supervisors in these firms will, therefore, be under pressure to improve productivity and act as managers rather than as promoted chargehands. Additionally, managers here will be more likely to allocate the more routine and predictable jobs to less skilled staff, while reserving complex and uncertain tasks to the more highly skilled workers and rewarding them accordingly. Greater differentiation of task type and stronger links between task complexity and skills are thus more probable in foreign-controlled firms, as is increasing supervisor distance from workers—especially the semi-skilled—and discretion over work-performance evaluation.

These interconnections between changing institutional structures and policies, on the one hand, and dominant enterprise type and behaviour in the first half of the 1990s, on the other hand, are illustrated in Fig. 8.3 for Hungarian enterprises. Despite the radical changes in the business environment of large enterprises in Hungary, the pervasive uncertainty and continued large presence of the state in the economy, have limited managers' willingness and capacities to alter prevalent patterns of behaviour.

Even with trade liberalization and the freedom to select suppliers, most large Hungarian enterprises did not change their largest suppliers for several years after 1990. Furthermore, foreign ownership and control had less impact on firms' strategies and structures in the early 1990s than might have been expected, although, as the next chapter will show, this began to have some effect by 1996. In general, then, the largest enterprises in Hungary continued to make the same products with inputs from the same suppliers for many of the same customers with the same technologies as in the late 1980s, but on a smaller scale and with fewer resources.

Similar continuities occurred in employment and work-organization practices. Only in the crisis SOEs and bankrupted enterprises did the numbers of employees and their composition change radically in the largest organizations (Whitley *et al.* 1996*a*). While some increase in supervisory control and reward differentials can be expected, especially in the foreign-controlled firms, continuing union involvement and state influence in most large enterprises limit the extent and speed of changes in work organization and managerial practices. In most cases, substantial alterations in these practices seemed to require major investments in production technologies as well as restructuring of top management personnel and procedures, which restricted them to foreign-controlled enterprises (Czaban and Whitley 1998; Whitley and Czaban 1998*b*).

CONCLUSIONS

This discussion of the institutional transformations and associated changes in enterprise type and behaviour in two former state socialist societies, Hungary and Slovenia, suggests four main conclusions. First, the extent and consistency of institutional changes in terms of their consequences for enterprises have been rather less radical than was expected by many in 1990. While generating considerable political upheaval and uncertainty, many tended to accelerate processes already set in train, especially in Slovenia, and did not amount to a wholesale and discontinuous transformation of all the key institutions that affect corporate structures and activities. Furthermore, as we have seen, liberalizing and decentralizing policies were not infrequently contradicted by political recentralization and party attempts to exercise control over key assets and positions.

Secondly, the impact of these institutional changes on enterprises varied according to the legacy of the state socialist period, and therefore between countries, and especially the extent of the economy's integration into the CMEA

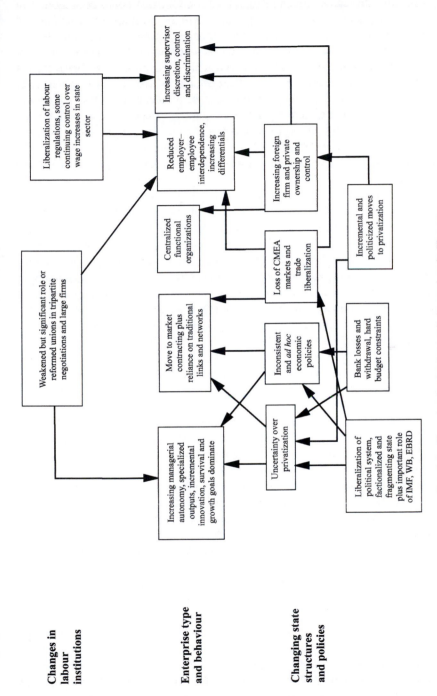

Changes in labour institutions

Enterprise type and behaviour

Changing state structures and policies

FIG. 8.3. Changing institutions and enterprises in Hungary

system and of the state's decentralization of control over economic activities. In Slovenia, the transformation of the political system and related institutions had limited impact on firms' structures and policies because of the considerable decentralization of control over economic activities already achieved and their considerable experience of, and involvement in, OECD markets. These factors were reinforced by the slow pace of privatization and extensive insider control of firms. They had more impact in Hungary because of the greater role of the central state in coordinating the economy, but here again contradictory state policies and considerable uncertainty over privatization procedures limited the extent of enterprise change in the early 1990s. Furthermore, it is arguable that the loss of CMEA markets had at least as significant an impact on firm behaviour, particularly in the short term.

Thirdly, the effects of institutional changes on organizations clearly vary according to the specific situation of each organization and industry. In particular, the financial position and economic viability of an enterprise in these economies had major effects on how their managers and workers responded to these changes. Major loss makers were both more dependent on the state for survival and less attractive to potential purchasers. They were thus unlikely to change their products and technologies but rather to survive by large-scale cost cutting and state support, remaining essentially the same but smaller. Less threatened enterprises remaining in state hands also were not likely to innovate significantly, because they usually lacked resources, including skills, for substantial product and technology upgrading, and could not easily obtain them from an indigent state. As long as sufficient surplus was made to service any outstanding loans and to provide working capital, incremental development was the safest policy for managers of these companies.

More successful enterprises that were, additionally, under internal control—as in Slovenia or some Employee Share Ownership Plan controlled firms in Hungary—on the other hand, can be expected to continue to develop in much the same way as they have learned in the past decade or so, and to avoid radical shifts in structure or behaviour. Foreign-firm-owned and controlled enterprises, on the other hand, have access to more knowledge of different ways of running firms and more capital for re-equipping plants and making new products. Potentially, then, these might change the most if the new owners want to develop their acquisitions into significant contributors to their international operations, which may not always be the case.

Finally, it is clear from this discussion that complex organizations should not be expected to change radically and immediately in response to institutional transformation, nor do they respond in a single manner to each particular change in their environment or ownership. No doubt the changed context in which Hungarian and Slovene firms operate, and the changing nature of the groups and interests controlling them, are altering their nature and behaviour. However, such alterations take time and vary according to specific circumstances and the groups involved.

Furthermore, contextual changes interact, so that anticipated deterministic relations between one type of change, such as ownership, and managerial behaviour are too simple, given the variety of additional factors intervening and the variability in managers' perceptions of their situation and abilities to act on them. This is especially so when many of the rules of the game have yet to be established and both managers and unions, as well as other groups in the process of becoming constituted as collective actors, are able to influence their development, albeit to varying degrees in different countries. As comparative analyses of industrialization indicate, the nature and roles of key interest groups during institutional transformation vary significantly, and these variations continue to affect patterns of social and economic organization for a considerable period (Kristensen 1997; Whitley 1992*b*; 1997).

9

Enterprise Change and Continuity in a Transforming Society: The Case of Hungary

INTRODUCTION

In this chapter I present some evidence about how leading Hungarian enterprises and their managers responded to the institutional and economic changes of the late 1980s and early 1990s that broadly confirms the analysis in Chapter 8. In addition to the limited and incremental nature of many changes to enterprises' structures and strategies in the early 1990s, the effects of changes in ownership were more varied and less sharp than many anticipated. Where privatization did result in significant changes in control and behaviour, typically when foreign firms bought a dominant shareholding, these took some time to be implemented. Additionally, many of the enterprises in severe financial difficulties that remained in state hands had restructured their activities quite substantially by 1996. Changing ownership *per se*, then, was not a prerequisite for reducing the labour force, disposing of business units, or reorganizing the managerial hierarchy. However, substantial investment in new technologies and products overwhelmingly occurred in those SOEs taken over by foreign firms, as was found in numerous case studies elsewhere (Carlin *et al.* 1995).

This chapter, then, presents some detailed information on how a number of substantial Hungarian companies dealt with the political reforms and market changes summarized in the previous chapter. Although the primary focus concerns how they responded to these changes, it is, of course, important to be aware that many managers and workers' representatives were active participants in the reconstruction of their society, both before and after the change of government in 1990. The ambiguous and often contradictory institutional changes of the first half of the 1990s enabled some managerial élites, and occasionally union leaders, to play a significant, if sometimes unpredictable, role in economic restructuring processes (Henderson *et al.* 1995; Szalai 1994; Voszka 1995). As Csanadi (1997: 71) suggests, the 'accumulated and overlapping uncertainties ... (of the transformation period) ... privilege agency over structure [but] also reduce the controlled and anticipated impact that individuals can have. The fluidity and therefore the openness of the system will simultaneously provide individuals with power and make them defenceless.'

Initially, I examine the relationships between owners and managers, focusing particularly on the degree of owner control and involvement as ownership was transferred to the private sector. This analysis of how different kinds of formal ownership were related to control over enterprise policies and practices will then be used to categorize the enterprises studied into four major kinds of owner control. These categories form the basis of the subsequent analysis of how organizations changed between 1990 and 1996. Three sets of changes will be considered here: first, top management teams and their perceptions of priorities, competitive strengths, and constraints; secondly, markets served, products sold, and technologies used, especially the kind and extent of innovations; thirdly, employment policies and organizational structures and procedures, including work-control strategies.

The data discussed here come from a three-and-a-half-year study of leading Hungarian enterprises between 1993 and 1997.[1] Senior managers from twenty-seven organizations were interviewed, in Hungarian, between the autumn of 1993 and the summer of 1994 on a wide range of topics. These included: their relations with owners, strategic decisions and priorities, financial policies and relations, product and technology strategies, inter-firm relationships, employment policies and work organization, and how their practices and policies had changed since 1990. Those in charge of eighteen of these enterprises were reinterviewed about these topics, and reasons for any further changes, in 1996. Shorter interviews on organizational matters were also conducted with sixty-five middle managers in 1994 and 1995, and 450 manual and clerical workers at fifteen enterprises were interviewed about work organization and control matters in 1995 and 1996.

By studying twenty-seven enterprises, it was possible to include a considerable variety of ownership and control types, reflecting the diversity of firm-ownership patterns that have developed in Hungary since 1968, as well as many different sectors and firm sizes. Both light and heavy manufacturing were included, as well as two service-sector firms, as is shown in Table 9.1. The eighteen enterprises reinterviewed in 1996 also covered a wide spectrum of industries and ownership types, although they were slightly more biased towards capital-intensive sectors.

CHANGING OWNERSHIP AND CONTROL RELATIONS IN HUNGARY

The analysis of enterprise ownership in Hungary is complicated by the changes in state ownership relations between 1990 and 1994, especially the establishment of the State Property Agency (SPA) in 1990 and the State Holding Company (SHC)—or State Asset Management Company—in 1992. The SPA was established by the last state socialist government before the 1990 elections to recentralize state control over the SOEs, in part as a response to the criticisms of so-called spontaneous privatization of public assets in 1988 and 1989. It was

[1]   This study was funded by the British Economic and Social Research Council. Fieldwork was organized and carried out by Laszlo Czaban with student assistants, and earlier results have been published in a number of papers (Czaban and Whitley 1998; Whitley and Czaban 1998*a*, 1998*b*; Whitley *et al.* 1996*a*, 1996*b*, 1997).

TABLE 9.1. Size and sector of 27 Hungarian enterprises studied in 1993–4 and of 18 studied in 1996

Enterprise sector	Enterprise size (no. of employees)															
	1–500		501–1,000		1,001–1,500		1,501–2,000		2,001–2,500		2,501–3,000		3,001+		Total	
	1993	1996	1993	1996	1993	1996	1993	1996	1993	1996	1993	1996	1993	1996	1993	1996
Food and drink	1		2				1			1					4	1
Textiles and garments			1												1	
Chemicals, inc. pharmaceuticals									1	1	1	1	2	2	4	4
Metallurgy	1	1											1	1	2	2
Non-electrical machinery						1			1				3	2	4	3
Electrical and electronic machinery	2	1					1			1			2	2	5	4
Other manufacturing	1		2	1	1	1								1	4	3
Construction			1												1	
Services													2	1	2	1
TOTAL	5	2	6	1	1	2	2		2	3	1	1	10	9	27	18

intended to prevent the effective transfer of these assets to enterprise managers and their contacts in the bureaucracy and the Party at low valuations, and without debt liabilities (Voszka 1994, 1995).

The SHC was set up by the new Antall government as the umbrella state agency for all SOEs that were regarded as strategic, and/or impossible to sell at an appropriate price, and intended to remain in state hands. The job of the SPA was then focused on privatization of the other SOEs. Although some differences between SPA- and SHC-owned enterprises were noticeable in our interviews, these were not so considerable and widespread as to warrant their separation in this analysis. Furthermore, the two agencies were re-merged in 1995 by the new socialist-dominated government elected in 1994. It seems sensible, then, to combine the ten enterprises owned by these and related state agencies in 1993 and 1994 under the general heading of state ownership.

The classification of the remaining seventeen enterprises by ownership type is more difficult because of the varying shareholdings of banks, top managers—sometimes facilitated by bank loans at favourable rates—foreign firms, foreign portfolio investors, employees, and private Hungarian investors. This variability and fluidity over time of ownership were characteristic of the Hungarian economy in the early 1990s, and probably of most of the former state socialist societies. Where one shareholder has over 50 per cent of the equity and none other has over 10 per cent, the identity of the leading owner seems fairly straightforward—as in the two Employee Share Ownership Plan (ESOP)-owned enterprises—and as in the six firms where majority shareholdings were held by foreign firms. Equally, the two firms where top managers own all the shares are straightforwardly classified as owner managed. There were, however, six enterprises with two or more large shareholders, and one where no individual shareholder or family owned more than 5 per cent of the issued shares.

Four enterprises were jointly owned by state agencies and foreign firms, such that the second largest owner could, and in many cases did, play a significant role in decision-making. In two of these the state was the largest owner and in two the foreign firms were. For the moment I shall classify these four organizations separately as jointly state–foreign firm owned while examining control relationships in more detail. A fifth enterprise was jointly owned by its top managers and a large state commercial bank. The leading owners of the sixth jointly owned enterprise were two German–Austrian holding companies who together held 50 per cent of the shares, with the rest spread in small lots among Hungarian and foreign private investors. Because this firm was not being turned into the subsidiary of a foreign firm, it is quite different from the foreign-firm-owned ones, and will be listed separately.

These varied kinds of ownership can be summarized as eight distinct types for investigating the role of owners in decision-making and controlling firm behaviour. The first four types were dominated by outside owners, while the last four had substantial, if not dominant 'insider' shareholdings. First, there were ten clearly state-owned enterprises. Next, there were four enterprises jointly owned by the state and by foreign firms. The third type, those dominated by foreign firm ownership, contained six enterprises. The fourth category consisted of the one company that was owned predominantly by two foreign portfolio investors. The four other types had varying degrees of manager ownership. In the fifth one, there was one enterprise with fragmented external ownership. The sixth type consisted of the firm jointly owned by the bank and top managers. The seventh comprised the two owned by their managers, while the last consisted of the two owned by ESOPs. In addition to differing in the type of ownership, these categories also varied according to the concentration of shareownership.

These ownership types varied greatly in size as measured by the number of employees. The SOEs and jointly state–foreign-firm-owned enterprises tended to be the largest, as Table 9.2 illustrates, although there were some large organizations under other forms of ownership. The two manager-owned firms were quite small, but so too were one of the ESOPs, an SOE, and a foreign-firm-owned enterprise. In general, the smaller firms were in the private sector in the early 1990s.

In 1996, six of the eighteen enterprises studied had changed their dominant ownership structure since their managers had been interviewed in 1993 and 1994. One of the SOEs had become quoted on the stock exchange and had a highly fragmented ownership pattern. Two of the eighteen that had been jointly state–foreign-firm-owned enterprises had become overwhelmingly foreign-firm owned. One of the firms that had been manager owned had collapsed and been taken over by its major foreign customer, and so was a foreign-owned subsidiary in 1996. The joint bank–top-manager-owned firm had effectively become a manager-owned one, and, lastly, the company dominated by foreign portfolio investors in 1993 was now quoted on the stock exchange and had a fragmented ownership pattern.

Overall, whereas eight of these eighteen had been state owned, seven were still SOEs in 1996. In line with many of the larger Hungarian enterprises, the proportion of foreign-owned subsidiaries had risen from 11 per cent in 1993–4 to 33 per cent in 1996. Two of the manager-owned firms in 1993 remained under direct owner control in 1996, and the ESOP-owned firm also had not changed its ownership. Finally, two of the eighteen had fragmented external shareownership in 1996, compared to none in 1993–4. Table 9.2 shows that the SOEs remained large in 1996, but so too were many of the foreign-owned ones, and one of the manager-owned firms now had over 9,000 employees.

Before I consider how these ownership types were related to the degree and form of owner control in leading Hungarian enterprises in the 1990s, their financial status needs to be analysed. In terms of enterprise debt, first of all, there were three major categories. First, enterprises whose short-term liabilities were more than the amount of authorized capital. Secondly, those where these liabilities were between 30 and 100 per cent of that amount and, thirdly, the rest, which had manageable debts. Enterprise profitability can also be broken down into a number of categories. First, there were enterprises that made both an operational and a

TABLE 9.2. Ownership type and firm size by number of employees, 1993 and 1996

Ownership type	Enterprise size (no. of employees)							
	1–500	501–1,000	1,001–1,500	1,501–2,000	2,001–2,500	2,501–3,000	3,001+	Total
1993								
State owned	1	2			2		5	10
Joint state–foreign-firm owned		1				1	2	4
Foreign-firm owned	1	3		1			1	6
Foreign-investor owned				1				1
Fragmented ownership							1	1
Joint bank–manager owned							1	1
Manager owned	2							2
ESOP owned	1		1					2
TOTAL	5	6	1	2	2	1	10	27
1996								
State owned	1						6	7
Foreign-firm owned		1	1		1	1	2	6
Fragmented ownership					2			2
Manager owned	1						1	2
ESOP owned			1					1
TOTAL	2	1	2	0	3	1	9	18

financial loss in 1993. Second were those that made an operational profit—however small—but had a financial loss because of their large debt burdens. A third group of enterprises just about broke even financially—i.e. plus or minus 50 HUF million, and did not have very large outstanding debts. Finally, there were those that made a significant profit of over 50 HUF million in 1993. The same categories were used to classify the eighteen firms studied in 1996, using inflation-adjusted figures.

These two indicators of financial status can be combined to form a single dimension of financial performance in 1993 and 1995. The best-performing companies had made significant profits and had limited or negligible debts. As can be seen from Table 9.3, there were sixteen of the twenty-seven companies studied in 1993–4 in that category. Most of these were privately owned to a significant extent. The three enterprises in the next group either were profitable but had substantial debts, or broke even over the year and only had limited debts. The third group consisted of three firms that were able to break even in 1993 but still had debt levels that required attention. Finally, five firms made operational and/or financial losses in 1993 and all these had significant levels of outstanding debt. They were all state owned or with a majority state share.

By 1996, eleven of the eighteen firms analysed were profitable and without major short-term liabilities, albeit in some cases because the state had written off their outstanding—and typically non-performing—debts, and in many cases had grown substantially in size. These profitable firms included five of the six foreign-owned companies, the three firms with fragmented ownership, and one of the manager-owned ones. Three enterprises remained in severe financial difficulties: two of these were state owned while the third was the collapsed owner-managed firm, now foreign owned.

The roles of owners and managers in these enterprises were analysed on a number of dimensions, both formal and informal. The formal aspects focused on the owners' veto powers, while the informal ones covered the extent of owners' involvement in operational and strategic issues, and their requests for information from managers. The major purpose of this analysis is to identify the extent of owner control over managerial decision-making—and how this varied between different kinds of owning groups—as these enterprises adapted to changing institutional and market conditions. Differences in the degree and type of owner control will be used to examine how these enterprises dealt with the transformation period and whether they followed the patterns outlined in the previous chapter.

The need to obtain the formal approval of owners for major decisions was assessed in terms of their veto powers in four areas: capital investment, new product introduction, top management appointments, and creating or closing major departments or business units. Most owners in 1993–4 had to approve capital expenditures involving 20 per cent or more of authorized capital, but four enterprises—all partly or fully owned by foreign firms—could make larger investments without formal approval from their parent companies. Fewer owners had

TABLE 9.3. Ownership and financial performance, 1993 and 1995

Ownership type	Financial performance				
	Profitable and with insignificant debts	Profitable with limited debts[a] or break-even[b] and insignificant debts	Break-even[a] with limited debts	Loss-making with significant debts	Total
1993					
State owned	4	1	1	4	10
State–foreign-firm owned	3	0	0	1	4
Foreign-firm owned	4	1	1	0	6
Bank/manager owned	0	1	0	0	1
Manager owned	1	0	1	0	2
ESOP owned	2	0	0	0	2
Foreign investor	1	0	0	0	1
Fragmented ownership	1	0	0	0	1
TOTAL	16	3	3	5	27
1995					
State owned	2	1	2	1	6
State–foreign-firm owned	2			1	3
Foreign-firm owned	3			1	4
Fragmented ownership	2				2
Owner managed	1		1		2
ESOP owned	1				1
TOTAL	11	1	3	3	18

[a] Short-term liabilities between 30% and 100% of authorized capital.
[b] Profits or losses of no more than 50 million HUF.

veto powers over the introduction of new products: apart from those with manager-owners the major firms where owners were involved in such decisions were foreign-owned ones and some SOEs—mostly the heavy loss makers.

The appointment of the CEO, on the other hand, required owner approval in all twenty-seven enterprises. Major organizational changes seemed to involve the owners in most of the SOEs and the joint management–bank-owned firm, as well as those managed by owners. Overall, the manager-owned and SOEs required formal owner approval of these kinds of decisions much more often than did the foreign-investor-owned, ESOP-owned, and fragmented-ownership firms. It is perhaps surprising that the foreign firms were less concerned to exercise their ownership rights formally than state agencies in the early 1990s, but this may reflect their relatively recent takeover of these Hungarian firms and lack of familiarity with the market.

In 1996 this relative decentralization of control over significant investment decisions by foreign firms had changed. Four of the six foreign-owned firms required their parent companies' agreement to invest over 20 per cent of their authorized capital and three of them also had to gain parent approval to introduce new products to the market. State owners, on the other hand, had slightly reduced their formal veto powers, with none requiring managers to gain their consent to introduce new products in 1996 and only four out of seven having formal powers to approve closures or sale of subunits. Chief executive appointments, as might be expected, remained the preserve of large shareholders in all cases.

A similar contrast was found when we asked about the frequency with which the largest owners requested information in 1993 and 1994. Over half received information about the enterprise's situation on a weekly or more frequent basis, especially the SOEs, the bank jointly owned firm, and, of course, owner-managed firms. Conversely, the foreign-investor owned, ESOP-owned, and fragmented-ownership firms provided information to their largest owners only on a quarterly or annual basis. In 1996, the overall frequency of information demands from owners had dropped, with only three of the eighteen enterprises reporting to their owners weekly or more often, and most providing information monthly or quarterly. As might be expected, the most intensive communication occurred in the manager-owned enterprises and those in financial crisis.

In terms of owners' involvement in everyday operational management issues, top managers in eight of these twenty-seven enterprises said that the largest owners were so involved in 1993 and 1994. Two of these, of course, were the owner-managed firms, while the other six had the state as the largest shareholder. In five of these six SOEs, the enterprise had been making losses, and usually also had substantial debts, so that the inclination of state owners to be concerned with their immediate problems may reflect severe financial pressures rather than state socialist legacies. It is worth noting here that none of the foreign firm owners was involved in day-to-day matters. In 1996, five of the eighteen sets of top managers said that their owners were concerned with operational issues. Three of these enterprises were still in severe financial difficulties, and the other two were manager owned. The involvement of outside owners in operational issues was, then, as much a product of financial distress as of ownership type.

Turning to consider the extent of owners' involvement in a range of strategic issues, we focused on eight areas: investment decisions, the approval of a business plan, top-management appointments below the CEO, prioritizing customers and suppliers, pricing policies, wage policies, and banking relationships. In the early 1990s most owners were directly involved in three major areas: investment decisions, approving the business plan, and top-management appointments. They were not, though, generally involved in the selection of customers or suppliers, or in determining pricing policies, although three of the foreign-firm-owned enterprises had experienced owner influence on supplier selection policies. Wages, on the other hand, were a matter of concern to some owners, particularly the manager-owners and one of the ESOPs, though not to the SOEs. Banking relations were also an area where manager-owners were involved, as were 40 per cent of the SOEs and one of the joint state–foreign-firm-owned firms. Overall, the external owners most involved in strategic decision-making were foreign firms and state agencies, with portfolio investors, small shareholders and the ESOPs delegating most to the top-management teams.

In 1996 most owners remained significantly involved in top-management appointments and investment decisions, but many of the outside owners had withdrawn somewhat from direct involvement in the other areas. In particular, state agencies were now less directly concerned with most of the decision-making areas considered than they had been earlier for the more financially stable SOEs. Those still in crisis, however, were subject to continuing high levels of owner intervention. Similarly, the collapsed firm taken over by its major foreign customer was closely monitored and controlled by its new owner. There was some evidence that foreign firms had increased their influence on firms' strategic behaviour, especially with regard to investment decisions, new product introduction, and banking relationships, and this may reflect an increasing integration of these Hungarian firms into their broader operations. On the whole, though, financial position seemed to be at least as influential as ownership type in encouraging owners to become significantly involved in strategic decision-making.

If we take into consideration owners' veto powers, information requests, and managerial involvement together, many of these Hungarian enterprises seemed to be quite tightly controlled by their external owners in the early 1990s, and not a great deal less so in 1996, especially where ownership was concentrated. Although the managers of the ESOP, foreign-investor, and fragmented-ownership firms had substantial *de facto* control, those in the SOEs were subject to frequent information requests and strong state influence on top-management appointments and organizational restructuring. This owner control was especially marked in the major loss-making SOEs. Foreign-owned firms seemed to have somewhat more autonomy on operational matters, and their managers were more often members of Boards of Directors, but usually the parent firm controlled senior-management appointments and, in half of the cases, influenced the choice of suppliers. Most of these foreign owners had, however, increased their involvement in firms' activities by the mid-1990s, while state agencies had become less involved in most strategic decisions of the financially stable SOEs.

This significant influence of large external shareholders on firms' strategies and actions was reflected in top managers' perceptions of the roles of other important groups and institutions, particularly banks. In general, they did not consider any other group or organization to be important sources of influence on their strategic priorities and decisions. Overwhelmingly, it was the ownership relation that was seen as dominant, despite shareholder wealth maximization not being given a particularly high priority by most managers. Although there had been some mutual shareholding between firms and banks before 1991—and this had led some observers to suggest that these connections would be an important feature of the Hungarian economy in the 1990s—hardly any managers saw their main banks as crucial influences on decision-making unless they remained large shareholders.

Furthermore, interviews with top managers at the larger banks in 1994 revealed a clear intention to reduce their holdings in companies and to distance themselves further from their clients. As soon as the bank consolidation programmes of the early 1990s allowed banks to reduce their shareholdings and to dispose of their large classified debts, they did so. While they are scarcely developing Anglo-Saxon sorts of market connections between banks and their large customers, there seems little doubt at the moment (1998) that Hungarian banks and firms are less closely connected than their counterparts in Japan, and perhaps Germany.

These differences in owner involvement and control, and their connections to the financial state of these companies, suggest four basic categories for exploring changes in the structures and practices of Hungarian enterprises since 1989. If we consider initially 'insider-controlled' firms, there were two types of these. In the first one, top managers exercised high levels of *de facto* control over major operational and strategic decisions, either because most shares were held by employees through an ESOP that they could largely control, or because ownership was so fragmented that shareholders could not readily be mobilized to oppose their actions.

The second group of insider-controlled firms consisted, of course, of those whose top managers owned most of the issued shares. In 1993–4 three of the twenty-seven enterprises analysed here displayed high levels of manager autonomy from ESOP and fragmented owners, and three were effectively controlled by their manager-owners, including the joint manager–bank-owned one. The foreign-investor-dominated enterprise can also be included in this set of insider-controlled firms, because in practice its managers had considerable freedom to decide what to do and how to do it, with the portfolio holders playing a relatively passive role. In 1996 there were five insider-controlled firms out of the eighteen studied. One of these was an ESOP, two had highly fragmented ownership, and two were owned by their top managers. These two kinds of insider-controlled firms will be combined in the analysis presented in this chapter, and characterized as 'manager controlled'.

The remaining twenty firms in the early 1990s all had substantial external influences on their strategic choices and, sometimes, on operational matters. They can, therefore, be characterized as outsider controlled. Since there were some differences in the extent of owner influence on decision-making and policies followed between SOEs and foreign-firm-owned enterprises, they will be separated into distinct categories. The four jointly owned enterprises can be divided between them according to the relative influence of the SHC or foreign firm. Three of these were effectively controlled by the foreign firm, while the fourth functioned more as an SOE. Thus, there were eleven SOEs and nine foreign-firm-controlled enterprises in the twenty-seven studied in 1993 and 1994. In 1996 there were six foreign-controlled firms and seven SOEs out of the eighteen considered.

Given the significant connections between financial situation and owner involvement, especially for the SOEs, it seems sensible to distinguish those in severe financial crisis from those in rather better financial health. Accordingly, the five enterprises which were making substantial operational and/or financial losses in 1993 and had large debts were classified as 'crisis SOEs', while the remaining six were considered to be relatively 'stable SOEs'. In 1996, two out of the seven SOEs analysed were still loss makers, and the collapsed manager-owned small firm which had been taken over by its largest, foreign, customer was also in a poor financial state.

Before we analyse how these Hungarian enterprises adapted to the radical institutional changes of 1989–90 and the collapse of many of their traditional markets, it is important to consider how the top-management teams of different control types changed. In particular, we would expect new owners to install their own top managers if they wished to implement significant changes, especially foreign ones (Carlin *et al.* 1995). In general, there were quite substantial changes in top-management personnel in the early 1990s, especially at the chief executive officer (CEO) level, but many of the replacements came from within the same enterprise.

Twenty-four of the twenty-seven firms studied in 1993–4 had changed their general directors at least once since 1989, and eleven had done so twice or more often, in one case four times. Of the three that still had the same CEO as in 1989, two were the small owner-managed enterprises and one was now foreign owned. Although both firms where the CEO had changed more than twice were state controlled, SOEs were not in general more prone to frequent changes. However, three of the five enterprises making losses in 1993 and with significant debts had changed their general director more than once since 1989. While a majority of the CEOs in 1993–4 came from within the enterprise, over three-quarters of those in foreign-firm-controlled companies were appointed from outside, compared to only 27 per cent of those in SOEs.

If we consider next changes in the composition of the top-management team, as defined by the chief executive, two-thirds of these firms had changed 80 per cent or more of their top managers since 1989, but again mostly from within. Nearly all (17) of these eighteen firms were state and foreign-firm controlled. There was a distinct tendency, however, for the foreign-controlled firms to replace more of their top managers from outside than state-controlled ones, with only 18 per cent of the latter having more than 40 per cent outsider top managers in 1993–4, compared to 55 per cent of the former. Overall, despite considerable movement among both managerial and non-managerial employees within most of these enterprises, the bulk of middle and senior management, and a majority of top managers, had little, if any, experience of working in other organizations or industries. The likelihood of radical change in their organizational routines and capabilities since 1989 was, then, rather limited.

Between 1993 and 1996, the turnover of top managers declined, although CEOs in the crisis firms continued to be replaced, often with their close collaborators. Ten companies still had the same chief executive in 1996 as in 1993, although four of the foreign-controlled firms had new ones. By 1996 over half of the CEOs of the eighteen firms had come from other companies. Only one, however, was from a different industry. As in 1993–4, it was especially the foreign-controlled firms that recruited their general director from outside the organization. Similarly, the rate of change of top-management teams fell in these three years. In eight firms less than 10 per cent of their membership had changed, and only four of the eighteen enterprises studied had replaced more than 40 per cent of their top managers in three years. Where changes had been made, recruitment practices continued to differ between control types. While most of the SOEs promoted managers internally, the majority of the foreign-controlled firms recruited them from outside, so that by 1996 four of these six firms had a majority of external top managers, although most were from the same industry. As might be expected, this seems to have led to some more significant changes in these firms compared to many of the SOEs.

These changes in ownership and top managers in the 1990s affected the sorts of strategic goals and objectives they espoused. Although top managers of almost three-quarters of the twenty-seven firms studied in 1993 and 1994 claimed that increasing shareholders' wealth was either extremely or very important to them, those in the privately owned and controlled firms were much more committed to this than those in the SOEs. Similarly, the SOEs appeared more committed to pursuing growth goals at the expense of short-term profits than did private firms in the early 1990s. By 1996, however, this contrast was reduced, as more of the manager- and foreign-controlled companies claimed that growth was a strong priority.

Another contrast between control types in late 1993 and early 1994 concerned top managers' focus on reducing direct labour costs. Those in SOEs regarded this as less important than nearly all those in private firms. However, by 1996 it was seen as a high priority by all top managers. This suggests that hard budget constraints and changes in attitudes by state élites had significantly affected SOE managers' views. Similarly, whereas fewer SOE than private-firm managers thought that low costs and prices were crucial to firm survival in 1993–4, they all did so in 1996, and in general they seemed to share common perceptions of the keys to competitive advantages to a greater extent in 1996 than earlier.

I now turn to an examination of how these different kinds of Hungarian enterprises adapted to the major institutional transformations since 1989 and the radical changes in domestic and foreign markets. Initially I consider the extent to which and ways in which they have actually changed their major product lines, entered new markets, changed major suppliers and customers, and become more flexible and responsive to customers' needs. Next, the scope and degree of changes in employment and organizational structures that these enterprises have implemented since 1989 will be described. The prevalent view of the transformation process in former state socialist societies would suggest that most firms have had to reduce considerably their labour force, dispose of many peripheral activities and units, and restructure their management. If ownership and control changes really are crucial to organizational transformation, then we would expect privately controlled enterprises to have altered more distinctly in these respects than the SOEs.

CHANGES IN PRODUCTS, MARKETS, CUSTOMERS, AND SUPPLIERS

The radical changes in dominant institutions and the collapse of the CMEA markets in 1989 and 1990 were expected to force the dominant enterprises of Eastern Europe to reorganize their product lines quite radically and redirect the improved outputs to Western markets at competitive prices. In line with this broad view, there was indeed a redirection of exports from the former CMEA countries to the OECD ones between 1986 and 1992 in many of the Central–Eastern European countries. Hungary, for example, moved from a ratio of 3:1 in the share of its exports going to CMEA countries relative to those going to EU countries in 1986 to a ratio of 1:2 in 1992 (Gross and Steinherr 1995: 136).

However, in many economies this change began before the collapse of the CMEA system, and the domestic market remained important for most companies in the 1990s. Additionally, the lack of investment capital on feasible terms limited the extent of radical changes in product lines, technologies, and diversification, as well as in customers and suppliers, in the enterprises studied here, and in many case studies (Carlin *et al.* 1995). Initially, I shall discuss product specialization and changes between 1989 and 1996; secondly, shifts in markets served; finally, changes in customers and suppliers.

As Table 9.4 shows, well over half (17) of the twenty-seven enterprises studied in 1993 and 1994 focused strongly on one product line that generated over 70 per cent of their sales. Seven of these had only one product line. Only ten had a second product line that contributed 20 per cent or more of total sales, and only one had a third line of activity which generated over 20 per cent of turnover—in this case trading and related financial services. The vast majority of these firms,

TABLE 9.4. Changes in product-line variety by control type 1990–1995

Percentage of sales	Control type				
	Stable SOEs	Crisis SOEs	Foreign	Manager	Total
Percentage of sales in 1993 generated by largest product line					
< 50	1	2		3	6
50–59		1			1
60–69	2			1	3
70–79			3	2	5
80–89	1		2		3
90–100	2	2	4	1	9
Percentage of sales in 1990 generated by 1993 largest product line					
< 50	2	1		1	4
50–59		1		1	2
60–69		1	1	3	5
70–79			2	1	3
80–89	2		1		3
90–100	2	2	5	1	10
Number of enterprises	6	5	9	7	27
Percentage of sales in 1995 generated by largest product line					
< 50	1			1	2
50–59	3				3
60–69	1			2	3
70–79			1		1
80–89			2	1	3
90–100		2	3	1	6
Number of firms	5	2	6	5	18

then, concentrated on quite a narrow range of products, and there is no indication that this was due to state control. In fact, foreign-firm-controlled ones appeared to be more narrowly concentrated than state-controlled ones. Similarly, most (21) of these firms produced standard lines with standard modifications rather than adapting them to customer specifications, and again foreign-firm-controlled firms were no more likely to adapt outputs for customers than state firms were. In fact, it was the smallest (< 1,000 employees) which were the most likely to adapt their outputs for customers' needs.

In all twenty-seven enterprises the largest product line in 1993 was also produced in 1990 and contributed almost the same proportion of total sales then, the product moment correlation coefficient between turnover percentages of these products in 1993 and 1990 being 0.92. Only two firms had changed the proportion of sales generated by their largest product line by more than 20 per cent in that period. Similarly, where there was a second product line producing over 10 per cent of sales, it was also produced in 1990 in all eighteen firms, and the correlation coefficient between turnover proportions was 0.54. Not only, then, were these firms highly concentrated around a small number of product lines in 1993, but their largest outputs had not changed greatly since 1990, and, indeed, the most important line generated very similar percentages of sales in 1993 as at the beginning of 1990. In terms of their dominant activities, few of these firms had changed significantly despite radical changes in their political and market environments, and in many cases in their ownership. Where major changes in products or services had occurred—in six cases—state firms had implemented these as often as privately controlled ones.

This continuity in product lines extended to 1995. Only two of the eighteen firms studied in 1996 changed the proportion of turnover contributed by their primary product line by more than 25 per cent between 1993 and 1995, and only a half of them changed it by over 10 per cent. Similarly, a half of this group of firms produced only one product line in 1996, and two-thirds only had two product lines. The most narrowly specialized enterprises were the foreign-controlled ones and those in severe financial crises. In contrast, many of the stable SOEs and the manager-controlled companies had three or more product lines. Overall, then, the products produced by most of these firms remained remarkably specialized and stable between 1990 and 1996. Only the manager-controlled enterprises had changed their major outputs significantly during this period, mostly in the early 1990s.

However, some firms had increased the integration of the production processes of their largest product lines between 1993 and 1996. Whereas, in 1993, most firms reported considerable flexibility in these processes, so that, for instance, buffer stocks were kept between different processes and breakdowns did not usually result in the entire production line coming to a halt, fewer did so in 1996. When six aspects of production-line flexibility—based on the Aston studies of technologies—were combined to form a single measure of workflow rigidity, nineteen of the twenty-seven firms interviewed in 1993 and 1994 said that their lines were relatively flexible. By 1996, only a half of the eighteen firms studied claimed a similar degree of flexibility. It was especially the manager-controlled and foreign-controlled firms that had become more rigid, partly because of new investments in production technologies and also because of a general tightening of production controls. In general, this shift can be seen as a reflection of the increasing managerial assurance that high-quality components would be delivered when needed, on the one hand, together with their capacity to control production processes, on the other hand. These two changes meant that the flexibility required by the shortage economy could be dispensed with in the more liberalized and competitive economy of the mid-1990s.

Some of these firms had introduced new products since 1989, but only six of the twenty-seven had made major product innovations that contributed over 20 per cent of sales in 1993. Five of these were foreign-controlled and one was manager controlled. A similar contrast between state and foreign-controlled firms was found for upgraded products. All nine foreign-controlled firms claimed that upgraded products generated over 20 per cent of total sales in 1993, whereas only five (45 per cent) of the state-controlled ones did so. This, however, appeared to be due more to the poor financial position of five of these state firms than to their ownership and control. Four of the seven firms which had not generated over 20 per cent of sales from upgraded products in 1993 were loss makers, and six of the seven enterprises which generated the overwhelming amount of their sales from unchanged or only marginally modified products were either loss making or else had large outstanding debts.

This contrast between the foreign-controlled firms and their state counterparts in terms of innovation and upgrading became more marked in 1996. All of the former had introduced new products that contributed over 20 per cent of turnover between 1993 and 1996, whereas none of the SOEs had done so. Similarly, all the foreign firms, except the formerly manager-owned collapsed one, had upgraded their products generating over 60 per cent of sales in that period, while only one of the crisis SOEs, and none of the stable SOEs, had done so. In contrast, over half of the turnover of the state firms in 1996 came from products that had not been changed in three years. The manager-controlled firms had not innovated quite to the same extent as the foreign firms between 1993 and 1996, but had done so much more than the SOEs. This suggests that private control, especially when coupled with competition, had encouraged significant levels of innovation and product change in these Hungarian companies.

As might be expected given the size of many of these firms, the share of the domestic market taken by their largest product line was considerable. In fourteen of the twenty-seven firms the major product line had over two-thirds of the Hungarian market in 1993, and in a further eight it had between one- and two-thirds. It is worth noting that six of the nine foreign-controlled enterprises had near monopolies of the domestic market, as did seven of the eleven SOEs, so that control changes here did not result in any significant alterations in market dominance. In fact, it echoes the findings of many case studies that foreign firms have been particularly interested in buying dominant positions in domestic markets (Carlin *et al.* 1995).

These dominant positions in the domestic market increased for most SOEs and foreign-controlled firms into the mid-1990s. The largest product line of thirteen of the eighteen firms analysed in 1996 (72 per cent) had over two-thirds of the domestic market then. All of the SOEs had over two-thirds of the Hungarian market for their largest product line in 1996, as did nearly all the foreign firms. In many cases their second largest product line also had very large market shares. It was only the smaller manager-controlled enterprises that tended to have smaller shares of the domestic market.

Similarly, most of these enterprises remained dependent on the domestic market. Whereas thirteen of the twenty-seven firms interviewed in 1993–4 sold over 60 per cent of their sales to Hungarian customers in 1989, eleven did so in 1993, as Table 9.5 shows. These were mostly the manager- and foreign-controlled ones. In 1996, slightly fewer of the eighteen firms were thus concentrated on domestic customers, with over a third selling less than a half of their outputs domestically. As expected, the other major markets were in Western countries, especially the EU states. Already in 1989, nearly half of the twenty-seven firms studied in 1993 and 1994 had over a fifth of their sales in these markets, and in 1993 ten firms were selling over 40 per cent of their products to these countries, mostly the SOEs. By 1996 this percentage had grown to 55 per cent, again dominated by SOEs, although three of the six foreign-controlled firms also sold extensively to OECD markets. In all three years, exposure to CMEA customers was very limited.

It seems, then, that most of these Hungarian enterprises had already substantially redirected their sales away from the Comecon countries by 1989, and most of the changes in markets served in the 1990s were incremental in nature, largely moving from domestic customers to those in OECD markets. While foreign-controlled firms in particular tended to produce a narrow range of products for the domestic market in the early 1990s, by 1995 they had become more oriented to Western markets.

The incremental pattern of change in products and markets served for most of these Hungarian enterprises extended to their major customers and suppliers. Most of the major customers—i.e. those that bought over 10 per cent of total sales—of the twenty-seven enterprises in 1989 tended to remain major customers in 1993. No less than forty-two of the sixty-three major customers in 1989 were still major customers in 1993–4. This relative stability of significant buyers was equally marked across all four control types, and reflects the dominance of domestic sales as well as the fact that most customers in the domestic market were large firms.

However, while there were only ten Western large customers in 1989, this had grown to twenty-three in 1993, mostly among the state- and foreign-controlled enterprises. This was especially noticeable in the latter firms, where the number of Western significant customers went up from one in seventeen in 1989 to seven in seventeen in 1993. Foreign control does, then, seem to have encouraged Western sales, often to subsidiaries and associate firms, but it should be borne in mind that the domestic market remained dominant in these companies. A further third of these major customers had changed between 1993 and 1996, often because of foreign firms changing their subcontracting relationships and/or entering the domestic market in a large way. On the whole, though, the customer base of most of these Hungarian firms does not seem to have changed radically since 1989.

A similar degree of stability was evident among the major suppliers of these Hungarian enterprises. Over two-thirds (69 per cent) of the fifty-five suppliers who provided over 10 per cent of their inputs in 1989 remained significant suppliers in 1993. The state firms, though, had changed more of these suppliers than had

TABLE 9.5. Changes in markets served by control type, 1989–1995

Percentage of sales to:	Control type in 1993–4 and 1995											
	Stable SOEs			Crisis SOEs			Foreign			Manager		
	1989	1993	1995	1989	1993	1995	1989	1993	1995	1989	1993	1995
Domestic market												
1–20	1	2	2		1	1	2	1	1	1	1	1
21–40	3	3	1	1	2			1	1	1	1	1
41–60	2	1	1	2			2	3	2	2	1	1
61–80			1	1	2		3	2	1		3	2
81–100				1		1	2	2	1	3	1	
CMEA markets												
1–20	5	6	5	4	4	1	6	9	6	5	6	5
21–40	1				1	1	3			2	1	
41–60												
61–80				1								
81–100												
OECD markets												
1–20	1		1	2	1		6	2	1	5	3	3
21–40	4	3	1	3	1		1	5	2	1	2	1
41–60	1	2	2		2	2	1		1		1	1
61–80		1	1		1		1	2	2	1	1	
81–100												
Number of firms	6	6	5	5	5	2	9	9	6	7	7	5

foreign-controlled ones. Nearly a half (44.5 per cent) of the twenty-seven major suppliers to the former group had changed by 1993, while only 12 per cent of the twenty major suppliers to the latter had altered. In most cases, these changes were from one domestic supplier to another—often because of the demise of many industrial units of agricultural cooperatives—and did not reflect a shift from CMEA ones to Western ones.

Indeed, the total number of Western major suppliers increased by only one, from three in 1989 to four in 1993, and there did not appear to be pressure from the new foreign-firm owners/controllers of Hungarian firms to increase their dependence on Western suppliers. As was the case for major customers, the bulk of these twenty-seven enterprises relied on domestic firms for most of their inputs, and the majority of large suppliers remained the same over the early transformation period. To some extent this stability reflects the sectors represented by our selected twenty-seven firms. Four are food processors and so unlikely to change their more significant suppliers, and three chemical firms process raw materials from Russia and ex-Soviet states which are still relatively cheap and abundant.

Again, further shifts in major suppliers after 1993 were incremental rather than radical. Less than a third of the three most significant suppliers to the eighteen firms studied in 1996 had changed in three years. Most of these changes stemmed from product innovations, with vertical disintegration, customer-specification alterations, and market-structure changes being the other reasons cited. Overall, then, the reorganization of customer and supplier relationships of these Hungarian firms was gradual rather than revolutionary, and often linked to product-line changes and incremental innovation. As might be expected, it was more evident in the foreign-controlled firms, which were becoming more integrated into the world economy.

EMPLOYMENT AND ORGANIZATION CHANGES

The capital-intensive nature of many firms' production processes and their domination of the domestic market might be thought to limit the extent of their technological changes in response to the transformation of their environments in the early 1990s. These factors should not, though, have restricted their ability to reorganize their work systems and management structures to the same extent, and many observers expected the combined effects of liberalization, privatization, and severe market loss to trigger large-scale organizational changes. I shall initially analyse changes in employment levels and structures before considering how these Hungarian enterprises had changed their internal organization.

Although the changes in the business environment of these firms were expected to have encouraged substantial reductions in employment as the state reduced subsidies and other forms of support, six of the twenty-seven firms studied in 1993 and 1994 had actually increased their labour force since the beginning of 1990. In five instances this was because of internal growth and/or adding specialist skills upon privatization, while the one SOE in this group had taken over one of its failing customers. Where the workforce had declined between 1 January 1990 and the end of 1993, it had not done so drastically in most cases, with only two firms cutting over a half of their employees. As Table 9.6 shows, state firms, especially those in severe financial difficulties, were no more reluctant to reduce their total labour force than were non-state controlled firms, and it is also important to bear in mind that some SOEs had already restructured themselves in the late 1980s. Privatization, then, was clearly not a necessary condition for significant labour-force reductions to be implemented.

Between 1993 and 1996, a third of the eighteen firms considered increased their workforces, in four cases by over 15 per cent. Two of these six were foreign controlled and three were manager owned—one of these latter companies had almost doubled its labour force. Most firms, though, did not change the total level of employment very much at all in this period, with only the two SOEs in severe financial crisis cutting employment by over 20 per cent. In most cases, then, major employment reductions, when they occurred at all, were carried out in the early 1990s, and employment levels had stabilized by the mid-1990s, with some firms increasing their staff numbers after earlier cuts.

In terms of which groups of employees had been most reduced, it seems clear from Table 9.6 that the recession and tightening of budget constraints had led to major reductions in the numbers of non-workflow employees by the end of 1993. Five firms had less than half the number of people in these support roles in 1993 than they had in 1990, while other groups had been cut much less. The largest reduction had occurred in the technical support area, which includes maintenance, production planning and scheduling, R&D, and ancillary services, including quite a number of unskilled workers. Eight firms had reduced the number of people in these roles by over 50 per cent—five of these were state controlled—and seventeen had cut them by over 20 per cent. Clerical workers had also been reduced quite significantly but perhaps not as much as might be expected given their considerable numbers in many of these enterprises. Although the foreign-owned and owner-managed firms had reduced non-workflow employees quite significantly, they did not seem to have done so more than the state-controlled enterprises, so that control type was not related to the apparent willingness to reduce staff numbers in ancillary functions in the early 1990s.

Financial position was a much stronger influence. The company that had been liquidated in 1991 retained only 7 per cent of its 1990 staff in non-workflow positions in 1993, and the three firms making operational losses in 1993—all state controlled—greatly reduced the number of employees in this category. As well as considerably cutting the number of directly employed maintenance workers—usually through subcontracting—these reductions were often achieved by dismissing the considerable number of ancillary workers who performed unskilled tasks in support of skilled production workers. Many of these had been engaged in carrying work materials to and from work stations, cleaning, etc., and

TABLE 9.6. Employment changes by control type at 27 Hungarian enterprises, January 1990–December 1993, and at 18 firms, December 1993–December 1995

Employment changes (% changes)	Control type							
	Stable SOE		Crisis SOE		Foreign[a]		Manager	
	1990–3	1993–5	1990–3	1993–5	1990–3	1993–5	1990–3	1993–5
Total employment								
Increase	0	1	1	0	2	2	3	3
1–20 reduction	4	4	0	0	3	4	2	2
21–40 reduction	1	0	2	0	3	0	1	0
>40 reduction	1	0	2	2	0	0	1	0
Direct production worker								
Increase	1	1	1	0	2	4	3	3
1–20 reduction	3	4	0	0	4	2	2	2
21–40 reduction	1	0	3	1	2	0	1	0
>40 reduction	1	0	1	1	0	0	1	0
First-line supervisors								
Increase	3	1	1	0	4	5	3	3
1–20 reduction	0	4	2	0	3	1	3	2
21–40 reduction	2	0	1	1	1	0	0	0
>40 reduction	1	0	1	1	0	0	1	0
Non-workflow employees								
Increase	0	0	1	0	0	2	3	2
1–20 reduction	3	5	0	0	3	3	1	3
21–40 reduction	2	0	2	0	3	1	2	0
> 40 reduction	1	0	2	2	2	0	1	0

[a] Omitting one foreign-firm-controlled enterprise that formed an integral part of an SOE in 1990 and could not be separated from it.

now the skilled workers in some—but by no means all—firms were undertaking these tasks.

In contrast, seven firms had increased the number of their direct production workers, and eleven had also added more first-line supervisors in the early 1990s. Indeed, nearly a half (13) of these enterprises had increased the overall number of line managers and only five had reduced them by over 30 per cent. These increases in supervisors and managers, both in absolute numbers and relative to the total workforce, were particularly marked for the foreign-firm and manager-controlled firms, which might suggest an intensification of managerial control over the work process and the organization as a whole. Certainly, the spans of control of first-line supervisors in operational areas had narrowed for most (21) firms, especially in the foreign-controlled firms.

The tendency to increase the proportion of employees engaged in direct production tasks and supervisory roles continued between 1993 and 1996. Five of the eighteen firms interviewed in 1996 employed over 80 per cent of their work-force in production, with a further six having between 70 and 79 per cent of their employees in this department. Two-thirds of these eleven firms were manager- or foreign-firm controlled. Similarly, nearly all of the eight firms that had increased the number of supervisors in this period were foreign or manager controlled. Equally, only four firms had over 20 per cent of their staff employed in technical support roles by 1996, of which three were stable SOEs. In general, then, most of these Hungarian enterprises seem to have radically reduced the proportion of indirect workers by the middle of the 1990s, especially those in private ownership and control and/or in severe financial difficulties.

Despite these changes in total employment, especially in support roles, the bulk of the middle management and technical staff remained the same in most firms between 1989 and 1993. In nearly three-quarters (74 per cent) of these twenty-seven enterprises, at least 60 per cent of these employees had not changed, although in many cases they had taken on additional responsibilities and their roles had altered significantly. However, there was a slight tendency for the 'outsider'-controlled firms to change more middle managers and technical staff than 'insider'-controlled ones. Four of the seven manager-owned and manager-controlled enterprises had changed less than 20 per cent of this group between 1989 and 1993, whereas only six of the twenty state- and foreign-firm controlled ones maintained such a high degree of continuity.

There was no indication, though, that SOEs sold to foreign firms were any more prone to changing middle managers than those remaining in state hands. Four of the state enterprises had changed over 40 per cent of this group, three of which were in 'crisis', while only two of the foreign-firm controlled ones had done so. In 1996, far fewer firms had experienced substantial changes in middle management and technical roles. Nearly two-thirds of the eighteen had changed less than 20 per cent of these staff since 1993, with the rest changing between 20 and 40 per cent of them. Those that had changed the most in this period were mostly in severe financial difficulties, as might be expected.

I suggested in the last chapter that the liberalization of the labour and product markets, together with changes in ownership and control, might be expected to increase wage differentials between groups of employees and encourage greater divergence in the ways they are rewarded and promoted. However, while some increases were recorded between 1993 and 1996, they were relatively minor in most cases. The median ratio of the chief executive's income to that of the average operative, for instance, rose only from 14 to 16 in this period. While enterprise size did affect this ratio, it was by no means the only factor. Foreign-controlled firms tended to reward their CEOs more than Hungarian owners did, perhaps because they appointed most of them from outside. The crisis SOEs had the lowest differentials in both years.

The foreign firms also maintained a slightly greater pay differential between first-line supervisors and operators in 1993 and 1996 than did the SOEs, but the contrast was small and the ratio did not change over this period. Differences in pay between technicians and university-educated staff and operators also remained the same between 1993 and 1996, with little variation across control types. If, then, liberalization of the wage payment system in Hungary had resulted in major increases in pay differentials between categories of staff, these had occurred before 1993, most probably in the late 1980s.

The traditional pattern of recruiting supervisors from skilled workers also did not change greatly in the 1990s. Over two-thirds of the twenty-seven enterprises studied in 1993 and 1994 claimed that more than two-thirds of their supervisors were former production workers, and this proportion remained at 67 per cent in 1996. In both years there was little difference between control types in this respect, and so the expectation that liberalization, competition, and privatization would result in the appointment of outsiders to first-line management posts was not borne out in these enterprises, possibly because of a shortage of appropriately skilled personnel.

Changes in employment structures and management personnel had been accompanied by some organizational restructuring in many of these enterprises, although not as far-reaching as once seemed likely. Two aspects of organizational change will be considered here. First, the extent to which managers have disposed of activities and units that are no longer needed with the end of the shortage economy, and rationalized their production facilities to deal with the much more competitive environment. Secondly, whether the decline in state control has resulted in decentralization of decision-making and control over activities to lower levels of the organization and the development of separate profit centres with substantial operational autonomy.

In analysing the restructuring of organizational units, it is useful to distinguish between those considered 'core' operations and those seen as more 'auxiliary' to the main activities of the organization. Top managers typically considered the former to be producing goods or services that were part of their main product line, mostly factories, while the latter were usually engaged in non-workflow activities. If we consider the reorganization of 'core' units first, remarkably few of the twenty-seven enterprises studied in the early 1990s had closed or sold any of these, despite the very severe trading conditions. Three of the five crisis SOEs, for instance, retained all their core units at the end of 1993. Furthermore, the size of the core units that had been closed or sold was usually quite small. On average they employed only 8.3 per cent of their 1990 labour force, and only four firms disposed of core units employing over 10 per cent of their total staff. Little differences between control types were evident in this respect, and most of the major disposals seemed to stem from special circumstances during liquidation or privatization.

Rather more firms had sold or closed core units between 1993 and 1996. Eight of the eighteen studied in 1996 had disposed of at least one such activity in that period and some of these were quite substantial. Three of those closed, for example, employed over 40 per cent of the workforce, and six contained over a fifth. Half of the firms that had closed these relatively large units were in financial crisis, suggesting that the state had altered its policy on such closures. None of the stable SOEs, however, closed a core unit in this period, and only one sold one—which was very small.

More firms had closed or sold auxiliary activities and/or units, however. Twenty-one had closed and a further two had sold at least one of these. Although state firms (64 per cent) appeared to be slightly more reluctant to close down such activities than non-state ones (87 per cent), the greatest difference in respect of control type was between foreign-firm-controlled ones and Hungarian ones. All the former had closed at least one auxiliary activity or unit, while only 67 per cent of the latter had done so. This greater willingness to dispose of ancillary units as opposed to core production facilities suggests that managers found it easier to disintegrate vertically than reduce output levels substantially, although the foreign-controlled ones seemed to implement closures more readily than their domestic counterparts. Between 1993 and 1996 only the foreign-controlled firms and crisis SOEs closed ancillary units, although all control types continued to sell them, in some cases to their employees.

Overall, then, despite the reductions in employment during the early 1990s, many firms still had many non-core activities and excess production units after 1993. Half of the eighteen reinterviewed in 1996 sold at least one ancillary unit and a third either sold and/or closed a production unit in the second period considered here. It was especially the foreign-controlled firms that seemed most able and willing to dispose of ancillary activities, and by 1996 they had become more specialized vertically and horizontally than the stable SOEs.

Organizational decentralization was analysed in two ways: first, whether firms had reallocated functional skills and resources from head office to subsidiaries and business units; secondly, the extent to which decision-making on a variety of issues was decentralized to unit managers. If we take the relocation of functional groups first, eight of the twenty-seven firms interviewed in 1993 and 1994 said there had been some decentralization of skills such as marketing and accounting to subunits, while fourteen claimed that most functional groupings were now decentralized to factories and other business units. As far as this last group was concerned, state firms were no less likely to claim such decentralization had occurred than privately controlled ones, but size did seem to be a factor. For instance, six of the nine enterprises that claimed to have allocated finance specialists to production units had over 3,000 employees. Over half of these enterprises, then, had restructured head-office departments and allocated some of their groups to subsidiaries and subunits. However, most still retained functional directors in the key areas of accounting, engineering, sales, and marketing at headquarters, and these typically were seen as members of top management, with subunit managers in practice being subordinated and having only limited decision-making powers.

Between 1993 and 1996, organizational structures remained more stable, with half of the eighteen firms reporting no substantial change. However, both of the crisis SOEs claimed they had undergone a considerable restructuring, and so did three of the six foreign-controlled firms. More of the stable SOEs had delegated substantial financial and purchasing/sales functions to their factory and similar subsidiary units in this period than had the crisis SOEs and the foreign firms. Overall, though, there did not seem to be many fully-fledged 'profit centres' with their own production, sales, purchasing, and accounting functions in these Hungarian enterprises, despite the general tendency for owners to delegate more decisions to managers. It is particularly striking that fewer of the foreign-controlled firms had delegated these additional functions to subunits than the SOEs.

In terms of the centralization of decision-making in specific areas, there did seem to be a general tendency to delegate many decisions to lower levels of the organization in 1996 than in the early 1990s, as Table 9.7 indicates. Following Lincoln and Kalleberg's (1990) study of commitment and control in American and Japanese firms, top managers were asked to identify the level of the organizational hierarchy at which twenty-four decisions were taken in practice. These ranged from routine production decisions to those dealing with major organizational restructuring. Six sets of these decisions can be identified: major organizational and administrative changes, financial management procedures, personnel management procedures, appointments and promotions at lower levels, production management, and marketing and purchasing. In all six of these areas, there had been an overall increase in decentralization away from the chief executive to functional heads of departments and plant managers.

Of the four control types considered here, it was the stable SOEs that showed the most delegation of decision-making to lower levels of their hierarchies between 1993–4 and 1996. This perhaps reflected their increasing autonomy from state agencies in this period and the more stable political environment. Foreign-controlled firms also appeared more willing to delegate control over administrative changes to functional directors, but did not change the location of decision-making in most other areas, presumably reflecting the greater degree of owner control in this period. Most of the manger-controlled firms were more similar to the SOEs in

TABLE 9.7. Centralization of decision-making, by control type, 1993–1996

Organizational level at which decision types made in practice	Control type							
	Stable SOEs		Crisis SOEs		Foreign controlled		Manager controlled	
	1993	1996	1993	1996	1993	1996	1993	1996
Major organizational and administrative changes								
Functional director	2	4	2	1	3	4	3	4
CEO	4	1	3	1	6	2	4	1
Financial management procedures								
Functional director	2	4	3	0	2	1	2	3
CEO and above	4	1	2	2	7	5	5	2
Personnel management procedures								
Functional director	3	3	2	0	6	4	3	4
CEO	3	2	3	2	3	2	4	1
Appointments and promotions								
Factory managers	4	5	2	1	7	4	3	5
Functional director	2	0	3	1	1	2	3	0
CEO	0	0	0	0	1	0	1	0
Production management								
Workflow manager	4	4	1	2	9	6	5	4
Factory manager	2	1	4	0	0	0	2	1
Marketing and purchasing decisions								
Factory manager	0	1	1	0	0	0	1	0
Functional director	3	4	0	1	8	5	5	5
CEO and above	3	0	4	1	1	1	1	0

terms of increasing decentralization in the mid-1990s, again perhaps reflecting the more stable economic environment. In contrast, the two crisis SOEs tended to remain fairly centralized in most areas, as might be expected.

This slight increase in decentralization did not, though, extend to the shopfloor. Both these sets of interviews with top managers and the 480 carried out with manual and white-collar employees in 1994 and 1995 revealed a general tendency to exert more managerial control over work processes, especially those conducted by unskilled and semi-skilled workers (Czaban and Whitley 1998; Whitley and Czaban 1998a). However, as with many of the other aspects of enterprise behaviour being discussed in this chapter, these changes were incremental and varied between firms rather than being radical and universal.

As already mentioned, many firms had increased the proportion of first-line supervisors in production functions in the early 1990s, and this had led to significant reductions in their spans of control in the privately controlled companies between 1990 and 1996. Most top managers expected their supervisors to control task allocation, but rather fewer in the early 1990s were insistent that they should also control how tasks were to be performed—no doubt reflecting the legacy of the shortage economy. By 1996, however, only one firm's top managers did not strongly expect supervisors to control how work was done. Interviews with production workers in 1995, on the other hand, revealed a more complex pattern of supervisory control.

First, many more of those in privately controlled firms said that supervisors exerted high levels of work control than did those in state enterprises. Secondly, when workers were given discretion over task performance, it was overwhelmingly the skilled workers who had most influence in the private firms and crisis SOEs, but not in the stable SOEs. In general, skilled workers were treated quite differently from unskilled and semi-skilled ones in the privatized firms, but not in the stable SOEs. Similarly, workers were involved in problem-solving and decision-making activities to a greater extent in the foreign-controlled firms, and again these were nearly all skilled staff. Access to supervisors and the ability to make complaints about supervisor behaviour were also easier in foreign firms, especially for skilled workers.

Overall, then, it seems that the top managers of the more stable SOEs had developed strong intentions to exert more control over task performance by the mid-1990s, but had not been able to translate that into practice to the extent found in privately owned firms. They also had not differentiated greatly between skill levels in terms of work control and involvement in problem-solving activities when compared to the foreign-owned firms and—to some extent—the crisis SOEs. Even in the latter, changes in prevailing systems of work organization and control seemed incremental rather than radical, and often depended on substantial investments in production facilities.

The general impression of employment and organizational change in these Hungarian enterprises is one of incremental restructuring and reduction in staffing and activities, especially in those controlled by foreign firms and in the crisis SOEs. Reductions in non-workflow personnel and the closure and/or sale of auxiliary activities in most firms have not been accompanied by large-scale rationalization of facilities or radical changes in operating departments. Similarly, the reshaping of most top-management teams and of many middle-management jobs have not yet led to the transformation of organizational structures or of the experience and skills of senior managers. In most firms, the bulk of senior and middle managers had worked in the same enterprise for most, if not all, their working lives, as had many top managers. Even in foreign-controlled firms this remained the case, and the appointment of outsiders had not, on the whole, led to radical changes, even when accompanied by investments in new machinery.

CONCLUSIONS

Many of these results bear out the general expectation of incremental changes in Hungarian enterprises in the 1990s outlined in the previous chapter. However, the varied connections between control type and patterns of change shown here suggest a more detailed set of conclusions, especially with regard to enterprise type and organizational matters. I shall first discuss issues concerning the 'governance' of enterprises and then consider changes to product, process, and market strategies. Thirdly, the implications of organizational restructuring and work-control changes will be discussed, and finally some more general points highlighted.

As expected, a key factor affecting the extent of managerial independence was the financial performance of the enterprise. In both 1993–4 and 1996, it was the worst performing companies that were most directly controlled by major shareholders, whether these were state agencies or foreign firms. The more financially stable SOEs were also quite tightly controlled in the early 1990s, but had gained more autonomy by 1996, while foreign owners had moved in the opposite direction. Foreign owners were also more inclined to recruit CEOs and other top managers from outside the company, and tended to impose new financial control procedures. However, this did not mean that centralization in general was greater in foreign-controlled firms; rather the extension of parent company procedures, and in some cases executives, to new Hungarian subsidiaries was often accompanied by internal decentralization of operating decisions, especially in the mid-1990s.

The divergence of espoused objectives and preferences between SOEs and private firms in 1993–4 had reduced somewhat by 1996. Most of these top managers claimed they were pursuing growth goals and were committed to improving employee skills as well as emphasizing profitability and shareholder returns by the mid-1990s. Similarly, the SOEs had moved closer to the private firms in seeking further cost reductions and competing on low prices. At least in terms of managerial rhetoric, then, the leaders of Hungarian firms seemed to have developed considerable consensus across control types in the course of the 1990s, perhaps because the state had withdrawn more decisively from enterprise control in 1994 and 1995.

Liberalization of imports and supply chains had encouraged some vertical disintegration of large enterprises, but at a slower rate than had been predicted in 1990 and notably more in the foreign-controlled firms than in the SOEs. Rather than leading to a broadening of product lines and entering new product markets, however, such reshaping of enterprise activities seemed to result in the already narrowly specialized firms focusing on a single product line for domestic and Western markets. Most of the companies acquired by foreign firms increased their product specialization in the 1990s and remained highly dependent on the domestic market. Although introducing new products and upgrading existing ones within current lines more than their state-controlled counterparts, they showed little intention of developing different product ranges.

Essentially, then, the reductions in employment and disposal of auxiliary units that most firms had carried out since 1990 had not changed their basic character. They were still producing much the same sorts of outputs in similar ways as they did in the late 1980s. Even the markets served had not changed a great deal, since most had already reduced their dependence on CMEA customers considerably by 1989. The radical institutional transformations and collapse of CMEA markets encouraged the new owners and managers to cut the scale of their operations and remove peripheral subunits, but did not lead them to alter their central activities very much at all. In the case of the SOEs this no doubt reflects their limited resources and often high sunk costs in capital-intensive technologies, together with the limited experience of their internally promoted managers with different activities. Foreign owners had more resources but, of course, decided to acquire most of these firms because of their products and the markets they dominated. They were unlikely, then, to alter their strategies radically, at least in the short term.

Within these Hungarian enterprises, changes to employment structures and policies, and to work-organization and control patterns, similarly were incremental rather than radical. They were also more marked in foreign-controlled firms and in those undergoing financial crises. Typically, increases in the relative proportion of direct production workers and supervisors accompanied large reductions in non-workflow employees. Foreign-controlled firms also reduced supervisors' spans of control and tended to increase managerial control over work processes more than other groups of firms, especially tasks carried out by the less skilled workers. This intensification of supervisory control was often accompanied by substantial investment in new production facilities and reorganization of work processes, but usually after the foreign firm had been in control for some time and the political environment had stabilized.

The tightening of managerial control over production flows and task performance in the foreign-controlled firms did not, though, seem to lead to increased distance between supervisors and skilled workers. Indeed, they were more likely to be seen as involving workers in decision-making and problem-solving than those in the SOEs, and to be more accessible in general. The increased formal-ization of many control procedures in these firms appeared to have facilitated managerial collaboration and communication with skilled workers, but much less so with the unskilled and semi-skilled. In contrast, the stable SOEs had decentralized decision-making a little between 1993 and 1996, but had not altered workplace relationships nearly as much.

This pattern of largely incremental changes in most of these Hungarian orga-nizations, and remarkable stability in their product strategies, between 1990 and 1996 emphasizes both the uncertainties of implementing major shifts in tech-nologies and markets and the mixed effects of institutional transformations on organizational restructuring (Csanadi 1997). In most of the companies studied here the substantial investments previously made in facilities and procedures for producing standardized goods in large quantities at relatively low costs meant that incremental improvements in production processes were much more attractive ways of dealing with the changing environment than radical innovations which required substantial investments. Price-based competitive strategies were more feasible in the situation of high market and institutional uncertainty than innova-tion-based ones that would necessitate the development of new technologies, new products, and new markets as well as new skills and knowledge amongst employ-ees. Even when capital and expertise for such investments were—in principle—available, as in the foreign-controlled enterprises, disposing of peripheral units, rationalizing production facilities, and focusing on reducing the costs of making, and upgrading the quality of, current products were more likely to be effective in the short term than committing large resources in an unpredictable environment.

Similarly, the liberalization of the economy and imposition of hard budget constraints did not automatically lead to rapid organizational changes in many of these Hungarian enterprises. This reflected the continued central role of the state in the economy, and the continuing legacy of many other aspects of the late state socialist period (Csanadi 1997). For many managers of Hungarian firms—as else-where in Eastern Europe—the dominance and fragmentation of the state, its shift-ing and often inconsistent policies, meant that incremental change coupled with divide and bargain tactics in negotiating with politicians, bureaucrats, and bankers seemed much more sensible policies than engaging upon radical restruc-turing, which involved considerable conflicts and high, unpredictable risks. Additionally, the memory of 1956 and consequent fear of substantial social unrest among the political class acted as considerable restraints on large-scale redun-dancies.

The implications of this study for the comparative analysis of business systems and economic change can be summarized in four points. First, just as institutional contexts structure economic coordination and control systems over considerable periods of time, so too changes in these contexts take time to affect prevalent patterns of economic organization and behaviour. Even radical trans-formations, as in Eastern Europe and occupied Germany and Japan after 1945, did not result in major changes in organizations instantaneously. Established routines and practices adapt political–economic changes at the same time as they adapt to them, and the institutionalization of new ways of doing things necessarily takes time.

Secondly, managers, technicians, skilled workers, and other employees of major enterprises are rarely passive and reactive groups during periods of major institutional change. While varying across countries and over time in their mobilization and active involvement in the restructuring of their societies, both old élites and new social groupings have unprecedented opportunities to influence the social order in the highly fluid and shifting environment. As old skills, networks, and practices lose their efficacy, newly constructed actors compete to institutionalize their developing rationalities and priorities as core components of the new social order. However, as Csanadi (1997) has emphasized, this very openness of the political and economic system during such times of radical change makes rational calculation and strategic decision-making very difficult, if not impossible. Because the nature of allies and opponents and the rules of the game for deciding outcomes are being reconstructed, groups, identities, and interests are constantly changing and uncertain. In such situations, individuals focus on short-term advantages and restrict their commitments to others as much as possible. The boundaries and behaviour of élites and organizations often become highly erratic and unpredictable in these kinds of environments.

Thirdly, because of the interdependence of institutional arrangements and coincidental events and phenomena, the consequences of particular institutional changes are rarely simple and straightforward. Even when policy-makers do have fairly clear objectives and are able to implement decisions effectively—neither of which are typical of most of the former state socialist societies of Eastern Europe—the resultant outcomes of institutional transformations usually diverge from their intentions. American reforms of the Japanese *Zaibatsu* and banking system during the post-war occupation of Japan, for instance, did not produce an Anglo-Saxon type of political economy. So too in Hungary, state withdrawal from the economy and the imposition of hard budget constraints did not greatly reduce large-enterprise dependence on the state, or the effectiveness of managerial lobbying. Indeed, the concomitant democratization of the political system and fragmentation of the state apparatus probably facilitated such divide and bargain tactics by managers, as the population expected the state to manage political and economic change. Similarly, the depression in Western Europe and attractiveness of investment opportunities in Pacific Asia in the early 1990s limited capital inflows to most of the former state socialist countries, just as the broader geopolitical environment reduced the likelihood of another Marshall Plan being implemented.

Finally, changes in ownership and control may reproduce many characteristics of enterprise structure and behaviour as much as change them radically. Although the foreign-controlled firms in this study did improve products more than SOEs, as well as tightening up production processes and managerial controls, they did not change substantially their products or markets served, nor did they engage upon the large-scale reshaping of their organizations. Major restructuring of the Hungarian economy thus seems unlikely to result from such transfers of control, at least in the short term. Since the attraction of many of these firms to foreign purchasers lies in their domestic near monopolies and low production costs, this is not too surprising. It does, however, mean that such privatization cannot fulfil expectations of transforming the former state socialist economies rapidly.

Furthermore, because many Hungarian-owned and controlled private firms are dependent on large foreign firms for product and technology licences, and also as large customers, they are not likely to initiate substantial restructuring and innovation in the short to medium term. Similarly, the inability of most states in Eastern Europe to coordinate economic development in a comparable manner to their Korean and Taiwanese counterparts in the post-war period means that radical and effective state-led economic reorganization is improbable. Most of these economies, then, will incrementally improve what they are currently doing rather than radically change their industrial structure, or generate high levels of growth and wealth creation in the near future.

REFERENCES

Abbott, A. (1988). *The System of Professions.* Chicago: University of Chicago Press.

Abegglen, J. C., and Stalk, G. (1985). *Kaisha, The Japanese Corporation.* New York: Basic Books.

Abel, I., and Bonin, J. P, (1994). 'Financial Sector Reforms in the Economies in Transition', in J. P. Bonin and I. P. Szekely (eds.), *The Development and Reform of Financial Systems in Central and Eastern Europe.* Aldershot: Edward Elgar.

Abo, T. (1994). *Hybrid Factory: The Japanese Production System in the United States.* New York: Oxford University Press.

Agh, Attila (1996). 'From Nomenclatura to Clientura: The Emergence of New Political Elites in East-Central Europe', in G. Pridham and P. Lewis (eds.), *Stabilising Fragile Democracies: Comparing New Party Systems in Southern and Eastern Europe.* London: Routledge.

Albert, M. (1993). *Capitalism vs. Capitalism.* New York: Four Walls Eight Windows.

Allen, G. C. (1981). *A Short Economic History of Modern Japan* (4th edn.). London: Macmillan.

Amsden, A. H. (1989). *Asia's Next Giant.* Oxford: Oxford University Press.

—— Kochanowicz, J., and Taylor L. (1994). *The Market Meets its Match.* Cambridge, Mass.: Harvard University Press.

Aoki, M. (1988). *Information, Incentives, and Bargaining in the Japanese Economy.* Cambridge: Cambridge University Press.

—— (1994). 'The Japanese Firm as a System of Attributes: A Survey and Research Agenda', in M. Aoki and R. P. Dore (eds.), *The Japanese Firm: The Sources of Competitive Strength.* Oxford: Oxford University Press.

Baden-Fuller, C. W. F., and Stopford J. M. (1991). 'Globalization Frustrated: The Case of White Goods', *Strategic Management Journal*, 12: 493–507.

Bae, K. (1987). *Automobile Workers in Korea.* Seoul: Seoul National University Press.

—— and Form, W. H. (1986). 'Payment Strategy in South Korea's Advanced Economic Sector', *American Economic Review*, 51: 120–31.

Barber, B. (1983). *The Logic and Limits of Trust.* New Brunswick, NJ: Rutgers University Press.

Barrett, R. E. (1988). 'Autonomy and Diversity in the American State on Taiwan', in E. A. Winckler and S. Greenhalgh (eds.), *Contending Approaches to the Political Economy of Taiwan.* Armonk, NY: M. E. Sharpe.

Bartlett, C. A., and Ghoshal S. (1989). *Managing across Borders: The Transnational Solution.* London: Hutchinson Business Books.

Batt, J. (1988). *Economic Reform and Political Change in Eastern Europe.* London: Macmillan.

Bauer, M. (1987). *Les 200.* Paris: Seuil.

—— and Cohen E. (1981). *Qui gouverne les groupes industriels?* Paris: Seuil.

Beattie, H. J. (1979). *Land and Lineage in China.* Cambridge: Cambridge University Press.

Beetham, D. (1991). *The Legitimation of Power.* London: Macmillan.

Berend, I. T. (1990). *The Hungarian Economic Reforms 1953–1988.* Cambridge: Cambridge University Press.

Best, M. (1990). *The New Competition: Institutions of Industrial Restructuring*. Oxford: Polity Press.

Biggart, N. W. (1997). 'Institutional Patrimonialism in Korean Business', in M. Orru *et al.* (eds.), *The Economic Organization of East Asian Capitalism*. Thousand Oaks, Calif.: Sage.

Bonifert, D. (1987). *A Berszabalyozas. Hogyan Kezdodott? Hova jutott? Merre tart?* (Wage Regulation. How it Started? Where it Got to? Where it Goes to?). Budapest: Közgazdasagi es Jogi Könyvkiadó.

Bonin, J. P., and Schaffer, M. E. (1995). 'Banks, Firms, Bad Debts and Bankruptcy in Hungary 1991–94', CEPR Discussion Paper No. 234, London: Centre for Economic Policy Research.

Boswell, J. S. (1983). *Business Policies in the Making: Three Steel Companies Compared*. London: Allen & Unwin.

Botti, H. (1995). 'Misunderstandings: A Japanese Transplant in Italy Strives for Lean Production', *Organization*, 2: 55–86.

Boyer, R. (1990). 'The Capital Labour Relations in OECD Countries', Document du Travail CEPREMAP, 9020, September.

—— (1991). 'Capital Labor Relation and Wage Formation: Continuities and Changes of National Trajectories', in T. Mizoguchi (ed.), *Making Economies More Efficient and More Equitable*. Tokyo: Kinokuniya.

—— (1994). 'Do Labour Institutions Matter for Economic Development? A "Regulation" Approach for the OECD and Latin America, with an extension to Asia', in G. Rodgers (ed.), *Workers, Institutions and Economic Growth in Asia*. Geneva: ILO.

—— (1997). 'French Statism at the Crossroads', in C. Crouch and W. Streeck (eds.), *Political Economy of Modern Capitalisms*. London: Sage.

—— and Durand, J.-P. (1997). *After Fordism*. London: Macmillan.

—— and Hollingsworth, J. R. (1997). 'From National Embeddedness to Spatial and Institutional Nestedness', in J. R. Hollingsworth and R. Boyer (eds.), *Contemporary Capitalism: The Embeddedness of Institutions*. Cambridge: Cambridge University Press.

Brandt, V. (1987). 'Korea', in G. C. Lodge and E. Vogel (eds.), *Ideology and National Competitiveness*. Boston: Harvard Business School.

Bunce, V., and Csanadi, M. (1993). 'Uncertainty in the Transition: Post Communism in Hungary', *East European Politics and Societies*, 7: 240–75.

Burawoy, M., and Lukacs, J. (1985). 'Mythologies of Work: A Comparison of Firms in State Socialism and Advanced Capitalism', *American Sociological Review*, 50: 723–37.

—— (1992). *The Radiant Past: Ideology and Reality in Hungary's Road to Capitalism*. Chicago: Chicago University Press.

Calder, K. E. (1993). *Strategic Capitalism: Private Business and Public Purpose in Japanese Industrial Finance*. Princeton: Princeton University Press.

Callon, M., and Vignolle, J. P. (1977). 'Breaking Down the Organization: Local Conflicts and Societal Systems of Action', *Social Science Information*, 16: 147–67.

Campagnac, E., and Winch, G. (1997). 'The Social Regulation of Technical Expertise: The Corporations and Professions in France and Great Britain', in R. Whitley and P. H. Kristensen (eds.), *Governance at Work: The Social Regulation of Economic Relations*. Oxford: Oxford University Press.

Campbell, J. L., and Lindberg, L. N. (1991). 'The Evolution of Governance Regimes', in

J. L. Campbell *et al.* (eds.), *Governance of the American Economy*. Cambridge: Cambridge University Press.

—— Hollingsworth, J. R., and Lindberg, L. N. (1991) (eds.). *Governance of the American Economy*. Cambridge: Cambridge University Press.

Carlin, W., van Reenen, J., and Wolfe, T. (1995). 'Enterprise Restructuring in Early Transition: The Case Study Evidence from Central and Eastern Europe', *Economics of Transition*, 3: 427–58.

Castells, M. (1992). 'Four Asian Tigers with a Dragon Head: A Comparative Analysis of the State, Economy and Society in the Asian Pacific Rim', in R. Appelbaum and J. Henderson (eds.), *States and Development in the Asian Pacific Rim*. London: Sage.

Chandler, A. D. (1977). *The Visible Hand*. Cambridge, Mass.: Harvard University Press.

—— (1980). 'The United States: Seedbed of Managerial Capitalism', in A. D. Chandler and H. Daems (eds.), *Managerial Hierarchies: Comparative Perspectives on the Rise of the Modern*. Cambridge, Mass.: Harvard University Press.

—— (1990). *Scale and Scope*. Cambridge, Mass.: Harvard University Press.

Cheng, T. J. (1990). 'Political Regimes and Development Strategies: South Korea and Taiwan', in G. Gereffi and D. L. Wyman (eds.), *Manufacturing Miracles: Paths of Industrialization in Latin America and East Asia*. Princeton: Princeton University Press.

Child, J. (1969). *British Management Thought*. London: Allen & Unwin.

—— (1972). 'Organization Structure, Environment and Performance: The Role of Strategic Choice', *Sociology*, 6: 1–22.

—— Fores, M., Glover, I., and Lawrence, P. (1983). 'A Price to Pay? Professionalism in Work Organization in Britain and West Germany', *Sociology*, 17: 63–78.

—— and Tayeb, M. (1983). 'Theoretical Perspectives in Cross-National Organizational Research', *International Studies of Management and Organization*, 12: 23–70.

Cho, D.-S. (1987). *The General Trading Company: Concept and Strategy*. Lexington, Mass.: D. C. Heath.

Cho, S. (1994). *The Dynamics of Korean Economic Development*. Washington: Institute for International Economics.

Chou, T. L., and Kirkby, R. J. R. (1998), 'Taiwan's Electronics Sector: Restructuring of Form and Space', *Competition and Change*, 2: 331–58.

Chu, Y.-h. (1994). 'The Realignment of Business–Government Relations and Regime Transition in Taiwan', in A. MacIntyre (ed.), *Business and Government in Industrializing Asia*. St Leonards, NSW: Allen & Unwin.

—— (1995). 'The East Asian NICs: A State-Led Path to the Developed World', in B. Stallings (ed.), *Global Change, Regional Response*. Cambridge: Cambridge University Press.

Chung, K. H., Lee, H. C., and Okumura, A. (1988). 'The Managerial Practices of Korean, American and Japanese Firms', *Journal of East and West Studies*, 17: 45–74.

Clark, G. L. (1995). 'Corporate Strategy and Industrial Restructuring', in G. L. Clark and W. B. Kim (eds.), *Asian NIEs and the Global Economy*. Baltimore: Johns Hopkins University Press.

—— and Kim, W. B. (1995). 'Introduction', in G. L. Clark and W. B. Kim (eds.), *Asian NIEs and the Global Economy*. Baltimore: Johns Hopkins University Press.

Clark, R. (1979). *The Japanese Company*. New Haven: Yale University Press.

Cotta, M. (1996). 'Structuring the New Party Systems after the Dictatorship: Coalitions, Alliances, Fusions and Splits during the Transition and Post-Transition Stages,' in

G. Pridham and P. Lewis (eds.), *Stabilizing Fragile Democracies*. London: Routledge.

Cox, A. (1986). 'State, Finance and Industry in Comparative Perspective', in A. Cox (ed.), *State, Finance and Industry*. Brighton: Wheatsheaf.

Crawford, B. (1995). 'Post-Communist Political Economy: A Framework for the Analysis of Reform', in B. Crawford (ed.), *Markets, States and Democracy*. Boulder, Colo.: Westview Press.

Csaba, L (1993). 'Economic Consequences of Soviet Disintegration for Hungary', in I. P. Szekely and D. M. G. Newbery (eds.), *Hungary: An Economy in Transition*. Cambridge: Cambridge University Press.

—— (1995). *The Capitalist Revolution in Eastern Europe*. Aldershot: Edward Elgar.

Csanadi, Maria (1997). 'The Legacy of Party-States for the Transformation', *Communist Economies and Economic Transformation*, 9: 61–85.

Csepeli, G., and Orkeny, A. (1992). *Ideology and Political Beliefs in Hungary*. London: Pinter.

Cumings, B. (1984). 'The Legacy of Japanese Colonialism in Korea', in R. H. Myers and M. A. Peattie (eds.), *The Japanese Colonial Empire, 1895–1945*. Princeton: Princeton University Press.

—— (1987). 'The Origins and Development of the Northeast Asian Political Economy', in F. C. Deyo (ed.), *The Political Economy of the New Asian Industrialism*. Ithaca, NY: Cornell University Press.

—— (1997). *Korea's Place in the Sun*. New York: Norton.

Cusumano, M. A. (1985). *The Japanese Automobile Industry: Technology and Management at Nissan and Toyota*. Cambridge, Mass.: Harvard University Press.

Czaban, L., and Whitley, R. (1998). 'The Transformation of Work Systems in Emergent Capitalism: The Case of Hungary', *Work, Employment and Society*, 12: 1–26.

Dabrowski, M. (1994). 'The Role of the Government in Postcommunist Economies', in L. Csaba (ed.), *Privatization, Liberalization and Destruction*. Aldershot: Dartmouth.

Daems, H. (1983). 'The Determinants of the Hierarchical Organization of Industry', in A. Francis *et al.* (eds.), *Power, Efficiency and Institutions*. London: Heinemann.

Daviddi, R. (1993). 'Discussion of Part One', in I. P. Szekely and D. M. G. Newbery (eds.), *Hungary: An Economy in Transition*. Cambridge: Cambridge University Press.

Deyo, F. C. (1987). 'Coalitions, Institutions and Linkage Sequencing—towards a Strategic Capacity Model of East Asian Developments', in F. C. Deyo (ed.), *The Political Economy of the New Asian Industrialism*. Ithaca, NY: Cornell University Press.

—— (1989). *Beneath the Miracle: Labour Subordination in the New Asian Industrialism*. Berkeley and Los Angeles: University of California Press.

DiMaggio, P., and Powell, W. W. (1991). 'Introduction', in W. W. Powell and P. DiMaggio (eds.), *The New Institutionalism in Organizational Analysis*. Chicago: University of Chicago Press.

Dicken, P. (1998). *Global Shift*. London: Paul Chapman Publishing.

Dietrich, M. (1994). *Transaction Cost Economics and Beyond*. London: Routledge.

D'Iribarne, P. (1989). *La Logique de l'honneur*. Paris: Seuil.

Dobak, M., and Tari, E. (1996). 'Evolution of Organizational Forms in the Transition Period of Hungary', *Journal for East European Management Studies*, 1: 7–35.

Dobbin, F. (1994). *Forging Industrial Policy: The United States, Britain, and France in the Railway Age*. Cambridge: Cambridge University Press.

—— (1995). 'The Origins of Economic Principles: Railway Entrepreneurs and Public

Policy in 19th Century America', in W. R. Scott and S. Christensen (eds.), *The Institutional Construction of Organizations*. Thousand Oaks, Calif.: Sage.

Donaldson, L. (1985). *In Defence of Organization Theory*. Cambridge: Cambridge University Press.

Dore, R. P. (1973). *British Factory—Japanese Factory*. London: Allen & Unwin.

—— (1986). *Flexible Rigidities*. Stanford, Calif.: Stanford University Press.

Doz, Y., and Prahalad, C. K. (1993). 'Managing DMNCs: A Search for a New Paradigm', in S. Ghoshal and E. Westney (eds.), *Organization Theory and the Multinational Corporation*. London: Macmillan.

Dunning, J. H. (1993). *The Globalization of Business*. London: Routledge.

Dyker, D. A. (1990). *Yugoslavia: Socialism, Development and Debt*. London: Routledge.

Dyson, K. (1980). *The State Tradition in Western Europe*. Oxford: Oxford University Press.

EBRD (1995). *Transition Report 1995*. London: European Bank for Reconstruction and Development.

Ebers, M. (1997). (ed.). *The Formation of Inter-Organizational Networks*. Oxford: Oxford University Press.

Eccleston, B. (1989). *State and Society in Post-War Japan*. Cambridge: Polity Press.

Eckert, C. J. (1993). 'The South Korean Bourgeoisie: A Class in Search of Hegemony', in H. Koo (ed.), *State and Society in Contemporary Korea*. Ithaca, NY: Cornell University Press.

Eckstein, H., and Gurr, T. R. (1975). *Patterns of Authority: A Structural Basis for Political Inquiry*. New York: J. Wiley.

The Economist (1997*a*). 'One World?', 18 October, 134–5.

—— (1997*b*). 'Capital Goes Global', 25 October, 139–40.

Elger, T., and Smith, C. (1994). *Global Japanization?* London: Routledge.

Elster, J. (1984). *Ulysses and the Sirens*. Cambridge: Cambridge University Press.

Emmott, B. (1992). *Japan's Global Reach: The Influences, Strategies and Weaknesses of Japan's Multinational Companies*. London: Century.

Enright, M. J., Scott, E. E., and Dodwell, D. (1997). *The Hong Kong Advantage*. Hong Kong: Oxford University Press.

Evans, P. (1995). *Embedded Autonomy: States and Industrial Transformation*. Princeton: Princeton University Press.

Feldenkirchen, W. (1997). 'Business Groups in the German Electrical Industry', in T. Shiba and M. Shimotani (eds.), *Beyond the Firm*. Oxford: Oxford University Press.

Fields, Karl J. (1995). *Enterprise and the State in Korea and Taiwan*. Ithaca, NY: Cornell University Press.

Figyelo (Observer) (1995). *The Largest Hungarian Companies*. Budapest: Figyelo.

Filtzer, D. (1992). 'Economic Reform and Production Relations in Soviet Industry, 1986–90', in C. Smith and P. Thompson (eds.), *Labour in Transition*. London: Routledge.

Fligstein, N. (1985). 'The Spread of the Multidivisional Form', *American Sociological Review*, 50: 377–91.

—— (1990). *The Transformation of Corporate Control*. Cambridge, Mass.: Harvard University Press.

—— (1996). 'Markets as Politics: A Political–Cultural Approach to Market Institutions', *American Sociological Review*, 61: 656–73.

Foss, N. J., and Knudsen, C. (1996) (eds.). *Towards a Competence Theory of the Firm*. London: Routledge.

Friedman, A. (1977). *Industry and Labour.* London: Macmillan.

Friedman, D. (1988). *The Misunderstood Miracle.* Ithaca, NY: Cornell University Press.

Fruin, M. (1992). *The Japanese Enterprise System.* Oxford: Oxford University Press.

Frydman, R., and Rapaczynski, A. (1993). 'Evolution and Design in the East European Transition', in M. Baldassarri *et al.* (eds.), *Privatization Processes in Eastern Europe.* London: Macmillan.

Fukutake, T. (1967). *Japanese Rural Society.* Ithaca, NY: Cornell University Press.

Gangopadhyay, P. (1998). 'Patterns of Trade, Investment and Migration in the Asia-Pacific Region', in G. Thompson (ed.), *Economic Dynamism in the Asia-Pacific.* London: Routledge.

Gates, H. (1987). *Chinese Working Class Lives: Getting By in Taiwan.* Ithaca, NY: Cornell University Press.

—— (1996). *China's Motor: A Thousand Years of Petty Capitalism.* Ithaca, NY: Cornell University Press.

Geddes, B. (1995). 'The Development of Accountancy Education, Training and Research in England', unpublished Ph.D. thesis, University of Manchester.

Gereffi, Gary (1994). 'The Organization of Buyer-Driven Global Commodity Chains', in G. Gereffi and M. Korzeniewicz (eds.), *Commodity Chains and Global Capitalism.* Westport, Conn.: Praeger.

—— (1995*a*). 'Global Commodity Chains and Third World Development', paper presented to ILO Forum on Labour in a Changing World Economy, Bangkok, 23–6 January.

—— (1995*b*). 'Contending Paradigms for Cross-Regional Comparison: Development Strategies and Commodity Chains in East Asia and Latin America', in P. H. Smith (ed.), *Latin America in Comparative Perspective.* Boulder, Colo.: Westview.

—— (1996). 'Commodity Chains and Regional Divisions of Labour in East Asia', *Journal of Asian Business,* 12: 75–112

Gerlach, M. (1992). *Alliance Capitalism.* Berkeley and Los Angeles: University of California Press.

Globokar, T. (1997). 'Eastern Europe Meets West: An Empirical Study on French Management in a Slovenian Plant', in S. Sackman (ed.), *Cultural Complexity in Organizations.* London: Sage.

Godley, M. R. (1981). *The Mandarin-Capitalists from Nanyang, Overseas Chinese Enterprise in the Modernization of China 1893–1911.* Cambridge: Cambridge University Press.

Gold, T. B. (1986). *State and Society in the Taiwan Miracle.* Armonk, NY: M. E. Sharpe.

—— (1988). 'Entrepreneurs, Multinationals and the State', in E. A. Winckler and S. Greenhalgh (eds.), *Contending Approaches to the Political Economy of Taiwan.* Armonk, NY: M. E. Sharpe.

—— (1996). 'Civil Society in Taiwan: The Confucian Dimension', in W. M. Tu (ed.), *Confucian Traditions in East Asian Modernity.* Cambridge, Mass.: Harvard University Press.

Grabher, G. (1993). 'The Weakness of Strong Ties: The Lock-In of Regional Development in the Ruhr Area', in G. Grabher (ed.), *The Embedded Firm: On the Socioeconomics of Industrial Networks.* London: Routledge.

—— (1995). 'The Elegance of Incoherence: Economic Transformation in East Germany and Hungary', in E. Dittrich *et al.* (eds.), *Industrial Transformation in Europe.* London: Sage.

Grancelli, B. (1995). 'Organizational Change: Towards a new East West Comparison', *Organization Studies*, 16: 1–26.

Granovetter, M. (1985). 'Economic Action and Social Structure: the Problem of Embeddedness', *American Journal of Sociology*, 91: 481–510.

—— (1996). 'Coase Revisited: Business Groups in the Modern Economy', *Industrial and Corporate Change*, 4: 93–130.

Greenhalgh, S. (1984). 'Networks and their Nodes: Urban Society on Taiwan', *China Quarterly*, 99: 529–52.

—— (1988). 'Families and Networks in Taiwan's Economic Development', in E. A. Winckler and S. Greenhalgh (eds.), *Contending Approaches to the Political Economy of Taiwan*. Armonk NY: M. E. Sharpe.

Gross, D., and Steinherr, A. (1995). *Winds of Change: Economic Transition in Central and Eastern Europe*. London: Longman.

Guillen, M. F. (1994). *Models of Management: Work, Authority and Organization in a Comparative Perspective*. Chicago: University of Chicago Press.

Haboush, J. K. (1991). 'The Confucianism of Korean Society', in G. Rozman (ed.), *The East Asian Region: Confucian Heritage and its Modern Adaptation*. Princeton: Princeton University Press.

Haggard, S. (1990). *Pathways from the Periphery: The Politics of Growth in the Newly Industrializing Countries*. Ithaca, NY: Cornell University Press.

—— and Moon, C.-i. (1993). 'The State, Politics and Economic Development in Postwar South Korea', in H. Koo (ed.), *State and Society in Contemporary Korea*. Ithaca, NY: Cornell University Press.

Halasz, G. (1993). *Alas es kozepfoku oktatas Magyarorszagon* (Basic and Intermediate Education in Hungary). Budapest: Egyetemi Konyvkiado.

Haley, J. O. (1992). 'Consensual Governance: A Study of Law, Culture and the Political Economy of Postwar Japan', in S. Kumon and H. Rosovsky (eds.), *The Political Economy of Japan 3: Culture and Social Dynamics*. Stanford, Calif.: Stanford University Press.

Hall, J. A. (1988). 'States and Societies: The Miracle in Comparative Perspective', in J. Baechler, J. A. Hall, and M. Mann (eds.), *Europe and the Rise of Capitalism*. Oxford: Blackwell.

—— (1995). 'After the Vacuum: Post-Communism in the Light of Tocqueville', in B. Crawford (ed.), *Markets, States and Democracy*. Boulder, Colo.: Westview.

Hamilton, G. (1991). 'The Organizational Foundations of Western and Chinese Commerce', in G. Hamilton (ed.), *Business Networks and Economic Development in East and Southeast Asia*. Hong Kong: Centre of Asian Studies, University of Hong Kong.

—— (1997). 'Organization and Market Processes in Taiwan's Capitalist Economy', in M. Orru *et al.*, *The Economic Organization of East Asian Capitalism*. Thousand Oaks, Calif.: Sage.

—— and Biggart, N. W. (1988). 'Market, Culture and Authority: A Comparative Analysis of Management and Organization in the Far East', *American Journal of Sociology*, 94 supplement: 552–94.

—— and Feenstra, R. C. (1997). 'Varieties of Hierarchies and Markets: An Introduction', in M. Orru *et al.* (eds.), *The Economic Organization of East Asian Capitalism*. Thousand Oaks, Calif.: Sage.

—— and Kao, C.-S. (1990). 'The Institutional Foundation of Chinese Business: The Family Firm in Taiwan', *Comparative Social Research*, 12: 95–112.

—— Zeile, W., and Kim, W. J. (1990). 'The Network Structures of East Asian Economies', in S. Clegg and G. Redding (eds.), *Capitalism in Contrasting Cultures*. Berlin: de Gruyter.

Hedlund, G. (1993). 'Assumptions of Hierarchy and Heterarchy, with Applications to the Management of the Multinational Corporation', in S. Ghoshal and E. Westney (eds.), *Organization Theory and the Multinational Corporation*. London: Macmillan.

Hellgren, B., and Melin, M. (1992). 'Business Systems, Industrial Wisdom and Corporate Strategies: The Case of the Pulp and Paper Industry', in R. Whitley (ed.), *European Business Systems: Firms and Markets in their National Contexts*. London: Sage.

Henderson, G. (1968). *Korea: The Politics of the Vortex*. Cambridge, Mass.: Harvard University Press.

Henderson, J. (1993). 'The Role of the State in the Economic Transformation of East Asia', in C. Dixon and D. Drakakis-Smith (eds.), *Economic and Social Development in Pacific Asia*. London: Routledge.

—— Whitley, R., Czaban, L., and Lengyel, G. (1995). 'Contention and Confusion in Industrial Transformation: Dilemmas of State Economic Management', in E. Dittrich, G. Schmidt, and R. Whitley (eds.), *Industrial Transformation in Europe*. London: Sage.

Herrigel, Gary (1989). 'Industrial Order and the Politics of Industrial Change: Mechanical Engineering', in P. J. Katzenstein (ed.), *Industry and Politics in West Germany*. Ithaca, NY: Cornell University Press.

—— (1993). 'Large Firms, Small Firms and the Governance of Flexible Specialization', in B. Kogut (ed.), *Country Competitiveness*. Oxford: Oxford University Press.

—— (1994). 'Industry as a Form of Order', in R. Hollingsworth *et al.* (eds.), *Governing Capitalist Economies*. Oxford: Oxford University Press.

—— (1996). *Industrial Constructions: The Sources of German Industrial Power*. Cambridge: Cambridge University Press.

Hethy, L. (1983). *Gazdasagpolitika es erdekeltseg* (Economic Policy and Interest). Budapest: Kossuth.

Hibino, B. (1997). 'The Transmission of Work Systems: A Comparison of US and Japan Auto's Human Resource Management Practices in Mexico', in R. Whitley and P. H. Kristensen (eds.), *Governance at Work: The Social Regulation of Economic Relations*. Oxford: Oxford University Press.

Hickson, D., McMillan, C. J., Azumi, K., and Horvath, D. (1979). 'Grounds for Comparative Organization Theory: Quicksands or Hard Core?', in C. J. Lammers and D. J. Hickson (eds.), *Organizations Alike and Unlike*. London: Routledge.

Higuchi, Yoshio (1997). 'Trends in Japanese Labour Markets', in M. Sako and H. Sato (eds.), *Japanese Labour and Management in Transition*. London: Routledge.

Hirschhausen, C. von (1995). 'No Privatization without Capitalization: Approaches to Post-Socialist Industrial Restructuring in Central and Eastern Europe', in E. Dittrich *et al.* (eds.), *Industrial Transformation in Europe*. London: Sage.

Hirschmeier, J., and Yui, T. (1981). *The Development of Japanese Business 1600–1980* (2nd edn.). London: Allen & Unwin.

Hirst, P., and Thompson, G. (1996). *Globalization in Question*. Oxford: Polity Press.

—— and Zeitlin, J. (1991). 'Flexible Specialization vs. Post-Fordism: Theory, Evidence and Policy Implications', *Economy and Society*. 20: 1–56.

Ho, D. Y. F. (1986). 'Chinese Patterns of Socialization: A Critical Review', in M. Bond (ed.), *The Psychology of the Chinese People*. Oxford: Oxford University Press.

Ho, S. P.-S. (1984). 'Colonialism and Development of Korea, Taiwan and Kwantung', in R. H. Myers and M. R. Peattie (eds.), *The Japanese Colonial Empire, 1895–1945.* Princeton: Princeton University Press.

Hollingsworth, J. R. (1991). 'The Logic of Coordinating American Manufacturing Sectors', in J. L. Campbell *et al.* (eds.), *Governance of the American Economy.* Cambridge: Cambridge University Press.

—— (1997). 'Continuities and Changes in Social Systems of Production: The Cases of Japan, Germany and the United States', in J. R. Hollingsworth and R. Boyer (eds.), *Comparing Capitalisms: The Embeddedness of Institutions.* Cambridge: Cambridge University Press.

—— and Boyer, R. (1997*a*) (eds.). *Comparing Capitalisms: The Embeddedness of Institutions.* Cambridge: Cambridge University Press.

—— —— (1997*b*). 'Coordination of Economic Actors and Social Systems of Production', in J. R. Hollingsworth and R. Boyer (eds.), *Comparing Capitalisms: The Embeddedness of Institutions.* Cambridge: Cambridge University Press.

—— and Streek, W. (1994). 'Counties and Sectors: Concluding Remarks on Performance, Convergence and Competitiveness', in J. R. Hollingsworth *et al.* (eds.), *Governing Capitalist Economies.* Oxford: Oxford University Press.

—— Schmitter, P., and Streeck, W. (1994) (eds.). *Governing Capitalist Economies.* Oxford: Oxford University Press.

Holmes, S. (1995). 'Cultural Legacies or State Collapse? Probing the Postcommunist Dilemma', public lecture delivered at the Collegium Budapest on 17 October, published as Public Lecture No. 13, Collegium Budapest, November.

Horvath, L. (1977). 'Uzemi demokracia es vallati strategia' (Work Place Democracy and Company Strategy), *Tarsadalmi Szemle*, 9: 72–7.

Hounshell, D. A. (1995). 'Planning and Executing "Automation" at Ford Motor Company, 1945–65', in H. Shiomi and K. Wada (eds.), *Fordism Transformed.* Oxford: Oxford University Press.

Hu, Y.-S. (1992). 'Global Firms are National Firms with International Operations', *California Management Review*, 34: 107–26.

Ingham, G. (1984). *Capitalism Divided? The City and Industry in British Social Development.* London: Macmillan.

Iterson, A. van (1996). 'Institutions and Types of Firm in Belgium: Regional and Sector Variations', in R. Whitley and P. H. Kristensen (eds.), *The Changing European Firm: Limits to Convergence.* London: Routledge.

—— (1997). 'The Development of National Governance Principles in the Netherlands', in R. Whitley and P. H. Kristensen (eds.), *Governance at Work: The Social Regulation of Economic Relations.* Oxford: Oxford University Press.

—— and Olie, R. (1992). 'European Business Systems: The Dutch Case', in R. Whitley (ed.), *European Business Systems: Firms and Markets in their National Contexts.* London: Sage.

Iwata, R. (1992). 'The Japanese Enterprise as a Unified Body of Employees: Origins and Development', in S. Kumon and H. Rosovsky (eds.), *The Political Economy of Japan 3: Social and Cultural Dynamics.* Stanford, Calif.: Stanford University Press.

Jacobs, N. (1958). *The Origin of Modern Capitalism and Eastern Asia.* Hong Kong: Hong Kong University Press.

—— (1985). *The Korean Road to Modernization and Development.* Urbana, Ill.: University of Illinois Press.

Jaklic, M. (1997). 'Changing Governance Structures and Work Organization in Slovenia', in R. Whitley and P. H. Kristensen (eds.), *Governance at Work: The Social Regulation of Economic Relations*. Oxford: Oxford University Press.

Janelli, R. L. (1993). *Making Capitalism: The Social and Cultural Construction of a South Korean Conglomerate*. Stanford, Calif.: Stanford University Press.

—— and Janelli, D. Y. (1982). *Ancestor Worship and Korean Society*. Stanford, Calif.: Stanford University Press.

Jansen, M. B. and Rozman, G. (1986). 'Overview', in M. B. Jansen and G. Rozman (eds.), *Japan in Transition: From Tokugawa to Meiji*. Princeton: Princeton University Press.

Johnson, C. (1982). *MITI and the Japanese Miracle*. Stanford, Calif.: Stanford University Press.

Jones, L., and Sakong, I. (1980). *Government, Business and Entrepreneurship in Economic Development: The Korean Case*. Cambridge, Mass.: Harvard University Press.

Jun, S. (1992). 'The Origins of the Developmental State in South Korea', *Asian Perspective*, 16: 181–204.

Jürgens, U. (1989). 'The Transfer of Japanese Management Concepts in the International Automobile Industry', in S. Wood (ed.), *The Transformation of Work?* London: Allen & Unwin.

Kagono, T., Alonaka, I., Sakakibara, K., and Okumara, A. (1985). *Strategic vs. Evolutionary Management*. Amsterdam: North Holland.

Kang, C.-K. (1997). 'Diversification Process and the Ownership Structure of Samsung *Chaebol*', in T. Shiba and M. Shimotani (eds.), *Beyond the Firm*. Oxford: Oxford University Press.

Kao, C.-S. (1991). 'Personal Trust in the Large Businesses in Taiwan', in G. Hamilton (ed.), *Business Networks and Economic Development in East and Southeast Asia*. Hong Kong: Centre of Asian Studies, University of Hong Kong.

Katzenstein, P. (1985). *Small States in World Markets*. Ithaca, NY: Cornell University Press.

Kemme, D. M. (1994). 'Banking in Central Europe during the Protomarket Period', in J. P. Bonin and I. P. Szekely (eds.), *The Development and Reform of Financial Systems in Central and Eastern Europe*. Aldershot: Edward Elgar.

Kenney, M., and Florida, R. (1993). *Beyond Mass Production*. Oxford: Oxford University Press.

Kenworthy, L. (1997). 'Globalization and Economic Convergence', *Competition and Change*, 2: 1–64.

Kim, C. S. (1992). *The Culture of Korean Industry*. Tucson, Ariz.: University of Arizona Press.

Kim, E.-m. (1989). 'Development, State Policy and Industrial Organizations: The Case of Korea's *chaebol*', paper presented to the International Conference on Business Groups and Economic Development in East Asia, Hong Kong, 20–2 June.

—— (1991). 'The Industrial Organization and Growth of the Korean *Chaebol*', in G. Hamilton (ed.), *Business Networks and Economic Development in East and Southeast Asia*. Hong Kong: Centre of Asian Studies, University of Hong Kong.

Kim, K.-d. (1988). 'The Distinctive Features of South Korea's Development', in P. L. Berger and H.-H. M. Hsiao (eds.), *In Search of an East Asian Development Model*. New Brunswick, NJ: Transaction.

Kim, K.-o. (1996). 'The Reproduction of Confucian Culture in Contemporary Korea', in

W.-M. Tu (ed.), *Confucian Traditions in East-Asian Modernity.* Cambridge, Mass.: Harvard University Press.

Kim, W. B. (1995). 'Patterns of Industrial Restructuring' in G. L. Clark and W. B. Kim (eds.), *Asian NIEs and the Global Economy.* Baltimore: Johns Hopkins University Press.

King, A. Y. C. (1996). 'State Confucianism and its Transformation: The Restructuring of the State–Society Relation in Taiwan', in W.-M. Tu (ed.), *Confucian Traditions in East-Asian Modernity.* Cambridge, Mass.: Harvard University Press.

Koechlin, T. (1995). 'The Globalization of Investment', *Contemporary Economic Policy,* 13: 92–100.

Koike, K. (1987). 'Human Resource Development and Labour–Management Relations', in K. Yamamura and Y. Yasuba (eds.), T*he Political Economy of Japan I.* Stanford, Calif.: Stanford University Press.

—— (1994). 'Learning and Incentive Systems in Japanese Industry', in M. Aoki and R. Dore (eds.), *The Japanese Firm.* Oxford: Oxford University Press.

—— and Inoki, Takenori (1990). *Skill Formation in Japan and South-East Asia.* Tokyo: University of Tokyo Press.

Kollo, J. (1993). 'The Transformation of Shopfloor Bargaining in Hungarian Industry', in I. P. Szekely and D. M. G. Newbery (eds.), *Hungary: An Economy in Transition.* Cambridge: Cambridge University Press.

Konjhodzic, I. (1996). 'The Patterns of Adjustment of Small Economies in the Process of Liberalization: The Finnish and Slovene Experience in Comparative Perspective', presented to a conference held at the Faculty of Economics, University of Ljubljana, September.

Koo, H. (1987). 'The Interplay of State, Social Class and World System in East Asian Development', in F. C. Deyo (ed.), *The Political Economy of the New Asian Industrialism.* Ithaca, NY: Cornell University Press.

—— (1993). 'Strong State and Contentious Society', in H. Koo (ed.), *State and Society in Contemporary Korea.* Ithaca, NY: Cornell University Press.

—— and Kim, E.-m. (1992). 'The Developmental State and Capital Accumulation in South Korea', in R. P. Applebaum and J. Henderson (eds.), *States and Development in the Asian Pacific Rim.* Newbury Park, Calif.: Sage.

Kornai, J. (1986). 'The Soft Budget Constraint', *Kyklos,* 39: 3–30.

—— (1996). 'Paying the Bill for Goulash Communism: Hungarian Development and Macro-Stabilization in a Political-Economy Perspective', discussion paper 1748, Harvard Institute for Economic Research, Harvard University.

Kovak, B. (1991). 'Entrepreneurship and Privatization of Social Ownership in Economic Reforms', in J. Simmie and J. Dekleva (eds.), ˉ*Yugoslavia in Turmoil: After Self Management?* London: Pinter.

Kozminski, A. K. (1995). 'From the Communist *Nomenklatura* to Transformational Leadership', in B. Grancelli (ed.), *Social Change and Modernization.* Berlin: de Gruyter.

Kraft, E., Vodopivec, M., and Cvikl, M. (1994). 'On its Own: The Economy of Independent Slovenia', in J. Benderly and E. Kraft (eds.), *Independent Slovenia.* London: Macmillan.

Kristensen, P. H. (1992). 'Strategies against Structure: Institutions and Economic Organization in Denmark', in R. Whitley (ed.), *European Business Systems: Firms and Markets in their National Contexts.* London: Sage.

—— (1994). 'Strategies in a Volatile World', *Economy and Society*, 23: 305–34.

—— (1996). 'On the Constitutions of Economic Actors in Denmark: Interacting Skill Containers and Project Coordinators', in R. Whitley and P. H. Kristensen (eds.), *The Changing European Firm: Limits to Convergence*. London: Routledge.

—— (1997). 'National Systems of Governance and Managerial Strategies in the Evolution of Work Systems: Britain, Germany and Denmark Compared', in R. Whitley and P. H. Kristensen (eds.), *Governance at Work: The Social Regulation of Economic Relations*. Oxford: Oxford University Press.

—— and Jaklic, M. (1997). 'Atlantis' Valleys: Local Continuity and Industrialization in Slovenia compared to West Jutland, Denmark and the Third Italy', unpublished paper, Copenhagen Business School, October.

Kuhn, Sarah (1989). 'The Limits to Industrialization: Computer Software Development in a Large Commercial Bank', in S. Wood (ed.), *The Transformation of Work?* London: Allen & Unwin.

Kukar, S., and Stanovnik, T. (1993). 'Analiza osnovnih ekonomskih elementov sistema pokojninskega zavaarovanja v Sloveniji' (The Analysis of the Economic Basis of the Social Insurance System in Slovenia), *IB Revija*, Ljubljana, 27: 8.

Kumazawa, M., and Yamada, J. (1989). 'Jobs and Skills under the Lifelong *nenko* Employment Practice', in S. Wood (ed.), *The Transformation of Work?* London: Allen & Unwin.

Kurgen-van Hentenryk, G. (1997). 'Structure and Strategy of Belgian Business Groups', in T. Shiba and M. Shimotami (eds.), *Beyond the Firm*. Oxford: Oxford University Press.

Kuzmanic, T. (1994). 'Strikes, Trade Unions and Slovene Independence', in J. Benderly and E. Kraft (eds.), *Independent Slovenia*. London: Macmillan.

Lado, M. (1994). 'Workers' and Employers' Interests—as they are Represented in the Changing Industrial Relations in Hungary', Krakow: University Council for Economic and Management Education Transfer Working Paper No. 3.

Laky, T. (1992). 'The Reality and Potential of Autonomous Entrepreneurship', in B. Dallago *et al.* (eds.), *Privatization and Entrepreneurship in Post Socialist Countries*. London: Macmillan.

Lampland, M. (1995). *The Object of Labor*. Chicago: Chicago University Press.

Lane, C. (1989). *Management and Labour in Europe*. Aldershot: Edward Elgar.

—— (1992). 'European Business Systems: Britain and Germany Compared', in R. Whitley (ed.), *European Business Systems: Firms and Markets in their National Contexts*. London: Sage.

—— (1997). 'The Governance of Interfirm Relations in Britain and Germany: Societal or Dominance Effects', in R. Whitley and P. H. Kristensen (eds.), *Governance at Work: The Social Regulation of Economic Relations*. Oxford: Oxford University Press.

Langlois, R. N. (1995). 'Capabilities and Coherence in Firms and Markets', in C. A. Montgomery (ed.), *Resource-Based and Evolutionary Theories of the Firm*. Dordrecht: Kluwer.

—— and Robertson, P. L. (1995). *Firms, Markets and Economic Change*. London: Routledge.

Lazarevic, Z. (1994). 'Economic History of Twentieth Century Slovenia', in J. Benderly and E. Kraft (eds.), *Independent Slovenia*. London: Macmillan.

Lazerson, M. H. (1988). 'Organizational Growth of Small Firms: An Outcome of Markets and Hierarchies', *American Sociological Review*, 53: 330–42.

—— (1995). 'A New Phoenix? Modern Putting Out in the Modena Knitwear Industry', *Administrative Science Quarterly*, 40: 34–59.

Lazonick, W. (1990). *Competitive Advantage on the Shop Floor*. Cambridge, Mass.: Harvard University Press.

—— (1991). *Business Organization and the Myth of the Market Economy*. Cambridge: Cambridge University Press.

—— and O'Sullivan, M. (1996). 'Organization, Finance and International Competition', *Industrial and Corporate Change*, 5: 1–49.

—— and West, J. (1998). 'Organizational Integration and Competitive Advantage', in G. Dosi *et al.* (eds.), *Technology, Organization and Competitiveness*. Oxford: Oxford University Press.

Liebenberg, R. D. (1982). ' "Japan Incorporated" and "The Korean Troops": A Comparative Analysis of Korean Business Organizations', unpublished MA thesis, Dept. of Asian Studies, University of Hawaii.

Lilja, K. (1997). 'Bargaining for the Future: The Changing Habitus of the Shop Steward System in the Pulp and Paper Mills of Finland', in R. Whitley and P. H. Kristensen (eds.), *Governance at Work: The Social Regulation of Economic Relations*. Oxford: Oxford University Press.

—— and Tainio, R. (1996). 'The Nature of the Typical Finnish Firm', in R. Whitley and P. H. Kristensen (eds.), *The Changing European Firm: Limits to Convergence*. London: Routledge.

Limlingan, V. S. (1986). *The Overseas Chinese in Asean: Business Strategies and Management Practices*. Pasig, Metro Manila: Vita Development Corporation.

Lin, H. (1991). 'Chinese Economic Familism and the Diversification of Economic Organizations: A Study of Taiwanese Business Groups', University of California, Davis, Research Program in East Asian Business and Development Working Paper No. 40.

Lincoln, J. R., and Kalleberg, A. L. (1990). *Culture, Control and Commitment*. Cambridge: Cambridge University Press.

Lindberg, L. N., and Campbell, J. L. (1991). 'The State and the Organization of Economic Activity', in J. L. Campbell *et al.* (eds.), *Governance of the American Economy*. Cambridge: Cambridge University Press.

—— —— and Hollingsworth, J. R. (1991). 'Economic Governance and the Analysis of Structural Change in the American Economy', in J. L. Campbell *et al.* (eds.), *Governance of the American Economy*. Cambridge: Cambridge University Press.

Lodge, G. C., and Vogel, E. F. (1987) (eds.). *Ideology and National Competitiveness*. Boston: Harvard Business School Press.

Luhmann, N. (1979). *Trust and Power*. Chichester: John Wiley.

—— (1988). 'Familiarity, Confidence, Trust: Problems and Alternatives', in D. Gambetta (ed.), *Trust*. Oxford: Blackwell.

Luksic, I. (1994). 'Liberalizem versus korporativizem' (Liberalism versus Corporatism), Ljubljana: Znanstveno publicistino sredisce.

Lydall, H. (1989). *Yugoslavia in Crisis*. Oxford: Oxford University Press.

Macfarlane, A. (1978). *The Origins of English Individualism*. Oxford: Blackwell.

McNamara, D. L. (1986). 'Comparative Colonial Response: Korea and Taiwan, 1895–1919', *Korean Studies*, 10: 54–68.

—— (1990). *The Colonial Origins of Korean Enterprise 1910–1945*. Cambridge: Cambridge University Press.

Mako, C., and Novoszath, P. (1995). 'Employment Relations in Multinational Companies: The Hungarian Case', in E. Dittrich *et al.* (eds.), *Industrial Transformation in Europe.* London: Sage.

Mann, S. (1987). *Local Merchants and the Chinese Bureaucracy, 1750–1950.* Stanford, Calif.: Stanford University Press.

Marceau, J. (1992). 'Small Country Business Systems: Australia, Denmark and Finland Compared', in R. D. Whitley (ed.), *European Business Systems: Firms and Markets in their National Contexts.* London: Sage.

Marody, M. (1997). 'Polish Society from the Perspective of European Integration', in J. H. Belka *et al.*, *The Polish Transformation from the Perspective of European Integration.* Warsaw: Friedrich Ebert Foundation.

Marris, R. (1964). *The Economic Theory of 'Managerial' Capitalism.* London: Macmillan.

Maurice, M. (1979). 'For a Study of "the Societal Effect": Universality and Specificity in Organization Research', in C. J. Lammers and D. J. Hickson (eds.), *Organizations Alike and Unlike.* London: Routledge.

—— Sorge, A., and Warner, M. (1980). 'Societal Differences in Organizing Manufacturing Units', *Organization Studies,* 1: 59–86.

—— Sellier, F., and Silvestre, J. J. (1986). *The Social Foundations of Industrial Power.* Cambridge, Mass.: MIT Press.

Merkle, J. A. (1980). *Management and Ideology.* Berkeley and Los Angeles: University of California Press.

Michell, T. (1988). *From a Developing to a Newly Industrialized Country: The Republic of Korea, 1961–82.* Geneva: ILO.

Moon, C. (1994). 'Changing Patterns of Business–Government Relations in South Korea', in A. MacIntyre (ed.), *Business and Government in Industrializing Asia.* St Leonards, NSW: Allen & Unwin.

Moore, B. (1966). *The Social Origins of Dictatorship and Democracy.* Boston: Beacon Press.

Moore, M. (1988). 'Economic Growth and the Rise of Civil Society: Agriculture in Taiwan and South Korea', in G. White (ed.), *Developmental States in East Asia.* London: Macmillan.

Mueller, F., and Loveridge, R. (1997). 'Institutional, Sectoral and Corporate Dynamics in the Creation of Global Supply Chains', in R. Whitley and P. H. Kristensen (eds.), *Governance at Work: The Social Regulation of Economic Relations.* Oxford: Oxford University Press.

Myant, M. (1993). *Transforming Socialist Economies.* Aldershot: Edward Elgar.

Nagy, K. (1989). 'New Technology and Work in Hungary: Technological Innovation without Organizational Adaptation', in A. Francis and P. Grootings (eds.), *New Technologies and Work.* London: Routledge.

Nishida, J. (1991). 'The Japanese Influence on the Shanghaiese Textile Industry and Implications for Hong Kong', M.Phil. thesis, University of Hong Kong.

North, D. C. (1990). *Institutions, Institutional Change and Economic Performance.* Cambridge: Cambridge University Press.

—— (1993). 'Institutions and Credible Commitment', *Journal of Institutional and Theoretical Economics,* 149: 11–23.

Numazaki, I. (1991). 'The Role of Personal Networks in the Making of Taiwan's *Guanxiqiye* Related Enterprises', in G. Hamilton (ed.), *Business Networks and Economic Development in East and South East Asia.* Hong Kong: Centre of Asian Studies, University of Hong Kong.

—— (1992). 'Networks and Partnerships: The Social Organization of the Chinese Business Elite in Taiwan', unpublished Ph.D. thesis, Department of Anthropology, Michigan State University.

Odagiri, H. (1992). *Growth through Competition, Competition through Growth*. Oxford: Oxford University Press.

Offe, C. (1976). *Industry and Inequality*. London: Edward Arnold.

—— (1997). *Varieties of Transition*. Cambridge: Polity Press.

Okada, Y. (1996). 'Institutional Arrangements and the Japanese Competitive–Cooperative Business Systems', paper presented to the Annual Conference of the Society for the Advancement of Socio-Economics, Geneva.

Orru, M. (1997). 'The Institutionalist Analysis of Capitalist Economices', in M. Orru *et al.* (eds.), *The Economic Organization of East Asian Capitalism*. Thousand Oaks, Calif.: Sage.

—— Hamilton, G. and Suzuki, M. (1989). 'Patterns of Inter-Firm Control in Japanese Business, *Organization Studies*, 10: 549–74.

—— Biggart, N., and Hamilton, G. (1991). 'Organizational Isomorphism in East Asia', in W. W. Powell and P. J. DiMaggio (eds.), *The New Institutionalism in Organizational Analysis*. University of Chicago Press, 361–89.

—— —— —— (1997) (eds.). *The Economic Organization of East Asian Capitalism*. Thousand Oaks, Calif.: Sage.

Palais, J. B. (1975). *Politics and Policy in Traditional Korea*. Cambridge, Mass.: Harvard University Press.

Pauly, L. W., and Reich, S. (1997). 'National Structures and Multinational Corporate Behavior', *International Organization*, 51: 1–30.

Penrose, E. (1959). *The Theory of the Growth of the Firm*. Oxford: Blackwell.

Pfeffer, J. (1993). 'Barriers to the Advance of Organizational Science', *Academy of Management Review*, 18: 599–620.

Piore, M. J., and Sabel, C. F. (1984). *The Second Industrial Divide*. New York: Basic Books.

Powell, W. W., and DiMaggio, P. J. (1991) (eds.). *The New Institutionalism in Organizational Analysis*. Chicago: Chicago University Press.

Pugh, D. S., and Redding, S. G. (1985). 'The Formal and the Informal: Japanese and Chinese Organization Structures', in S. R. Clegg *et al.* (eds.), *The Enterprise and Management in East Asia*. Hong Kong: Centre for Asian Studies, University of Hong Kong.

Pye, L. (1985). *Asian Power and Politics: The Cultural Dimensions of Authority*. Cambridge, Mass.: Harvard University Press.

Ramstetter, E. (1998). 'Measuring the Size of Foreign Multinationals in the Asia Pacific', in G. Thompson (ed.), *Economic Dynamism in the Asia-Pacific*. London: Routledge.

Rasanen, K., and Whipp, R. (1992). 'National Business: A Sector Perspective', in Richard Whitley (ed.), *European Business Systems: Firms and Markets in their National Contexts*. London: Sage.

Redding, S. G. (1990). *The Spirit of Chinese Capitalism*. Berlin: de Gruyter.

Revesz, G. (1990). *Perestroika in Eastern Europe: Hungary's Economic Transformation 1945–1988*. Boulder, Colo.: Westview.

Richardson, G. (1972). 'The Organization of Industry', *Economic Journal*, 82: 883–96.

Robinson, M. (1991). 'Perceptions of Confucianism in Twentieth-Century Korea', in G. Rozman (ed.), *The East Asian Region: Confucian Heritage and its Modern Adaptation*. Princeton: Princeton University Press.

Rohlen, T. P. (1974). *For Harmony and Strength: Japanese White-Collar Organization in Anthropological Perspective.* Berkeley and Los Angeles: University of California Press.

Ross, G. (1995). *Jacques Delors and European Integration.* Oxford: Polity Press.

Rus, A. (1994). 'Quasi-Privatization: From Class Struggle to a Scuffle of Small Particularisms', in J. Benderly and E. Kraft (eds.), *Independent Slovenia.* London: Macmillan.

Sajo, A. (1994). 'Has State Ownership Truly Abandoned Socialism? The Survival of Socialist Economy and Law in Postcommunist Hungary', in G. S. Alexander and G. Skapska (eds.), *A Fourth Way: Privatization, Property and the Emergence of New Market Economics.* London: Routledge.

Sako, M. (1992). *Prices, Quality and Trust.* Cambridge: Cambridge University Press.

—— (1997). 'Introduction: Forces for Homogeneity and Diversity in the Japanese Industrial Relations System', in M. Sako and H. Sato (eds.), *Japanese Labour and Management in Transition.* London: Routledge.

Sakudo, Y. (1990). 'The Management Practices of Family Business', in C. Nakane and S. Oishi (eds.), *Tokugawa Japan.* Tokyo: University of Tokyo Press.

Salaff, J. W. (1991). 'The Chinese Connection: Management Control Structures and the Search for Labor in Taiwan', in E. K. Y. Chen *et al.* (eds.), *Taiwan: Economy, Society and History.* Hong Kong: Centre of Asian Studies, University of Hong Kong.

Samuels, R. J. (1987). *The Business of the Japanese State.* Ithaca, NY: Cornell University Press.

Sato, H. (1997). 'Human Resource Management Systems in Large Firms', in M. Sako and H. Sato (eds.), *Japanese Labour and Management in Transition.* London: Routledge.

Sato, T. (1990). 'Tokugawa Villages and Agriculture', in C. Nakane and S. Oishi (eds.), *Tokugawa Japan.* Tokyo: University of Tokyo Press.

Schienstock, G. (1997). 'The Transformation of Regional Governance: Institutional Lock-Ins and the Development of Lean Production in Baden-Württemberg', in R. Whitley and P. H. Kristensen (eds.), *Governance at Work: The Social Regulation of Economic Relations.* Oxford: Oxford University Press.

Scott, W. R. (1995). *Institutions and Organizations.* London: Sage.

Sharpe, D. R. (1997). 'Compromise Solutions: A Japanese Multinational Comes to the UK', in R. Whitley and P. H. Kristensen (eds.), *Governance at Work: The Social Regulation of Economic Relations.* Oxford: Oxford University Press.

Sheard, P. (1994). 'Interlocking Shareholdings and Corporate Governance in Japan', in M. Aoki and R. Dore (eds.), *The Japanese Firm: The Sources of Competitive Strength.* Oxford: Oxford University Press.

Sher, M. (1996). 'Japanese Governance Structures and the Western Paradigm: The Origins and Practices of Japanese Industrial Groups and their Main Bank Relationship', paper presented to an EMOT workshop, Barcelona, 25–8 January.

Shieh, G. S. (1992). *'Boss' Island: The Subcontracting Network and Micro-Entrepreneurship in Taiwan's Development.* New York: Peter Lang.

Shin, E. H., and Chin S. W. (1989). 'Social Affinity among Top Managerial Executives of Large Corporations in Korea', *Sociological Forum,* 4: 3–26.

Silin, R. H. (1972). 'Marketing and Credit in a Hong Kong Wholesale Market', in W. E. Willmott (ed.), *Economic Organization in Chinese Society.* Stanford, Calif.: Stanford University Press.

—— (1976). *Leadership and Values: The Organization of Large Scale Taiwanese Enterprises*. Cambridge, Mass.: Harvard University Press.

Smidovnik, J. (1991). 'Disfunctions of the System of Self Management in the Economy, in Local Territorial Communities and in Public Administration', in J. Simmie and J. Dekleva (eds.), *Yugoslavia in Turmoil: After Self Management?* London: Pinter.

Smith, C., and Meiksins, P. (1995). 'System, Society and Dominance Effects in Cross-National Organizational Analysis', *Work, Employment and Society*, 9: 241–67.

Smith, T. C. (1959). *The Agrarian Origins of Modern Japan*. Stanford, Calif.: Stanford University Press.

Smitka, M. (1991). *Competitive Ties: Subcontracting in the Japanese Automotive Industry*. New York: Columbia University Press.

Sorensen, C. W. (1988). *Over the Mountain are Mountains: Korean Peasant Households and their Adaptation to Rapid Industrialization*. Seattle: University of Washington Press.

Sorge, A. (1991). 'Strategic Fit and the Social Effect: Interpreting Cross-National Comparisons of Technology, Organization and Human Resources', *Organization Studies*, 12: 161–90.

—— (1996). 'Societal Effects in Cross-National Organization Studies: Conceptualizing Diversity in Actors and Systems', in R. Whitley and P. H. Kristensen (eds.), *The Changing European Firm: Limits to Convergence*. London: Routledge.

—— and Warner, M. (1986). *Comparative Factory Organization*. Aldershot: Gower.

Stark, D. (1989). 'Bending the Bars of the Iron Cage: Bureaucratization and Informalization in Capitalism and Socialism', *Sociological Forum*, 4: 637–64.

Steers, R. M., Shin, Y. K., and Ungson, G. R. (1989). *The Chaebol*. New York: Harper & Row.

Steinberg, D. I. (1989). *The Republic of Korea*. Boulder, Colo.: Westview Press.

Stewart, P. (1996) (ed.). *Beyond Japanese Management*, special issue of *Asia Pacific Business Review*, 2 (4): 1–204.

Stewart, R., Barsoux, J.-L., Kieser, A., Ganter H.-D., and Walgenbach, P. (1994). *Managing in Britain and Germany*. London: Macmillan.

Storper, M., and Salais, R. (1997). *Worlds of Production: The Action Frameworks of the Economy*. Cambridge, Mass.: Harvard University Press.

Strange, R. (1993). *Japanese Manufacturing Investment in Europe*. London: Routledge.

Streeck, W. (1997). 'German Capitalism: Does it Exist? Can it Survive?' in C. Crouch and W. Streeck (eds.), *Political Economy of Modern Capitalism*. London: Sage.

Svetlicic, M. and Rojec, M. (1996). 'Kolektor', case study of foreign direct investment in Slovenia, Faculty of Social Sciences, University of Ljubljana.

Swaan, W. (1993). *Behaviour and Institutions under Economic Reform*. Tinbergen Research Series, No. 46, Amsterdam: Thesis Publishers.

Szalai, E. (1994). 'Political and Social Conflicts Arising from the Transformation of Property Relations in Hungary', *Journal of Communist Studies and Transition Politics*. 10: 56–77.

Tainio, R. (1997). 'Does Foreign Ownership Matter? Organizational Responses to Ownership Changes in Finnish Companies', paper presented to the 13th EGOS Colloquium, Budapest, 2–5 July.

Tam, S. (1990). 'Centrifugal versus Centripetal Growth Processes', in S. Clegg and G. Redding (eds.), *Capitalism in Contrasting Cultures*. Berlin: de Gruyter.

Taylor, L. (1997). 'Editorial—The Revival of the Liberal Creed—the IMF and the World Bank in a Globalized Economy', *World Development*, 25: 145–52.

Teece, D. J., Rumelt, R., Dosi, G., and Winter, S. (1994). 'Understanding Corporate Coherence: Theory and Evidence', *Journal of Economic Behaviour and Organization*, 23: 1–30.

Trigilia, C. (1990). 'Work and Politics in the Third Italy's Industrial Politics', in F. Pyke *et al.* (eds.), *Industrial Districts and Inter-Firm Cooperation in Italy*. Geneva: ILO.

UNCTAD (1996). *World Investment Report 1996*. New York and Geneva: United Nations.

Upham, F. K. (1987). *Law and Social Change in Post-War Japan*. Cambridge, Mass.: Harvard University Press.

Varhegyi, E. (1993). 'The Modernization of the Hungarian Banking Sector', in I. P. Szekely and D. M. Newberg (eds.), *Hungary: An Economy in Transition*. Cambridge: Cambridge University Press.

Voszka, E. (1992). 'Spontaneous Privatization in Hungary: Preconditions and Real Issues', in G. Lengyel *et al.* (eds.), *Economic Institutions, Actors and Attitudes: East Central Europe in Transition*. Sociological Working Papers, 8; Budapest: University of Economic Sciences.

—— (1994). 'Centralization, Renationalization, Redistribution: The Role of the Government in Changing the Ownership Structure in Hungary, 1989–93', CEPR Discussion Paper No. 916; London: Centre for Economic Policy Research.

—— (1995). *Agyaglabakon allo orias. Az AV Rt letrehozasa es mukodese* (The Giant with Feet of Clay). Budapest: Penzugykutato.

Wade, R. (1988). 'The Role of Government in Overcoming Market Failures: Taiwan, Republic of Korea and Japan', in H. Hughes (ed.), *Achieving Industrialization in East Asia*. Cambridge: Cambridge University Press.

—— (1990). *Governing the Market*. Princeton: Princeton University Press.

—— (1996). 'Globalization and its Limits: Reports of the Death of the National Economy are Greatly Exaggerated', in S. Berger and R. Dore (eds.), *National Diversity and Global Capitalism*. Ithaca, NY: Cornell University Press.

Webber, M. (1995). 'Changing Places in East Asia', in G. L. Clark and W. B. Kim (eds.), *Asian NIEs and the Global Economy*. Baltimore: Johns Hopkins University Press.

Weiss, L. (1988). *Creating Capitalism: The State and Small Business Since 1945*. Oxford: Blackwell.

Westney, E. (1996). 'The Japanese Business System: Key Features and Prospects for Changes', *Journal of Asian Business*, 12: 21–50.

Whitley, R. (1992*a*). *Business Systems in East Asia: Firms, Markets and Societies*. London: Sage.

—— (1992*b*) (ed.). *European Business Systems: Firms and Markets in their National Contexts*. London: Sage.

—— (1992*c*). 'Societies, Firms and Markets: The Social Structuring of Business Systems', in R. Whitley (ed.), *European Business Systems: Firms and Markets in their National Contexts*. London: Sage.

—— (1996*a*). 'The Social Construction of Economic Actors: Institutions and Types of Firm in Europe and other Market Economies', in R. Whitley and P. H. Kristensen (eds.), *The Changing European Firm: Limits to Convergence*. London: Routledge.

—— (1996*b*). 'Business Systems and Global Commodity Chains: Competing or Complementary Forms of Economic Organization?', *Competition and Change*, 1: 411–25.

—— (1997). 'The Social Regulation of Work Systems: Institutions, Interest Groups, and Varieties of Work Organization in Capitalist Societies', in R. Whitley and P. H.

Kristensen (eds.), *Governance at Work: The Social Regulation of Economic Relations*. Oxford: Oxford University Press.

—— and Czaban, L. (1998*a*). 'Ownership, Control and Authority in Emergent Capitalism: Changing Supervisory Relations in Hungarian Industry', *International Journal of Human Resource Management*, 9: 99–113.

—— —— (1998*b*). 'Institutional Transformation and Enterprise Change in an Emergent Capitalist Economy: The Case of Hungary', *Organization Studies*, 19: 259–80.

—— and Kristensen, P. H. (1996) (eds.). *The Changing European Firm: Limits to Convergence*. London: Routledge.

—— —— (1997) (eds.). *Governance at Work: The Social Regulation of Economic Relations*. Oxford: Oxford University Press.

—— Henderson, J., Czaban, L., and Lengyel, G. (1996*a*). 'Continuity and Change in an Emergent Market Economy: The Limited Transformation of Large Enterprises in Hungary', in R. Whitley and P. H. Kristensen (eds.), *The Changing European Firm: Limits to Convergence*. London: Routledge.

—— —— —— —— (1996*b*). 'Trust and Contractual Relations in an Emerging Capitalist Economy', *Organization Studies*, 17: 397–420.

—— —— —— (1997). 'Ownership, Control and the Management of Labour in an Emergent Capitalist Economy: The Case of Hungary', *Organization*, 4(1): 75–98.

—— Jaklic, M., and Hocevar, M. (1999). 'Success without Shock Therapy in Eastern Europe: The Case of Slovenia', in S. Quack *et al.* (eds.), *National Capitalisms, Global Competition and Economic Performance*. Berlin: de Gruyter.

Whittaker, D. H. (1990*a*). 'The End of Japanese-Style Employment?', *Work, Employment and Society*, 4: 321–47.

—— (1990*b*). *Managing Innovation*. Cambridge: Cambridge University Press.

Wilkinson, B. (1994). *Labour and Industry in the Asia-Pacific*. Berlin: de Gruyter.

—— Morris, J., and Munday, M. (1995). 'The Iron Fist in the Velvet Glove: Management and Organization in Japanese Manufacturing Transplants in Wales', *Journal of Management Studies*, 32: 819–30.

Williamson, O. E. (1975). *Market and Hierarchies*. New York: Free Press.

Winch, G. (1996). 'Contracting Systems in the European Construction Industry', in R. Whitley and P. H. Kristensen (eds.), *The Changing European Firm: Limits to Convergence*. London: Routledge.

Winckler, E. A. (1988). 'Elite Political Struggle, 1945–1985', in E. A. Winckler and S. Greenhalgh (eds.), *Contending Approaches to the Political Economy of Taiwan*. Armonk, NY: M. E. Sharpe.

Winter, S. (1988). 'On Coase, Competence and the Corporation', *Journal of Law, Economics and Organization*, 4: 163–80.

Wolf, M. (1970). 'Child Training and the Chinese Family', in M. Freedman (ed.), *Family and Kinship in Chinese Society*. Stanford, Calif.: Stanford University Press.

Wong, S.-L. (1985). 'The Chinese Family Firm: A Model', *British Journal of Sociology*. 36: 58–72.

—— (1988). 'The Applicability of Asian Family Values to other Sociocultural Settings', in P. L. Berger and H.-H. M. Hsiao (eds.), *In Search of an East Asian Development Model*. New Brunswick, NJ: Transaction Books.

—— (1996). 'Chinese Entrepreneurs and Business Trust', in G. Hamilton (ed.), *Asian Business Networks*. Berlin: de Gruyter.

Woo, J.-E. (1991). *Race to the Swift*. New York: Columbia University Press.

294   *References*

Wood, S. (1989). 'The Transformation of Work?', in S. Wood (ed.), *The Transformation of Work?* London: Allen & Unwin.

Wu, Y.-L., and Wu, C.-L. (1980). *Economic Development in Southeast Asia: The Chinese Dimension.* Stanford, Calif.: Hoover Institution Press.

Yoo, S., and Lee, S. M. (1987). 'Management Style and Practice in Korean Chaebols', *California Management Review*, 29: 95–110.

Yoshino, M. Y., and Lifson, T. B. (1986). *The Invisible Link: Japan's Sogo Shosha and the Organization of Trade.* Cambridge, Mass.: MIT Press.

You, J.-i. (1994). 'Labour Institutions and Economic Development in the Republic of Korea', in G. Rodgers (ed.), *Workers, Institutions and Economic Growth in Asia.* Geneva: ILO.

Zeile, W. (1991). 'Industrial Policy and Organizational Efficiency: The Korean *Chaebol* Examined', in G. Hamilton (ed.), *Business Networks and Economic Development in East and Southeast Asia.* Hong Kong: Centre for Asian Studies, University of Hong Kong.

Zucker, L. (1986). 'Production of Trust: Institutional Sources of Economic Structure, 1840–1920', *Research in Organizational Behaviour*, 8: 53–111.

—— (1987). 'Institutional Theories of Organization', *Annual Review of Sociology*, 13: 443–64.

Zysman, John (1983). *Governments, Markets and Growth.* Ithaca, NY: Cornell University Press.

INDEX